DTP'S
2021 NFL DRAFT GUIDE

DANIEL PARLEGRECO

TABLE OF CONTENTS

Chapter 1: Introduction 1

Chapter 2: QB's 3

Chapter 3: RB's 14

Chapter 4: FB's 28

Chapter 5: WR's 32

Chapter 6: TE's 63

Chapter 7: OT's 75

Chapter 8: Interior Offensive Lineman (Guards or Centers) 93

Chapter 9: Edge Players (4-3 DE's and 3-4 OLB's) 111

Chapter 10: Defensive Tackles (Includes 3-4 DE's) 135

Chapter 11: Middle Linebackers 153

Chapter 12: Outside Linebackers (Strong Side or Weak Side) 164

Chapter 13: Cornerbacks 176

Chapter 14: Safeties 205

Chapter 15: Conclusion 223

Chapter 16: Glossary of Terms and Top 50 Big Board 224

Chapter 1

Introduction

Wow, here we are 2021! What a ride it's been. I can't believe another draft season is upon us and this is surely going to be another good one. Certainly, we've seen several changes over the college football season throughout this past season. A pandemic certainly doesn't help. Sure, it's made evaluations a bit harder with fewer games and a lot of sicknesses. I've had to rely a lot more on 2019 and even 2018 game tape for a lot of these guys that either opted out this season or only played in a handful of games.

What can I promise you this year?

- The most prospects I've ever evaluated throughout my last 6 years of evaluating prospects
- More in-depth reports and analysis. Each report is significantly longer than in previous years
- As always, my evaluations are written in clear to understand phrasing and sentence structure
- Why I 'LOVE 'or 'HATE 'certain prospects
- Scouting glossary of terms used. Here you'll find terms you might be unfamiliar with explained in the back as a reference

Due to a somewhat unique pre-draft process, I wanted to get this out to you even SOONER than previous years. If you've never read my draft guide previously, you'll notice a lot of my viewpoints and evaluations are significantly different than mainstream media. Don't worry, that isn't necessarily a bad thing.

Over the last 6 years, I've put my blood, sweat, and tears into this draft guide. I work tirelessly from the morning hours until the late evening hours watching game tape after game tape. It's truly been a passion of mine. While you might strongly disagree with some of my assessments, I guarantee you that I came to my assessment through watching the game tape, while not having any preconceived ideas of any of these players. Hence the reason, a lot of my grades are different than 'NFL personalities 'or 'talking heads 'on television.

Why should you trust me?

Well to put it simply, I rely on the film, and the film only! Rather than being overly reliant and overly affected by pre-draft workouts in underwear, I base my evaluations STRICTLY on the tape. I generally watch anywhere from 2-6 games on every single prospect in this class.

Doing it this way prevents me from overvaluing guys who can run impressive times or can win athletic competitions. We know football players play football, and the best way to evaluate them is by watching them play it. While this is risky, I'm the only one who stands completely by his convictions of 'watching the tape ' only.

Talk to any of my past readers and they still marvel at some of my outstanding evaluations of former players that weren't talked up enough before the draft. Who are some of these players? Well just last year, two of my absolute favorites in the draft were Antoine Winfield Jr and Chase Claypool. Both of them turned out to be STUDS for their respective teams their rookie season.

Who else? Well in previous years, I was FAR higher on guys like DK Metcalf, Aaron Donald, and Patrick Mahomes. The list can go on and on, I promise you that.

That's not to say I hit a home run on every one of these players and I'll be transparent about that as well. Like most evaluators, QB's can be very very tough. And I've missed on a few of those. And perhaps you'll notice right away looking at the QB position that I differ greatly from most evaluators.

What excites me from this class?

Every draft class has a unique and unparalleled feel to it. I'm so excited about a number of these players in this particular class and there's tremendous depth at a wide variety of positions. I'm intrigued by the fact that we could have 5 first-round quarterbacks, yes 5!

So many teams throughout the NFL this past season needed an upgrade at quarterback, even teams that made it into the playoffs. This is going to cause several intriguing opportunities for playoff-caliber teams in the early to middle parts of the draft with potential trade scenarios. Could we see a QB run go early?

There's far better depth this season along the offensive line, tight end, and linebacker position groups. Those immediately stood out to me. Perhaps I'm not as high on the defensive line talent in this class, it's a bit of a down year as far as TOP-END talent. But there's going to be a plethora of starters taken in this draft class on Day 3. *That gets me excited just thinking about it.*

I can't wait to see which sleepers drop into the 5th and 6th rounds! With that being said, let's dig deep into these players. Read this with an open mind and you won't be disappointed. Every single NFL season I get numerous messages saying "wow you were so right on this player!" I GUARANTEE that will happen again. Nothing gives me more satisfaction than that. I put everything I have into all of this for you guys. Here we go, the 2021 NFL Draft!

Chapter 2

QB's

1 - Trevor Lawrence - Clemson - 6'6 220 lbs

Strengths: Lawrence has been the starter for the Tigers ever since his true freshman campaign, taking over midway through the season and then taking the Tigers all the way, winning the national championship. Lawrence possesses an impressive frame with good height and length with room in his frame for additional muscle if he chooses. Will only be 21 years old during the beginning of his rookie season. Lawrence is a physically gifted kid that has all the tools of an elite passer, both in arm talent, football intelligence, and athletically. He utilizes good ball placement and precise touch combined with the needed velocity to accurately make all the throws. Standing tall in the pocket, Lawrence shows good pocket presence and footwork while pressure weighs down with the ability to quickly get the ball out, rarely looking rattled. A quick decision maker that wastes very little time. Is comfortable throwing at multiple release points and to all different angles and areas on the football field. Much tougher than his size would appear to indicate, Lawrence shows fearlessness when working as a runner, both on designed and broken-down plays. Comfortable with making tight-window throws showing the ability to challenge even the narrowest of windows. Doesn't look rattled on broken-down plays, and appears to be very comfortable in creating something for himself. Lawrence is advanced in the mental areas of the game, showing good pre-snap awareness and defensive recognition abilities to quickly diagnose. After the snap, Lawrence quickly reads coverages, always keeping his eyes down the field. A leader of men, Lawrence is beloved by his fellow teammates and coaches for his blue-chip characteristics and leadership abilities.

Weaknesses: Missed a couple of games in his junior season due to getting Covid-19. Some will argue that Lawrence has a very lanky frame, lacking great body armor to hold up from NFL-quality hits consistently. Lawrence has had some issues with his deeper ball, lacking consistent accuracy to place the ball for his teammate to have a chance to make a play on it. At times, he can appear to be a bit pre-meditated with his intended target before the snap, forcing his throws quickly before he's even looked at an available 2nd option. On other occasions, he will keep his eyes fixated on the intended target waiting for an opening, and then being very late with his 2nd read with the passing lane closed already.

Best Fit: Starting QB that can play in any system

Player Ranking (1-100): 97.4 - Lawrence has all the tools of an elite QB. We haven't seen a QB prospect that is as well-rounded and physically gifted as Lawrence since Andrew Luck. He's got every single tool you'd want in a player. His personality traits, leadership abilities, and blue-chip characteristics make him even more admirable. Lawrence could ultimately be an elite next-level QB that will warrant a starting role immediately. Top-5 Player.

2 - Trey Lance - North Dakota State - 6'3 224 lbs

Strengths: A tall, well-built, and tough as nails prospect, Lance has the NFL size and strength evaluators look for. After coming onto the scene as the main starter during his redshirt freshman season, Lance certainly didn't disappoint setting records with the highest amount of touchdowns (28) without an interception in FCS history. Not solely a passer, Lance is a gifted runner with the ball, running for over 1,000 yards during his redshirt freshman campaign. As a developed and pro-style system experienced passer, Lance looks mature beyond his years. Showing tremendous poise both inside and outside the pocket, Lance never looks rattled even in the biggest of game situations. What I loved about Lance is his patience and comfort in the pocket, waiting for an available read to open up while constantly scanning the field. And if nothing did, he was perfectly content taking the safer check-down option. Lance is a playmaker at every available opportunity, creating both on designed and broken-down plays. When Lance decides to tuck the ball and run, his physicality and lower-body strength are on full display, frequently bouncing off and picking up additional yardage after contact. Not just a bruiser, Lance is a gifted athlete showcasing stellar open-field speed. Tremendous ball skills with the ability to utilize excellent ball fakes to force 2nd level misreads for defensive backs. Will only be 20 years old on draft day. Has all the arm potential for continued development at the next level, showing terrific ball placement, touch, and deep ball strength. Lance's decision-making is far beyond his years as evidenced by his ridiculously low career interceptions.

Weaknesses: The biggest knock and concern with Lance is his lack of game experience, only having 17 career starts. Evaluators will be concerned about his lack of experience going up against big-time college programs during his time. There are too many games on film where he is overly reliant on his running ability, far too quickly getting into 'flight mode 'and ditching the pocket. While there's no arguing with Lance's lack of mistakes, there were several times where he was a little late with his delivery or became overly confident in his ball velocity, giving defenders opportunities to make plays on the ball.

Best Fit Ready to Start NFL QB

Player Ranking (1-100): 88.9 - Was not expecting to like him as much as I did. Lance is the true definition of an all-around prospect showcasing the athleticism for today's NFL with the passing developmental upside that coaches will love. While he's not the finished article, Lance will give a team 15 years of continued growth. And if he reaches his ceiling, watch out! He's going to be good. 1st round player.

3 - Zach Wilson - BYU - 6'3 210 lbs

Strengths: A 3-year starter for the Cougars that has been tremendous for them this season, finishing with over a 70% completion percentage and a ridiculously low touchdown to interception ratio. Wilson has good height for the position with a trim middle and a tapered midsection. A well-rounded and highly competitive gunslinging QB that has good physical attributes as both an athlete and as a passer. A confident kid that thinks he can make a play on every snap of the ball, showing fearlessness when playing with extensive experience in a pro-style offensive system. Quickly getting rid of the football, Wilson has a rocket release. Good overall pocket poise, showing good patience while he scans the field, never settling on his 1st read, and keeping his vision downfield. Navigates well through the pocket with good footwork, sliding his feet to buy himself extra time. Has shown dramatic improvement during each campaign. Shows little hesitancy when it comes to throwing through tight, narrow windows. Excellent at throwing receivers open on comeback or sidelines timing routes. Comfortable throwing the ball off-platform, Wilson shows good accuracy on the move. Very quick when escaping the pocket, showing the ability to pick up chunks of yards on the ground. Impressive open-field abilities to create in space with good shiftiness and natural running abilities.

Weaknesses: Has had some minor injury concerns, including needing surgery to fix his fractured thumb during his sophomore season. He also needed offseason shoulder surgery to fix a torn labrum in his shoulder. Wilson has more of a wiry-built frame and appears to look like he could use some additional bulk on his frame to hold up at the next level, especially considering his durability concerns. Overall arm strength and ball velocity aren't elite and he tends to put too much air under the ball when throwing the ball down the field. Can be a bit frustrating as he attempts to do too much on every play, leading to some poor sacks or forcing bad throws when his intended target is covered. Has competed in very few games against NFL competition.

Best Fit: Starting QB

Player Ranking (1-100): 87.7 - I really really like Wilson. He's gotten so much better during each season. He's a playmaker that shows tremendous accuracy. While he doesn't have elite arm talent, he's a really good athlete and he will create and make a lot of plays at the next level. My only slight worry is his durability. 1st round player.

4 - Justin Fields - Ohio State - 6'3 228 las

Strengths: A former Georgia recruit that backed up Jake Fromm before transferring to Ohio State and being granted immediate eligibility to play for the Buckeyes, finishing with a tremendous sophomore season with the Buckeyes. Fields is a well-built prospect with prototypical NFL size and weight to play at the next level. A former shortstop baseball player that plays with natural passing ability on the move. Experienced and comfortable in a pro-style system with taking the ball under center, Fields displays a rare blend of excellent athleticism and natural arm talent. Fields has very good pocket awareness with instinctive movement abilities and quick feet to create valuable time in the backfield, while seemingly having eyes behind his head to feel external pressure. Sees things developing quickly and has excellent zip on the ball to make tight-window throws, making it seemingly impossible for defenders to get their hands on the football. Short to medium level accuracy is tremendous. Very comfortable on broken-down plays, Fields shows improvisational skills coupled with good straight-line speed to threaten if given an opening. Physicality is evident with good lower body strength to fall forward through contact and gain additional yardage. Impresses when playing in RPO settings with an advanced understanding of timing, nuance, and deception to fool defenders. A tough as nails kid that played through some big-time injuries, gutting it out on the field. A big-game and big-moments QB that has played at his best during some of the biggest games of his career.

Weaknesses: The Buckeyes offensive system is predicated on getting rid of the ball quickly and to shorter-to-intermediate levels of the field and he lacks a ton of experience on deeper developing routes. When he does throw deeper, his accuracy and ball placement are very sporadic, sometimes great and other times poor. Very reliant on throwing the ball to his 1st read and will struggle if he's continually forced to look off his initial target. Has a bad habit of holding onto the ball for far too long if his 1st read isn't open while taking some unnecessary sacks. I worry about his overall lack of field vision down the field, he misses open receivers quite a bit. Has the tendency of abandoning the pocket too quickly and getting into 'flight mode 'and attempting to gain yards with his feet. Overall decision-making abilities are suspect as he will force some terrible throws when the receiver isn't open. A rhythm quarterback that tends to get rolling, and if he doesn't start games well, his entire game can be out of sync.

Best Fit: Starting QB

Player Ranking (1-100): 86.6 - Fields reminds me of Dak Prescott. Not quite as sturdy physically as Dak but he's a better overall thrower of the football than Dak. Equally effective on the move and a really good athlete, Fields has really impressed me. He's a smart, 'tough as nails' kid that has a good understanding of how to attack a defense. 1st round player.

5 - Mac Jones - Alabama - 6'3 217 lbs

Strengths: Took over the starting role during his sophomore season after Tua suffered his season-ending injury, starting the Tide's final 4 games of the season. Jones took the Tide to win the championship this game, playing terrific down the stretch. Jones plays the game like an old veteran, showing tremendous poise and pocket awareness at all times, having experience playing under center at times. Good footwork within the pocket to slide and maneuver to buy himself additional time. Excelling at the mental sides of the game, Jones shows excellent pre-snap awareness and recognition abilities. After the snap, Jones does a nice job of utilizing his eyes to look off receivers, rarely settling on the 1st read unnecessarily. He always keeps his vision down the field. A highly intelligent kid both on and off the field. Rarely gets jittery when pressure weighs down, showing good patience. He does a nice job of using both his head and pump-fakes to create openings for down the field targets to create some spacing. A good decision-maker that has impressed both in his completion percentage and his ridiculously low touchdown to interception numbers. He rarely gives the defense an opportunity to make a play on the ball. Places the ball well down the field, showing good touch, timing, and accuracy at all levels. Wastes very little motion in his release, getting rid of the football quickly.

Weaknesses: Took advantage of superior athletes that could consistently separate at the college level with some of the best-skilled players in college football. Overall arm talent is just 'OK 'and lacks an elite-level arm to make all of the throws. This is especially evident by his balls downfield continually hanging in the air, lacking the ability to add more zip to his ball. He gets a lot of balls batted down at the line of scrimmage due to his low release point. An average athlete that cannot consistently threaten with his feet, tending to be a bit of a statue in the pocket. Overall size is average, lacking much body armor on his frame or prototypical height.

Best Fit: Mid-level starter ability

Player Ranking (1-100): 79.1 - Jones lacks elite arm talent and athleticism to be a top-flight starting QB but he could be a very solid mid of the pack starter at the next level. He has a lot of Andy Dalton to his game. Solid in mostly everything. His touch, accuracy, and ball location impressed this year. He will make very very few mistakes. 3rd round player.

6 - Kyle Trask - Florida - 6'5 240 lbs

Strengths: An intriguing blend of size and power, Trask has shown some promise over the last couple of seasons starting for the Gators, impressing in many big-time SEC battles. Despite never having started a game in high school, Trask's developmental upside is high, starting his first game in 2019. Trask is a 'tough as nails ' QB that plays his best when the game is on the line, as he repeatedly fought through injuries, playing injured and leading his team to some big-time games in the final embers of a game. A good decision-maker that rarely makes unnecessary mistakes, as evidenced by his stellar touchdown to interceptions numbers each campaign. Trask is a highly-intelligent reader of the game, having advanced concepts of utilizing his eyes to look off safeties and rarely allow defenders to know where he's going with the ball. When his mechanics are dialed in and his feet set, his short to medium levels of accuracy are top-notch, delivering the ball where only his receiver has a chance to make a play on the ball. Trask is a playmaker that rarely settles, frequently extending and picking up additional yardage with his ability to fight through tackles and get the ball out. Trask has played in a pro-style setup preparing him to play in an NFL-style offense.

Weaknesses: Trask's most frustrating downside is his overall lack of a pocket presence. While he has gotten better since his initial starts, his lack of ability to feel a rush and take unnecessary sacks can be beyond frustrating. This leads to him easily giving up the fumble and sack/strips by opportunistic defenders. Trask runs into trouble with his foot mechanics, leading him to some inaccuracies with his throws on occasion. He hasn't quite developed the ability to alter arm mechanics to change trajectory and ball speed to adjust to different routes. An average arm, lacking ideal strength. When he 'sees 'the rush, he gets a bit panicky failing to take necessary sacks and oftentimes throwing the ball up in the air leading to some interception opportunities for defensive backs. Trask has had a couple of minor knee problems both in his freshman campaign and last season.

Best Fit: Starter potential

Player Ranking (1-100): 78.3 - Trask certainly has some impressive traits considering he's still learning the QB position. He's a smart, nuanced, and big-bodied QB that evaluators will like. He's had some impressive success against big-time SEC defenses as well. He doesn't have the 'WOW 'factors and there's little to love about him but there's a certain belief that he can get better and be a starter at the next level. 3rd round player.

7 - Kellen Mond - Texas A&M - 6'2 205 lbs

Strengths: A 4-year starter for the Aggies that took over during his freshman season, showing good consistency and reliability. A well-built dual-threat QB that shows prototypical and excellent size for the transition to the next level while displaying the frame for additional girth. A terrific athlete, Mond is one of the better running QB's in college football, as evidenced by his 500 yards rushing in 2 separate seasons. Unique throwing mechanics allow him to get out the ball quickly. Possesses plus skills as a pure thrower of the football, showing impressive overall talent to test all levels of a defense with the needed velocity. A tough as nails prospect that has regularly been beaten up in the SEC and continues to get back on his feet and battle throughout. Most of his best throws come while he's on the move, showing terrific accuracy outside the pocket to make downfield throws.

Weaknesses: Major question marks about his overall decision making, having a bad habit of releasing the ball when panicked, launching it into the air. Regularly throws the ball into double teams, showing too much trust in his teammates in almost impossible situations. Poor pocket presence that shows very little patience as plays break down, frequently getting into 'flight 'mode and abandoning the pocket at the first opportunity. Erratic footwork that fails to create and buy additional seconds when staying in the pocket. Limited ability to read coverages with coaches only requiring him to make half-field reads. Ball placement and accuracy are incredibly sporadic, especially when within the pocket, especially notable when throws are beyond 15 yards. Has played in a college-style spread offense throughout his career, failing to have any experience under center.

Best Fit: Backup QB

Player Ranking (1-100): 69.8 - Mond has had a nice college career but his mechanics and consistency are all over the place. He struggled against the better teams on the schedule. He does possess an intriguing mix of size, arm talent, and athleticism which will make him potentially go much higher. 5th round player.

8 - Jamie Newman - Wake Forest - 6'3 235 lbs

Strengths: Before transitioning to Georgia and deciding to sit out the season, Newman played 1.5 seasons with the Demon Deacons, donning some impressive performances. Possessing a well-developed frame, Newman shows the size and girth evaluators look for in a starting QB. Newman flashed at times, showing impressive down the field touch on some long balls, placing the ball perfectly. A very good athlete that shows the ability to create and pick-up yardage with his feet. Possesses good pocket presence with the ability to stand tall in the pocket with pressure weighing heavily and making a tight window throw. Newman is known to possess leadership-style intangibles to an NFL team. Newman certainly possesses an NFL arm, showing the ability to alter ball velocity to make tight-window throws as well as utilizing more touch on down the field shots.

Weaknesses: Newman is a developmental prospect that has minimal tape at this point. While he has 'flashed' in certain games, scouts will be hesitant about the sporadic nature of his play. When competing against better defenses, Newman looked completely lost. His mechanics in the pocket continually let him down, creating accuracy issues at all levels of the field. Newman can be frustrating with how difficult he makes easy throws make, missing wide-open targets at times. Even though Wake Forest coaches tried to give Newman easy assignments and consistent 1-read underneath reads, he still faltered far too many times.

Best Fit: Developmental prospect

Player Ranking (1-100): 69.2 - I'm not as high on Newman as others are. While you can make the case he didn't have the talent around him as other QB's in this draft class, he's just far too inconsistent for my liking. There's nothing 'stellar 'or 'overly excitable 'about his game. He has some above-average physical tools but at best, he's a backup QB. Unfortunately, he didn't get a chance to play for Georgia. I know many scouts were waiting for that to see how he did with more talent around him and competing against better defenses routinely. 5th round player.

9 - Sam Ehlinger - Texas - 6'2 222 lbs

Strengths: Ehlinger is a 4-year starter for the Longhorns that is the definition of a football player that just loves the game. Ehlinger brings intangibles, leadership, and commitment to a football team. Built tough with a power-packed frame and thick limbs, Ehlinger presents a dual-threat option for the next-level. A power runner that quickly leaves the pocket upon pressure weighing down. He's also a threat on designed running plays, showing the lower-body strength to run over or through uncommitted tacklers. Ehlinger is at his best when playing as an option-style QB that is given some freeness at the line of scrimmage to create and utilize his extemporaneous nature to play-make. While he's still raw as a passer, he has shown some improvement in his mechanics during his 4 seasons. Often utilizing impressive anticipation and touch, Ehlinger is comfortable throwing the ball on vertical plains, practically laying the ball in the hands of his receivers.

Weaknesses: Ehlinger is a very limited passer at this point that lacks the arm strength and the ideal accuracy to consistently win at the next level. While he's a strong kid, he lacks the needed size and body to withstand the physical nature he enjoys playing with at the next level. His accuracy is sporadic oftentimes struggling on intermediate-based routes that require needed velocity and placement. He fails to possess the overall needed arm strength to make the tight-window throws, both on the sidelines, and in the tight middle of the field windows. Was protected by an offense that allowed him dual-options at the line of scrimmage, frequently relying on simple screen and receiver-option routes to pick-up his yardage. His deep-ball accuracy is a huge question mark and looked wide of the mark on far too many occasions on film.

Best Fit: Backup at the next level.

Player Ranking (1-100): 68.4 - Ehlinger is a football player that will give his heart and soul to a team but he lacks the ideal throwing potential to develop into a starting quality QB at the next level. He reminds me so much of Tim Tebow it's scary. 5th round player.

10 - Davis Mills - Stanford - 6'4 225 lbs

Strengths: Took over as the starter for the Cardinals after Costello went down with a knee injury towards the end of the 2019 season. He then started in 5 games as a senior for the Cardinals. Mills has a really nice frame for a QB, displaying good height and size. Mills had a good year this year for the Cardinals, finishing with a 66% completion percentage and an average of over 300 yards passing per game. Very much a rhythm quarterback, Mills has the most success when he's able to get in a zone, getting rid of the ball quickly. Excelling in the shorter to intermediate areas of the game, Mills possesses the arm strength to be able to squeeze balls into tight windows, showing confidence in his abilities. Is effective placing the ball on timing routes, showing good anticipation and ball placement allowing his receiver the only chance to make a play. Good footwork within the pocket, showing subtle little movements to buy himself extra seconds. Above-average functional athleticism that allows him to extend plays outside of the pocket on occasion. Appears to have good pocket presence, showing fearlessness in the pocket when pressure is bearing down.

Weaknesses: Struggled with some knee injuries his first couple of seasons at Stanford. Has only started 11 games during his college career, lacking ideal experience. Didn't have to make too many full read throws, Stanford coaches allowed him to generally throw to the 1st intended target, only making half reads. Will need to learn how to utilize his eyes to look off safeties and linebackers in the 2nd and 3rd level of a defense. His field vision is a concern as he frequently will miss open targets down the field. Appeared to have some accuracy concerns when working the deeper areas of the field.

Best Fit: Backup QB with some developmental upside

Player Ranking (1-100): 68.1 - Mills is a hard player to evaluate because of his lack of game time. He has gotten progressively better it's appeared in each start but he's still a work in progress. He's neither a great thrower of the football nor is he a great athlete, so his physical tools don't appear to have major upside, but he's fairly solid all-around. 5th round player.

11 - Brady White - Memphis - 6'3 210 las

Strengths: A former Arizona State recruit that ended up losing the starting QB battle and thus transferring to Memphis. White has been really solid for Memphis, finishing with over 4,000 yards passing his junior season with a 64% completion percentage. A good-sized athlete that shows terrific size for the position. White is a playmaker that loves to get on a roll quickly, playing in a classic 'gunslinger 'role. Memphis offensive coaches always had him on the move, whether it was on sneaks, waggles, boots, or play-action style plays. Has a little bit of Baker Mayfield to his game, almost as if he's playing backyard football. A really tough kid that plays with a fearlessness when tucking the ball and running. Accuracy is good when working 15 yards and under, and doesn't need to be 'on a platform 'when getting rid of the football. Appears to have suitable arm strength, albeit, not great. Was impressed at his ball location on timing routes, placing the ball in spots where the defensive back has no chance of making the play. Appears to have good pre-snap awareness picking out defensive schematics quickly, eating up big chunks of yards when against zone.

Weaknesses: An older prospect that will be 25 years old during his rookie NFL season. White is a rhythm QB, and when he's ON he's really good. When he's off, he's off. A 1-read QB that is reliant on getting rid of the football very quickly, rarely having to make full-field reads. At times he gets far too aggressive, leading to needless mistakes when he had a better option that was in a good opportunity to make a play. Careless when tucking the ball and running, leading to unnecessary fumbles. Not always the best at perceiving pressure, panicking unnecessarily which leads to poor accuracy and placement. Arm mechanics and release are inconsistent, allowing the ball to flutter in the air, throwing entirely off of his back foot. Benefitted by having some of the best offensive playmakers in college football during his time at Memphis, where he just had to put the ball in their hands.

Best Fit: Backup QB

Player Ranking (1-100): 66.9 - White is fun to watch play but he's erratic and extremely inconsistent. I wish I could've seen him play in a different style of offense to see how he translated when having to read full fields and go through his progressions but he didn't. But something is intriguing about this kid. 5th round player.

12 - Shane Buechele - SMU - 6'1 207 lbs

Strengths: A 5th-year starter that played his final 2 seasons for SMU after playing his first three seasons with the Texas Longhorns. Buechele has gotten better and better during each of his seasons, improving in his completion percentage, yards per game, and overall QBR. A high-character guy that is loved by everyone that knows him, showing terrific leadership qualities and hard-working blue-chip characteristics. Buechele is a solid athlete that shows good quickness when working inside and outside of the pocket, with some ability to create for himself while on the move. Always has an escape plan when pressure is weighing down, showing good pocket presence and awareness. Plays with fearlessness, rarely taking unnecessary sacks. A highly-intelligent QB that more often than not makes really good decisions with the football. Does a nice job of utilizing his eyes, and keeping them down the field, rarely locking onto his first target and showing a willingness to throw the ball in all different areas of the field. Generally speaking, he places the ball well in shorter to intermediate areas of the field, allowing his targets to pick up additional yardage after receiving the ball.

Weaknesses: Struggled terribly with consistency and injuries during his time with Texas. Buechele lacks any kind of top-notch physical tools that project him as a 'high upside prospect.'Undersized and lacks the 'live' arm that will threaten all different points on the field. Elongated release point limits his ability to get the ball out in ample time.

Best Fit: Backup QB

Player Ranking (1-100): 64.5 - Reminds me of Colt McCoy. Not going to light the world on fire physically but he could end up being a really solid backup for 10+ years at the next level. He's gotten better and better during his career which shows me there's still some developmental upside. 6th round player.

13 - Feleipe Franks - Arkansas - 6'6 234 lbs

Strengths: A 2-year starter for the Florida Gators before transferring and playing his final year for the Razorbacks. Franks had his best year this year, finishing with an impressive 68% completion percentage and excellent touchdown to interception numbers. Franks is a physical specimen, featuring rare size and height for the position. Has all the physical tools you want in a QB. While not an elite athlete, Franks is a good functional athlete that shows some good footwork within the pocket to buy additional time. Not afraid to tuck the ball and run on broken-down plays. Featuring a tremendous arm, Franks can make all the throws, showing 0 intimidation of tight windows or sidelines throws. Will make beautiful touch passes down the field, showing good anticipation and timing. Understands how to utilize his eyes down the field to manipulate safeties to create extra space.

Weaknesses: Franks broke his leg early on in his final season at Florida causing him to miss most of his junior season. Very thin and could stand to gain some additional functional weight. Franks has struggled with most of the mental aspects of the QB position, failing to go through his progressions and make whole field reads. Very slow reading things, taking far too much time in the pocket. Very much a hot and cold football player that shows very little consistency. Accuracy is as sporadic with his consistency. Has had significant decision-making concerns, making some boneheaded throws in double coverage, leading to poor interceptions.

Best Fit: Developmental prospect

Player Ranking (1-100): 63.4 - Franks has shown some upside this year for the Razorbacks. There's never been any denying his physical tools but he's very very frustrating as a prospect, as both Florida and Arkansas saw. He's worth taking a chance on though for some developmental upside.

14 - K.J. Costello - Mississippi State - 6'5 222 lbs

Strengths: A former starting QB for the Stanford Cardinals before transitioning to Mississippi State and playing his final year of eligibility with the Bulldogs. It's rare for a college QB to come into the NFL with a legitimate 4-years of starting experience. The first thing that stands out about Costello is his rare size and height, possessing an NFL frame with room for additional growth and weight on his frame. Has experience playing in two different offensive systems, including a pro-style system while at Stanford. Costello has some physical talents, including an active arm capable of making all of the throws. Shows the ball velocity abilities to rip the ball in highly contested parts of the field or throw beautifully lofted red-zone throws. Good overall mechanics, both in his feet and his arms, allowing him to alter his throwing motion to make throws to all parts of the field. While he's not a great athlete, he does show some impressive pocket awareness with the ability to shuffle his feet in the pocket to create extra seconds for himself in the pocket. Good pre-snap awareness allows him to signal call and identify defensive alignments, quickly pointing out potential blitzes or trouble areas for the offensive line. Keeps his eyes downfield at all times, waiting patiently for one of his targets to create some spacing. Very confident and trustworthy in both his physical gifts and his teammates, allowing them opportunities to win 50/50 balls.

Weaknesses: Struggled significantly at times this year in the SEC this season and got benched due to very high interception numbers. This has caused many to seriously question his overall decision making. On far too many occasions when the play breaks down, Costello throws the ball carelessly into the air as opposed to taking sacks or getting rid of the football. Costello is a lanky built guy that needs to add additional weight onto his frame to have suitable body armor for the next level. Overall mobility when attempting to escape the pocket is extremely limited, failing to offer much of a Plan B option when plays break down.

Best Fit: Backup QB

Player Ranking (1-100): 60.4 - Costello has physical gifts but he's just as frustrating when it comes to his ability to be consistent. He will flash for a game or two and then be dreadful for 3 or 4 straight games. Coaches will think there are traits to work with and he could potentially develop into a nice solid backup. 6th round player.

15 - Ian Book - Notre Dame - 6'0 210 lbs

Strengths: A 5th-year player and 3-year starter for the Fighting Irish, Book has been a consistent presence for their offense the last few seasons. A true gun-slinger, Book is one of the most mobile escape artists we've seen play the QB position, showing tremendous ability with his legs. Regularly making plays to extend plays with his feet, Book buys himself additional time inside and outside the pocket. As a pocket passer, Book shows good short to medium level accuracy, placing the necessary zip on his balls. Very quick release with an efficient set-up. Appears to throw with some nice touch on seam routes and over the shoulder balls. Rarely makes a bad mistake, only having 2 interceptions in his final season.

Weaknesses: Lacks ideal size and measurements. Doesn't have the prototypical arm strength and appears to struggle with some down-the-field routes. Footwork and pocket awareness are over the place, getting far too hurried with perceived pressure. This leads to hit or miss accuracy. A run-first QB that is too reliant on his feet. Treats every play like it's the last and this leads to taking big losses unnecessarily. Locks onto targets pre-snap, failing to adjust after the snap.

Best Fit: Backup QB

Player Ranking (1-100): 57.1 - Book is a fun watch but he's basically a glorified backyard QB that has excelled mostly with his feet while extending plays. He lacks the physical tools to be a starter at the next level. But he could be a nice backup in the right system. 7th round player.

TOP-10 QBs

1. Trevor Lawrence
2. Trey Lance
3. Zach Wilson
4. Justin Fields
5. Mac Jones
6. Kyle Trask
7. Kellen Mond
8. Jamie Newman
9. Sam Ehlinger
10. Davis Mills

Chapter 3

RB's

1 - Najee Harris - Alabama - 6'2 230 lbs

Strengths: A 4-year contributor to the Tide offense that finally saw his chance to start during his junior season, certainly not disappointing with over 1200 yards rushing and 300 yards receiving. Harris a multi-faceted back that instantly stands out due to his bellcow makeup, showcasing incredible thickness and density throughout his rock-solid frame. The very definition of an intense and high energy worker, fighting for every single yard and fighting until the whistle blows, oftentimes risking his body in the process. He continually keeps his legs pushing and prodding through contact, engaging his lower body to gain additional yardage and push piles forward. A violent runner that will run with reckless abandon and utilize his upper-body power and hands to stiff-arm defenders away from the ball. A bit reminiscent of Derrick Henry in his long speed, showing the ability to break off big runs and rarely getting caught from behind. Was impressive when used as a receiver, showing surprising agility when running routes, soft hands, and the ability to snatch the ball out of the air. Has a good sense of spatial awareness and field vision at both the 1st and 2nd levels, seeing and recognizing things quickly to create in the open field. Flashes in his pass protection, showing some upper-body power and willingness but just needs to be more consistent.

Weaknesses: Due to his large and upright frame, he has some leverage concerns failing to keep his pads down through contact, leaving a large surface area for defenders when working through the hashes. Has taken a lot of big hits throughout his career due to his frame size. Long speed is good but initial quickness out of his stance is clunky, leading to some behind the yard of scrimmage takedowns. Will need to learn to more consistently widen his base when pass protecting to sustain blocks.

Best Fit: Bellcow Back

Player Ranking (1-100): 85.2 - I love Harris. I know people are going to compare him to other Tide backs and it's very very tough to do so. Harris is just so exciting to watch. He's a guy you want on your team because he's a battler and will fight for every single yard. There's some Derrick Henry to his game but his tenacious attitude and physique remind me a bit of Marion Barber from the Cowboys. Barber was outstanding for a couple of seasons before injuries took him out of the league. I love Harris and think he's worth a borderline 1st round pick. He's going to dominate short-yardage situations and be a true 20+ back at the next level that has shown consistency and little injury worries.

2 - Travis Etienne - Clemson - 5'10 210 lbs

Strengths: A 4-year starter for the Tigers that has been a huge part of their success in each of those seasons. During his junior campaign, he showed his ability to catch the ball out of the backfield, greatly impressing with over 400 yards receiving and 4 touchdowns. During his freshman season, Etienne showcased experience on special teams', being utilized extensively on kickoff returns. Etienne is a top-flight athlete showcasing both the initial acceleration out of his stance and the long-speed to turn the tiniest of creases into 20-30 yard runs routinely. A constant big-play threat that will force committed tackles, frequently plowing forward through contact and breaking the initial tackle in the open field. An experienced pass protector that routinely will be used to dig out linebackers in blitz situations, showing good pre-snap awareness. Certainly not a 1-trick pony as a runner, showing comfort bouncing runs outside in addition to playing in a more traditional north/south role. A more physical than expected runner for his size, always pushing piles forward, showing to be effective in short-yardage responsibilities. Has had no injury concerns at all during his 4 years, showing reliability.

Weaknesses: Despite his smaller nature, he far too often runs upright through holes, failing to keep his pads down through contact. This affects his ability in pass protection as well, failing to maintain the point of attack, easily losing sustain due to his inability to stay square and leveraged. His vision isn't exceptional and he will get caught crossing the field too often. This happens at both the 1st and 2nd levels, failing to read things quickly and getting overly reliant on his speed. Some might be concerned about his usage during his 4 seasons, having quite a bit of wear and tear on his frame already.

Best Fit: A true bellcow that can start from Day 1

Player Ranking (1-100): 84.4 - I like Etienne quite a bit. He's a dynamic playmaker that is somewhere between Alvin Kamara and Dalvin Cook in playing style. His receiving ability is only going to get more and more refined with additional experience. He's not a top-tier runner in my estimation but a very, very good one. High 2nd round player.

3 - Chuba Hubbard - Oklahoma State - 6'0 208 lbs

Strengths: After finishing with over 2,000 yards and 21 touchdowns during his sophomore campaign, Hubbard finished as a finalist for the Heisman. Has valuable experience in the return game, doing it quite a bit during his freshman season. A lean and athletically-built runner that has a track background. That background is obvious every time he touches the ball, showing the rare explosiveness to burst through the hole and the 2nd level speed to destroy angles from defensive backs in the open field. Not just an athlete, Hubbard shows ability as a runner with excellent patience in the backfield and good vision to spot fading lanes. Hubbard follows his blocks well, picking up chunks of yards in a flash, taking advantage of every possible opening. Terrific lateral mobility and change of direction to redirect his frame and cross-field on broken down plays. Does a nice job of avoiding big hits in the hole with his elusiveness and shifty limbs in space.

Weaknesses: Struggled through a lower leg injury during his junior season. Hubbard lacks ideal body armor to be an every-down back at the next level. When staying in the backfield to pass protect, he will get completely engulfed by blitzers, lacking the anchorage power to sustain and absorb. Not a finisher and lacks any kind of power when playing, failing to fall forward through contact or gain any additional yardage. Contact balance as a whole is underwhelming. Hasn't consistently shown upside as a receiver, having some very poor drops on his resume.

Best Fit: Change of pace offensive weapon and return specialist

Player Ranking (1-100): 79.3 - Hubbard is an explosive and fun player to watch. He isn't just explosive but he also is a natural runner. He would best be suited in a zone style offensive system where he can run outside-zone. 3rd round player.

4 - Kenneth Gainwell - Memphis - 5'11 191 lbs

Strengths: Gainwell, another of Memphis 'long line of impressive running backs, showcased an equally impressive redshirt freshman season. Finishing with over 1400 yards rushing and 600 yards receiving, Gainwell is a 3-down running back showcasing explosive big-play potential every time he touches the ball. As a receiver, Gainwell shows rare receiving abilities, oftentimes being used as a slot receiver and showing the ability to run terrific routes and track the ball. His soft hands are generally pretty reliable as a last resort in bailouts by the quarterback as well. As a runner, Gainwell drops his pads and maintains excellent contact balance through contact. A tougher than expected runner that shows decisiveness while wasting very little time in the backfield. He explodes through narrowing holes, picking up chunks of yardage with relative ease. With only 200 carries on his frame, he's got very little wear and tear on his frame and will only be a redshirt sophomore coming into the league.

Weaknesses: After opting out of his final season, Gainwell has only had 14 career starts and came out of nowhere for his monster redshirt freshman campaign. As a blocker, Gainwell is raw with very limited experience during his college career. When used, he struggled to maintain leverage and sustain blocks, likely stemming from his size. Most of Gainwell's larger runs come from ditching interior lanes and bouncing to the outside edges. Not sure he's truly a 'win inside 'type of back. There were too many times on film where Gainwell lacked the patience needed to allow plays to open up, not showcasing the ideal vision for a top-flight back. Shiftier and quicker than he is fast, his long speed is a major question mark.

Best Fit: Explosive change of pace back and return specialist

Player Ranking (1-100): 79.0 - Gainwell is a solid prospect that can likely get significant snaps for a team while offering some upside on special teams. He's a versatile niche player that is one of the best receiving backs in this draft class. 3rd round player.

5 - Jaret Patterson - Buffalo - 5'9 195 lbs

Strengths: A 3-year starter for MAC-Conference program Buffalo, Patterson has been incredibly productive during his time with the Bulls. Each successive season has been better than the last, producing some of the gaudiest rushing numbers you'll ever see. Built with a small and low center-of-gravity cut frame, Patterson possesses good compactness and lower-body power to dice his way through defenses. Plays far bigger than his listed size, Patterson doesn't shy away from contact. A 1-cut runner that plants his outside foot and explodes up the field, wasting very little time or steps. Possesses really good power through his frame, rarely going down upon 1st contact. Very good in short-yardage situations, running behind his pads and keeping his legs moving through contact. Patient upon receiving the ball, Patterson allows his blockers to open up things for him at the 1st level before he explodes through contact. Quick feet allow him to evade defenders both behind the line of scrimmage and down the field. Impressive change of directional ability that routinely allows him to cut-back in the open field and flips his hips to cross the field. Played in a two-back system and showed his ability to be used as a lead blocker at times. Shows upside as a pass protector, showing willingness and toughness to give rushers a good 'POP 'with his hands.

Weaknesses: Patterson wasn't used much at all in the passing game, failing to offer much 3rd down abilities. When he was used, his routes and hands showed very little development. An undersized runner that likely isn't a bell cow at the next level. Overall speed is just 'OK 'and appears to run out of gas 15-20 yards into his longer runs. Can get a bit too patient in waiting for plays to develop, allowing himself to get caught from behind. For being an undersized runner, he isn't quite as explosive as you would want him to be.

Best Fit: Change of pace back

Player Ranking (1-100): 78.3 - There's no denying the kind of year Patterson had this past season statistically. He's been tremendous and has gotten better each year. Yes, he doesn't excite you for the next level with his size or his athleticism, but the kid makes plays almost every time he touches the ball. I want him on my team even if he's just a change of pace back on Day 1. 3rd round player.

6 - Demetric Felton - UCLA - 5'9 189 lbs

Strengths: A multi-faceted weapon for the Bruins offense, Felton has been a hybrid running back/receiver that has both carried the ball and caught the ball extensively. As a return specialist, Felton showed dynamic ability while finishing with some big returns. Getting his chance as a runner during his senior season, Felton didn't disappoint, averaging over 5 yards per carry. While running the ball, Felton shows big-play potential every time he touches the ball, planting his foot and exploding up the field. Requires committed tacklers to bring him down showing the ability to slip out of tackles on occasion. Not just fast, Felton has rare elusive abilities to create for himself down the field. Has the coordinated feet to start, stop, and redirect quickly. Very good open-field vision and change of directional skills that allow him to cross-field with ease. As a receiver, Felton shows impressive abilities to do damage when working in the slot. An explosive route runner that showcases his quickness to separate on shorter routes, frequently utilizing his entire wingspan to make plays outside of his frame, showing reliable hands.

Weaknesses: Felton isn't a true bellcow runner and needs to be utilized in a niche role for a team at the next level. Attempts to do too much every time he has the ball, taking unnecessary losses far too much. Questionable vision, failing to have the jump-cut instincts to feel things and change course. Lacks the patience to allow things to develop, getting to top speed too quickly while running out of room. Not a power player and fails to push piles or gain much additional yardage after contact. As a pass protector, Felton plays very upright, easily getting knocked off balance.

Best Fit: Change of pace back, receiving back and return specialist

Player Ranking (1-100): 74.9 - Felton is a nice gadget player that offers plenty of versatility in all aspects of playing football. An explosive offensive playmaker that should be a 4th round pick.

7 - Javonte Williams - North Carolina - 5'10 220 lbs

Strengths: A 2-year split carry back for the Tar Heels that has proved to be an impressive dual-threat option both as a runner and a receiver. Williams has improved statistically in each season with yards, per carry average, and touchdowns. Featuring a short and compact frame, Williams possesses bellcow capabilities at the next level. Running behind his pads and keeping and utilizing his low and natural center of gravity to hammer through expiring lanes. Staying on his feet as he goes through contact, Williams is almost like a bowling ball through traffic, showing the impressive balance to stay on his feet. A direct and 1-cut runner that wastes very limited steps in the backfield, quickly getting upfield. Very good in short-yardage situations. Shows good vision to navigate and work through the correct lanes. An absolute load to handle in 1 v 1 situations for defensive backs due to his lower body strength and thick frame. Runs hard with a terrific motor, playing with competitiveness. Has some long speed and had some really good long runs where he was able to outrun defensive backs that had the angle on him. Very comfortable in the receiving game, showing good and smooth hands in space. Functional strength is noticeable while in pass protection, maintaining a good base, and showing the ability to absorb rushers with his anchor.

Weaknesses: Took advantage of sharing carries and beating up on defenses that were worn out already. Not a dynamic big-play guy as it takes him a minute to get to 2nd gear. Struggles redirecting his frame when trying to cross-field laterally, and he will instantly slow down when he's not playing north/south. Has had several ball security issues throughout college.

Best Fit: Starting RB

Player Ranking (1-100): 74.8 - I think Williams best years'are ahead of him. He's a true physical beast that can play all 3 downs for a team. He's shown improved ability in the passing games during each subsequent year. And he can be a good pass protector. 4th round player.

8 - Kylin Hill – Mississippi State – 5'10 214 lbs

Strengths: Hill, coming off a monster year where he tallied over 1300 yards rushing and 11 touchdowns is an intriguing back that has bellcow capabilities. Built with a low center of gravity and tremendously thick lower half, showing the ability to bully and play with power. A bruising back that shows impressive foot quickness and initial acceleration, perfectly comfortable playing north/south or bouncing to the outside and attacking the perimeter. Not content with simply avoiding contact, Hill is a bruiser and that's the only way he knows how to play. Without a doubt his best characteristic is his contact balance, displaying the ability to routinely break 2, 3, or even 4 tackles in a single carry. He will maintain leverage, keeping his pads low and his shoulders down, and run over and plow right through uncommitted tacklers with ease, making them look foolish. A part-time starter in his first two seasons, Hill has minimal wear and tear on his body at the college level. While he didn't have gaudy receiving statistics, Hill is an accomplished receiver that shows impressive route-running potential and soft hands to be used on 3rd downs.

Weaknesses: Quicker than he is fast, Hill lacks the home-run abilities to threaten the back half of a defense. At times he can get too aggressive with his frame, always seeking out and looking for contact. At some point, he will need to learn body preservation and taking what the defense gives you. Has very minimal experience in pass protection, almost always getting used as a receiver on 3rd downs. He can be too aggressive in looking for big plays, resulting in negative plays behind the line of scrimmage when he tries to work laterally and bounce outside.

Best Fit: Great #2 back but can start as well

Player Ranking (1-100): 74.6 – Hill is a good prospect that has an impressive blend of size and power, but he isn't a dynamic playmaking back. He can be a poor decision-maker at all levels of a run and generally a major risk-taker when it comes to picking a lane. I think he'll be a solid #2 back for a team that should warrant 10-15 carries a game as a rookie. 4th round player.

9 - Trey Sermon - Ohio State - 6'0 213 lbs

Strengths: After featuring for the Sooners his first three seasons, Sermon decided to transfer to Ohio State for his final year of eligibility. Sermon has had 4 seasons of solid production but had his best year as a sophomore with the Sooners finishing with almost 1,000 yards rushing. A compactly-built runner that shows great muscularity throughout his frame, possessing excellent NFL body armor. A one-cut runner that plants his foot into the ground and decisively makes a decision in the backfield. Has a good secondary burst for a guy of his size, showing impressive suddenness in the way he can change speeds up. Slippery in the way he runs, showing good lateral mobility to make guys miss in the open field. An excellent competitor that will fight for additional yardage through contact. Does a nice job of playing through uncommitted tacklers, showing good contact balance to stay on his feet. Violent with the ball in his hands, dropping his pads and delivering big blows to unsuspecting defenders. Possesses good lower body strength to hold up in pass protection, showing good technique with the anchor to withstand blocks. Played his best during some of the biggest opportunities and in the biggest games of his career.

Weaknesses: Missed the end of his 2019 season with Oklahoma due to a knee injury. Needs to do a better job of dropping his pads in space, leaving his surface area far too big when working through gaps. Very frustrating in short-yardage situations as he attempts to do too much, missing the hole, attempting to get outside the hashes, and bouncing his runs. In the passing game, he's a bit limited and cannot run good routes in space. Has some struggles catching the football. Quicker than he is fast, Sermon lacks top-end speed.

Best Fit: Change of pace back

Player Ranking (1-100): 74.2 - Sermon was very good for both the Sooners and the Buckeyes. While he lacks any defining elite characteristics, he'll be a solid back for the next level. 4th round player.

10 - Larry Rountree III - Missouri - 5'11 216 lbs

Strengths: A 4-year contributor to the Tigers offense, Rountree has been on the field every game of his career, playing a valuable role in every game. Solid production in every campaign, finishing with nearly 4000 yards rushing between his 4 seasons with a few of those seasons playing in a running back committee role. Has experience as a return specialist. A well-built runner, showing developed muscle tone and good overall weight distribution, Rountree has the compactness and size to be an every-down back. While not having great receiving production, Rountree impressed me when given an opportunity. Shows good smoothness and fluidity running routes combined with the soft hands to catch the ball comfortably as a last resort. The first thing that stands out as a runner for Rountree is his excellent vision, sensing his surroundings well and anticipating spacing in his runs. A quick-footed runner that gets to top-gear quickly. Runs behind his pads, maintaining good leverage through contact, making him a difficult guy to reach in space. A patient back that allows things to develop in front of him before planting his foot and exploding through narrowing gaps. Packs good power and contact balance when playing north/south, capable of staying on his feet and picking up additional yardage after contact. Has shown upside in pass protection, having a good anchor to absorb.

Weaknesses: Limited as an athlete. Rountree is quicker than fast and has questionable overall long speed. Not a big-play runner and was caught from behind several times, running out of gas. Not a great open-field runner, failing to offer any kind of shiftiness to create for himself when reaching the 2nd level. Can be too quick to abandon the inside lanes, relying on bouncing his runs frequently to the perimeter.

> **Best Fit: Potential starter in a zone-style offensive system**

Player Ranking (1-100): 74.0 - Rountree is a back with very very few flaws. He's a safe pick and could be a Day 1 starter. He's not an electric or dynamic game-changing type but he's incredibly reliable. I like Rountree quite a bit and believe he could be a truly good value pick in the 4th round.

11 - Javian Hawkins - Louisville - 5'9 196 lbs

Strengths: As a redshirt freshman, Hawkins exploded onto the scene, finishing with over 1500 yards rushing. He picked up right where he left off during his final season as a sophomore, before opting out of the final few games of the season. A versatile prospect that is an experienced return specialist as well as an improved receiver during the 2020 season. As a receiver, Hawkins shows dynamism with the ball in his hands, creating something out of nothing multiple times this past season. Hawkins is a small, low center of gravity back that is an absolute mismatch of a player due to his rare athletic abilities. Utilizes his stature to stay on his feet, showing good contact balance through traffic. A human joystick, Hawkins bounces off defenders, showing ridiculous change of directional abilities and acceleration. He limits his surface area and plays with good leverage, running behind his pads and keeping his frame low to the ground, rarely allowing a defender to get two hands on him.

Weaknesses: Lack of power is prevalent in all aspects of the game. Still needs continued work in the receiving game, was more of a check-down option in the flat than he was a receiving back that can run good routes. Questionable hands, appearing to be more comfortable corralling the ball into his frame than he was snatching the ball out of the air. A complete liability if asked to stay in and pass protect, getting completely overwhelmed at the point of attack. A bit reckless as a runner at times, failing to always have a plan, appearing to lack some vision behind the line of scrimmage. This caused him to run into his blockers frequently. Not going to offer much as a between the tackles runner, strictly an outside-zone runner.

> **Best Fit: Change of pace back and return specialist**

Player Ranking (1-100): 72.4 - Hawkins is a niche player at the next level. He's not a guy that you're going to want to carry the ball 15+ times a game but he's a fit for a team that already has an established bellcow. He could be a very good return specialist on Day 1 and a nice change of pace back. If he gets better as a receiver, he could be terrific. 4th round player.

12 - Jermar Jefferson - Oregon State - 5'10 217 lbs

Strengths: A 3-year starter for the Beavers, Jefferson has been a consistent factor for their offense in the running game, averaging 5.7 yards per carry during his three years. Built with a rock-solid physique, Jefferson has a compact frame capable of handling the NFL rigors. There's no mistaking the kind of back Jefferson is, he's a power back that drops his pads and maximizes every opportunity given to him. He picks up yardage in chunks, utilizing his powerful lower-body to fall forward to push piles. Rarely goes down to the first contact, showing excellent contact balance when working through the line of scrimmage, bouncing off uncommitted tacklers. A scheme versatile back that possesses the traits to play in any system. Tremendous vision allows him to quickly make decisions, knowing exactly which hole he should take advantage of while displaying the jump-cut ability to switch if a more advantageous lane opens. Displays good traits with the ball in his hands, showing the agility to change directions and create additional yardage when reaching the 2nd and 3rd levels. While he hasn't shown tremendous receiving production, he's shown reliability on check-downs catching the ball cleanly.

Weaknesses: Has been very sporadically used in the receiving game, finishing with less than 300 career receiving yards during his three years. Despite his size, he's a liability in pass protection, lacking reliable recognition abilities. He routinely whiffs on blitzers that he's supposed to pick up. Quicker than he is fast, Jefferson isn't a top-notch athlete and lacks home-run ability when he hits the open field.

> **Best Fit: Solid # 2 back and change of pace**

Player Ranking (1-100): 71.8 - Jefferson is a good runner that displays a lot of really impressive traits. He lacks the top-end explosive abilities to be a dynamic runner at the next level. But his size, vision, and contact balance make him a really attractive 4th round pick. If he had 3-down abilities, he could go higher.

13 - Michael Carter - North Carolina - 5'8 202 lbs

Strengths: Carter is a 4-year significant contributor for the Tar Heels that has been a valuable commodity both on offense and in the return game. An athletically-built runner that utilizes his natural leverage advantages to make it extremely difficult for defenders to get their hands on him. Competitive with the ball in his hands, dropping his pads and pushing piles forward while keeping his legs moving at all times. A fluid moving athlete that has loose limbs allowing him to change direction and cross-field on a dime, showing tremendous all-around agility. Possesses a hard-working motor that will fight and scrap for every single yard. Very patient, rarely making false steps in the backfield, awaiting the perfect time to explode through the hole. Has shown upside as a receiving back, showing the ability to separate against linebackers in space. A terrific return specialist that shows great field vision with the ball to create by himself. Has shown improvement in pass protection, dropping his pads, and delivering good POP, while remaining leveraged at all times. A tough kid that minus his wrist injury in 2018 hasn't missed a game during his 4-year career.

Weaknesses: Broke his wrist in 2018 and missed 3 games. A 'jack of all trades 'runner that doesn't excel in any one area. Lacks the body armor abilities to be a true bellcow runner at the next level. Will get thrown around a bit due to his size, and lacks great functional strength to consistently be a power runner. Overall deep speed is good but isn't great and lacks the home-run abilities to take the ball to the house. Doesn't always show consistency catching the ball, focusing on corralling the ball into his chest, as opposed to attacking the ball out of the air. Not exactly a tackle breaker and will struggle to gain additional yardage after contact consistently.

Best Fit: Change of pace back

Player Ranking (1-100): 70.3 - I like Carter quite a bit when used in the right role. He'll likely never be a 20+ carry a game player. But he can be a good return specialist that will bring considerable versatility to an offense. He's one of the most agile and shifty runners in space in this draft class. 4th round player.

14 - Pooka Williams - Kansas- 5'10 170 lbs

Strengths: A 2-year starter for the Jayhawks that begin playing from Day 1 during his true freshman campaign. Exploded immediately for Kansas finishing with over 1600 yards from scrimmage his freshman season. An athlete that shows big-play potential every time he touches the ball, including in the return game as well. Williams is a human joystick, possessing rare change of directional ability and agility. He can make a guy miss in a phone booth routinely with his fluidity and looseness through his lower body. His start/stop quickness and 0-60 acceleration are unlike anything I've seen. Not just quick, Williams has the terrific long speed to take plays to the house. It's impressive how well Williams stays on his feet through contact despite being so small. Strong lower body and leveraged shoulders force tacklers to wrap-up from his ankles, if they take too high an approach, they will bounce off of him. Better than expected toughness in short-yardage situations, keeping his feet always moving through contact to fall forward. As a pass-catcher, Williams is also impressive. Displaying good hands, Williams can run some nice routes and create after the catch. He's dynamic playing out of the slot with his ability to create for himself on screens.

Weaknesses: Only played in 4 games for Kansas this past season after deciding to sit out the remainder of the year to prepare for the draft. Williams is small, very small for the next level. Was involved in a domestic violence case back in 2018 that caused him to eventually serve a one-game suspension. Will offer very little as a pass protector due to his lack of size and functional strength. Can be a bit frustrating behind the line of scrimmage with his indecisiveness and he lacks elite-level vision.

Player Ranking (1-100): 69.9 - Williams is a fun player to watch but I do have some concerns. He's likely only a fit as a gadget player for an offense. His concerns off the field with domestic violence will likely cause him to get taken off many teams 'draft boards. If a team can find a defined role for him there's no denying what he can bring to an offense. 5th round player.

15 - Khalil Herbert - Virginia Tech - 5'9 204 lbs

Strengths: A 5th year senior for the Hokies that ended up transferring from Kansas, where he played his first 4 years. As a senior with the Hokies, Herbert was tremendous, despite battling through a hamstring injury. He played as the teams 'primary kickoff return specialist as well this past season. A smart runner that shows discipline and precision upon receiving the ball, awaiting the perfect time to explode through narrowing gaps in the offensive line. A smooth operator that gets to top gear in a flash, showing good initial quickness. Runs balanced with a natural and low center of gravity to escape ankle swipers. Stays square through congested traffic to keep or regain his momentum if engaged. Senses his surroundings well and anticipates spacing in his runs. Excellent overall body control and instincts in his jump cut to find creases. A shifty and loose-limbed frame allows him to find and navigate through the tiniest of creases at the 1st level. Very good navigator in space, showing good field vision and instincts to find the best and most direct angles to take.

Weaknesses: Has dealt with some soft tissue injuries through his legs. Has very limited experience as a pass-catcher during his time. A scatback that prefers to play outside the hashes and bounce his runs to the perimeters. Doesn't play as physical as you would expect for a guy with his frame. More of a finesse runner that lacks the nastiness or the aggression to win with power through the 'A 'gap. Very limited experience in pass protection.

Best Fit: Scatback and return specialist

Player Ranking (1-100): 68.2 - Herbert was a really good player for the Hokies this year despite playing through some hamstring injuries. He offers upside as a return specialist and is a good scatback that will create for himself and pick-up yardage in the open field. He's not a bellcow runner and shouldn't be treated as such. But there's no reason why he can't have success playing 15-20 snaps a game. 5th round player.

16 - Elijah Mitchell - Louisiana - 5'10 215 lbs

Strengths: A 4-year contributor to the Ragin 'Cajuns offense, Mitchell mostly split carries his first few seasons and still produced tremendous production. Mitchell was used extensively in the receiving game during his sophomore campaign as well, finishing with 350 yards and an additional 3 touchdowns. Built with a rock-solid frame, Mitchell shows NFL size and toughness through his frame. The true definition of a dual-threat back, Mitchell shows tremendous all-around skills to be a significant contributor from Day 1 at the NFL level. In the receiving game, Mitchell shows a good understanding of simple routes to create a cushion for his QB, displaying good and reliable hands. Competitive with the ball, Mitchell shows toughness and fight to pick-up additional yards while always falling forward. Does a good job of fighting off ankle swipes and staying on his feet through contact. A decisive runner that reads the backfield quickly, maintaining squareness when rushing between the tackles, minimizing his pad level to find narrow creases. Has a good bounce in his step to create for himself in space, showing good agility and loose hips to change directions. Shows good reactionary ability and instincts when in pass protection, keeping his head on a swivel. A really good overall athlete that displays some good long speed to take the ball to the house.

Weaknesses: Had a foot injury during the end of his freshman season that caused him to miss the end of the season. Very reliant on bouncing his runs to the outside, failing to take what's given to him within interior lanes on too many occasions. Upright to a fault when bouncing his runs outside, allowing defenders to wrap him up securely when he fails to drop his pads. Took advantage of being able to stay fresh through games as he was mostly a rotational back with their offensive system.

Best Fit: Change of pace back

Player Ranking (1-100): 63.8 - I like Mitchell quite a bit. He's got almost everything you want in a runner. Size, toughness, physicality, and athleticism. While he hasn't proven it as a standalone back, he should get a chance to impress for a team in the NFL. 6th round player.

17 - Brenden Knox - Marshall - 6'0 223 lbs

Strengths: A 3-year contributor to the Thundering's Herd's backfield committee, Knox exploded during his sophomore campaign. He finished that year averaging over 5 yards per carry and nearly 1400 yards rushing and 11 touchdowns. Featuring a tank of a frame, Knox has tremendous compactness and size throughout his physique. Knox doesn't run like a typical power back, he's incredibly loose through his frame, showing outstanding shiftiness and agility. He limits his surface area, rarely allowing defenders to get two hands on him. Knox shows some explosiveness through his frame, utilizing his built-up momentum to deliver punishing blows to tacklers. He keeps his legs churning through contact, falling forward and gaining additional yardage. Wastes very little movement or time in the backfield, showing decisiveness and conviction upon receiving the ball. Will blow through uncommitted arm tacklers, forcing defenders to be completely invested to bring him down.

Weaknesses: Limited experience and production as a receiver, failing to have hardly any kind of production catching the ball during all 3 seasons. An upright runner that will need to do a better job of dropping his pads and playing with better leverage when working between the hashes. Didn't compete against top-tier competition. Even though he has some explosiveness to his game, he's not a top-tier athlete. He lacks the game-changing speed to routinely threaten the 3rd level of a defense.

Best Fit: Change of pace back

Player Ranking (1-100): 59.9 - Knox is a solid runner that dominated the Conference-USA in the last few seasons. He's got very few flaws and could challenge for a backup role during training camp. 7th round player.

18 - CJ Marable - Coastal Carolina - 5'8 200 lbs

Strengths: A former Arkansas State recruit that ended up transferring to Coastal Carolina following his freshman season, having to sit out the 2017 season. Marable has been impressive while starting every season the last 3 seasons, showing proficiency in both the running and receiving games. Also served as the team's kickoff return specialist at times. A short and compactly-built runner, Marable uses his size to his advantage. Staying low out of his stance, Marable drops his shoulder pads and maintains good leverage through contact, allowing him to stay balanced through congested gaps. Despite being undersized, Marable makes most of his living running through the hashes. Quickly reading the 1st level and finding any expiring lanes, Marable shows terrific vision to identify things developing. As a receiver, Marable runs nice routes out of the backfield, showing confidence to extend and snatch the football out of the air with ease. A good athlete that shows fluidity in his movement to get to top gear in a flash. With the ball in his hands, Marable shows loose hips and good agility to limit his surface area to create additional yardage down the field.

Weaknesses: Has improved when pass protecting but still needs to get better with his technique and recognition skills. Quicker than he is fast, Marable lacks top-end long speed. Not a power back and will have a hard time in short-yardage situations to push piles forward. An undersized back that will likely be limited to a niche role at the next level.

Best Fit: Change of pace back

Player Ranking (1-100): 58.2 - Marable is a versatile weapon for a team that can be used in all aspects of the game. A short and shifty runner that shows good change of pace abilities for the next level. While he's small and lacks great power, he shows upside as a receiver and a special teams 'return specialist. 7th round player.

19 - Brian Robinson - Alabama - 6'1 228 lbs

Strengths: Robinson, known as the Tide's power back, had a solid final couple of seasons for the Tide while playing in a cleanup role. Built with tremendous thickness throughout his frame, Robinson is a load to handle for defenders. Robinson also has experience being the teams 'rotational kickoff return specialist for two seasons. He showed during his junior season the ability to be used in the receiving game with natural pass-catching ability. Robinson is your classic 1-cut north/south runner that plays with directness from the very snap of the ball. Excellent when used in short-yardage situations, pushing piles forward and keeping his legs churning through contact. Robinson very much is a momentum runner that takes pride in getting more and more carries to wear a defense down towards the end of games. Anticipating contact well and rarely going down upon the first contact, Robinson plows through tackles while staying on his feet with terrific contact balance and a powerfully-built lower body. Shows a surprising ability to make the 1st defenders miss in space behind the line of scrimmage. His power is on display when pass protecting, showing the ability to anchor with his lower half and absorb contact. Excellent motor and effort when blocking for his teammates down the field.

Weaknesses: A limited athlete that will get chased down from behind on occasion, failing to offer any kind of big-play ability in any facet. At times he is far too aggressive to attack the interior of the 'A 'gap, failing to allow his lineman to open up a 1st level hole. Overall his decision-making is very hit or miss and he frequently picks wrong, opting for the potential bigger play and taking some negative yardage runs.

Best Fit: Short-yardage back

Player Ranking (1-100): 56.3 - Robinson is likely limited to a short-yardage role at the next level. His lack of explosiveness or true 3rd down ability limits his effectiveness for most teams. He's a tough-as-nails runner though that should get 5-10 carries a game. 7th round player.

20 - Rakeem Boyd - Arkansas - 6'0 206 lbs

Strengths: A former Aggie that transferred following his freshman season to a junior college before transferring to Arkansas. A 3-year starter for the Razorbacks that was tremendous during his junior campaign where he tallied over 1100 yards rushing and an additional 160 yards receiving. An athletically-built and lean back that possesses dual-threat opportunities at the next level. Despite not having elite receiving production, Boyd has flashed impressive upside as a receiver with natural hands to extend and catch the ball with ease away from his frame. A terrific athlete that picks up chunks of yards in a flash with his long stride lengths, showing real breakaway abilities. Patient in the backfield while he awaits 1st level openings and quickly explodes through. Boyd runs tougher than his size would seem to indicate, showing a nonstop attitude and motor to relentlessly fight for additional yardage. Quickly dropping his pads upon receiving the ball, Boyd powers through contact, showing good leg drive while utilizing forward momentum to create additional yardage. Shows willingness as a blocker with good timing and instincts to recognize things quickly.

Weaknesses: Struggled with a foot injury during his senior season. A bit of a straight-line runner that will struggle when being asked to change directions or flip his hips. This limits his ability to create in the open field and makes him strictly a 1-angle pursuant. Disappointing contact balance in the open field as he struggles to stay on his feet through weak and uncommitted tackles. Razorbacks coaches didn't trust him frequently on 3rd downs, taking him off the field.

Best Fit: Chance of pace back

Player Ranking (1-100): 54.0 - Boyd is a good mix of explosiveness and toughness as a runner. My main worry is he's a bit of a straight-line athlete and lacks the looseness and contact balance you like to see in a smaller back. Has a chance to catch on in training camp. Undrafted free agent.

TOP-10 RBs

1. Najee Harris
2. Travis Etienne
3. Chuba Hubbard
4. Kenneth Gainwell
5. Jaret Patterson
6. Demetric Felton
7. Javonte Williams
8. Kylin Hill

9. Trey Sermon
10. Larry Rountree III

Chapter 4

FB's

1 - Rhamondre Stevenson - Oklahoma - 6'0 227 lbs

Strengths: One of the best former JUCO prospects in the country that transferred to Oklahoma to play his final two seasons, seeing significant snaps for them in each season. Instantly impressing for the Sooners, Stevenson averaged a tremendous 8 yards per carry as a junior. Built with a powerful and physically-imposing frame, Stevenson shows true versatility to be effective in short-yardage situations, blocking, and in the receiving game. Breaking tackles for fun, Stevenson rarely goes down upon the first contact, playing like a man on a mission. Plays with terrific leverage at all times, pushing piles forward while keeping his legs churning through contact. A true north/south runner that runs direct, hitting expiring holes in a flash while completely maximizing each available opportunity. Good vision when receiving the ball, sensing his surroundings well, and wasting little time finding cutback lanes. Shiftier than you would imagine for a guy of his size, showing good open-field wiggle to create at the 2nd level. Possesses a nasty stiff-arm to keep his frame clean while working on the perimeter. Has impressed when working in pass protection showing willingness and power at the point of attack to absorb contact well through his lower half. Flashes upside as a run blocker, which would ideally suit him at FB at the next level, maintaining positioning and opening up 1st level opportunities for his back.

Weaknesses: Stevenson was one of the Sooners suspended for failed drug tests before the Peach Bowl at the end of his junior campaign, causing him to be suspended for the college football playoff and 5 games during his senior year. A bit of a build-up speed runner that lacks the initial juice to explode out of his cuts, most notable when working in outside lanes. His overall change of directional ability and short-area quickness are average. Struggles to separate when working consistently in the receiving game against linebackers due to lack of agility and quickness.

Best Fit: Starting FB

Player Ranking (1-100): 68.4 - Stevenson could be a nice asset for an offense due to his versatility to assist. His suspension concerns will need to be looked into, but there's no denying there's a good player here. He could offer a nice #2 option that could stay on the field to assist in pass protection or open up holes while working in 2-back sets. 5th round player.

2 - Tory Carter - LSU - 6'1 250 lbs

Strengths: Carter is a physical presence for the Tigers team that has seen snaps at fullback, tight end, and all the special teams' units. Carter is built incredibly tough with a big and compact frame, appearing to love all the physical aspects of playing football as evidenced by his violent nature. Special teams 'coaches will love his hard-working and blue-chip characteristics to play with aggression and nastiness. As a blocker, Carter displays the mentality and the finishing ability to clear out run lanes while opening up blocking holes. Displays powerful POP-on contact with his upper body when reaching his blocks. When he's not on the field, it's noticeable for the LSU runners. Possesses the body armor and the lower body power to explode out of his stance to deliver devastating blows while on the move to create real displacement push. His former experience as a backup tight end will enable him to routinely be used as a receiver to run routes, showing good and reliable hands as a last option.

Weaknesses: Has had some off-field concerns, including being suspended by the team for a game. (Unknown reasons) He was also ejected from a game during his junior season for targeting. Has essentially had no experience as a runner and likely won't offer any upside in short-yardage situations or as a Plan-B alternative when he's on the field. Minimal overall athleticism and isn't going to blow anyone away with physical qualities, limiting his effectiveness to create separation when used as a receiver.

Best Fit: Blocking FB

Player Ranking (1-100): 66.2 - Carter knows what he is and that's why he's valuable. There are no projections or necessarily upside with the player but he'll be a Day 1 starter on all the special teams 'units for a team. He can also be used immediately on offense to open up holes. I like this kid and he's going to make a nice NFL role player for a team. 5th round.

3 - Ben Mason - Michigan - 6'3 256 lbs

Strengths: Mason, a team captain, has been a reliable and valuable member of the Wolverines team during all 4 seasons of his career. The definition of versatile, Mason has switched between playing at FB, defensive line, and then FB again for his final season. He's also played extensively on special teams and has been used at tight end as well. Mason's size and length are an asset, possessing a larger frame, allowing him to play as an emergency tight end if needed at the next level. A very good lead blocker, that utilizes his length effectively when working in space while run blocking, showing the ability to quickly win inside hand placement and control defenders to open up holes for his backs. Understands leverages and playing with angles. Packs some power throughout his frame with good upper and lower body power. As a sophomore, Mason was used quite a bit as a straight-line runner on the goal-line and also in short-yardage situations, showing really good production with 7 rushing touchdowns. Terrific toughness and competitiveness to fight for every inch on the field with the ball in his hands. A reliable catcher of the ball showing soft hands to catch the ball in traffic.

Weaknesses: After having 2 solid seasons being the teams 'main blocker, between switching positions and not being used as extensively on offense, Mason has been a bit underwhelming production-wise. Mason is more of an athlete fullback than he is a dominating physical presence. He's not going to blow-up running lanes, he's more of a 'reach 'blocker that will utilize his length to win. Just an 'OK 'overall athlete and isn't much of a threat on offense other than in short-yardage situations.

Best Fit: Athletic versatile FB

Player Ranking (1-100): 59.5 - Mason is a solid football player and a versatile contributor to any team. He's a good lead blocker and a solid special teams player. He's not going to light the world on fire as a production player but his valuable goal-line experience can make him attractive to teams. 7th round player.

4 - Spencer Brown - UAB - 5'11 220 lbs

Strengths: Brown is an impressive 4-year starter for Conference-USA program UAB, where he has been a mainstay for their offense since his freshman campaign. Considered a weight-room warrior by his teammates, Brown is incredibly powerful throughout his frame. His weight has fluctuated throughout his career and he's played at 240 pounds at times, which could suit him nicely as a fullback at the next level. Brown is a bulldozer with the ball in his hands, showing terrific toughness as a runner to push piles forward through contact. A 1-cut and direct runner that wastes no time. He keeps his legs churning at all times and always falls forward to gain an additional yard or two. He stays balanced while keeping his pads low and playing with a low center of gravity to escape tackle attempts. He shrugs off ankle tackles with relative ease, rarely going down to uncommitted tackles. While not used much in the passing game, he has shown the ability to run routes and present an available target for his quarterback. He has flashed while being used to pass protect, showing terrific lower body strength to be able to absorb and hunker down.

Weaknesses: Brown has very little experience being used in the receiving game, with single-digit receptions during each campaign. Does not have a lot of experience being used as a lead back or in opening up holes. He needs considerably more recognition work when in pass protection, appearing to have some lapses in concentration, responding late to pressure situations. Brown has played in a triple-threat backfield where he was often used to wear out defenses or take advantage of tired defenses, allowing him to stay fresh. Not a great athlete and lacks the short-area quickness to separate in the receiving game or be a home-run hitter while running the ball.

Best Fit: FB or change of pace back

Player Ranking (1-100): 58.3 - Brown is a powerful runner that offers some upside as a change of pace and short-yardage runner. His lack of overall experience in the receiving game and protection situations limits his upside as an immediate contributor for a team at the next level. He's going to need to prove he can a great special teams player as a rookie to make a team. 7th round player.

5 - Adam Prentice - South Carolina - 6'0 245 lbs

Strengths: A graduate transfer who played his first 4 seasons with Mountain-West program Colorado State before transitioning and playing his final year with the Gamecocks. Prentice is a compactly-built and stout fullback that is built like a bowling ball. He's a very difficult guy to bring down to the ground due to his width and strength through his lower half. Was used quite a bit as a runner during this sophomore season, showing experience to be relied upon in short-yardage situations. A very well-rounded lead-blocker that remains square while blocking, utilizing very good field vision to pick up defenders at both the 1st and 2nd levels. Very strong that loves the physical areas of the game, bringing a violent nature to deliver punishment at the point of attack when reaching defenders. When being used as a receiver, he shows reliable hands to snatch the ball out of the air away from his frame.

Weaknesses: An older prospect who will be 24 years old his rookie season. Tore his ACL during the early part of his career, causing him to get a medical redshirt year. Doesn't have a load of experience catching the ball, with only single-digit receptions during each year. Limited athletically and fails to offer much upside after the catch due to lack of short-area quickness or up-the-field speed.

Best Fit: Blocking FB and Special Teams

Player Ranking (1-100): 54.5 - Prentice is limited athletically but will maximize every aspect of his positive traits due to his hardworking nature. He's going to need to make a roster on special teams.

6 - Mason Stokke - Wisconsin - 6'2 239 lbs

Strengths: After starting his career as a linebacker, Stokke transitioned to fullback the last two seasons. A versatile offensive weapon that has been used as a lead blocker, in the running game and in the receiving game successfully. Stokke's former experience at linebacker is evident in the way he plays fullback, showing good ease of movement skills and fluidity when working laterally. A good overall athlete that will be a valuable 3rd down piece for an offense. When being used as the lead blocker, Stokke maintains squareness with defenders to keep spacing and distance between the defender and the runner. Understands how to play with leverage to generate good point of attack control and power. Commits himself to winning inside hand fits to control the defender throughout the duration. When working the flats in the receiving game, Stokke shows good comfort and initial quickness to get open quickly. His soft hands rarely let him down. As a runner, Stokke has proven the ability to successfully be used both on the goal-line and in short-yardage situations.

Weaknesses: Stokke is still relatively new to the position and is still learning how to play in all the facets of fullback. More of a technician in his style of play than a bulldozer that will plow large running lanes at the point of attack. A bit of a 'jack of all trades but master of none' player that lacks a defining characteristic.

Best Fit: Versatile offensive chess piece

Player Ranking (1-100): 54.3 - Stokke is a good player that has some athleticism to his game. As a runner he's shown the ability to play with some power. But he lacks the overall physicality and strength to be a dominant point of attack blocker in either the run or passing game. Undrafted free agent.

TOP-5 FBs

1. Rhamondre Stevenson
2. Tory Carter
3. Ben Mason
4. Spencer Brown
5. Adam Prentice

Chapter 5

WR's

1 - Ja'Marr Chase - LSU - 6'1 208 lbs

Strengths: After being a rotational receiver in his freshman campaign, Chase lit the world on fire in 2019 as a sophomore, setting SEC records in yards and touchdowns. He finished that year with just under 1,800 yards receiving and 20 touchdowns. Chase decided to sit out his final season before entering the draft where he will have just turned 21 a few days before his draft day. Built with good weight distribution, Chase carries his weight excellently with tremendous compactness and muscularity through his frame. Chase has practically 0 overwhelming concerns on his tape and for only having 1 year of starting experience his levels of nuance are quite incredible. Playing the game like a flat-out bully, Chase is a beast both with the ball in his hands and without. Equally comfortable and adept playing both outside as the 'X 'or kicking inside and playing in the slot. Excellent physicality, jam technique, and hand strength allow him to routinely handle press-man corners, quickly disengaging and utilizing different release points to keep defensive points on their heels. His ball skills, leaping ability, and flexible body control allow him to consistently time the ball to perfection at the top of its flight. Incredibly consistent in 50/50 situations where he can be trusted across the middle or with multiple defenders on him to make a play. An excellent overall athlete that shows both the start/stop quickness and good long speed to threaten all levels of a defense. He combines this with his stellar and advanced route-running technique to utilize excellent footwork in and out of his breaks to hide patterns and create and keep defenders on their heels. Chase is a total team player that shows toughness and reliability when used to block in-line for his backs.

Weaknesses: Some will look at Chase's only 1-year of starting experience as a weakness. While he doesn't have elite height, it won't look recognizable on tape because of the way he plays. He will suffer from an occasional concentration lapse leading to a few drops on tape. While he is a willing blocker, he will occasionally utilize poor technique leading to misses when lining up in the slot.

Best Fit: 'X 'receiver

Player Ranking (1-100): 90.2 - Chase has all the skills you want in a receiver. His advanced route-running ability, coupled with his natural athleticism, strength, and ball dominance makes him a #1 receiver at the next level. He has very few flaws on tape and will only get better with additional snaps at the next level. I'm excited about his future. High 1st round player.

2 - De'Vonta Smith - Alabama - 6'1 175 lbs

Strengths: A 3-year contributor to the Tide offense that has been one of the most explosive playmakers in all of college football the last couple of years. Came onto the scene following his game-winning touchdown in the national title game during his sophomore season. Then he completely blew up his junior season with over 1200 yards receiving and 14 touchdowns. Smith has some experience in the return side of the game, returning kickoffs during his senior season. Smith is equally effective on the inside and the outside, showing comfort in playing any of the Alabama receiver roles. Smith is an explosive and slippery athlete that looks effortless running by defenders and is smooth as ice in the way in which he runs routes. He fluidly alters route speeds creating separation at all areas of his routes, leaving defenders caught in the mud when choosing to cross-field or run inside an in-breaking route. Invites press coverage, showing terrific wiggle and releases to instantly separate. Despite his lanky frame, his yards after catch ability is certainly above average showing elusive characteristics in the open-field. Alabama coaches did whatever they could to get him the ball quickly so he could showcase his post-catch ability to create and pick up yards in a flash. Fearless when playing in the middle of the field, rarely going down upon the first contact. Terrific body control, concentration, and balance to adjust to the ball in mid-flight and routinely out-jump or post-up defenders to make plays in the air. His strong hands at the catch point allow him to pluck the ball out of the air routinely. Smith had some stellar games against cornerbacks that have been drafted very high in the last few seasons.

Weaknesses: Smith is rail-thin that lacks much muscle mass on any part of his frame and will likely get bullied at the next level both at the line of scrimmage and at the catch point. Top-end speed is good but isn't elite. He was protected quite often as the 'move 'receiver at the line of scrimmage failing to have to take on cornerbacks on the line of scrimmage. When he doesn't gain considerable separation, he struggles. Needs to improve functional strength and hand strength when competing at the catch point.

Best Fit:'Z 'receiver that can play in the slot

Player Ranking (1-100): 88.9 - Smith is a smooth route-runner that offers versatility for an offense. He would be ideally suited as a 'z 'move receiver that can occasionally bump inside and play in the slot as well. I'd like to see him gain an additional 5-10 pounds of solid muscle for the next level as long as it doesn't sacrifice his explosive quickness. His success in the championship game and in crucial moments this year will elevate him even more. Has some Marvin Harrison to his game. 1st round player.

3 - Rashod Bateman - Minnesota - 6'2 210 lbs

Strengths: A 3-year starter for the Gophers that had a ridiculous sophomore campaign in 2019 where he finished with over 1200 yards and 11 touchdowns. He originally opted out for the 2020 season but opted back in. Bateman possesses an NFL physique with a good frame and muscularity through his frame. Bateman is one of the more refined college receiver prospects you'll find. Showcasing a variety of different releases at the line of scrimmage, Bateman can bully smaller receivers with his hands or keep his frame clean with good quickness. Bateman has experience playing both on the outside and in the slot, and he runs a full route tree already. A reliable catcher of the football that utilizes his entire wingspan to make catches confidently outside of his frame. Strong hands allow him to snatch the ball away from defenders. Good red-zone target with his ability to go vertical and high-point the ball. Very good and reliable in tight spaces. A nuanced and diversified route-runner that shows deception at all levels of his routes, utilizing terrific footwork at the top of routes to create separation. Dangerous after the catch, showing a good secondary burst to explode through uncommitted tackles and has broken a lot of tackles. A physical blocker that takes it personally, showing toughness and upper-body power to sustain through the duration of plays.

Weaknesses: By no means is he slow but Bateman doesn't possess elite long speed nor does he have great initial acceleration out of his stance. He can be a bit too aggressive at all levels and will be called for some offensive pass interference with his continued reliance on pushing off. There appears to be some lower body stiffness through his frame that is manifest on lateral movements and in-breaking routes. Bateman could stand to put on some additional weight on his frame to play in the physical manner that he enjoys playing in.

Best Fit: 'X 'receiver

Player Ranking (1-100): 86.3 - I really really like Bateman. I don't remember seeing a receiver that is as polished as him at all the advanced areas of the game as Bateman is. He doesn't have any clear-cut deficiencies as a receiver. Perhaps he's not an elite athlete but he's still a very good one. The most important thing is he separates constantly! 1st round player.

4 - Jaylen Waddle - Alabama - 5'10 182 lbs

Strengths: Waddle is a 3-year starter for the Tide that immediately began gaining significant snaps during his freshman season, proving his big-play potential both in the receiving game and in the return game. He's had several special teams 'return touchdowns. Despite not having the ideal and prototypical size, Waddle makes up for it in his game-changing abilities every time he touches the ball. Quickly getting to speed, Waddle plays with a relentless motor on every snap of the ball. Not just quick, Waddle has breakaway speed to threaten all levels of the defense. A smooth and fluid athlete that can play both vertically and laterally, showing the ability to cross-field and change directions with ease. Playing all over the offensive formation, Waddle plays both inside and outside in college. Excellent on broken-down plays showing good awareness down the field to present a QB-friendly option. When defenders fail to get their hands on him early in his routes, Waddle makes them pay for it, quickly putting them on skis and separating. His sharp footwork and varied release points make him an extremely difficult cover from the beginning to the end of his route. After the catch, Waddle utilizes his breakaway abilities, 5th gear, and his good field vision to gain the most out of every touch of the ball. Waddle maximizes his frame, showing good length with the ability to snatch the ball away from his frame and extend. A passionate blocker that takes the physical sides of the game personally, showing aggression and willingness to seal edge rush lanes for his teammates.

Weaknesses: Waddle fractured his ankle midway through his junior season causing him to need surgery and miss the rest of the season. Production numbers came down quite a bit during his sophomore campaign. Took advantage of being the 3rd or 4th option early in his career, rarely getting significant defensive attention. Picked up a lot of his yards on manufactured plays, such as on screens and RPOs. Needs to continue to widen his route tree, running only a handful of routes. Waddle is short and lacks the prototypical receiver frame to play on the outside, leaving him likely in a niche or slot role strictly. He needs to continue to refine his route-running technique, relying solely on his speed instead of setting up his routes through his stems. A bit of a body catcher that relies on corralling the ball into his chest instead of attacking it with his hands.

Player Ranking (1-100): 84.9 - Waddle could have possibly put himself into the Day 1 discussion if not for the injury. He was having a really impressive junior campaign before the injury. A dynamic game-changing athlete that will produce every time he touches the ball. 2nd round player.

5 - Dyami Brown - North Carolina - 6'0 185 lbs

Strengths: A 2-year starter for the Tar Heels that has posted two really impressive seasons of over 1,000 yards receiving. A good-sized and leanly-built athlete that possesses the frame to play on the outside at the next level, with above-average length. A savvy route-runner that moves fluidity out of his stance with good initial acceleration out of his stance. He sells his routes nicely, possessing some devastating double moves to create openings down the field. Long-speed is a constant threat for defenders, showing the ability to threaten vertically up the seams and create separation against defensive backs. Very good lateral agility to separate in/out of his break, showing looseness in his hips to not have to gear down when changing direction. This allows him to consistently find pockets of space in slants and other in-breaking routes. Has an understanding of how to regularly find pockets of space against zone coverage, presenting a nice QB-friendly option in the middle of the field. Maximizes out his frame physically, showing the good post-catch ability to pick up additional yardage after the catch. I love how physical Brown plays when blocking downfield for his teammates, never giving up on a play and showing the physicality to sustain and hold his perimeter blocks.

Weaknesses: The biggest concern with Brown is his frequent issues with drops, failing to reliably extend and snatch the football out of the air. He's overly reliant on bringing the ball into his chest and utilizing his body to secure the ball. This limits him in 50/50 situations where he will get the ball knocked away from his hands. Has played almost exclusively on the left side of the formation, having very little experience in the different receiver spots. Would like to see him widen his route tree to keep defenders guessing.

Best Fit: 'X 'receiver

Player Ranking (1-100): 82.7 - Brown was stellar this past season showing his ability to potentially be a solid starter from Day 1 at the next level. He's fluid, smart, and a really good athlete that can separate on all different points of a football field. His hands need to get better when catching the football and he hasn't been consistently tested at the line of scrimmage, which could present a problem. I would take him in the 2nd round.

6 - Cornell Powell - Clemson - 6'0 205 lbs

Strengths: Before his senior season, Powell was mostly a role player and return specialist for the Tigers. As a senior, Powell put himself firmly into the draft discussion, finishing with nearly 900 yards receiving and 7 touchdowns. Possessing good overall size with a developed build, Powell shows next-level readiness. A really good athlete that accelerates smoothly into his routes, Powell can take the top off a defense, possessing great long speed as well. Dynamic with the ball in his hands, Powell doesn't go down easily, showing good competitive toughness and leg strength to fight for every yard while staying on his feet. Good body control and ball skills, showing the ability to contort his body while locating the ball down the field. Varies up his speeds through his stems, creating good deception to separate at various levels of his route. Versatile, as he's played all over the offensive front, playing both inside and outside and on both sides of the line of scrimmage. Excellent catcher of the football, showing good reliability to make grabs outside of his frame. Understands how to beat jams at the line of scrimmage, utilizing a wide range of hand techniques and wiggle to keep his frame clean. A willing and aggressive blocker that shows good ability as a stalk blocker.

Weaknesses: A one-year wonder that had virtually no production his entire career before finally living up to his former high school billing during his final season. Picked up the vast majority of his yards this year from screens and manufactured plays designed to get him the ball quickly. Lacks a vast arsenal of routes. Still developing as a route runner, getting a bit lazy with his technique, far too often rounding off his routes.

Best Fit: Outside receiver

Player Ranking (1-100): 82.3 - I liked Powell a lot more than I was expecting to. Athletic, physical, and reliable. These are three traits that every receiver should possess and Powell has all 3 in heaps. He was stellar this year and did a lot of damage by his own creation, purely on willpower. He would be an ideal #2 target for an offense. 2nd round player.

7 - Tamorrion Terry - Florida State - 6'4 210 lbs

Strengths: Has started virtually every game since his redshirt freshman season, showing to be a reliable target for the Seminoles offense. He put himself on the draft radar following his stellar sophomore season where he tallied 1200 yards receiving and 9 touchdowns. Terry is a big-bodied receiver with rare length and size for the position. He's not just your typical possession receiver, as Terry possesses really impressive overall athleticism. Seminoles coaches used Terry every opportunity they could to get the ball in his hands with his ability to create after the catch. Violent after the catch, Terry utilizes nasty stiff arms and long strides to pick up chunks of yardage in a flash. Utilizes good field vision to pick the right angles to pick up additional yardage. A savvy route-runner that possesses a diversified route tree, capable of winning at all levels of the field. Shows sharpness at the top of his routes, capable of creating separation when working laterally. Combines good initial acceleration out of his stance with above-average long speed to separate on vertical routes. Understands how to utilize his frame to create leverage and open up inside releases to box-out defenders at the catch point. Long arms allow him to make plays outside of his frame.

Weaknesses: Needs to continue to develop his frame as he lacks sufficient body armor for the next level, having a bit of a lankier physique. Has had several issues with his hands, failing to secure the ball with his hands. He's too reliant on attempting to body catch the ball by securing it into his chest. Doesn't always show aggression at the catch point, failing to accurately attack the ball. I wish he showed more physicality when blocking, at times looking disinterested if the ball wasn't coming in his direction. Has lined up almost exclusively on the right side of the formation, failing to play anywhere else on the line of scrimmage.

Best Fit: 'X 'receiver

Player Ranking (1-100): 80.2 - Terry is a big and talented receiver that possesses a wide range of ability to play at the next level. I was impressed with his ability to win in several different ways. He's a really good football player that can consistently create after the catch as well. 2nd round player.

8 - Rondale Moore - Purdue - 5'9 180 lbs

Strengths: Moore exploded onto the scene during his true freshman season after being one of the most highly touted high school players finishing his freshman year with nearly 1300 yards. He added an additional 200 yards rushing and several big plays in the return game as well. Moore is a short but tough kid that is one of the most dynamic athletes in all of college football. Excelling every time, he gets the ball in his hands, Moore is almost impossible for defenders to get two hands on due to his shifty and agile nature. Keeping his pads leveraged and his frame practically on the ground at all times, Moore is like a bouncy ball that rarely goes down upon 1st contact with rare contact balance. Rare acceleration to instantly get to top gear, Moore excels the most at the shorter to more intermediate levels of the field, utilizing his short-area quickness and agility to create for himself. Quick feet allow him to keep his frame clean at the line of scrimmage. A good route-runner that shows sharpness to his routes, showing the terrific change of direction and transitional quickness. Moore isn't just 'quick 'he also has top-tier speed and this will be showcased when a narrow window opens up for himself. Purdue coaches utilized him in a lot of screens and manufactured plays where he was able to take a 5-yard gain and get 20-30 yards routinely due to his field vision and toughness.

Weaknesses: Missed most of the 2019 season due to an ongoing hamstring issue. Durability concerns will be a major question mark. Size concerns will be a problem for many teams and he certainly won't be considered an outside receiver for many teams. Lacks the length to be able to win the majority of 50/50 balls at the next level, failing to have the wingspan. Has had several concentrations drops. A little too aggressive at times, taking far too many unnecessary hits. Not exactly a 'down the field 'threat with the majority of his route being less than 10 yards, despite his great speed. Doesn't always appear engaged when it comes to blocking downfield for his teammates.

Best Fit: 'Niche 'player that can be used in a variety of different roles including special teams', designated running plays, and in the slot

Player Ranking (1-100): 79.9 - If Moore's health checks out 'OK 'he's a fun player to watch. He'll make any offense better and more explosive. There's some Tyreek Hill to his game. He's small but he will make plays every time he can touch the ball. I want him on my team. 3rd round player.

9 - Terrace Marshall - LSU - 6'3 200 lbs

Strengths: A solid role player his first two seasons at LSU before playing in a featured role for the Tigers offense in 2020. Marshall is a good-framed athlete that displays a long and lean physique. Marshall has shown the ability to continue his stellar sophomore production into his junior year despite no longer having elite-level QB play as he did in 2019. Marshall is a versatile threat, having extensive experience in the slot as well as playing on the perimeter too. A very good athlete that can threaten the deep halves of the field. Has a good understanding of how to beat press coverage with his hands, showing good physicality and nuance against man coverage. Strong hands allow him to win 50/50 balls and dominate at the catch point. Marshall utilizes his entire catch radius to frequently extend and make difficult grabs look routine. Runs a diversified route-tree with the ability to set-up his routes very nicely. Very good ball skills with his ability to locate the ball down the field and high-point it and snatch it away from defensive backs. Dynamic in the red-zone with his combination of size and leaping ability, as evidenced by his high touchdown numbers. Good after the catch showing physicality and aggression to fight for additional yardage and fall forward through contact.

Weaknesses: A 1-year starter that was very much a role player before his junior season. A build-up speed athlete that takes a few seconds to get to top gear. Could stand to gain some additional sharpness through his routes, lacking great footwork at the top. Fails to consistently separate and tends to be more of a 'fight at the catch point receiver 'than someone who can consistently separate with precise routes. Doesn't offer much interest or toughness as a blocker. Fails to always look engaged and actively interested when the play isn't designed for him.

> ### Best Fit: Versatile receiving threat that can be a # 3 receiver for a team

Player Ranking (1-100): 79.8 - Marshall is a talented receiver that brings a ton of versatility to the table, showing the ability to play anywhere. He lacks a ton of starting experience but he's been very good when he's played. He's a nice combination of size, athleticism, and skill. He should immediately fight for valuable snaps. 3rd round player.

10 - Sage Surratt - Wake Forest - 6'3 215 lbs

Strengths: Surratt burst onto the scene after a stellar sophomore year where he finished with over 1000 yards and 11 touchdowns. A smart kid, both on and off the field, that chose Wake Forest over Harvard because of Wake's business program. Built with tremendous size, muscularity, and thick limbs, Surratt is a powerhouse receiver that plays with strength throughout his frame. Uses his size in every aspect of the game, especially post-catch where he will routinely pick up additional yards after contact. Loves and takes blocking seriously, showing the good technique to clear run lanes on the perimeter. Despite his size, Surratt is smooth as ice in the way he plays, quickly and seamlessly getting downhill and into full stride. Possesses tremendous body control and ball tracking abilities to be able to adjust to the ball while it is in flight while utilizing his body to box out and give himself the only opportunity to make a play. An excellent leaper that uses his length and sticky hands to go up and snatch the ball out of the air. Comfortable when taking on press-coverage, showing enough hand strength, and wiggle at the line of scrimmage to beat jams.

Weaknesses: Missed the final 4 games of his career with a shoulder injury during his sophomore campaign. While Surratt is a good athlete, he lacks elite athleticism and explosive twitchiness to be able to consistently separate against more agile corners at the next level. Hip flexibility and tightness limit his effectiveness when working on lateral plains. Will require QB's to make tightly contested balls on most occasions as he rarely creates substantial separation.

Best Fit: #2 possession receiver

Player Ranking (1-100): 79.3 - Surratt is a solid player that will instantly merit starting consideration for a team. While he's not an elite athlete, he's got very very few flaws to his game. For only playing 2 seasons in the ACC, he's very refined. He will be a dynamic red-zone threat immediately and consistently bully smaller corners at the next level.

11 - KadariusToney - Florida - 5'11 189 lbs

Strengths: Toney is a 4-year contributor to the Gators offense and special teams that has done it all. Playing in every kind of formation and being used as a wildcat QB, a running back and a receiver, Toney brings versatility and unquestioned playmaking ability to a team. Toney is dynamic with the ball in his hands, being able to alter and cross-field with loose hips and unparalleled agility. Despite his lankier build, Toney is surprisingly strong through his lower half, rarely getting brought down by the first guy. His ability to stay on his feet and remain balanced through congested traffic is impressive. Outstanding start/stop quickness and acceleration allow him to evade defenders and generally almost always make the 1st guy miss. Gators did whatever they could to get the ball in his hands to take advantage of his skillset in the open field. Toney also has extensive experience in both kickoff and punt return duties. Fearless when working in the middle of the field, Toney shows trustworthiness in congested spots. I was impressed when watching him as a blocker, showing toughness and physicality to handle outside zone runs and seal off the edges.

Weaknesses: Toney is a 'jack of all trades 'kind of player that doesn't truly have one dominant position nor has he ever put up exceptional statistics in any one season. Toney doesn't appear to have the frame for much additional muscle mass. Not a reliable 'hands 'catcher as he almost always has to corral the ball into his chest upon receiving it. He's still learning and raw when it comes to the route-running aspects of his game, only recently learning how to play receiver, formerly a high school QB. Long-speed is just 'OK 'and generally is quicker than he is fast, having been caught from behind on occasion. Almost always used as a slot receiver when lined up as a receiver with very little outside experience. There are concerns with Toney off-the-field that will need to be addressed with evaluators.

Best Fit: Slot receiver that can be used on special teams'

Player Ranking (1-100): 78.8 - Toney had a really good senior season where he showcased an ability to have a significant role as a receiver at the next level. He's a fun player that will make some plays for an offense no matter where he is used. I'm a little bit worried about him off-the-field so he drops a round for me. I'd take him in the 3rd round player.

12 - Elijah Moore - Ole Miss - 5'9 185 lbs

Strengths: After churning out successful NFL pass-catchers the last few years, Ole Miss has produced another highly-exciting prospect in Moore. Moore has been a two-year starter for the Rebels, exploding during his final year as a junior finishing with nearly 1200 yards receiving in only 8 games. He's also had extensive experience in the return game, returning both kickoffs and punts. Moore is a short and highly-explosive slot receiver that excels in a wide variety of traits. Has shown success at both slot and outside receiver in college.

Though small, you would never know it the way Moore plays. He shows outstanding physicality and toughness for his size, competing and fighting for everything. Excellent quickness off the line of scrimmage, showing the precise footwork to create separation through all levels of his route. A very good route-runner that understands how to manipulate defensive backs while putting them on their heels, consistently creating leverage for himself. Very good at utilizing the perimeter, showing good awareness along the sidelines. Elusive with the ball in his hands, showing the agility and quick-footed abilities to create additional yardage. Fearless when working in the middle of the field.

Weaknesses: Will likely be limited to a slot role at the next level due to his size, lacking ideal height or length. He will get bullied by larger NFL cornerbacks that can hamper his release at the line of scrimmage or rough him up in the contact window. He lacks the hand strength to beat jams. Quicker than he is fast, lacking the elite speed to be a vertical target at the next level. Needs to do a better job of varying up his releases, creating some predictability through his stems. Shows very little willingness to offer any kind of blocking downfield for his teammates, looking completely disengaged at times.

Best Fit: Slot receiver

Player Ranking (1-100): 77.3 - Moore is one of the best slot receivers in this draft class. He consistently finds creases in the middle parts of the field. He's tough and elusive. It's hard not to love Moore after watching him his final year at Ole Miss He was electric and completely dominated the SEC. 3rd round player.

13 - Jonathan Adams Jr - Arkansas State - 6'3 220 lbs

Strengths: A 2-year starter for Sun-Belt program Arkansas State, Adams has been the number 1 target each of the last two seasons showing terrific production, especially in his final season. Adams was the teams 'kickoff return specialist during his freshman season as well. Built with a tremendously stacked physique, showing physicality and muscle from his head to his toe. Adams dominates in the physical areas of the game, showing the ability to consistently win 50/50 balls while playing through traffic in the middle of the field. Plays like a bully the way he attacks the football, boxing out at the catch point and utilizing his body as a shield to protect the ball. Shows sticky hands to make catches away from his frame with some highlight reel 1-handed catches on his resume. An excellent red-zone target that shows terrific jump-ball abilities to win and pluck the ball out of the air like an NBA power forward. A good tracker of the football down the field, regularly contorting his body and adjust to the football with his back towards the ball. Physically dominant after the catch showing toughness and aggression to pick up and fight for additional yardage after the catch. Has won both with shorter routes and deeper routes down the field.

Weaknesses: Not a separator and will frequently need to win contested catches due to his lack of elite twitchiness to separate at any level of the defense. Overall deep speed is just OK and he needs to build-up to get to top gear. Tightness is evident throughout his lower body when asking him to play laterally or flip his hips, showing a limited range of motion and change of directional quickness.

Player Ranking (1-100): 76.3 - Adams is a physical specimen that is an absolute bully both before the balls' arrival and after receiving the catch. So difficult to handle down the field for opposing cornerbacks. He's going to need to win with physicality on every snap due to his lack of elite athleticism. But I wouldn't bet against him. 3rd round player.

14 - Marlon Williams - Central Florida - 6'0 215 lbs

Strengths: A 4-year contributor to UCF that has had really good production during each of the last 2 seasons since taking over the starting duties. Williams has experience as a return specialist as well, returning both kickoffs and punts. Williams is built incredibly thick, showing rare width with a rock-solid physique. An absolute bully in the way he plays, brushing off uncommitted tacklers with relative ease, picking up significant amounts of yards after the catch. A finisher that will fight for every single yard, rarely leaving an inch on the field. Playing as an oversized slot receiver, Williams takes advantage of mismatches against smaller corners, dominating them at the catch point. Frequently utilizing his big frame to box out, Williams shows comfort in extending and utilizing his entire catch radius to make tremendous grabs away from his body. His sticky hands allow him to make difficult over the shoulder grabs look routine or extend and high-point the football. Excellent in the middle of the field, showing reliability and trustworthiness through traffic. While he doesn't possess great explosiveness, a nice burst is evident after catching the ball while showing good field vision to search out desirable open-field angles.

Weaknesses: Possesses a very limited route arsenal. Williams plays almost entirely out of the slot or in bunch formations, allowing him to focus on shorter routes designed to get him the ball quickly. Lacks elite acceleration off the line of scrimmage or deep speed to offer any kind of vertical separation. Tightness in his lower half is abundant as he fails to be able to consistently separate or change direction without gearing down. Doesn't always show his physicality when it comes to run blocking, looking uncommitted, and disinterested at times.

Best Fit: Oversized slot receiver

Player Ranking (1-100): 75.9 - Williams reminds me of a combination of Anquan Boldin and LaviskaShenault last season with his blend of size and physicality. He takes advantage of size mismatches to dominate in the shorter areas of the field. A real load to have to handle in the open field, he forces committed tacklers. I like this kid quite a bit. 3rd round player.

15 - D'Wayne Eskridge - Western Michigan - 5'9 188 lbs

Strengths: A 5th year senior that is following in the footsteps of former teammate Corey Davis. Eskridge is a completely different type of receiver and shows definite NFL characteristics. Has experience playing on both sides of the line of scrimmage, playing both receiver and cornerback. A short and explosive target, Eskridge shows the big-play potential to threaten at all levels of a defense. Excelling most when playing in the intermediate parts of the field, showing the ability to catch and then pick-up additional yardage after contact. Shifty and agile, Eskridge effortlessly flips his hips to separate on in-breaking routes. A track athlete that has blur speed in straight lines. A reliable target, Eskridge typically has very good hands and is very tough when competing on contested balls against bigger defenders. Has good wiggle and initial quickness off the line of scrimmage to beat jams. A dynamic playmaker that makes plays whenever he has the ball in his hands, proving to be an outstanding return specialist.

Weaknesses: Missed most of the 2019 season after suffering a broken clavicle in the 4th game of the season. For all his speed, I don't see a guy that consistently separates as much as you would expect. Very limited route tree. Doesn't appear to consistently run his routes with as much sharpness as you would like. Has played mostly in an outside role, despite being greatly undersized and projecting more to a slot role at the next level. Needs to do a better job of altering his releases, allowing cornerbacks to jump his routes.

Best Fit: Slot receiver and return specialist

Player Ranking (1-100): 74.9 - Eskridge is a fun player that shows dynamic abilities with the ball in his hands. He's a tremendous athlete and can make plays on special teams. 4th round player.

16 - Amari Rodgers - Clemson - 5'10 211 lbs

Strengths: Rodgers has been a dynamic playmaker for the Tigers during the last 3 seasons, showing big-play ability both on special teams and in the receiving game. Rodgers exploded during his sophomore season with 55 catches with nearly 600 yards receiving getting himself noticed. But Rodgers saved the best for last with his final year as a senior, dominating and posting his best statistical production to-date. Built with a short, low center of gravity physique, Rodgers possesses a running back frame with receiver-like traits. This is noticeable when he has the ball in his hands, showing terrific lower-body strength and power to plow forward through contact and fight through ankle tacklers. His field vision is on display with the ball as he quickly looks up and scans for 2nd and 3rd level openings. Very sudden in the way he moves, showing tremendous lateral quickness and change of direction abilities. Initial acceleration is terrific showing the ability to beat jams with wiggle and hand strength, instantly creating separation. A physical kid that will utilize his natural leverage advantage to open up holes for his teammates with good blocking abilities at both the 1st and 2nd levels. A reliable pass catcher that shows good and sticky hands to pluck the ball out of the air through traffic.

Weaknesses: Tore his ACL during the spring football season before his junior campaign and remarkably came back to play football during that season. Has significant height and wingspan concerns which will likely limit him to a 'niche 'player that can be used in a slot role. While Rodgers has improved in his diversity of a route tree, he still needs to continue to improve. He runs the majority of his routes within 10 yards of the line of scrimmage, focusing on simple shorter routes designed to get him the football. Picked up a number of his yards on manufactured play-calls including jet sweeps and simple screens. Quicker than he is fast, Rodgers needs to win initially at the line of scrimmage if he wants to gain any separation. Will struggle winning anything vertically against bigger defenders. If challenged at the catch point, Rodgers will struggle to win with lack of length and play strength. Doesn't always play with the physicality you would expect for his frame.

Player Ranking (1-100): 74.7 - Rodgers was dynamic for Clemson this year with tremendous production. He's one of the most electric slot receivers in this draft class, showing the ability to win whenever he has the ball in his hands. The further he is away from the line of scrimmage the more he will struggle. Don't expect a pure receiver, expect a niche player that will make a lot of plays for your offense and special teams 'units. 4th round player.

17 - Austin Watkins - UAB - 6'2 207 lbs

Strengths: A JUCO transfer that played his final two years of eligibility for UAB, despite having offers from many other top schools. While having good family roots and being a relative of Sammy Watkins, Austin has been incredibly productive the last two seasons playing in the Conference USA, finishing with nearly 1100 yards his junior season and 6 touchdowns. An explosive big-play guy that averaged over 19 yards per catch, Watkins shows down the field speed to stretch the back half of defenses. Watkins is built with really good size, showing a tall and filled-out frame with good overall weight distribution. Has the versatility to line up as an 'X 'or can kick inside and play in the slot as well. A physical player that shows fearlessness when working through the middle of the field and playing through contact. Skilled with the ball in his hands, both explosively and physically. Rarely going down upon the first contact, Watkins puts his head down and plows through safeties, showing competitiveness with the ball in his hand. Isn't stiff like most 6'3 receivers, showing good transitional quickness and agility when working on laterally-breaking routes. Good in contested situations, showing the ability to utilize his entire wingspan to extend and snatch the ball out of the air. A good ball-tracker when playing with his back towards the ball, showing flexible body control and ball awareness abilities.

Weaknesses: A limited route-runner that runs a lot of simple deeper routes and lacks experience in shorter and more intermediate-based routes. He was also utilized on several manufactured offense gadgetry type of plays, designed to get him the ball in space. Needs to add more refinement to his routes, lacking the precision at the top of his routes to consistently separate. I would like to see him show more nuance through his stems, tending to only play with 1-speed making him a fairly easy cover for more athletic corners.

Player Ranking (1-100): 74.3 - I like Watkins quite a bit. He can do almost everything well. He will need to add more precision and experience running a wider variety of routes but other than that, he's a good football player. He's got speed, size, and impressive receiver traits. 4th round player.

18 - Warren Jackson - Colorado State - 6'6 215 lbs

Strengths: Jackson came onto the scene after a dominating junior campaign where he posted over 1100 yards receiving and 8 touchdowns. He missed his final season as a senior after opting out before the season. One of the biggest receivers in college football in terms of height coupled with wingspan. But despite his somewhat lengthy frame, Jackson shouldn't be labeled as soft or lacking strength. Showing his willingness to play with physicality and toughness when asked to run block on the perimeter. Jackson is a versatile threat capable of winning inside or outside. Playing like an NBA Power Forward, Jackson is dominant with the ball in flight, showing tremendous body control and vertical leaping ability to out snatch any defensive back in flight. A natural hands 'catcher that snatches the ball out of the air with outstretched hands. While not an elite athlete, Jackson moves well in straight-line situations, showing the big-play threat in vertical settings to create huge chunk plays. Jackson thrives against tight press-man coverage with the ability to utilize his length to fight through jams, while also winning the vast majority of the 50/50 balls thrown in his direction.

Weaknesses: Still a very limited route-runner at the point in time, focusing more on vertical plains than truly threatening in the shorter to intermediate areas of the game. His long legs and huge frame make him a large moving target for defenders, limiting his effectiveness after the catch. Has some hip stiffness to his game, limiting his lack of change of direction and agility. This limits his effectiveness both as a route-runner and after the catch.

Best Fit: Has developmental upside to be a starting receiver

Player Ranking (1-100): 73.5 - I like Jackson quite a bit. He's dominant in the air and he's more physical than you would expect for a guy of his size. He could be a real red-zone nightmare for teams at the next level. 4th round player.

19 - Frank Darby - Arizona State - 6'0 194 lbs

Strengths: A 5th year senior for the Sun Devils that improved during each campaign. Beloved by his coaches for his hard-working and blue-chip nature, Darby has shown the willingness to get better each year. A squatty built prospect that shows compactness and thickness through his frame to play at the next level. A big-play weapon that shows tremendous toughness and leadership qualities for the Sun Devils offense. A twitchy athlete that has really quick feet, making him a difficult cover at the line of scrimmage due to his release variances. His wiggle in his frame makes his routes unpredictable, making him a difficult cover assignment at all levels of his route. Really good ball skills and body control allow him to constantly make impressive plays down the field, showing the tracking abilities and reliable hands to make tough catches. Understands how to run routes both while in man and zone coverages. Shows impressive short-area quickness and lower body flexibility to turn on a dime and cross-field with very minimal speed reduction when flipping his hips. A willing blocker that shows good timing and block instincts to seal edges and block perimeter lanes.

Weaknesses: Struggled with a rib injury during his final season causing him to miss a huge chunk of the season. While he's a compactly-built prospect, Darby lacks prototypical NFL length and height. His lack of length comes into play when QB's are forced to make tighter space throws to Darby and he fails to win enough of the 50/50 contests. This is also partly because he seems more comfortable corralling the ball into his frame as opposed to reliably using his hands. Quicker than he is fast, Darby will struggle to separate consistently on vertical routes. While typically his quickness allows him to beat jams, when corners can matchup man-to-man, he will struggle with tight jams, due to lack of technique and upper-body strength. Inconsistent play due to large chunks of concentration lapses during games, seemingly looking disinterested. Functional strength is subpar and he will get overwhelmed at the point of attack in the run game, and he lacks the ideal post-catch ability to win significantly after the catch.

Player Ranking (1-100): 73.3 - I like Darby and he has some impressive traits, most notably his quickness and loose hips. He's a tough guy to cover in space with his ability to change directions and play laterally. While his college production was never top-end, I think he can be a nice role player and compete for a #3 receiver role immediately.

20 - Rico Bussey Jr - North Texas - 6'2 194 lbs

Strengths: Bussey Jr came onto the scene as a junior totaling over 1,000 yards and 12 touchdowns. Bussey Jr is an athletically-built and lean receiver that shows versatility and nuance in the way in which he plays. A smooth accelerator off the line of scrimmage showing good quickness and balance to keep his frame clean against most defensive backs. An impressive route-runner that will show variance in his releases and his ability to alter speeds at different breakpoints in his routes. Good footwork both in and out of his breaks to hide patterns and create separation in the shorter and intermediate areas of the field. He has experience both inside and outside and might be best suited inside at the slot at the next level with his skill set. Really smart kid that will never give up on plays and has a good understanding of where to sit against zone coverages. Reliable in the middle of the field, showing some toughness and reliability in contested situations.

Weaknesses: Tore his ACL in the 2nd game of his senior year. Thankfully he was given a redshirt medical season to play one more time in college before getting drafted. He will need to be monitored and teams will be concerned with him coming off an ACL injury. Generally, he isn't a down the field guy and relies on intermediate routes and shorter routes. Quicker than fast and will struggle to separate down the field in vertical settings. On far too many occasions, he waits for the ball to come into his chest rather than being proactive and attacking the football. When going up against physical corners, he will get roughed up at the line of scrimmage showing some trouble in utilizing his jam technique. Limited upside after the catch and almost always goes down to the first contact.

Best Fit: Slot or outside

Player Ranking (1-100): 72.2 – Bussey Jr is a good route-runner and has a great understanding of how to get open. While not the most physical or the fastest, he's a good overall player. He showed he can have success against top-tier defenses when he went against them. 4th round player.

21 - Chatarius (Tutu) Atwell - Louisville - 5'9 165 lbs

Strengths: After getting his chance to be the full-time starter in 2019, Atwell exploded setting receiving records for the Tigers, finishing with almost 1300 yards receiving and 11 touchdowns. Atwell is a versatile threat that has lined up at every receiver position for the Tigers, also have some experience returning punts as well. Atwell is a small but athletically-built receiver that will threaten to take the top off the defense every time he's on the field. Offensive coaches did whatever they could to get the ball in his hands, utilizing him on jet sweeps and screens. He's been one of the best big-play receivers in college football. Getting to top gear in a flash, Atwell accelerates into his routes and does a nice job of creating separation at all areas of the field. A savvy route-runner that sets up his routes well, utilizing terrific footwork and nuance through his stems. Don't let his size fool you, Atwell is tougher than you would imagine. He plays with an aggressive and feisty mentality that will fight for every yard. He's capable of breaking tackles and creating for himself in the open field with his start/stop quickness. He has terrific field vision when he has the ball, taking good angles in the open field.

Weaknesses: Atwell is small, very small. Some teams 'will shy away because of his lack of ideal body armor. He struggles against bigger and physical corners who are willing to rough him up at the line of scrimmage and disrupt his route timing. Lacks an ideal catch radius to extend and make plays outside of his frame. Limited in 50/50 situations and will get outmuscled at the catch point. Questionable hands on tape and had several poor concentration drops. Needs to bring more value as a route-runner by diversifying his route tree.

Best Fit: Slot receiver and occasionally outside

Player Ranking (1-100): 72.0 - Atwell is a dynamic big-play receiver. He's likely to go higher in this draft than in previous years due to the recent success of smaller and more explosive receivers. He can immediately play a role on special teams as a return specialist and be used occasionally as a method to keep the defense honest. 4th round player.

22 - Tylan Wallace - Oklahoma State - 5'11 193 lbs

Strengths: A 3-year starter for the Cowboys that came onto the scene following a massive 1500 yard, 12 touchdown sophomore campaign. Wallace was used at times as a punt returner and has experience in doing so as well. While not having elite long-speed, Wallace shows above-average quickness in and out of his breaks to sell his routes to create for himself. Has a very good awareness of zonal coverage concepts, finding soft zones in spacing to sit in, and create chunks of yardage. A force with the ball in his hands, Wallace is always looking to create something out of nothing. Being used in a variety of roles, mostly designed at getting him the ball quickly to make plays post-catch. While with the ball post-catch, Wallace is incredibly feisty and competitive at racking up tons of yards 'after the catch. Wallace is a QB friendly target that works tirelessly on broken-down plays to get open down the field. A willing and aggressive blocker on the outside that is often used as the 'point of attack 'blocker on outside zone-style runs. Wallace makes the majority of his catches in tightly congested areas in the middle areas of the field, showing reliability and strong hands in tight windows.

Weaknesses: Wallace has had some minor injury concerns, including battling through a groin injury during his final senior campaign. He also tore his ACL midway through his junior campaign. A very slightly-built guy that will struggle with some of the physical aspects of playing the receiver position at the next level, especially in the physical style in which he prefers playing. Fails to have any kind of experience or ability to defeat press-cover corners. The overwhelming majority of his catches in college were on manufactured screens and quick-outs that allowed him to skew his numbers favorably. While a good athlete, there is the concern with added strength/size at the next level he will lose some of his explosiveness, albeit which isn't elite as it is. Fails to offer any kind of separation on vertical routes, forcing his QB to make tight-window throws or 50/50 balls in double coverage.

Player Ranking (1-100): 71.2 - Wallace is a good prospect but not a great one. He took advantage of subpar Big-12 defenses that rarely forced him to create quickly or defeat physicality at the line of scrimmage. He has a chance to be a solid cog in a wheel for a team but certainly not a #1 or 2 target. 4th round player.

23 - Amon-Ra St. Brown - USC- 6'1 195 lbs

Strengths: The brother of Packers receiver, St. Brown is a former five-star college recruit out of California that has lived up to his billing so far at USC. St. Brown has been tremendous since his true freshman season, totaling his best year as a sophomore where he tallied over 1000 yards and 6 touchdowns. Was used in the rushing game and also has some experience being used in the return department as well, with both punts and kickoffs. St. Brown is a long and leaner framed receiver that has been extensively used as an oversized slot receiver. St. Brown excels in zone coverage, having good zonal instincts, and finds soft zones in coverage routinely. A 'move the sticks 'receiver that plays with veteran savvy and football intelligence to always create openings. Quick feet allow him to keep his frame clean through the line of scrimmage. Very good in short-yardage plays, showing terrific agility and short-area quickness to create for himself at all levels. Plays with a very diversified route tree and can win in a variety of different ways. Overall change of direction is impressive, playing with leverage at all times and never needing to gear down when going in-and-out of transitions. Reliable catcher of the football, showing flexible body control and the ability to fully extend to adjust to the ball at all levels. Very physical blocker that appears to take it personally, rarely giving up on a play until after the whistle.

Weaknesses: St. Brown is mostly just a slot receiver and has very limited experience playing on the outside. His functional strength is minimal and he will get overwhelmed at the line of scrimmage if he has to play as an 'X. 'Poses very minimal threat after the catch, lacking great physicality, contact balance, or open-field vision to create. Quicker than he is fast and he's not much of a deep-play guy that is going to stretch the field vertically. Struggles against press-man coverage and prefers playing and finding soft zones in space.

Player Ranking (1-100): 70.9 - St. Brown is a savvy slot receiver that will continuously take advantage of short-yardage situations and zone coverage. He's highly intelligent and catches mostly everything thrown in his direction. 4th round player.

24 - Trevon Grimes - Florida - 6'4 217 lbs

Strengths: A former highly-touted five-star Ohio State recruit that transferred following his freshman season. A big-bodied receiver that displays impressive measurables for the position, showing ideal size and wingspan to play as a prototypical possession-based receiver. Uses his physicality impressively in the blocking game, showing tenacity and willingness to latch on and control the shoulder pads of the defender through the duration of a play. Uses his size well to box-out at the catch point, showing good physicality with his entire wingspan to catch the ball with outstretched arms. I was impressed when watching Grimes foot usage at the top of routes, showing some suddenness and separation quickness to create some spacing. Is comfortable in different receiver positions, showing a propensity for playing both inside in bunch formations as well at outside. Strong with the ball in his hands, showing toughness and a strong stiff arm to threaten winning additional yardage. Following his freshman campaign, he hasn't missed a game in his career.

Weaknesses: Lack of explosive characteristics are evident throughout his style of play, causing little concern post-catch for defensive backs, other than physical nature. His overall statistics have been marginal at best throughout his 3-year career at Florida, despite never having missed any game time. Grimes is prone to some poor concentration and subpar hand strength, leading to him getting the ball knocked out on occasion. Runs a very limited route tree that lacks much variety or nuance.

Best Fit: Outside possession receiver

Player Ranking (1-100): 70.3 - Grimes size will make him an attractive prospect in addition to his former five-star credentials out of high school. He never quite lived up to his billing in college, but he certainly has had some moments. He's a 4th round player.

25 - Shi Smith - South Carolina - 5'10 186 lbs

Strengths: A 4-year contributor to the Gamecocks offense, Smith has done a nice job in a limited role for their offense. Smith was the team's primary kickoff return specialist during his time as well. Featuring a small but squatty build, Smith shows good compactness and muscularity in his frame despite being undersized. The Gamecocks coaches utilize Smith in a niche role, attempting to get him the ball any opportunity they had including in screens, in motion, etc. Smith plays almost entirely in the slot, but unlike most slot receiver, Smith shows true vertical ability to win up the seams down the field due to his good speed. Not just fast, Smith's lower body explosiveness is evident in his lateral abilities, showing smoothness throughout his hips to stop on a dime and flip his hips to change directions. Smith shows outstanding vertical leaping ability with the ability to high point the ball in the air while out jumping defensive backs and snatching the ball out of flight. Smith maximizes his frame out, showing an advanced understanding of how to post-up and box out at the catch point, making it impossible for defenders to make a play on the ball. Dynamic with the ball in his hands, Smith shows toughness while dropping his shoulder pads, showing the ability to plow through guys and pick-up additional yardage after contact.

Weaknesses: A very limited route-runner that picks up the majority of his yardage through manufactured plays as opposed to winning with his routes. Needs to clean up some of his technique in his footwork when working through transitions and at the top of routes, lacking nuance and precision in minimizing false steps. Catches the most ridiculous and impossible catches but is prone to some poor concentration drops during his career. Smith has size limitations due to lack of ideal length and height and will be limited to slot/special teams 'duties at the next level.

Best Fit: Slot receiver and special teams 'return specialist

Player Ranking (1-100): 70.2 - I like Smith quite a bit and he's been very very successful against some big-time SEC defenses during his career. While he was rarely the #1 target for opposing defenses, he still made the most of every opportunity he got. He needs to become more polished as an overall route-runner to be an elite slot receiver but he's got the traits to fight for snaps very quickly. 4th round player.

26 - Nico Collins - Michigan - 6'4 215 lbs

Strengths: A 2-year starter for the Wolverines that didn't play his final year of eligibility due to opting out before the season beginning. Collins was an impressive target for the Wolverines, finishing with over 1300 yards combined and 13 touchdowns during his sophomore and junior campaigns. Collins is a big-bodied receiver that displays tremendous size and physicality for the position. A hard-working presence that gives everything he has on every snap of the ball. An absolute bully that loves all the physical sides of the game, showing great trustworthiness in contested situations. Fearless when playing across the middle of the field, rarely hesitating to make a big catch before get taking a big hit. Collins utilizes his size and wingspan to consistently play above the rim and outreach defenders in the passing game, showing aggressiveness at the catch point to attack the football. These traits make him a dynamic red-zone target, showing tremendous upside when working in tight spaces. Has a good understanding of utilizing proper jam technique coupled with his great length to keep his frame clean at the line of scrimmage to allow himself to get into his route. After the catch, Collins shows toughness to plow throw ankle tackles and gain additional yardage after contact.

Weaknesses: Tore his groin during the spring of the 2019 season, but it didn't cause him to miss any game time. Collins isn't a great speed athlete and true north/south speed is marginal despite showing the ability to win on vertical routes with size. A build-up speed runner that takes a few seconds to get to top gear, forcing his quarterback to hold onto the football a bit longer if he's the 1st read. Lower body tightness is on display as he struggles when asked to play laterally and flip his hips to cross the field. Collins was never the number 1 target with the Wolverines and always the number 2 or 3 option on the team, allowing him to take advantage of 1 v 1 matchups regularly. Will be reliant on playing with an accurate QB due to his inabilities to create spacing for himself at the top of routes.

Best Fit: Outside receiver

Player Ranking (1-100): 69.3 - Collins is a big-bodied receiver that shows upside as an outside receiver. While he's certainly got the NFL frame, he's not a great overall athlete. He will need to consistently dominant NFL physicality and I'm worried he's not going to be able to consistently do that. But he'll immediately compete for a #4 or 5 receiver role on a team if he can contribute on special teams. 5th round player.

27 - DamonteCoxie - Memphis - 6'3 200 lbs

Strengths: A 3-year starter for the Tigers that had tremendous sophomore and junior campaigns tallying over 1,100 yards receiving during each campaign, setting receiving yard and reception records at the school. Coxie is a well-built receiver with a terrific frame, showing good height and length with additional room on his frame for more muscle. Loving the physical aspects of the game is what Coxie is most known for, showing tremendous aggressiveness and 'want 'when it comes to laying it all on the line every snap. This is especially evident in run support, taking it personally and opening up holes for his running backs. He also shows this when it comes to winning at the top of routes, rarely getting outmuscled or bullied for the football. Coxie is at his best when the ball is in the air, showing tremendous instincts, ball skills, and body control to time the balls 'arrival to perfection. He almost always puts himself in a position to make a play on the ball, utilizing his wingspan to box out at the catch point and pluck the ball out of the air. Appears to have a good plan to fight through jam technique, showing good upper-body strength and elusiveness to keep his frame clean through contact. A better than average athlete that shows good deep speed to threaten vertically when given opportunities.

Weaknesses: Coxie played the first couple of games during his senior season and then decided to sit out the rest of the campaign for unknown reasons. A 'build-up 'speed athlete that takes a few seconds to get to top gear. Lower body tightness is on display when attempting to redirect his frame or run in-breaking routes. Lacks the separation quickness in-and-out of his breaks to create any kind of separation consistently. Overall speed is 'OK 'and isn't top end. Plays in a high-powered offense that is known for racking up significant amounts of yards in a flash and he took advantage of that.

Best Fit: Possession outside receiver

Player Ranking (1-100): 68.9 - I like Coxie and he's got the toughness and nastiness you want in a player. He has the frame to continue filling out and adding additional functional size and strength. He's got a chance to be a develop into a nice #3 receiver for a team. He's certainly got the traits to be a valuable special teams ' commodity from Day 1. 5th round player.

28 - Dazz Newsome - North Carolina - 5'11 190 lbs

Strengths: A 4-year contributor to the Tar Heels offense that exploded onto the scene during his junior season where he finished with over 1,000 yards receiving and 10 touchdowns. Newsome is also an experienced and explosive punt and kickoff return specialist with several long returns, including a return touchdown. While Newsome doesn't have the largest prototypical NFL physique nor the fastest and most explosive 40 time, he makes up for it in his nuanced receiver play. A skilled route-runner that efficiently runs a wide diversity of routes, showing terrific craftiness at all levels. Utilizing smooth transitions and good separation quickness, Newsome is a 'separator 'in being able to create spacing for himself at the top of routes. Relentless in the way in which he plays, showing a terrific motor. always working to get open downfield on broken plays. Does a nice job of utilizing body control and awareness to make sidelines grabs. Good with the ball in his hands, showing the post-catch ability to win additional yards after contact. Very willing and aggressive blocker down the field showing a good 'team spirit 'in his willingness to handle some of the dirty work.

Weaknesses: Newsome plays almost entirely in the slot and has very little outside experience. When having to defeat jam technique or more physical corners, Newsome will struggle at all levels. Lacking the ideal physicality at the catch point, he will give up contested grabs to more physical press corners. A bit of a body catcher that doesn't attack the football aggressively, preferring to secure it with his body. This leads to many drops. Not a speed maven and lacks the 2nd gear to attack a defense vertically.

Best Fit: Slot receiver

Player Ranking (1-100): 68.2 - Newsome is one of the best pure route-runners in this draft class. He's skilled and crafty and will create separation. His versatility as a return specialist certainly makes him a valuable commodity. I would feel comfortable with him in the 5th round.

29 - Tim Jones - Southern Mississippi - 6'1 202 lbs

Strengths: A 3-year starter for Conference-USA program Southern Mississippi, Jones had a stellar junior campaign where he tallied over 900 yards receiving. Jones is a versatile weapon that plays mostly in the slot but has also shown the ability to play on the perimeter as well. A smaller but compactly-built kid that has good lower body strength and twitch. An explosive athlete that quickly accelerates off the line of scrimmage, Jones shows terrific wiggle and hand strength to beat jams. A smooth operator that navigates in-and-out of his transitions with relative ease, rarely needing to gear down, showing the ability to quickly separate. Does the bulk of his damage in the middle of the field, showing reliability and toughness in traffic. Does a nice job of locating and tracking the football down the field, showing an impressive vertical ability to high-point the ball. Gets to top speed in a flash. Precise and sharp footwork allows him to create separation at the top of his routes. Impressive with the ball in his hands, Jones 'lower body power allows him to plow through uncommitted tacklers and pick-up additional yardage after contact. He also has elusive hips and impressive change of directional ability to make guys miss in small spaces, showing the ability to win with power or finesse in space.

Weaknesses: Jones is quicker than he is fast, winning the majority of his reps in the middle of the field. He lacks the elite top-end vertical speed to threaten vertically. Lacks ideal and prototypical NFL size/wingspan to play on the perimeters. He's almost entirely a slot receiver, lacking a ton of experience playing on the outside. Has had some soft tissue issues that have caused him some issues during his career. His touchdowns numbers throughout his career have been very underwhelming despite good overall production.

Best Fit: Slot receiver

Player Ranking (1-100): 67.5 - I like Jones and he's impressive in the way he moves in and out of his breaks. Has a real feel for playing inside and shows fearlessness when working through traffic and catching the ball in tight spaces. He's got a good chance to make an NFL roster. 5th round player.

30 - Blake Proehl - East Carolina - 6'1 186 lbs

Strengths: The brother of now NFL receiver Austin and son of former receiver Ricky, Blake possesses good family lineage as he progresses to the next level. After suffering a season-ending knee injury during his true freshman campaign, Proehl has been a steady performer for East Carolina the past three seasons on both offense and punt returns. The definition of versatile, Proehl can play a valuable role for any offense having experience at all 3 wide receivers positions. A smart and nuanced prospect that shows good initial quickness and wiggle out of his stance to beat jams. Does a ton of damage when working in the middle of the field or on the sidelines, showing terrific awareness against zone or on broken-down plays. Very good field vision with the ball in his hands to create for himself in the open field and is a real threat post-catch as evidenced by his dynamism in the return game. Very reliable hands 'catcher that shows stickiness to extend and snatch the ball out of the air. A QB-friendly target that is trustworthy in the middle of the field or contested situations. Change of direction is sudden, showing smoothness through his lower body to transition and change direction without needing to gear down.

Weaknesses: Overall production has been reminiscent of a good role player in college and was never a true number one target for defenses to have to gear down on. His frame is still very wiry and he lacks ideal body armor to handle NFL rigors. Still needs to continue to refine his physicality and toughness in the blocking parts of the game. Route-running has gotten better but he needs to improve his sharpness at the top of routes and learn a more diversified route-tree. Quicker than he is fast and he is strictly a shorter to an intermediate-route receiver, failing to have the long speed to be a threat down the field.

Best Fit: All-around receiver and special teams 'returner

Player Ranking (1-100): 66.9 - I like Proehl quite a bit. I think if he played in a higher-powered college offense he could have had even better production. He's open a lot! He's a reliable and consistent performer that could be a nice #3 or 4 option for an offense. 5th round player that can immediately be a return specialist.

31 - Jaelon Darden - North Texas - 5'9 174 lbs

Strengths: A former high-school QB, Darden transitioned to receiver his freshman season at North Texas, never looking back. Darden has been very productive during each of his seasons since his freshman year, showcasing dynamism both in the receiving game and also on special teams. One of the best punt return specialists in college football, Darden showed the ability to break out a big play any time he touched the ball. Darden is a flat-out playmaker that is incredibly gifted with the ball in his hands. Showing the ability to make guys miss in a phone-booth, Darden is loose-hipped, elusive, and crazy quick. He was utilized as a 'jack of all trades 'player that has even taken snaps as a runner. Once Darden gets his hands on the football he immediately looks up and tries to create. He limits his surface area due to his natural leverage advantage, rarely allowing tacklers to get clean tackles on him. Best used as a slot receiver where he can quickly get defenders on their heels due to his change of directional ability coupled with his lateral quickness. He's such a difficult guy to cover due to his shiftiness and transitional quickness. He shows a good understanding of how to beat both man-to-man and zonal coverages.

Weaknesses: Darden is limited due to his stubby arms and his overall lack of height, making him strictly a 'niche 'or a slot receiver at the next level. While he's quick and can quickly separate, he's limited to 5-10 yard routes due to a lack of long speed to separate on intermediate or longer developing routes. A 'niche 'player that has never been the sole focus of a defense and took advantage of manufactured offensive plays designed to get the ball in his hands.

Best Fit: Slot receiver and return specialist

Player Ranking (1-100): 65.6 - I like Darden and his skillset. He's a niche player that brings the big-play potential to both special teams and offense. He's a quick guy that can make almost any defender miss in space. While he isn't gifted with the best size he makes the best use of his available tools. 5th round player.

32 - Seth Williams - Auburn - 6'3 211 lbs

Strengths: A 3-year starter for the Tigers that took over a starting role fairly early on during his true freshman season in 2018, showing good and reliable offensive production during each campaign. Williams is built with prototypical possession receiver size and a very impressive wingspan. Utilizing his size and big frame to continuously box-out at the catch point, Williams is a very hard matchup for smaller defensive backs. A very nice safety blanket for QBs, Williams catches almost every 50/50 ball and is trustworthy through congested traffic. He catches absolutely everything, showing rare body control with the ability to adjust to all kinds of throws. Has made some spectacular one-handed catches while on the move. Excellent red-zone target with his ability to track the ball and get vertical to win jump-balls. Moves well out of his stance and is dynamic when he's able to run comeback or slant type of routes, making it impossible for defenders to make plays on the ball. Has some post-catch ability showing toughness and willingness to fight for additional yardage. Clever in his way to utilize his hands and head fakes to create some deception through his stems and to create tiny bits of cushions for himself.

Weaknesses: Limited down the field due to lack of great speed. Despite his good overall size and strength, he will get disrupted and re-routed against more physical press corners, failing to have great jam technique to fight through coverage. Lacks much nuance in his routes with very limited separation quickness to separate from defensive backs consistently. A north/south runner that will struggle when asked to change directions to redirect his frame.

Best Fit: Possession receiver

Player Ranking (1-100): 65.4 - Williams has been a solid receiver for the Tigers that has made his living on shorter routes and jump-ball situations where he can routinely win at the catch point with his size and frame. He's not a separator nor does he offer a ton of overall athletic upside to get much better. Not as physical as you'd expect for someone with his frame. 5th round player.

33 - Anthony Schwartz - Auburn - 6'0 180 lbs

Strengths: A 3-year contributor to the Tigers offense, Schwartz is a high school track and field state record-setter with tremendous all-around speed. A dual-threat player for the Tigers offense having experience both in the receiving game as well as the running game, recording big plays in both facets. Schwartz is a danger to the defense any time he touches the ball, showcasing an ability to hit a home run every single chance he gets. Not just fast, Schwartz has unreal initial acceleration going from 0-60 in the blink of an eye. Plays mostly in the slot, showing the rare change of directional ability with loose hips and terrific agility. Can separate purely with speed, even when his routes aren't precise. Does a nice job of altering his speeds through his stem to create some good deception before transitioning to top gear and separating. Can routinely be open for 5-7 yard outs or comeback routes due to the respect defensive backs give to him because of his speed. Generally is a very reliable hands 'catcher that shows good sticky hands to extend and make most catches.

Weaknesses: Broke his hand before the start of the 2019 season but he didn't miss any game time. Possesses a very wiry high-cut frame with the possibility of injury if taking any significant hits. Lacks much power through his frame and will get manhandled at the line of scrimmage against bigger press-man corners that will prevent him from getting into his routes. This lack of power is evident at the catch point too, failing to offer much ability in contested situations. Most of his big plays came on manufactured plays, such as option-style runs or trickery and he will need to be more refined at all the roles of a receiver at the next level. Limited with the ball in his hands and having to fight through blocks, generally going down upon the first contact.

Best Fit: Explosive slot receiver and gadget-style player

Player Ranking (1-100): 64.9 - Schwartz lacks true nuance as a receiver but he makes up for it in elite athletic traits. He's a home-run threat every time he touches the ball. He needs to gain more power through his frame to hold up consistently but he'd be an intriguing 4th or 5th option for a team. One of the fastest players in college football. 6th round player.

34 - Ihmir Smith-Marsette - Iowa - 6'1 179 lbs

Strengths: A 4-year contributor to the Hawkeyes offense and special teams 'units that has had really solid production during each campaign since his freshman season. As a junior, Smith-Marsette was arguably one of the best return specialists in college football, returning 2 kickoffs for touchdowns. A dynamic big-play threat, Smith-Marsette will continually threaten the back half of a defense with the impressive deep speed with long strides to eat up cushions of space. Iowa coaches frequently used him off the line of scrimmage where he can utilize his quick feet to create instant separation at the line of scrimmage. These quick feet are also noticeable at the top of his routes, showing terrific snap and sharpness to create small creases in spacing. A very fluid mover that shows terrific looseness throughout his lower body to flip his hips and change direction without needing to gear down. Shows good spatial awareness when playing through zone coverage, often finding some soft zones in coverage to sit in and present a QB-friendly target. A nuanced route-runner that understands how to get defenders on their heels with terrific subtlety through his body movements to create good deception through different levels of his stem. A good ball tracker that shows good awareness down the field coupled with good body control.

Weaknesses: Smith-Marsette is very undersized and will struggle with the physical aspects of playing the position at the next level. He was protected by typically playing off the line of scrimmage or being used as the 'move 'receiver but if he has to handle NFL press, he will struggle to disengage due to lack of functional strength. Struggles when competing against physical corners at the catch point, getting outmuscled by more physical corners. While he shows good nuance in his routes, he's limited with his route tree, failing to have a wide array of 'go-to moves. 'Tends to struggle when he's playing in the middle of the field, lacking the dominant box-out abilities to win 50/50 balls. Doesn't always play with good levels of aggression or physicality in the run game, looking far too passive.

Player Ranking (1-100): 63.4 - Smith-Marsette is a good athlete that will offer a big-play option for a team. His functional strength, lack of physicality, and toughness make me worry if he can offer a role immediately. He will have to compete for a #4 or 5 role for a team during training camp, showing he can play some special teams'to earn himself a spot and valuable snaps. 6th round player.

35 - Emeka Emezie - North Carolina State - 6'3 220 lbs

Strengths: Emezie came onto the scene impressing greatly during his sophomore season in 2018 while being the #3 target behind Kelvin Harmon and Jakobi Meyers. Built with tremendous physicality and size throughout his frame, possessing a muscled-up physique. Emezie has experience playing all over the offensive formation, playing both inside and outside. A classic possession-based receiver, Emezie is very physical in all areas of the game. Comfortable handling press coverage, Emezie utilizes good wiggle at the line of scrimmage to keep his frame clean. Excellent in contested situations showing the 'alpha mentality,' winning the majority of his 50/50 opportunities. Strong hands allow him to routinely extend and make plays outside of his frame. Routinely has to adjust to badly thrown balls while playing with inept quarterback play the last two seasons. A smooth route runner that shows sharpness with his footwork in-and-out of transitions to create a QB friendly target to always be at the right place at the right time. Smart football intelligence allows him to create for himself down the field on broken down plays while playing against soft zones. A willing blocker that shows toughness and 'want' when it comes to blocking downfield for his teammates.

Weaknesses: After greatly impressing while being the #3 option during his sophomore season, Emezie never quite developed into the number 1 target many were expecting him to following Harmon and Meyers' departures. His touchdown numbers have been just 'OK' throughout his career. Overall athleticism is minimal, lacking the deep speed to threaten vertically. Not a separator, lacking the separation quickness to consistently get open down the field.

Player Ranking (1-100): 62.5 - I like Emezie and I think he can be a better NFL receiver than he was college. Coaches rave about his work ethic and drive. If he had a better QB the last two years I'm convinced he would have had better production. 6th round player.

36 - Jhamon Ausbon - Texas A&M - 6'2 220 lbs

Strengths: Ausbon is a 3-year starter for the Aggies that has had a very solid 3-year career before opting out of his final season. His junior and final campaign was stellar finishing with nearly 900 yards and 5 touchdowns. A big and physically imposing player that looks to be more of an H-back than a receiver with his frame. Ausbon is a workout warrior that has won strength &conditioning awards while with the Aggies in the offseason. Ausbon appears to have an understanding of how to run routes with precision and body manipulation, showing good forward lean while utilizing his head and eyes to throw off defensive backs. A good hands ' catcher that shows the sticky hands to make contested catches away from his frame or make tight-coverage 50/50 grabs in traffic. Has comfort and experience both in the slot and to the outside. Surprisingly quick feet and change of directional ability. Has improved during each season in his ability to sharpen his footwork in/out of his breaks to hide his patterns. His physicality is best-showcased post-catch showing some feisty characteristics to win additional yards after contact.

Weaknesses: Missed some game time during his sophomore campaign after suffering a nagging foot injury. Explosive characteristics are greatly underwhelming, lacking the foot speed or the separation quickness to create any kind of spacing at the next level. Despite his physically imposing size, Ausbon fails to adequately use it at the college level, allowing defensive backs to bully him both at the line of scrimmage and at the catch point. Limited to a short-route receiver, lacking the long speed or the nuance to create on double-moves. Gives his QB very narrow windows where they generally need to time the ball to perfection to give him a chance to win.

Best Fit: Oversized slot receiver

Player Ranking (1-100): 59.3 - A big receiver that could bump down a bit after sitting out his senior campaign. His best chance of getting drafted is playing a bit closer to 210 than 220 as he lacks the explosive nature at the bigger size. He's worth a gamble after his solid junior campaign.

37 - Isaiah McKoy - Kent State - 6'3 200 lbs

Strengths: A 3-year starter for MAC-Conference program Kent State, exploding onto the draft scene during his sophomore year with nearly 900 yards and 8 touchdowns. Has experience in the return game the last two seasons as well, showing good toughness and willingness. McKoy has excellent size, featuring vines for arms and a nice-sized frame with room for continued muscular development. A former high-school track athlete, McKoy has excellent long speed, showing the ability to be a big-play threat down the field. Dynamic when running vertical routes, routinely getting behind defenses. McKoy accelerates well through his routes, showing deceptive speed with his long strides. Not just a vertical runner, McKoy does a nice job of sinking in his hips and gearing down to change direction, showing good looseness through his lower body when used in lateral breaking routes. A large wing-span allows him to dominate at the catch point against smaller cornerbacks, showing the ability to extend and makes catches outside of his frame. Very physical and aggressive in run support, showing willingness to do the dirty work.

Weaknesses: Has had a number of really poor penalties during his career, due to lack of field discipline. Very raw as a route runner, lacking a large diversified route-tree. Appears to round off his routes at the top, making them easy to jump on for good defensive backs. Inconsistent hands lead to far too many concentration drops. Didn't compete against top-tier players in the MAC. Needs to continue filling out his frame with more muscle and is a little bit lanky right now.

Best Fit: Developmental outside speed receiver

Player Ranking (1-100): 59.1 - McKoy is a good football player that has the athletic ability coupled with the frame to be a fun developmental-type player. While he's still raw and needs refinement on the technical aspects of the game, there's traits to develop here. 7th round player.

38 - Cade Johnson - South Dakota State - 5'10 186 lbs

Strengths: Johnson has been one of the most dynamic players throughout the FCS the last few seasons, shining on both offense and special teams. Due to there being no FCS season this past season, Johnson hasn't played since 2019 but he was stellar during his career finishing with nearly 3,000 career receiving yards and 28 touchdowns. He also is a dynamic return specialist, finishing with 2 kickoff returns for touchdowns as well. Johnson does his damage almost exclusively out of the slot, showing dynamic abilities to get open. An explosive athlete that quickly gets from 0-60, Johnson is one of the best overall athletes in his conference, dominating his level of competition. Not just possessing long speed, Johnson shows a terrific initial release off the line of scrimmage, quickly accelerating and creating separation at the bottom of his stems. His loose hips and shifty frame allows him to create separation against man coverage. Dynamic with the ball in his hands, the coaching staff utilizes his dynamism on jet-sweeps and screens quite a bit, showing his ability to pick up chunks of yards in a flash. Has great zonal instincts, quickly finding soft zones in coverage to sit in and create a QB-friendly target down the field. Maximizes his frame in the running game, showing good toughness and aggression to block down the field.

Weaknesses: Johnson looked like a man amongst boys in the FCS but if he played in a more competitive conference, he would struggle against similar level of athletes. Size limitations will prevent him from playing an outside role at the next level and he will be limited to strictly slot duties. Despite his athleticism, Johnson isn't great at making guys miss in the open field, taking far too many hits. Could continue to improve his functional strength. His hands are hit or miss and he'll miss some inopportune catches on occasion.

> **Best Fit: Slot receiver and special teams 'return specialist**

Player Ranking (1-100): 57.3 - Johnson is a good athlete and a really good return specialist. I'm worried his overall athleticism isn't as great as it appeared to be due to inferior competition. There's no denying his production especially his junior campaign but I wouldn't feel comfortable drafting him until the 7th round.

39 - Adrian Hardy - Louisiana Tech - 6'2 205 lbs

Strengths: An impressive 4-year contributor to the Louisiana Tech offense that has been a consistent presence on their offense in each of the last 4 seasons. Hardy had a stellar sophomore year where he finished with over 1100 yards and 6 touchdowns, firmly putting himself on the NFL Draft map. A good-sized prospect that has the height and frame that teams'covet to play on the outside, showing the frame to continue to add more muscle to his frame. Hardy utilizes his long frame to dominate smaller receivers at the catch point, extending and grabbing the ball away from his frame. Good body control and down the field awareness to track the ball in flight and make some really nice grabs while in double coverage. Better than expected yards after the catch ability, consistently shrugging off ankle swipers and gaining additional yardage after contact. A reliable target in the middle of the field who appears to have good spatial awareness when playing against zone coverage. Had one of the best games of his career against LSU's defense in 2018.

Weaknesses: Hardy has had notable concerns catching the ball routinely, especially his first couple of seasons, dropping several balls. While he's got a big frame, he needs to continue to add more muscle to play at the next level, especially to handle NFL press coverage. Strictly an outside receiver that lacks the experience playing inside at all. Mostly a chains 'mover that lacks the big play-ability to create consistent big plays at the next level. Overall movement skills are just OK and he lacks the short-area quickness and agility to consistently create any kind of separation against more athletic cornerbacks. Not a vertical threat to attack the back half of a defense in a vertical setting.

Best Fit: Outside possession receiver

Player Ranking (1-100): 56.9 - Hardy is an interesting outside receiver prospect. He's had some really good games but he's been a bit inconsistent through his career. He's not a separator and will need to be relied upon in highly contested situations routinely and his questionable hands make me a bit worried. But there are developmental traits to work with. 7th round player.

40 - Damon Hazelton - Virginia Tech - 6'2 215 lbs

Strengths: Hazelton has had a unique college career, transferring twice and finishing up his college career with the Missouri Tigers. Hazelton has shown production during each of his stops and showing impressive overall numbers with 3 different programs and in 3 different football conferences. Hazelton has a broad-shouldered and prototypical NFL possession receiver build, showing terrific size and wingspan for the position. Where Hazelton sF is down the field with a nice combination of rare ball tracking ability and body control to routinely make over the shoulder grabs and contested catches down the field. Shows complete confidence in his hands, regularly extending and making catches outside of his frame while fully stretched out. Physical at the catch point while showing terrific hands to outmuscle defensive backs. Excellent when working back towards the football or boxing out at the top of his route while fully utilizing his massive frame to shield the ball. Flashes violence and physicality when blocking for his teammates. He shows some variance in his releases and a surprising amount of nuance to how he runs routes while setting up defenders on subsequent plays. Very good after the catch utilizing good vision and aggression to fight and pick up additional yards down the field.

Weaknesses: Teams are going to be concerned about why he needed to transfer on two different occasions. Has dealt with several soft tissue injuries during his career that have caused him to miss some game time. A build-up speed runner that lacks true acceleration off the line of scrimmage to create a ton of separation quickly. Will force quarterbacks to make contested throws quite a bit due to his overall lack of separation quickness. A bit of a frustrating player that will drop some routine catches due to poor concentration. I would like to see him more routinely utilize his physicality in all aspects of the game, flashing it at times and going long stretches of appearing passive. Didn't have to deal with a ton of jam coverage in college and was given free access to routes on most of his receptions.

Best Fit: Outside receiver

Player Ranking (1-100): 55.6 - Hazelton is a big-bodied receiver that has been good in 3 different places. While he's not a great athlete he's a physical specimen that shows some intriguing traits as a developmental option. He's going to need to prove he can be a reliable special teams player to make an NFL roster. 7th round player.

41 - Ben Skowronek - Notre Dame- 6'3 211 lbs

Strengths: A 2-year starter at Northwestern before being a graduate transfer and playing his final season with the Irish. In his final year, in a shortened season, Skowronek was impressive, finishing with 6 touchdowns and nearly 500 total yards on offense. Good intangibles and leadership qualities, as he was a captain both in high school and in college. Top-end special teams player in college. A massive target that possesses a rare combination of size, physicality, and length. A big-game player that has had some of his best receptions and touchdowns in the biggest moments and the biggest games. Looks almost like a tight end the way he runs down the field, understanding how to utilize his frame to dominate at the catch point. Very good red-zone target. Strong hands, reliability in traffic, and good body control allow him to box-out to regularly make plays in the middle of the field. Wins the majority of 50/50 scenarios. Maximizes his frame to consistently extend and make grabs outside of his frame.

Weaknesses: Took a medical redshirt his final season at Northwestern after suffering a bad ankle injury, requiring surgery. Overall production has been just 'OK 'failing to have top-end production. An older prospect that will be 24 years old this summer. Not a great athlete, lacking short-area quickness to separate in-and-out of transition. Deep speed is just 'OK 'failing to have the vertical ability to test the back half of a defense. Will require QB's to repeatedly make tight-window throws or trust him in contested situations.

Best Fit: Possession receiver and special teams

Player Ranking (1-100): 55.2 - Will have to earn his keep on special teams, which he's very good at. He had a good season this past year at Notre Dame but he lacks a truly defining characteristic other than being able to bully with his size. But you have to love his frame and the physicality he brings to a football team. 7th round player.

42 - Marquez Stevenson - Houston - 5'10 182 lbs

Strengths: A 5th year senior that won the starting job during his sophomore season, Stevenson played tremendously, finishing with over 1000 yards and 14 touchdowns that season. Not just a gifted receiver, Stevenson is a great return specialist as well, finishing with 3 kickoff returns for touchdowns as well. Stevenson plays almost entirely in the slot for the Houston offense, constantly being used 'in-motion 'to create mismatches in the defense. Used in a variety of option-style plays as well, showing terrific ability with the ball in his hands. A tremendously gifted athlete that will take many of his routes vertically while playing up the seams showing blow-by speed, almost as if the defensive backs were frozen in their tracks. Does an excellent job of tracking the football down the field, showing terrific awareness and body control to quickly locate and snatch the ball out of the air. Stevenson gets to top gear in a flash, quickly accelerating through his stem and smoothly going in and out of transitions.

Weaknesses: Stevenson missed some game time during his senior season for an ankle issue. Also missed his entire 2017 season with a torn ACL and was given a medical redshirt due to injury. Missed all but two games as well in 2016 with a broken collarbone. Lacks ideal size with a thinner physique that lacks any kind of lower body strength. Easily misdirected and disrupted at the line of scrimmage if he's not 'in-motion. 'Lacks any kind of nuance in his style of play, failing to be able to offer consistent route-running abilities or precision at the top of his routes. A body-catcher that attempts to always corral the ball into his chest as opposed to utilizing his hands.

Best Fit: Slot receiver and niche player

Player Ranking (1-100): 54.3 - An explosive athlete that is more of an athlete than a refined football player at this point. His injury history is very worrisome as well. There are certainly athletic traits to work with but he's a major work in progress. His best chance is winning a roster spot on special teams. Undrafted free agent.

43 - Josh Palmer - Tennessee - 6'1 210 lbs

Strengths: A 4-year contributor to the Vols offense, Palmer is a leader both on and off the field. Being raised in Canada and playing high school football there before transferring to Florida during his high school season. Built with prototypical size and wingspan, Palmer is a nice fit for an outside possession-based receiver role for a team. A physical offense presence that works with a tireless motor on every snap of the ball. Does a nice job of utilizing his big frame at the catch point to box out and control the rep throughout. An excellent 'hands' catcher that utilizes his big mitts to snatch the ball out of the air, showing terrific hand strength to win the majority of the 50/50 balls in congested parts of the field. Good ability to win the ball in the air, attacking the football at the highest point. Shows some nice ability after the catch with physicality and aggression while running with the ball. The best word to describe Palmer is reliable, showing a willingness to handle not always showing up on the stat sheet but willing to put the team first. This is especially noticeable when being used as a perimeter blocker when sealing off edges and opening up holes for his backs, as Palmer takes it personally.

Weaknesses: Palmer struggles when it comes to his route-running mostly due to his poor pad level when working in and out of transitions, leading to clunky routes towards the top. Lacks the ideal explosive characteristics, both with long speed and with separation quickness to consistently generate any kind of separation. Has mostly been a 'share the load' receiver and has taken advantage of having very little defensive attention before his senior season. Production-wise, he's just been 'OK' and certainly hasn't produced anything reminiscent of a #1 receiver. Consistency has been a major problem for Palmer as he shows up for big games and then disappears for others.

Best Fit: Possession outside receiver

Player Ranking (1-100): 54.0 - Palmer had a nice final season showing he can be relied upon to some extent. While his production has been just subpar throughout his career, his physical components make him an intriguing option as an undrafted free agent.

44 - Dez Fitzpatrick - Louisville - 6'2 202 lbs

Strengths: A reliable and consistent presence for the Cardinals for the last 4 seasons, Fitzpatrick has rarely missed a snap of football during his time. Built with a nice frame, Fitzpatrick shows good overall size and muscle for the next level. Fitzpatrick is a hard worker and is known to be incredibly detail-oriented to consistently improve at all levels. A physical kid that shows good toughness and reliability in contested situations, showing reliable hands through traffic. He's very confident in his hands, showing stickiness with the ability to high-point and extend while utilizing his entire catch radius. A really good athlete that has averaged over 18 yards per catch during each of the last two seasons, showing big-play abilities with good straight-line speed. Does a nice job working in-and-out of transitions, showing smoothness and fluidity throughout his movements. A skilled technician in how he plays the position, showcasing good football intelligence to beat jams and vary his releases through his stems to create separation. Impressive after the catch, quickly locating defenders and finding soft openings to attack. A willing blocker that appears to take it personally, showing toughness and a feisty nature to sustain at 1st and 2nd level openings.

Weaknesses: An older prospect that will be 24 years old during his rookie season. The production throughout his career has been 'OK 'but nothing stellar or dominant reminiscent of a #1 receiver. Functional football speed isn't evident even if timed speed is good. Fitzpatrick rarely shows the ability to separate and attack vertical seams in college against interior athletes. A build-up speed athlete that takes a second to get to top gear. Aggression and physicality are there, but functional strength has room to improve. He will struggle to beat jam technique against more physical corners at the line of scrimmage. He lacks the ideal box-out ability to dominate smaller athletes, failing to utilize his frame and consistently win at the catch point.

Best Fit: 'Z 'receiver

Player Ranking (1-100): 53.9 - Fitzpatrick is a skilled and nuanced route-runner with some nice traits as an athlete. His size is impressive but his overall functional strength doesn't match his physique. His lack of production despite never missing any games is just marginal at best. Undrafted free agent.

45 - Danny Davis - Wisconsin - 6'0 194 lbs

Strengths: A 4-year contributor to the Badgers offense that has been mostly a #2 or 3 option for their offense. A former four-star recruit that immediately contributed to the offense from Day 1. Davis offers versatility for a team, having been a return specialist as well as playing both in the slot and on the outside. Used quite a bit his last few seasons as a gadget player, having taken some snaps as a runner as well. Davis maximizes his physique out in the way he plays, showing good reliability when fighting for contested balls. A good ball locator with his back to the ball, showing the ability to track the ball and high-point. Has a great understanding of how to utilize the sidelines while keeping his feet in-bounds. A varied and nuanced route-runner that shows a wide diversity of routes, showcasing the ability to alter release points while creating deception at all levels. Has good zonal awareness and will find soft zones in coverage and sit in and present a QB-friendly target down the field. A physical blocker that shows willingness and aggression to sustain perimeter blocks.

Weaknesses: Production hasn't improved much during his career, failing to ever have a great statistical season. Was suspended for 2 seasons for allegedly being present in the QuinezCephus sexual assault incident, even though he was eventually acquitted. A long line of lower-body injuries throughout his career, most of them he didn't miss any game time from. A wiry physique that lacks the necessary upper-body strength and wiggle to defeat jams at the line of scrimmage. Not a great athlete and struggles to quickly get into his routes, lacking acceleration off the line of scrimmage. Most of his catches are on highly contested grabs, failing to have the transitional quickness to separate out of his routes.

Best Fit: Slot receiver and special teams 'contributor

Player Ranking (1-100): 53.4 - Lacks a defining trait for the next level. Is neither a great athlete nor a great physical specimen. He brings toughness and willingness to handle the dirty work which could earn him a shot on special teams 'in training camp. Undrafted free agent.

46 - Racey McMath - LSU - 6'3 224 lbs

Strengths: McMath finally got his chance for significant snaps during his senior season, where he showed an ability to play receiver and potentially prove to be a better NFL receiver than a college one. Has a ton of experience on special teams 'playing on all the units and was one of the best all-around special teams 'players. Built with terrific and rare physical tools, possessing broad shoulders and long limbs. McMath plays both on the outside and in the slot. McMath loves the physical sides of the game, showing tremendous toughness and physicality through all phases of the game. Understands how to handle jam technique, showing terrific hand strength and wiggle to quickly get into his routes. Physical with the ball in his hands, showing the ability to pick up additional yardage through contact. An excellent athlete that displays impressive deep-speed to threaten all levels of the defense.

Weaknesses: Production and snaps are not things that McMath has had a ton of throughout college, failing to impress considerably when on the field. Has been mostly a special team and a role player throughout college. A bit of a straight-line athlete that lacks lateral abilities to separate in-and-out of transitions when working on in-breaking routes. Lacks a ton of experience and valuable snaps throughout college. Needs refinement in all phases of the game.

Best Fit: Can play anywhere and will be a special teams 'maven

Player Ranking (1-100): 53.0 - Lacks great experience while playing the receiver position. Will be an immediate special teams 'beast. He has upside with his physical tools if he can get continued refinement and development with additional reps. Undrafted free agent.

TOP-10 WRs

1. Ja'Marr Chase
2. De'Vonta Smith
3. Rashod Bateman
4. Jaylen Waddle
5. Dyami Brown
6. Cornell Powell
7. Tamorrion Terry
8. Rondale Moore
9. Terrace Marshall
10. Sage Surratt

Chapter 6

TE's

1- Kyle Pitts - Florida - 6'5 240 lbs

Strengths: Starter for the Gators for the last two seasons, having his breakout campaign as a sophomore, finishing with 650 yards and 5 touchdowns. An athletically-built tight end that possesses a long and lean physique. His versatility allows him to be used all over the offensive formation, including in the slot, in-line, or just off of the tackle. A nifty route-runner that utilizes a wide variety of head and body movements to create deception at all levels of his route. Flexible body control and good ball skills allow him to make adjustments to the ball. An excellent athlete that shows the speed to separate on linebackers and the lateral agility to create separation on in-breaking routes. Utilizes his entire catch radius to make plays away from his frame or extend and high-point the football, showing good hands. Has a good understanding of how to utilize his size in the red-zone, as evidenced by his high touchdowns numbers the last two seasons. Does the majority of his damage in the middle of the field with good reliability and trustworthiness in contested situations? A good run blocker that shows 'want 'when it comes to blocking with good physicality to quickly win inside hand fits and generate lower body torque to plow backward to clear running lanes.

Weaknesses: Missed some games during his junior season for a concussion and needing nasal surgery. Overall functional strength needs to improve, especially to assist in pass protection. Gets a bit reckless when blocking, quickly losing control and getting over his skis. His route running could use more consistency and he needs to show a little more sharpness and nuance in setting up back-to-back routes. Has had some poor concentration drops over the last few seasons.

Best Fit: Receiving TE

Player Ranking (1-100): 89.5 - Pitts is a dynamic receiving tight end that shows a willingness to get better while blocking. He will need to continue to add muscle and strength to his frame, but he's a dynamic receiving weapon. One of the best pure receiving tight ends we've seen in years. He's always battling his butt off to create an opening for his QB. 1st round player.

2 - Pat Freiermuth - Penn State - 6'5 260 lbs

Strengths: A 3-year starter for the Nittany Lions that took over towards the beginning of his freshman season. Freiermuth has been impressive during his time, improving on his production each season. A well-built prospect that has prototypical NFL tight end size, with good compactness and length for the position. Loves all the physical aspects of the game. Very comfortable utilizing his entire wingspan, showing reliability in the middle of the field to snatch the ball while fully extended with ease. Rarely drops the ball through contact, showing good and strong hands. Freiermuth is violent with the ball in his hands, showing impressive post-catch nastiness to do real damage in the open-field with his devastating stiff arms and competitiveness. He routinely ran over defensive backs for fun, reminiscent of Rob Gronkowski. Penn State coaches often lines him up on the outside proving to be a mismatch for linebackers or defensive backs. A smooth and fluid route runner that sets up his routes nicely and consistently creates separation for himself at the top of his routes with good separation quickness. Had to deal with poor and sporadic quarterback play during his time and still put-up excellent production. A good run blocker that appears to take it personally, showing good technique, angles, and power at the point of attack through his lower body.

Weaknesses: Freiermuth is an all-around tight end but lacks the defining athletic traits to excite, as he's only an average straight-lined athlete. Doesn't always attack the football the way you liked to see him do so, appearing to at times, wait for the ball to reach his frame. Could stand to improve a bit as a blocker, he will occasionally lose sustain despite good positioning. Needs continued refinement when fighting through press coverage, he will occasionally get bullied and re-rerouted at the line of scrimmage.

Best Fit: All-around TE

Player Ranking (1-100): 83.3 - A solid and well-rounded prospect that while he doesn't have elite athletic abilities, he's a nuanced player. He consistently gets open and he catches everything thrown in his direction. Plus, he plays with a massive chip on his shoulder and he will bully smaller defenders for fun. 2nd round player.

3 - Brevin Jordan - Miami - 6'3 245 lbs

Strengths: Jordan has started almost every single game for the Hurricanes since his freshman campaign, showing good reliability and consistency for their offense the last 3 seasons. Built like an oversized receiver, Jordan has an athletic frame with very little body fat. Playing all over the offensive formation, Jordan is comfortable playing off the shoulder of the tackle, in the slot, or split out wide. A really good athlete that does a ton of damage as a receiver when working up the seam, exploding out of his stance and showing the ability to separate from linebackers vertically very quickly. He can separate at all levels of the field. Runs a wide diversity of routes, showing fairly good precision and sharpness to his routes. Possesses strong hands and reliability to win in contested situations. Runs with violence after the catch, possessing a nasty stiff-arm to create additional yardage. Difficult to bring down showing good contact balance to bounce off tacklers. A competitive run blocker that does a nice job of showing good physicality and point of attack power to set the edge and create openings along the perimeter for outside-zone runs.

Weaknesses: Pass blocking could stand to improve quite a bit. While he's willing, he fails to consistently play with leverage and win inside hand leverage, causing him to struggle to sustain for any period. Doesn't extend and make plays outside of his frame consistently, tending to prefer to wait for balls to reach his body. Needs to continue to refine some of his footwork in his routes, at times he can look clunky and disinterested.

Best Fit: Receiving TE

Player Ranking (1-100): 79.4 - Jordan is a nice blend of athleticism and toughness. While he's raw as a blocker, I think there are traits there for development. He looked really bad at times but other times he looked dominant. He wants to be good and that's clear. Jordan is a nice mix for today's NFL. He's not an elite athlete but he's a very good one. 3rd round player.

4 - Tre McKitty - Georgia - 6'4 247 lbs

Strengths: A 2-year starter for the Seminoles before transitioning to the Bulldogs and playing his final year of eligibility. McKitty is built with a twitched-up and incredibly muscular physique, showing the compactness and build to handle the next-level. McKitty plays with a relentless passion and motor, working hard on every snap of the ball. A versatile tight end that was used almost exclusively as a blocking tight end for the Seminoles, but has experience playing in the backfield as well as playing split out wide. A willing blocker that shows experience and physicality while run blocking, McKitty plays with a good understanding of positioning, angles, and leverage. While in pass protection, McKitty plays with good leverage, anchorage strength in his lower half, and a wide base that allows him to anchor and hold the point of attack. McKitty is a terrific athlete that accelerates well out of his stance, showing good separation quickness in and out of his transitions to create separation against man coverage. Impressive route-runner that shows an understanding of how to create spacing at all levels, selling his routes well with head/body manipulation.

Weaknesses: Lacks confidence in his hands and has far too many body catches on tape, would like to see him utilize full extension to snatch the ball away from his frame more consistently. Overall production during his time in college was disappointing. Solid blocker but has noticeable room for improvement especially in the run game where he fails to utilize full extension to keep defenders off of his chest plate. Lacks the snap on his routes and tends to round them off, lacking the precise footwork needed. Not a great 50/50 ball catcher and will get outmuscled by linebackers and safeties at the catch point.

Best Fit: All-around TE

Player Ranking (1-100): 75.4 - McKitty certainly wasn't helped by quarterback play during his time with the Seminoles but he's got all the physical tools to have success. A nice combination of blocking experience coupled with the raw physical tools to get better and better as a receiver, with the proper coaching. 3rd round player.

5 - Kenny Yeboah - Ole Miss - 6'4 247 lbs

Strengths: A former Temple Owl and 5th year senior who transferred to play his final season of eligibility for Ole Miss, having an impressive senior season in the SEC. Yeboah had his coming out party against Alabama this season, finishing with almost 200 yards receiving. A versatile all-around tight end that was one of the best blocking tight ends in college football before transitioning and showing his proficiency as a receiver this past season at Alabama. As a pass blocker, Yeboah shows physicality and toughness, maintaining squareness and discipline throughout the rep. He keeps his pads down and commits himself to win the shoulder pads of pass rushers while controlling them. Yeboah played mostly as a split back tight end, even blocking as a fullback in college up the middle. A very good athlete that eases out of his stance and gets to top speed in a flash. Shows the speed to separate up the seams against linebackers. Tough and competitive with the ball in his hands, Yeboah fights for every single yard, gaining a ton of yards after contact. Comfortable utilizing his entire wingspan to make outstretched catches, Yeboah shows reliability snatching the ball outside of his frame.

Weaknesses: Yeboah was a former wide receiver and cornerback in high school that transitioned to a tight end in college. He's still growing into his frame and could stand to gain an additional 10-15 pounds of muscle at the next level. Lacks elite size and length. A little bit of a clunky route runner with a very limited route tree due to not playing a traditional in-line tight end role. Needs to continue to refine his footwork in his routes, relying on coming out of the backfield from a split formation and running simple seam routes that were designed to get him in space.

Best Fit: Hybrid TE

Player Ranking (1-100): 74.7 - Yeboah impressed me this season for the Rebels. He dominated in some big-time games. He's a truly 'do everything 'TE that isn't just an outstanding blocker but he's shown this year in the SEC he can be a very solid pass-catching hybrid WR/TE as well. A ridiculously competitive kid that shows all the traits you want in a draft pick in the 1st round. I love Yeboah and would take him in the 4th.

6 - Kylen Granson - SMU - 6'2 242 lbs

Strengths: A 2-year starter with Conference-USA program Rice before transitioning and starting his final 2 seasons with SMU, posting tremendous receiving production at SMU with 1300 yards receiving and 14 touchdowns the last two seasons. An athletically-built tight end and former receiver, Granson features an oversized receiver's frame with a tapered midsection while carrying room for additional muscle. Has shown the versatility to line up all over the offense; playing inline, in the slot, as an H-back or on the outside. A fluid accelerator that gets to top gear in an instant. A skilled and nuanced route runner that runs with precision and sharpness throughout his stems, while utilizing quick feet at the top to create separation for himself. An excellent athlete that shows rare speed and athleticism to separate at all levels of a defense. Utilizes his body to shield defenders while winning at the catch point with his strong hands. Physical and dominant with the ball in his hands, showing excellent competitive toughness to fight for every inch.

Weaknesses: A bit of a tweener that lacks the ideal prototypical frame to handle in-line duties at the next level. Will get manhandled at the point of attack in the passing game, lacking anchorage power to sit on blockers. In the running game, Granson frequently gets over his skis, losing balance upon making contact.

Best Fit: Receiving TE

Player Ranking (1-100): 74.0 - Granson is one of the best receiving tight ends in this class. He's not going to provide traditional tight end traits as far as blocking, but if coaches can wrap their heads around this, he can be a tremendous receiving TE. A true mismatch for linebackers, Granson is too explosive to be misused. 4th round player.

7 - Hunter Long - Boston College - 6'5 254 lbs

Strengths: A 2-year full-time starter for the Owls, Long has been incredibly productive during each of the last 2 campaigns with over 500 yards receiving combined. A big-bodied tight end that has played all over the offensive formation, including as an in-line blocker, in the slot, or split out wide. Long is an instinctual and smart football player that understands how to beat zone coverages, quickly finding some soft spacing and sitting in and presenting a QB-friendly target immediately. Understands how to win with good positioning and leverage down the field against defensive backs. Will adjust on the fly on broken-down plays. Strength and physicality are evident after the catch, fighting for additional yards after contact. Long really excels in the blocking department. Showcasing a strong and powerful lower body, Long does a nice job of holding the point of attack with good positioning when being used in-line to pass protect. A very experienced run blocker at Boston College, Long commits himself to dominating and taking out his opponent to clear perimeter rush lanes for his backs.

Weaknesses: Overall red-zone production has been very minimal in the last few years despite his gaudy receiving yards. Waits for the ball to reach his frame so he can corral it with his body, rather than attacking the football with his hands. Has had several simple concentration drops on film. Limited as an athlete, mostly just a north/south mover that struggles if asked to redirect his frame and play laterally. Not going to create any kind of separation against man coverage and will be tasked with winning at the catch point by boxing out or winning with physicality if he wants to have any kind of NFL production. Most of his big plays were on broken down plays where he simply worked hard at being open down the field.

Best Fit: All-around TE

Player Ranking (1-100): 73.5 - I don't think Long has the traits to be a dominating receiver at the next level but he's good enough at a combination of blocking AND receiving that he could be a nice #2 tight end for a team. Don't expect him to be a high-volume big-play receiving threat though. Good football player. 4th round player.

8 - Noah Gray - Duke - 6'4 240 lbs

Strengths: A 2-year starter and team captain for the Blue Devils that has been a consistent performer during each of the last 3 seasons, gaining significant playing time during his sophomore campaign as well. A former high-school QB that transitioned to TE. Gray is an athletically-built tight end that runs and moves almost like a wide receiver, creating a nightmare mismatch for linebackers. Gray is a versatile 'move 'tight end playing all over the offensive formation, playing as an H-back, an in-line TE, split out wide, and also in the slot. Dynamic in the red-zone, Gray shows proficiency to be able to line up and find the tiniest little creases in coverage. Gray is a savvy route-runner that understands how to utilize the subtlest of movements to create spacing through all levels of his routes. Excellent footwork allows him to run very precise and sharp routes. Does a nice job of catching tightly congested balls, showing terrific hands. Impressive and physical when used as a blocker, Gray understands utilizing positioning and angles to seal edges and open up lanes. He does a nice job of engaging his lower body to get some good power and torque at the 1st level when being used as an H-back.

Weaknesses: A lot of his receptions came from manufactured play designs which allowed him to work out of the backfield. While he's shown upside as a blocker, he lacks a ton of experience in pass protection and could stand to gain additional experience. A good athlete but isn't great and he struggled consistently creating separation against most athletic linebackers.

Best Fit: All-around TE

Player Ranking (1-100): 73.4 - I like Gray quite a bit and he's been a consistent performer that rarely leaves the field for the last 2 seasons. He shows upside to be a 3-down player that can stay on the field to assist in protection. A hard-working kid that has developmental ability. I love how deceptive he is with his footwork. He's a hard guy to cover in space. 4th round player.

9 - Nick Eubanks - Michigan - 6'5 256 lbs

Strengths: A 4-year contributor to the Wolverines offense, Eubanks shows the physical tools to play at the next level. Built like an NBA Power Forward, Eubanks shows the length and raw physical tools to be a high ceiling guy at the next level. Eubanks smoothly accelerates out of his stance with good initial quickness coupled with impressive long speed to threaten all levels of the defense. Transitional quickness while working through his stems is impressive, showing fluidity and ease of movement. Displays reliable and strong hands at the catch point to pluck the ball out of the air with outstretched arms. Shows toughness, focus, and finish to be a reliable target on 50/50 balls or in congested situations in the middle of the field. Impressive with the ball in his hands, Eubanks shows some post-catch upside to pick up additional yardage after contact. A red-zone nightmare that will merit extra consideration due to his frame and athletic ability to go vertical. Run blocking has shown promise, showing good aggressiveness and physicality to close off and seal perimeter run lanes.

Weaknesses: Eubanks missed some game time during his senior season for an undisclosed injury. Suffered a lower back injury during his junior season that he played through. Had a season-ending elbow injury his freshman season causing him to get redshirted. Eubanks is raw and lacks the nuance or the finesse to be an immediate Day 1 contributor. Production during his career has been subpar at best, never completely dominating against Big-10 competition despite starting his final two seasons. Inconsistent routes due to poor footwork in and out of his breaks, failing to sell out his routes and create any kind of deception. Pass protection and finishing ability are a giant work in progress at this point.

Best Fit: Athletic TE

Player Ranking (1-100): 72.3 - Eubanks is all potential at this point, rarely showing that consistency on the field. He certainly has impressive physical tools but he's a giant 'work in progress 'and will need time developing both in the receiving ends and also while blocking. 4th round player.

10 - Cary Angeline - North Carolina State - 6'7 250 lbs

Strengths: A former USC recruit that transferred after redshirting his freshman season in 2016. After transferring he began starting games for the Wolfpack at the end of his redshirt sophomore season in 2018 and hasn't looked back since. A long and rangy built kid that has length for days, making him a complete size mismatch for most defenders. A dynamic red-zone target with his long frame that has racked up high amounts of touchdowns during each season. Moves all over the offensive formation, playing mostly as an oversized slot though. But he will occasionally show some proficiency when playing as an H-back with good run blocking ability when working through the 'A 'gap. Runs like a receiver when accelerating out of his stance with good initial smoothness and fluidity when working through his stems. Runs a variety of different route concepts, showing an understanding of how to beat both zone and man coverage defensive setups. An excellent overall athlete that shows both initial quickness and good long speed to separate on linebackers vertically.

Weaknesses: An older prospect that will be 24 during his rookie season. A better run blocker than pass protector and will get swallowed up when attempting to pass block due to poor leverage concerns. Needs more experience and understanding of how to utilize his hands when taking on blocks in pass protection while quickly dropping his anchor. Lacks toughness and physicality for the position and tends to be purely a finesse player. Functional strength appears 'OK 'and could stand to gain more muscle on his frame.

Best Fit: Receiving TE

Player Ranking (1-100): 71.8 - Angeline has impressed the last 3 years for the Wolfpack showing good athleticism, size, and overall movement skills. He's shown the ability to consistently separate against linebackers and box out safeties and defensive backs with his size. The problem is he's going to need to improve functional strength and physicality to get snaps at the next level. But the receiving upside is exciting. 4th round player.

11 - Tony Poljan - Virginia - 6'7 265 lbs

Strengths: A former QB for Central Michigan before transitioning to TE and then eventually transferring to Virginia for his final season. Poljan had a really solid abbreviated season as a senior, still finishing with over 400 yards receiving and 6 touchdowns. Featuring rare size, Poljan has the height and length that teams covet to present a mismatched offensive weapon for the next level. Former QB characteristics are on display, as he's a highly intelligent and nuanced football player. Shows some good footwork when working in/out of breaks, doing a nice job of hiding patterns. A natural athlete, Poljan moves effortlessly and smoothly for a guy as large as him. A tough as nails prospect that plays with excellent competitive toughness to fight for additional yards with the ball in his hands. A very good catcher of the football, Poljan shows comfort utilizing his entire wingspan to routinely snatch the ball and extend away from his frame. Could be a very good red-zone player with traits that translate at the next level. Utilizes his large frame to box-out and dominate at the catch point, showing reliability in 50/50 scenarios.

Weaknesses: Still learning how to play TE. Needs to learn some of the finer details. Still very raw as a blocker and fails to understand how to properly utilize his hands both in the passing game and when attempting to open up holes in the run game. Rare height makes leverage concerns exacerbated when attempting to hold up against shorter defenders that can get underneath him. A build-up speed runner that lacks great initial acceleration out of his stance. Long-levered frame with an extremely high-cut torso, limiting his effectiveness in lateral scenarios. Has to really gear down if wanting to change directions, making it easy for defensive backs to recover.

Player Ranking (1-100): 70.2 - Poljan has been surprisingly really impressive in the receiving game despite being completely new to the position. He's got an extremely intriguing frame that is a bit reminiscent of Scott Chandler. If he can develop into a solid blocker, there's no reason why he can't see significant snaps by his 2nd season. 4th round player.

12 - Matt Bushman - BYU - 6'5 245 lbs

Strengths: A 3-year starter for the Cougars that has been a consistent offensive presence for them since his freshman season. Bushman had a terrific final season as a junior in 2019 finishing with about 700 yards and 4 touchdowns. Bushman is a long and rangy athlete that shows good size with the frame for additional muscle. Has the flexibility to be used both in-line or flexed out wide. A really good receiver that understands how to utilize his frame to box out smaller defenders. His large catch radius makes him a dynamic receiving presence that will present a QB-friendly target even when he's covered. His excellent reliability and strong hands allow him to make impossible catches, showing excellent body control and contortion abilities. Has good zonal instincts showing the ability to find soft creases in coverage and then sitting in and creating a nice opening opportunity. A good overall athlete that will separate vertically on linebackers. When used as a run blocker, Bushman shows physicality and the ability to get some movement at the 1st level. Hasn't always been helped by good QB play and still has produced year-after-year.

Weaknesses: Ruptured his Achilles before his senior season and will likely not be ready for the start of offseason activities for a team. An older prospect that is already 25 years old. Light in his lower body, lacking the lower body strength to be able to hold the point of attack in the passing game. When going up against man coverage, Bushman has struggled against more physical defenses, effectively taking him out of plays.

Best Fit: Receiving TE

Player Ranking (1-100): 69.7 - If Bushman didn't have the injury he likely would have been a Day 2 pick. He will get pushed down a couple of rounds due to the unknowns of his injury and when he'll be ready. If he comes back 100% he could be a really solid starting receiver at the next level. He just needs to improve functional strength and be a more consistent pass protector. 5th round player.

13 - Pro Wells - TCU - 6'4 250 lbs

Strengths: Wells, a 2-year starter for the Horned Frogs, has continued the tradition of athletic tight ends that the program continually puts out. Built like an absolute tank, Wells possesses an intriguing mix of size, length and freakish athleticism. A red-zone monster that showcases his ability to get vertical and high-point the ball in the air to out-jump defenders in the back of the end zone. He combines his leaping ability with his ball skills to adjust to the football showing good body control. A smooth moving athlete that eases out of his stance showing good initial quickness to transition well into his stems. Fluidity and agility are prevalent in his transitions as he moves in and out of his breaks, showing the ability to separate at different levels of the field. Has shown impressive yards after the catch ability and contact balance with several broken tackles during the last couple of seasons, showing good competitiveness, field vision and toughness.

Weaknesses: Overall receiving production has been a major disappointment, only finishing with about 400 yards the last two seasons combined despite starting in 15 games. Very raw when it comes to protection situations, failing to have ideal experience. When doing so, he looks completely out of his element, failing to offer any kind of sustainability. Wasn't used much in the running game either. Still raw as a route runner and needs to learn more nuance and a more diversified route tree if he wants to be able to win at the next level.

Best Fit: Receiving TE

Player Ranking (1-100): 69.6 - There's no denying the physical talent that Wells has but he's a developmental project in the truest sense of the word. He's never lived up to his potential in college but there's certainly hope he can end up being a better NFL player than college. 5th round.

14 - Tommy Tremble - Notre Dame - 6'4 248 lbs

Strengths: A 2-year contributor to the Fighting Irish offense, Tremble played more in a fullback/H-back role his final season to assist in the run game. An athletically-built prospect that possesses a lean and well-developed frame with very little body fat. A smooth mover that effortlessly gets to top gear, showing good initial acceleration and quickness off the line. Despite his lack of great production, Tremble shows good athletic upside, possessing the deep speed to threaten linebackers vertically. Shows some agility and looseness in his lower body to change direction and separate on in-breaking routes. Comfortable while extending to make plays outside of his frame, showing good soft hands. At his best in the running game where he shows his physical nature to get downhill and blow defenders off the ball while utilizing his built-up momentum. Very good on the move when blocking for screens, showing good body control and balance while making 2nd level contact. Plays far bigger and more powerful than his size would suggest.

Weaknesses: Tremble has been mostly used as a rotational tight end, rarely carrying the load in production, only finishing with 400 career yards. Hasn't played much of a traditional in-line role, since he was deployed mostly as an H-back this past season. A bit undersized and could struggle in pass protection situations attempting to hold up in 1 v 1 situations, lacking ideal bulk.

Best Fit: In-line blocking TE

Player Ranking (1-100) 64.7 - Tremble is a really really good run blocker. He shows the physicality and nastiness to open up 1st level run lanes and can be used as a hybrid TE/FB at the next level. He's a bit undersized but he's got a nice frame for continued bulk. There's absolutely athletic traits in the player, which could be exciting for development. 6th round player.

15 - Quintin Morris - Bowling Green - 6'2 251 lbs

Strengths: The leading receiver for MAC-Conference Bowling Green, Morris had tremendous sophomore and junior campaigns, tallying nearly 1200 yards and 11 touchdowns combined. Morris is built with an athletic frame, featuring a muscled-up physique with good compactness. Played entirely as a receiver his first few seasons before transitioning to more of a traditional tight end role for his final year. Receiver athleticism is on display as he uses his acceleration and long speed to be a sizable mismatch against linebackers. A former high school basketball player, Morris showcases his post-up abilities to dominate at the catch point. Comfortable with multiple bodies around him, Morris utilizes his large catchers 'mitts to snatch the ball with strong hands and tremendous concentration. These traits make him a very good red-zone target. A willing run blocker that shows good leg drive, committing himself to win inside hand fits to drive back with his lower body.

Weaknesses: Still very raw at the tight end position and learning the position. His production this year when handling tight end duties was significantly lessened. Lacks top-end competition experience having played in the MAC-Conference all his career. Got exposed when handling pass protection responsibilities, getting overmatched and consistently dominated at the point of attack.

Best Fit: Developmental receiving TE

Player Ranking (1-100): 61.2 - Morris has been really good in the MAC-Conference as a receiver. He flashes upside in the receiving parts of the game but he's a LONG way away from being a starter at tight end. He had a very disappointing final campaign. 6th round player.

16 - Shaun Beyer - Iowa - 6'4 244 lbs

Strengths: Beyer is the next in line from a long and successful string of NFL tight ends that got their start at Iowa. A terrific high school football player that hasn't quite lived up to his billing during his college career. Beyer is a strong, low center of gravity kid that is built with good thickness through his lower body. Beyer is at his best when blocking in-line, showing the ability to work the edges with good angles and positioning. Does a nice job of crossing the face of defenders and latching on, showing good lower-body strength to anchor down. A finisher that rarely loses sustain, showing good upper-body strength and iron-grip strength in his hands to latch on. As a receiver, Beyer flashes the ability to win 50/50 balls in traffic. Good overall body control allows him to adjust to badly thrown footballs.

Weaknesses: Tore his meniscus in 2018 causing him to miss the season. Production-wise Beyer has been limited throughout his college career, never being relied on heavily in the passing game. Limited explosiveness out of his stance lacking elite quick-twitch to be a dominant physical presence as a receiver. Offers very little once he catches the ball, lacking the competitive toughness to be a force to break tackles and pick up additional yardage. Very limited route tree that is predicated on 2 or 3 routes.

Best Fit: In-line blocker TE

Player Ranking (1-100): 56.2 - Beyer will likely get drafted due to Iowa's tight end lineage and he's worth a gamble. He's not a great athlete but he's a tough kid that will offer upside as a blocker. He's not a bad athlete but he just isn't a great one. There's developmental upside with him. 7th round player.

17 - Luke Farrell - Ohio State - 6'6 258 lbs

Strengths: A 3-year contributor to the Buckeyes offense that has handled a lot of the "ugly" work for the Buckeyes offense during that time. A well-built kid that shows physicality with a compact and dense frame. A tough as nails kid that shows toughness, competitive drive, and a relentless edge. Farrell is the ultimate team player showing the willingness to do all the dirty work, including consistently being used as the lead blocker both in the running game and getting out in front of screens. A technician that understands how to utilize full extension to keep defenders off of his frame. A smart and disciplined blocker that plays with excellent blocking awareness and instincts, almost always being in the right positions. As a receiver, he flashes some upside athletically, showing some smoothness when working up the seams or vertically. Does a nice job of utilizing his physicality at the catch point, showing "box-out ability" to post-up smaller defensive backs.

Weaknesses: Farrell has been mostly used in a blocking role for Ohio State during each of the last 3 seasons with very minimal receiving production during that time. Has struggled with a nagging ankle injury at times, most notably during his sophomore season. Not a great sideline-to-sideline athlete and will struggle when asked to change directions or show variance in his speeds through his transitions. A 1-speed runner that won't separate from quicker and more athletic defenders. Limited post-catch, lacking the ability to pick up sufficient yardage after the catch.

Best Fit: In-line Blocking TE

Player Ranking (1-100): 55.4 - Farrell is a hard-working blue-chip prospect that will fight his butt off on every snap of the ball. He's limited athletically but he could serve a nice role as a #2 tight end at the next level. 7th round player.

18 - Miller Forristall - Alabama - 6'5 244 lbs

Strengths: Forristall is a 5th year senior that began getting significant snaps during his junior season where he took over some starting duties for the Tide. A well-built kid that displays strength and physicality beyond what his size measurements are. Forristall was often used in an H-block role to create openings on running plays and screens. He's an excellent all-around blocker that displays a terrific ability to make 2nd level strikes in space, showing good body control and excellent length. Lower body strength is noticeable in pass protection, showing the ability to quickly drop his anchor and grant very little movement. He utilizes his length to keep his frame clean and virtually untouched. While offensive production was limited during his time, Forristall showed reliable hands to make some nice catches.

Weaknesses: Forristall has suffered several injuries during his time at Alabama. He was sidelined for multiple games last season after suffering a broken throat muscle. He's missed game time due to foot, knee, and shoulder injuries as well. A limited receiver that has offered very little in terms of production catching the ball. Overall athleticism is subpar, lacking the flexibility or the lateral quickness to create any kind of separation against man coverage. Needs to maximize his frame and add additional muscle for the next level to be a reliable blocker against NFL defenders.

Best Fit: Blocking TE

Player Ranking (1-100): 54.2 - Forristall is strictly a blocking TE at this point. While he's experienced and is terrific at making 2nd level contacts while on the move, he offers very little as a receiving option. He will have to prove dependability with his injury history and earn a spot on special teams.

TOP-10 TEs

1. Kyle Pitts
2. Pat Freiermuth
3. Brevin Jordan
4. Tre McKitty
5. Kenny Yeboah
6. KylenGranson
7. Hunter Long
8. Noah Gray
9. Nick Eubanks
10. Cary Angeline

Chapter 7

OT's

1 - Penei Sewell - Oregon - 6'6 330 lbs

Strengths: A 3-year starter for the Ducks that has won practically every award the Pac-12 has to offer. Built with a monstrous frame with powerful limbs, Sewell possesses the ideal and prototypical NFL physique for the next level. A competitive blocker that shows a fiery nature that battles and possesses the mean streak offensive coaches will love. Easing out of his stance and into his kick slide in the passing game, Sewell effortlessly mirrors in space while maintaining proper spacing and staying square against his matchup. His incredibly powerful upper body and iron-grip strength in his hands allow him to lock onto defenders, rarely losing sustain once latched on. If he does lose, he shows the recovery ability to quickly reset. A very aware blocker that shows good awareness against late coming blitzers and stunts/gains. When unoccupied, he's quick to look for an assignment. In the run game, Sewell utilizes built up momentum to roll his hips forward and drive his legs to be a true 'people mover.' Quickly getting downhill and into the 2nd level, Sewell shows good overall anticipation and change of direction on the move to hit moving targets. Nastiness is shown when he makes 2nd level contacts, blowing defenders off the ball. Excellent when used on screens, showing true naturalness when playing on the move. Will be 20 years old on draft day and into his first NFL season as well.

Weaknesses: There are times when his overall lateral agility and redirection abilities look to be a continued work in progress. His lower body strength is good but not quite to the same level as his upper-body power. Can occasionally struggler against shorter/stouter rushers who can win inside hand leverage on him, putting him on skates. He has a tendency to leave his chest plate far too exposed with far too wide hand placement.

> **Best Fit: Prototypical franchise LT**

Player Ranking (1-100): 93.4 - I have a hard time seeing Sewell not being a Top-10 player in this draft class. With very few flaws and with one of the highest ceilings in this whole draft class while only being 20 years old, how can you pass up on this kid? Smooth, strong, and a very very good athlete. He's a franchise LT.

2 - Christian Darrisaw - Virginia Tech - 6'5 314 lbs

Strengths: A 3-year starter for the Hokies that took over the starting LT role a few games into his true freshman campaign, having never looked back. Possessing prototypical left tackle size with good overall weight distribution and a tapered midsection, Darrisaw certainly is NFL ready. The first thing that stands out with Darrisaw is his terrific initial movement, easing off the snap of the ball with quick feet. Possesses the recovery ability to quickly reset and regain the point of attack if he has any missteps. Maintains good leverage through contact allowing him to keep his wide base and terrific balance throughout. Commits himself very quickly to winning hand placement, controlling defenders with full extension. Loose lower body movements allow him to play laterally and smoothly change direction to cross face to pick up any late blitzes. Terrific hand strength that allows him to latch on, rarely losing sustain. Shows good patience in the passing game, rarely playing over his toes. In the run game, Darrisaw works combo blocks nicely with his teammates, smoothly and effectively transitioning while passing them. An easy mover when climbing to the 2nd level, showing terrific anticipation and balance in space to make contact.

Weaknesses: Has notably put-on strength and muscle during his time but he could stand to continue gaining functional strength in his lower half. He will get bullied on bull rushes occasionally when he fails to drop his pads. Lacks consistent finishing ability. Doesn't possess any kind of 'nastiness' as a blocker and lacks the dominating mentality or mean streak. Pre-snap awareness and recognition can improve as he at times will be late to adjust to oncoming blitzes or delayed rushes.

Best Fit: Zone-blocking LT

Player Ranking (1-100): 90.1 - I love Darrisaw. He struggled with power and strength early on in his career at Virginia Tech but it's noticeable he's gotten considerably better when handling power. His footwork and smoothness in the way he plays are impressive, completely wiping out athletic rushers routinely. Rarely will you see him get dominated in a rep. He's got Pro-Bowl talent. 1st round player.

3 - Rashawn Slater - Northwestern - 6'3 307 lbs

Strengths: A 4-year starter for Northwestern that has played on both sides of the line, having started his first two seasons on the right side before moving to the left side his final two seasons. After playing guard in high school, Slater shows the ability to kick back inside at the next level. One of the things I noticed right away about Slater is how quickly he thinks and reacts. Routinely he will handle a combination block with a guard and then pick up the late-onset rusher. A smooth and efficient mover that shows good lateral movement ability to handle athletic rushers. If initially beaten, Slater shows the secondary quickness to reset and recover to quickly regain his footing to anchor back down. Rarely loses the leverage battle, keeping his knees bent through contact. A fluid operator in the running game, quickly firing off the ball. Often used as the lead blocker on pulls, showing impressive 2nd level reach ability to make contact and hit moving targets in space.

Weaknesses: Lacks the ideal measurables both height and length to play on the outside at the next level. On far too many occasions I would like to see him show more patience. He often gets too aggressive in passing sets which causes some balance and leverage issues. Shows some tightness in his hips and lower body which forces him to lose some of his power when playing face-up with a defender. Showed adequate power as a tackle, but will need to add additional anchorage ability if he's to kick inside and handle bigger interior players.

Player Ranking (1-100): 85.6 - Slater has a lot of really good experience playing against some high-profile guys like Chase Young and having some success. I think his measurables could push him inside for some teams and that's 'OK' because he could be a tremendous starting interior player. He just needs to continue to get stronger through his lower half to handle NFL power. 1st round player.

4 - Alex Leatherwood - Alabama - 6'5 312 lbs

Strengths: A 3-year starter for the Roll Tide that has played both at left tackle and guard. Built with a power-packed frame and excellent overall weight distribution. Positional versatility will help him when working at the next level, allowing him to get early playtime. Leatherwood is strong as an ox, likely one of the strongest prospects in this entire class. When defenders even attempt a bull rush on him, Leatherwood stops them in their tracks almost immediately. An aggressive blocker that plays with reckless fire and aggression, bringing toughness to an offensive line. Leatherwood moves well on his kick-slide, as well as showing impressive recovery quickness to reset and regain control at the line of scrimmage if initially beaten. In the run game, Leatherwood is a 'people mover 'in the truest sense of the word. Bullying his opponents, Leatherwood uses his forward momentum to roll his hips and drive his legs to steer opponents away from the football.

Weaknesses: The biggest area of weakness with Leatherwood is his slower reaction times coupled with poor hand placement. This especially shows up in passing sets where he gives far too easy access to the QB almost instantaneously off the snap off the ball. Overall, his body control is suspect, showing a bit of recklessness in his style of play, leading to whiffs in space while allowing defenders to catch him off-balance. Plays on his toes quite a bit, leading to some poor balance issues. Not a great space player due to his poor balance and taking some poor 2nd level angles.

Best Fit: Tackle but can kick inside in a pinch

Player Ranking (1-100): 84.3 - Leatherwood is a really solid prospect that will be dominant in the run game on Day 1. While he's not an elite athlete in space, he will certainly move piles forward and create movement at the 1st level. He has enough functional athleticism to be a solid pass protector coupled with his size and length to continue to grow into it. 2nd round player.

5 - Samuel Cosmi - Texas - 6'7 300 lbs

Strengths: Cosmi, a 3-year starter at both right and left tackle that has impressed at both positions in college. Cosmi is built with a long and rangier build, showing good overall length with the frame for continued growth. Cosmi plays the game intelligently, utilizing good angles in the run game to open up 1st hole lanes. A real technician in his style of play that understands fundamentals, anticipation, and leverage. Plays with excellent awareness throughout a play when left without an assignment, always looking to assist and notice late coming blitzers. A scrappy and physical blocker that plays with a nasty mean streak, finishing on every play, oftentimes bringing his opponents to the ground. In the passing game, his overall athleticism and quick feet are on full display. Showing easy movement skills, agility, and smooth footwork to mirror in space. Good lower-body flexibility and smooth hips allow him to play laterally and cross the face of defenders. Has the secondary burst to recovery if he is late off the snap of the ball.

Weaknesses: The biggest issue with Cosmi is his repeated leverage concerns when attempting to get his large frame into a lower stance. His upright nature allows smaller, stout rushers to get under him and bully him at the line of scrimmage. Not a dominant point of attack blocker that will consistently clear lanes and relies more on technique than power. Cosmi needs to continue to maximize his frame by adding some additional mass to his lower body to handle the point of attack power for the next level. Not a natural 'move 'blocker in space and struggles consistently getting to the 2nd level.

Best Fit: Tackle in either scheme

Player Ranking (1-100): 83.7 - I was impressed watching Cosmi this year. While he's not a dominant physical presence and isn't an outstanding athlete either, he's just a solid all-around prospect. Rarely will you see him make a major mistake. The best word you can describe him is: smooth. If he continues to maximize his frame with additional strength and muscle without sacrificing athleticism, he could be a solid NFL starter. 2nd round player.

6 - Teven Jenkins - Oklahoma State - 6'6 320 lbs

Strengths: Jenkins a full-time starter that is experienced in playing both sides of the offensive line the last 3 seasons for the Cowboys. Built with terrific and prototypical size, Jenkins has all the makings of a potential starting left tackle at the next level. Excellent movement skills and quick feet allow him to mirror amongst the best of them. Loose-hipped and lower body flexibility allow him to move laterally and quickly re-shuffle and redirect his frame to maintain good positioning against quick-twitch rushers. Active hands allow him to keep his frame clean through contact. Iron-grip hand strength allows Jenkins to latch on, rarely losing sustain. Really good lower-body strength allows him to sit down and anchor against squatty and explosive bull rushers, rarely giving up much ground. Utilizes all of his size in both aspects of the game, playing with full extension and maintaining the point of attack with length. In the running game, Jenkins drives and rolls his hips forward through contact to create movement at the 1st level. 2nd level movement skills show him to be an effective zone-style fit at the next level as he consistently reaches blockers while on the move. A finisher that has a nasty mean streak.

Weaknesses: Jenkins gets too aggressive in pass sets, overreaching and getting on his toes, limiting his balance. This makes him especially vulnerable to longer-armed athletes or ones that can counter his well. Has had several leverage issues due to poor pad level, getting exposed on occasion against bendy athletes that can get under his pads. Has had some weight distribution issues while on the move. Overall hand placement is hit or miss and sometimes can get too wide with his technique, leading to some holding calls.

Best Fit: LT or RT in any system

Player Ranking (1-100): 81.0 - Jenkins has all the potential to be a high-end starting tackle at the next level. Has the power, movement skills, and experience to be effective. While some of his technique needs to improve, he has the raw athletic traits to get better with additional refinement. 2nd round player.

7 - Jackson Carman - Clemson - 6'5 335 lbs

Strengths: A former five-star recruit out of high school; Carman took over the starting LT job for the Tigers during his sophomore campaign. Built with a massive frame, Carman possesses rare width and size for the next level. While in pass protection, Carman shows the ability to consistently eliminate defenders. Experienced in playing against some of the pass rushers, some of which now play in the NFL, Carman rarely loses off the snap of the ball. Moving well for his size, Carman stays square while remaining in control for every rep. Plays with a nasty mean streak, showing aggressiveness and physicality at every step of the way. Understands how to utilize his hands at the snap of the ball showing a heavy-handed punch to offset defenders. Iron-grip strength is prevalent in his hands, rarely losing sustain once they initially reach a defender. Lower-body strength is on display when working against defenders that attempt to bull rush him, absorbing rushes with relative ease. Recovery ability is good too, quickly re-setting and re-anchoring. An absolute bully in the run game that is your classic 'road grader 'when working vertically. Power is manifest throughout his frame. Rolls his hips forward while bringing impressive torque from his lower body to drive and move piles forward.

Weaknesses: Carman isn't a great 'move 'blocker and can struggle consistently making 2nd level contact. He allows his base to be too narrow when off of his spot, limiting his effectiveness when on the move. Overall length isn't great and he might have to kick inside at the next level. It was notable when attempting to win hand placement battles against longer defenders. A belly-to-belly blocker that doesn't frequently utilize full extension and keep his frame clean. Not a great athlete and struggles when playing laterally or attempting to cross the face of a defender, failing to stay square. Will have some issues on counter moves with lack of balance and change of directional abilities.

Best Fit: RT or guard

Player Ranking (1-100): 79.3 - Carman is a powerful, powerful man. His five-star high school credentials were on display quite a bit for the Tigers the last few years. He has some mobility issues and lacks great length for the tackle position. Some teams'will likely want to kick him inside or over to RT. I think he can do either. I love the violent nature and nastiness with which he plays. 3rd round player.

8 - Jalen Mayfield - Michigan - 6'5 320 lbs

Strengths: A 2-year full-time starter for the Wolverines at RT that has had several big-time starts against now NFL edge rushers, including Chase Young. Has left tackle potential and played there some snaps for the Wolverines. Mayfield has continuously added to his frame since arriving at Michigan, possessing an athletic and big frame for the next level. Mayfield is a good athlete that eases off the snap of the ball with bent knees, keeping his arms fully extended to keep his chest plate clean. Possesses good lateral mobility and foot quickness to mirror in space and effectively limit potential pass rush reps when playing on an island. Strong hands and good placement allow him to latch on while rarely losing sustain through the duration. A finisher that plays until the echoes of the whistle. Easy movement skills are on display in the running game, showing comfort on down blocks. Does a nice job of rolling his hips forward through contact to create some movement? Good comfort and experience at the 2nd level showing the ability to reach/hook/pull while connecting with linebackers.

Weaknesses: While he's a good athlete he will tend to take too wide a kick-slide in his initial footwork when attempting to overcompensate against speed rushers, making him vulnerable to inside moves. His footwork needs refinement and can get a bit clunky at times. Has several balance issues in the passing game. Over-pursues and lunges at defenders on occasion, playing on his toes. When he fails to keep his pads down at the point of attack, he will be caught off-balanced on the counter. Can get his hands too wide on occasion, limiting his effectiveness at holding his anchor. Lower body strength is erratic and at times it is really impressive, and other times he appears to give up significant ground against speed-to-power rushers.

Best Fit: RT in a zone-style system

Player Ranking (1-100): 79.0 - I'm not as high on Mayfield as some others are. While he doesn't have any immense weaknesses, he doesn't have any bonafide strengths either. He's strong and somewhat athletic but he's great at either. He's a bit inconsistent on tape which is frustrating for an evaluator. He should compete for a starting gig immediately but I don't think he's a top-notch tackle prospect. 3rd round player.

9 - Liam Eichenberg - Notre Dame - 6'6 302 lbs

Strengths: A 5th-year graduate senior and a 3rd-year starter at left tackle for the Irish, Eichenberg possesses plenty of experience to play at the next level. Eichenberg is a well-built prospect with next-level credentials, including good overall size and length for the position. A smart kid that plays disciplined while remaining in control at every play. A technician in the way he plays utilizing his frame well and playing with good depth and angles. While in the passing game, his quick feet and smooth footwork allow him to remain perfectly positioned with arms extended to keep his frame clean. Does a nice job of keeping his pads leveraged and his stance wide with perfectly bended knees. Can handle power when working against powerful rushers, showing the ability to drop the anchor and absorb bull rushers. Has gained notable power each season at Notre Dame and that is especially evident in the running game. Quickly seals off the perimeter to clear outside-zone runs, controlling with good technique and length. Keeps himself composed and controlled when working in space, remaining balanced and square when working on 2nd level blocks. Frequently used and entrusted to be the lead dog on screens, doing a nice job of consistently making 2nd level contact, without losing balance.

Weaknesses: Can be a tad late off the snap of the ball, allowing him to quickly give up pressure. Inconsistent strike accuracy and placement. This has led to some holding calls and will also lead more explosive rushers to quickly disengage on the counter move. Not a great lateral athlete and can struggle at times playing sideways, showing some lower body stiffness when attempting to work across the face of defenders, most notably when against slanted fronts. Not a bully while on the move in the run game, certainly not a 'people mover.'

Best Fit: LT or RT in any offensive system

Player Ranking (1-100): 77.4 - Eichenberg is a smart and experienced LT that can play in any offensive line system. He has a ton of experience playing out of a zone-style system but perhaps he could be better suited when he's not on the move as much. He's not a great pass protector and will likely struggle against more athletic quick-twitch rushers. But he's not 'BAD 'per se either. A technician that plays with smarts and intangibles, not a great athlete or mauler type. 3rd round player.

10 - Daniel Faalele - Minnesota - 6'9 400 lbs

Strengths: Faalele started almost every game during his first 2 seasons with the Gophers at right tackle. The first thing you'll notice about Faalele is his rare size. He's one of the biggest players I've ever evaluated. His combination of height, length, power, and athletic ability is something you'll rarely see. His former rugby experience growing up in Australia is evident in the way he moves, showing the impressive change of directional abilities. An absolute bully in the running game that utilizes built-up momentum, hip torque, and lower body power to clear out large rush lanes. Utilizes his rare wingspan to quickly attach himself to defenders and win inside hand placement. Terrific range in space that shows consistency in making 2nd level contact. If he's able to reach your frame and latch on to you while on the move, it's almost impossible to be able to disengage yourself. In the passing game, Faalele showcases his power when working against powerful edge defenders. If rushers even attempt to bull rush him, he quickly drops his anchor and controls the entire snap of the ball. Powerful upper-body is manifest in his initial 'POP' with his hands. Good against counter moves, rarely letting defenders get around his frame. Shows good foot quickness and length when working against rushers that will attempt to win outside leverage, easily walking them backward, forcing them to take wide depths in pursuit.

Weaknesses: Missed most of his junior season for covid-related reasons. Due to his frame, he will be a bit inconsistent with both his hand timing and placement, getting too high at times. Balance issues will be exposed on occasion. Pad level can sometimes struggle, limiting his effectiveness to play laterally against shorter and quicker rushers that can get underneath him. Still very raw and learning how to play the position.

Best Fit: RT

Player Ranking (1-100): 76.4 - It's hard not to like Faalele with his rare size, power, and mobility. For as raw as he is, he surprisingly didn't get exposed as much as you'd expect. If he's able to put it all together and clean up some of the technical ends of his game, watch out! 3rd round player.

11 - Brenden Jaimes - Nebraska - 6'6 300 lbs

Strengths: A rare 4-year starter for the Cornhuskers, Jaimes has rotated on both sides of the line of scrimmage, having extensive experience playing both on the right and left sides. Set Nebraska record for starting in 40 consecutive games. Jaimes possesses a solid frame for the position with good length and functional strength throughout. In the passing game, Jaimes shows very good initial quickness, gaining good depths on his initial kick-step, sliding with ease. Very good at mirroring all kinds of rushers, showing good lateral agility. Maintains good positioning, playing with full extension to maintain separation between him and rushers, rarely letting defenders into his frame. Iron-grip strength in his hands allows him to control blockers, rarely losing sustain. Will force-wide rush lanes against speedier quick-twitch rushers, utilizing his length to push them past the pocket. Very good at recognizing things pre-snap, adjusting quickly to stunts and gains. In the run game, Jaimes fires off the ball, showing the ability to locate and lock onto defenders at the 2nd level. Maintains good anticipation and change of directional abilities while on the move, offering upside as a reach and hook blocker. Has schematic versatility with experience playing both in power and zone blocking concepts.

Weaknesses: Can be a bit too grabby in the run game, getting called for a number of holding penalties when runs go to the perimeter. Could still stand to gain some lower body strength and will occasionally get put on skates when his leverage isn't on point. Has been inconsistent with his pad level and will allow his pads to rise mid-play on occasion. Will overset to the outside at times attempting to handle speedier rushes, leaving the inside counter lanes vulnerable and wide open. Doesn't always play with good strike accuracy and will allow his hands to get easily knocked away by rushers that have quick and active hands.

Best Fit: Starting tackle in either scheme

Player Ranking (1-100): 76.1 - I like Jaimes quite a bit. The consistency and level of experience he brings in addition to his experience playing in any system and on both sides of the line is tremendous. The guy was never hurt! He's not an elite prospect but he rarely makes a mistake. 3rd round player.

12 - James Hudson - Cincinnati - 6'4 302 lbs

Strengths: A former defensive line four-star recruit by Michigan, Hudson transferred to Cincinnati for his final year, after sitting out the 2019 season due to NCAA regulations. He came on strong for the Bearcats after starting every single game for them at LT this past season. Hudson has a nice-sized frame with very good length for the next level, having put on significant amounts of clean muscle over the last few years. Hudson has all the athletic traits for development, including terrific athleticism and movement abilities. He eases off the snap of the ball with bent knees, showing quick feet, perfectly capable of mirroring in space in the passing game. Gains good depth on his initial kick-step, sliding easily. Good recovery ability if initially beaten. Plays with full extension, quickly controlling the pads of defenders. Uses his iron-grip strength in his hands to rarely lose sustain. In the running game, Hudson fires off the ball flashing impressive lateral mobility to consistently be used as the 'move' blocker on reach and hook blocks. Shows excellent change of direction, body control and anticipation while on the move.

Weaknesses: Made a really stupid decision in his final game of his career, getting ejected for targeting in the Bowl Game against Georgia, hurting their chances significantly of winning the game. He still is very new to the position and is learning the finer nuances of playing on the offensive side of the ball. Has only started in one season, albeit it wasn't even a full season. Needs to continue adding additional bulk and size to his frame to handle the NFL rigors of playing at the next level. Could stand to gain additional strength in his lower body, as he repeatedly had struggles against more powerful, squattier rushers. Allows his pads to rise mid-play, causing some point of attack power concerns as he allows defenders to get under his pads.

Best Fit: Developmental LT

Player Ranking (1-100): 75.8 - Hudson has arguably one of the highest ceilings in this draft class. If he starts immediately, he will struggle. But I'm convinced with more development and NFL coaching, he could be an outstanding starter in a year or two. He's one of the better athletes in this tackle class. 3rd round player.

13 - Abraham Lucas - Washington State - 6'7 328 lbs

Strengths: Lucas is a 3-year starter for the Cougars at right tackle that has greatly impressed during each of the 3 seasons. Built with a giant frame and thickness and length throughout, Lucas has all the size you would want for a next-level starter. Very skilled and effective in pass sets, showing good quickness and smoothness through his kick-slide. Natural in his movements, Lucas maintains good spacing and technique with bent knees and arms fully extended to keep defenders off of his frame. Good reset and recovery ability if initially beaten. Mirrors excellently in space, maintaining a good position to stay square with defenders. Appears to have a solid anchor with considerable strength being added since his freshman campaign, showing the ability to sit down on rushers. Places his hands well through contact, showing good hand placement coupled with iron-grip strength to hold sustain. Good awareness throughout the play, having a good understanding of when to pass on twists and stunts by the defensive line. A busy blocker that always looks for an assignment when left without one, keeping his head on a swivel at all times. Showed some 2nd level ability in the run game when being used in space, with good balance and acceleration while on the move.

Weaknesses: Inconsistent with his leverage, allowing his pads to rise mid-rush, limiting his effectiveness against quicker-twitch rushers that can grab the edges. Played mostly in a pass-first offense his first few seasons and overall experience in the running game is very limited and will need to be refined at the next level. More of a technique player when he is used in the run game, not a 'people mover 'that shows tremendous explosion off the ball to clear rush lanes. Lacks any kind of aggression or mean streak to his play, failing to ever overwhelm his opponents with pure power.

Best Fit: LT or RT

Player Ranking (1-100): 75.3 - Lucas is a smooth and effective pass protector. He's not quite refined in the run game nor is he the most overly powerful player. But he typically maintains good positioning and technique. 3rd round player.

14 - Cole Van Lanen - Wisconsin - 6'5 312 lbs

Strengths: Van Lanen began getting significant game-time during his sophomore year, splitting time at LT. He's taken over full-time duties ever since and not looking back. Possessing a next-level frame, Van Lanen displays a power-packed physique with excellent overall weight distribution. Van Lanen is an intriguing blend of both raw strength and athleticism. One of the strongest prospects in this class, physicality and pure country strength is evident throughout Van Lanen's style of play. Excelling in the run game, Van Lanen is a flat-out bully in his ability to be a true 'people mover. 'Showing good initial quickness to climb to the 2nd level in an instant, Van Lanen utilizes built-up momentum to generate significant displacement power. Bows his back and shows really good leg drive to move piles at the 1st level. In the passing game, Van Lanen shows solid technique to stay square while keeping defenders off of his frame with full extension. Plays with a nasty mean streak finishing his blocks to the echoes of the whistle.

Weaknesses: After being one of the highest-graded linemen in college football during his sophomore season, Van Lanen has dropped off a bit for evaluators the last two seasons. Lacks confidence in his ability to mirror in space, oftentimes oversetting to his outside leaving interior gaps completely exposed for counters. Stiffness is evident throughout his frame in the passing game, lacking the looseness and flexibility in his frame. Lacks the quickness and recovery ability to reset after losing initially on the rep. Gets overaggressive reaching for blocks due to his lack of length.

Best Fit: Power-blocking RT

Player Ranking (1-100): 73.4 - Van Lanen is a really good run blocking tackle having loads of experience playing in Wisconsin's run-heavy offense. He lacks the ideal athleticism to be a dominant pass-blocking tackle at this point, hence the reason I think he's better suited on the right side of the line. There's no denying the player's toughness, strength, and mean streak. 4th round player.

15 - Dillon Radunz - North Dakota State - 6'6 304 lbs

Strengths: Coming from a long-line of NFL prospects from the FCS level, Radunz shows outstanding traits to be the next one. Starting and dominating FCS competition for 3 straight seasons at LT, Radunz has more than enough experience for the next level. Possessing a solid frame to play outside at the next level, Radunz displays an athletic profile with long limbs and additional room in his frame for muscle. In the passing game, Radunz shows above-average movement ability, easing off the snap of the ball and remaining in control. Lateral agility allows him to move sideways with relative ease to cross face and play face up. Does a nice job of keeping his frame clean while blocking and getting to full extension while controlling the shoulder pads of defenders with his iron-grip strength in his hands. Aggressiveness and physicality are two traits that Radunz has in baskets full, bringing a nasty mean streak to an offensive line. A smart blocker that quickly communicates with his teammates to call things out pre-snap and identifies protections and defensive alignments. In the run game, Radunz fires out of his stance quickly to generate displacement power from his lower body, moving defenders out of the way. Does a nice job of getting to the 2nd level and making contact in space.

Weaknesses: Suffered a season-ending ACL injury the very first game of his sophomore campaign. There will always be concerns about someone coming from FCS level competition and transitioning directly into a role in the NFL. While he's got physicality and athleticism, he isn't 'elite 'in any one facet of his game. At times, his overaggressive nature in the passing game will hurt him when he lunges into blockers, getting over his toes, leaving him susceptible to counter moves.

Best Fit: Tackle in any scheme

Player Ranking (1-100): 72.1 - Radunz could end up being a real steal in this draft class. He has the size, experience, and physicality to be a solid starter down the road. There's always the question mark of his transition from the FCS to the NFL. 4th round player.

16 - Robert Hainsey - Notre Dame - 6'5 302 lbs

Strengths: A 3-year starter and team captain for the Irish that has played exclusively at right tackle. Hainsey is a developed prospect that features a well-built frame, showing the ability to be a positionally-versatile prospect in any scheme or multiple spots along the front. A very clean prospect that excels in the passing game.

Hainsey eases off the snap of the ball showing good initial quickness while maintaining good depth on his kick-slides to mirror in space. Understands how to utilize his hands, showing good accuracy and timing with his punches. Utilizes his full arm extension that allows him to keep defenders off of his frame and maintain the point of attack in passing sets. Excellent agility and lateral quickness that allows him to mirror when working in space. Plays with nastiness in the running game, showing good toughness and finish. He shows the strength with his hands and upper body to bully at the 1st level and clear run lanes.

Weaknesses: Missed the second half of his junior season after suffering a broken ankle. Lacks the ideal frame of a tackle, appearing to have somewhat stubby limbs and lack of elite length. A bit of a top-heavy prospect with a large upper body but severely lacking the ideal bulk and anchorage strength through his lower body. This gets exposed when his pads rise mid-play, getting bullied against squatty-built rushers that can win the leverage battle against him. He struggles re-setting and re-anchoring when initially losing the rep. More of a positional run blocker than a space clearer, failing to equip his lower body and hips into his down blocks.

Best Fit: RT or kick inside and play guard

Player Ranking (1-100): 72.0 - Hainsey will likely be evaluated differently by different teams. Due to his lack of ideal length, some might view him better inside. He's another stellar Notre Dame offensive lineman that could get overvalued because of it. He's not one of the better Irish blockers but he's a very solid one. 4th round player.

17 - Josh Ball - Marshall - 6'8 310 lbs

Strengths: A former Seminoles four-star recruit and starting left tackle, Ball ended up being dismissed from the program following some off-the-field incidents with a former girlfriend. After Florida State dismissed Ball, he played community college and then transferred back to the FBS level and played his last two years of eligibility with Marshall. Ball is built with a massively long and athletic frame, showing the length and size requisites to play at the next level. Ball moves well for his size, showing terrific initial quickness out of his stance. Good lateral agility coupled with a smooth kick-slide allows him to mirror in space. Active and heavy-handed showing the power through his upper body to ease rushers off the snap. Really impressive movement skills in the run game, showing good initial acceleration off the line of scrimmage to get into the 2nd level. Good length and balance allow him to reach targets with relative ease. Not content simply reaching, Ball is violent and will completely wash them out with overwhelming power.

Weaknesses: His off-the-field things will need to be looked into by evaluators. There are serious question marks over his character issues. Like most lineman that are over 6'6, he will have continued struggles with leverage concerns. If he doesn't drop his pads and make it a concerted effort, he will struggle against quicker-twitched bendy athletes that can get underneath his pad level. Has a bit of a lanky frame and will need to gain some more anchorage strength through his lower body so that he can sit down on bigger NFL defenders. He will get bullied at times against bull rushers.

Player Ranking (1-100): 71.9 - The biggest thing with Ball is going to be his former removal at Florida State. There's no denying the pure physical talent that Ball possesses. He can be a really good starter at the next level if there aren't considerable concerns about him off the field. He possesses the size, length, and movement skills to easily translate. 4th round player.

18 - Walker Little - Stanford - 6'7 309 lbs

Strengths: Little only had 1 full season of starting during his sophomore campaign where he played as the LT for the Cardinals, making it to the All Pac-12 First Team. Little is possessed with a long-levered frame showing good overall weight distribution and tremendous length. Length eases off the snap of the ball in passing sets, utilizing his length to force speed rushers to far wide rush lanes. An aware and instinctive blocker that is quick to diagnose and read disguised or delayed onset blitzes. He does a nice job of working in combination with his teammates, seeing things quickly, and working well with combo blocks. Despite his height and frame, Little is impressive the way he keeps his pads squared and leveraged, rarely being overwhelmed with shorter defenders. Shows good hand strength in his abilities to stunt defenders if he gets his hands fitted on them.

Weaknesses: Little sat out his final season due to personal choice and missed practically all of his junior campaign after suffering a bad knee injury. Evaluators are going to be very concerned about his previous medical issues, having only played one full season of college football. When he fails to get his hands on speedier rushers on the edges, he fails to have the recovery quickness to reset. An average athlete that lacks elite foot quickness to mirror against more athletic rushers and will struggle in the passing game at the next level. Limited in a zone-style set up where he would need to play in space, failing to have ideal change of directional ability.

Player Ranking (1-100): 68.3 - Little is a decent prospect but nowhere near starter quality at this point. Teams' will likely vary on what his best position is and his medical evaluation will likely be the difference between whether he gets drafted or not. If his medical checks out 'OK 'he's a 5th round player.

19 - Adrian Ealy - Oklahoma - 6'7 326 lbs

Strengths: A former four-star recruit that has started at right tackle during each of the last two seasons for the Sooners. A massive man that displays all the physical tools you want in a tackle, including vines for arms and terrific width. Ealy utilizes his wide body in the passing game, making it very difficult for defenders to get around him as he limits available angles. Better quickness out of his stance than you would imagine for a man of his size, showing some agility and footwork to mirror while working in space. Forces wide rushes due to his length, perfectly utilizing his long arms and body positioning to work defenders too far outside. Excellent lower body strength and power are on display against bull rushes, as he rarely grants any space after dropping his anchor down. Possesses a nasty mean streak with powerful hands to deliver devastating blows to defenders. Good awareness to quickly react to blitzes, stunts or gains, keeping his head on a swivel at all times.

Shows some movement ability when working in space in the running game, quickly getting downhill and making some good 2nd level contact. Utilizes his length to quickly control defenders while working in space, winning inside hand fits and controlling throughout the duration.

Weaknesses: The biggest thing repeatedly on display for Ealy is his continual leverage concerns, frequently struggling against shorter defenders that can get underneath his pads. Shows some tightness when having to work laterally and will get caught out of position against good counter rushers. Will overset at times in the passing game, lacking ideal patience, causing him some repeated balance issues. Is bailed out quite a bit with his length, appearing to have some slow reaction times off the snap of the ball. Still very raw as a lineman despite being with the Sooners for 4 seasons.

Best Fit: Power-blocking scheme RT

Player Ranking (1-100): 68.0 - Ealy has been a solid player for the Sooners but he's not a fit in a zone-style offense. He lacks ideal movement abilities and still has major work to do in terms of being a starter at the next level, most notably in the passing game.

20 - Calvin Ashley - Florida A&M - 6'7 330 lbs

Strengths: A former five-star recruit for Auburn player that transitioned to Florida A&M following his redshirt freshman campaign after only seeing a little bit of playing time. Ashley chose to sit out his final campaign to prepare for the draft. Guys like Ashley don't grow on trees with his rare combination of size, length, and overall power through his frame. Ashley shows tremendous strength in his lower-body, handling power with power with ease. Easily absorbing bull rushes, Ashley resets and re-anchors rarely losing much footing. A physical blocker that shows good initial 'POP' in his hands to displace at the 1st level in the run game. Fires off the ball in the running game, rolling his hips and driving his legs forward to clear run lanes. Good awareness to notice late oncoming blitzers and react to stunts/gains.

Weaknesses: Ashley has battled several minor nagging injuries during his time at Auburn that caused him to have some playtime issues leading to his wanting to transfer. His medical will be very important. Hand placement is a continuous problem for Ashley, oftentimes placing them too narrow leading to easy counters for explosive rushers. Ashley's upper-body power isn't on the same level as his lower-body power, and he will quickly lose sustain even after being in a good initial position. Lateral quickness and agility are serious question marks and he will get toasted by explosive quick-twitch speed rushers that can win the outside edges. Limited to a man-blocking role at the next level as his 2nd level and zonal abilities are suspect at best.

Best Fit: Developmental tackle

Player Ranking (1-100): 65.3 - The talent is certainly there with Ashley as evidenced by his high school five-star status but he needs refinement and development. Ashley will get drafted with his talent. He's not anywhere near being ready to start at the next level but he will get his opportunities to impress.

21 - Spencer Brown - Northern Iowa - 6'9 314 lbs

Strengths: Brown, another FCS tackle prospect, is one of the rarest physical specimens in this draft class. A 4-year starter for Northern Iowa since his freshman campaign at RT. Equipped with an absolutely monstrous frame, Brown not only has the height but he has vines for arms. Known for his lifting accolades, Brown has tremendous power through his frame, most notably in his upper body. This power is on display when he finishes, showing the ability to routinely bring FCS defenders down to the ground when he finishes them off. In the passing game, Brown moves surprisingly well for his size, showing the ability to redirect and reset his frame if initially beaten. He utilizes his vines to keep defenders off of his frame and force wide pursuit lanes. Shows patience to handle counters, rarely allowing himself to get caught off-balanced. In the running game, he shows impressive change of directional ability with good 2nd level accuracy while on the move.

Weaknesses: Missed his entire sophomore campaign after suffering a bad injury. Brown's level of competition will always be a question mark until he competes against top-flight competition. He's still growing into his frame, having gained 90 pounds in the last few years. He's going to have constant leverage concerns due to his height, he needs to consistently fight to keep his pads down. Strike timing and accuracy are inconsistent, surprisingly not having ideal hand strength as you would expect. Needs to play with a wider base, playing far too narrow on occasion allowing himself to get caught off-balanced on occasion.

Best Fit: Developmental tackle

Player Ranking (1-100): 64.6 - Brown shows impressive flashes of strength and athleticism. But he's going to have an uphill climb coming from the FCS level and due to his height and size. NFL defenses will constantly be putting him on skates and forcing him to play laterally. 6th round player.

22 - Brady Christensen - BYU - 6'6 300 lbs

Strengths: A 3-year starter at BYU that was entrusted with protecting the blind side for Zach Wilson and their offense. Built with a long and lean physique, Christensen shows NFL quality movement skills in his frame. Possessing good range and easy movement skills, Christensen easily and effectively kick-slides to mirror in space, even against athletic rushers. Lower body flexibility allows him to handle more explosive rushers, maintaining good positioning throughout. Utilizes his length nicely with good hand placement and technique, playing with full extension to keep rushers off of his frame. Understands how to play with angles and leverage in the run game, maintaining good positioning and opening up perimeters lanes for his backs. His athleticism is on display in the run game as well, showing him to get out of his stance quickly and into the 2nd level with ease.

Weaknesses: While Christensen has put on noticeable muscle mass during his time, he still possesses a very slender position. He could and likely should continue to add additional muscle mass and size as long as it doesn't negatively affect his movement skills. His lack of overall muscle and strength is pressing as he gets bullied at the point of attack. He lacks a great anchor and if he initially gets beat off the line, he struggled to regain his footing to re-anchor down. Gets a little overaggressive in the passing game, playing over his toes and getting caught off-balanced by good rushers that have a counter plan. Appears to be a bit late in recognizing things post-snap, failing to adjust for blitzes or stunts. An older prospect that will be 24 years old during his rookie season. Hasn't competed against top-tier rushers.

Best Fit: Athletic outside tackle

Player Ranking (1-100): 64.1 - Christensen has been one of the more consistent and reliable pass protecting offensive tackles in college football the last few seasons. He's not elite nor has he competed against great competition but he's solid and helped stabilize the BYU offensive line. 6th round player

23 - Tommy Doyle - Miami (OH) - 6'8 326 lbs

Strengths: After missing most of his freshman campaign with a bad foot injury, Doyle went on to play both right and left tackle for MAC conference Miami (OH) and did so at a very high level the next subsequent years. Doyle is built with a massive physique with tremendous height and length. Doyle shows good initial quickness while getting into his stance to mirror, properly using his frame to keep defenders off his frame. In the run game, Doyle shows above-average zonal abilities. He gets out of his stance quickly while pulling, showing some agility and change of directional abilities to make contact in space. A mauler that quickly engages his lower-body power to generate displacement power to drive backward. Quick to recognize blitzing and pre-snap defensive alignments, Doyle communicates well with his teammates, rarely reacting late.

Weaknesses: Doyle will, on occasion, overset to his outside shoulder, leading to some interior gaps being exposed in the passing game. Doyle is a waist bender that has repeated issues with balance due to far too narrow a stance. His overaggressive nature causes him to get caught lunging while misplacing his punches at the line of scrimmage. Takes far too many short and choppy steps in his kick-slide leading to some struggles with mirroring quicker-twitch rushers. Doyle notably really struggles with pad level due to his size, allowing shorter and stockier rushers to control him at the point of attack.

Best Fit: Developmental tackle in a zone-style system

Player Ranking (1-100): 61.2 - Doyle is a solid MAC prospect that shows developmental upside but he's a major work in progress when it comes to the passing game. His repeated technique and leverage concerns will make him a liability initially but there's likely something to work with down the road. 6th round player.

24 - Jake Curhan - California - 6'6 323 lbs

Strengths: A 5th year senior and 4-year starter for the Golden Bears at right tackle. Had a streak of starting in 38 consecutive games, showing incredible reliability and consistency. Curhan is a mountain of a man, possessing incredible size, compactness through his frame, and vines for arms. A smart blocker that quickly recognizes things, always keeping his head on a swivel while being aware of blitzes or stunts. An aggressive finisher that plays to the echoes of the whistle on every snap. Understands how to play with full extension, rarely allowing defenders into his pads. In the passing game, Curhan eases off the snap of the ball utilizing his width to seal off interior lanes. Does a nice job of forcing wide arcs for pass rushers, playing with a good understanding of angles while walking defenders past the QB. Good lower-body strength allows him to anchor against bull rushes. Has the iron-grip strength in his hands to latch on, rarely losing sustain. In the running game, Curhan shows good initial get-off, showing the ability to generate good displacement power through his hips, rolling his hips forward, and driving opponents away from the ball carrier. Moves better than you would expect for a man of his size, showing good north/south movement ability to reach 2nd level linebackers in space.

Weaknesses: Curhan has repeated issues with leverage, coming out of his stance far too high. This causes defenders to routinely get underneath his pads and control him through the snap of the ball. A waist bender that doesn't appear to play with great coordination between his upper and lower body. Not a great lateral athlete and struggles mirroring in pass protection, failing to have ideal agility. Shows significant tightness concerns through his lower body.

Best Fit: RT or can kick inside and play guard

Player Ranking (1-100): 60.5 - Curhan is a powerful man that has shown good consistency to play in almost every game of his career. While he's not a great athlete, he's a mauler. He could be a nice fit as a RT or kicking inside and playing guard in a power-blocking system. 6th round player.

25 - Jaylon Moore - Western Michigan - 6'4 311 lbs

Strengths: A 3-year starter at left tackle that has been a consistent presence on their offensive line since his sophomore season. Was originally recruited as a tight end before transitioning to the offensive line and putting on significant amounts of muscle. Moore has an athletically-built frame, possessing a lean and trim midsection, with very little unnecessary body fat. His former basketball background is on display with his smooth movement skills. Maintains good technique, playing with a wide base while keeping his pads leveraged. Plays with a nastiness, showing good physicality coupled with a violent mean streak. Does a nice job in the running game of walling off with his frame, playing with good angles while opening up perimeter lanes. Commits himself to winning inside hand fits in the running game, utilizing his hips and lower body to drive and push piles forward. A finisher that stays locked in, rarely letting blockers off with very good hand strength in the running game.

Weaknesses: Has some balance concerns. He routinely gets far too aggressive in his pass sets, getting caught lunging and off-balanced. Has all kinds of issues with his footwork, either oversetting to the outside or taking short and choppy steps. This allows savvy pass rushers to counter him with ease. He gives up his chest plate at times due to firing high out of stance and completely whiffing with his hands. He needs to learn how to utilize his hands better in pass sets. Still very raw as a pass protector and needs significant time and development, as he's still growing into his frame.

Best Fit: Developmental right tackle

Player Ranking (1-100): 59.3 - Moore impressed me at times in the running game but he got exposed quite a bit in the passing game. He possesses power through his frame but his lack of technical refinement makes me think he's going to get destroyed if he's asked to play too soon. He'd be better transitioning to the right side of the line. 7th round pick.

26 - Landon Young - Kentucky - 6'7 321 lbs

Strengths: Young took over the starting role during his true freshman season and never looking back, starting for 4 straight seasons. A former five-star recruit, Young is a talented tackle that has continued developmental upside to improve. Possessing good size, Young has vines for arms, showing the ability to control the point of attack with his length. In the passing game, Young utilizes full extension to keep his frame clean. He will walk rushers backward forcing them to take wide rush pursuit angles. Powerful man that has excellent and rare upper-body power and strength possessing strong hands that allow him to latch on, rarely losing sustain. Quick to drop the anchor, Young will drop his pads and anchor down, allowing very little movement against bull rushes. In the run game, Young has a good understanding of zone concepts, maintaining disciplined technique while playing with angles and leverage. A fairly good athlete in space, oftentimes being used as the lead blocker on hook and trap blocks at the 1st level.

Weaknesses: Was redshirted during his 2018 campaign after a season-ending knee injury. A slow-footed pass protector that will struggle against more athletic quick-twitch rushers that can play with bend. Despite his size, Young will occasionally get too wide, leaving his chest plate completely exposed. Limited when asked to move laterally, getting caught on his heels and off-balanced. Limited as a 2nd level blocker, lacking the necessary balance and straight-line explosiveness to make contact.

Best Fit: Developmental tackle

Player Ranking (1-100): 57.3 - Young has looked good at times but lacks a defining characteristic for the next level. He's got good size and upper body power, but he lacks the overall movement ability to be effective when he has to move off of his spot. 7th round player.

27 - Alaric Jackson - Iowa - 6'6 318 lbs

Strengths: A 3-year starter for the Hawkeyes that has played on both sides of the line of scrimmage. A good athlete that eases out of his stance with impressive quickness to get out into his stance. Excels the most when having to handle bigger and powerful rushers, showing the ability to stay square and hunker down into his anchor. Maintains good balance when working through contact, rarely giving up leeway. He shows the recovery strength to reset himself if initially losing ground. In the run game, Jackson shows flashes of being an effective edge blocker. I was impressed when seeing him seal off outside edges with smooth cut blocks. Has the initial quickness out of his stance to reach 2nd level defenders in space.

Weaknesses: Has some sloppy weight on his frame and could stand to drop a few pounds to help his overall movement ability. Played through a bad knee injury that never completely healed in 2019, limiting his overall effectiveness. Lacks the ideal length for his size to play on the outside and could get bumped inside by some teams at the next level. Lower body stiffness is evident throughout, struggles when having to play on an island in space, lacking necessary lateral agility to mirror in space. Attempts to overcompensate in his kick-slide but that leaves him susceptible to counter inside moves where he frequently gets caught on his heels. Reactionary time is just 'OK' and is often a tick late when responding to blitzes or stunts.

Best Fit: RT or Guard

Player Ranking (1-100): 56.4 - Jackson is a decent prospect that could have developmental upside in the right system. He will likely get drafted higher due to Iowa's offensive line lineage, but his play on tape isn't good enough for me to feel comfortable drafting him higher than the 7th round.

28 - Dan Moore - Texas A&M - 6'6 309 lbs

Strengths: A 3-year starter for the Aggies at left tackle, Moore is an experienced prospect that has loads of game time playing against SEC competition. He also has some experience playing on the right side of the line as well during his freshman season. A systematically-versatile prospect that has experience both in zone and power concepts. Moore possesses a stout frame with very good thickness through his core and lower body, almost reminiscent of a guard. A smooth mover, Moore shows good ability as a pass protector, utilizing good fundamentals and solid overall movement skills to handle playing in space. Patient in protection, rarely oversetting his feet, remaining balanced and squared at all times. Understands how to utilize his hands, placing them well and with good timing and accuracy. Very smart and instinctual blocker that is quick to react to things, keeping his head on a swivel at all times. Keeps a wide base when handling bull rushes, utilizing his good lower body strength to anchor down and hold the point of attack.

Weaknesses: Lacks ideal length to play tackle and could bounce inside. A major liability in the running game, failing to have the ideal tenacity and power to uproot defenders off the spot. Fails to have the initial quickness to generate displacement through his lower half. A good athlete but not a great one, appearing to have some difficulties recovering if initially beaten off the snap.

Best Fit: Developmental tackle or guard

Player Ranking (1-100): 55.1 - Moore is a major liability in the run game and just OK in the passing game. The fact that he has extensive experience against SEC competition and could play guard or tackle allows him to get drafted. But his tape is very subpar. 7th round player.

TOP-10 OTs

1. Penei Sewell
2. Christian Darrisaw
3. Rashawn Slater
4. Alex Leatherwood
5. Samuel Cosmi
6. Teven Jenkins
7. Jackson Carman
8. Jalen Mayfield
9. Liam Eichenberg
10. Daniel Faalele

Chapter 8

Interior Offensive Lineman
(Guards or Centers)

1 - Wyatt Davis - Ohio State - 6'4 315 lbs

Strengths: A full-time starter and former five-star recruit that took over full-time responsibilities during his junior season in 2019 where he was arguably one of the best offensive linemen in college football. An absolute bully that is built like a refrigerator that plays with a relentless mean streak while finishing to the echoes of every single whistle. Eases off the snap of the ball showing good initial quickness into his stance to mirror in space. Handles power easily even from the strongest of nose tackle. Davis utilizes his upper-body power on every snap of the ball, showing iron-grip strength in his hands to latch on, rarely losing sustain on counter moves. While in the run game, Davis shows fluidity and 2nd level movement abilities. A real people mover that shows terrific power the point of attack to open up first level holes. Very quick to respond to things both pre- and post-snap. Does a nice job in working combination blocks with the center, maintaining good communication throughout? Not simply a 'physically dominant 'player as he shows loose lower body flexibility and agility to handle the change of directional type of movements in open-field situations.

Weaknesses: At times Davis can be overly aggressive, getting caught flailing and losing his balance in space. While he's gotten better, he's still not a great 'space 'player and is better-suited playing in a man-blocking assignment where he can physically impose himself on a specific assignment. A good athlete but I don't believe he's an elite one. Lacks elite arm length to keep defenders off of his frame. Shows some hesitancy when it comes to handling blitzes and stunts from linebackers.

Best Fit: Guard in any offensive line setup

Player Ranking (1-100): 84.9 - Davis has less than 2 full years of starting experience, but despite that, he showed dominance. A really good player that will attract teams in any offensive system. Smart, strong, and agile. While he's not a comparable guard in terms of athleticism of some other former 1st round guards, he's a solid 2nd round player.

2 - Josh Myers - Ohio State - 6'5 312 lbs

Strengths: A two-year starter for the Buckeyes at center, Myers has consistently been one of the best centers in all of college football the last two seasons. Built with excellent size for the center position, Myers possesses the length and the stoutness teams require for their interior players. Utilizing his length to hold the point of attack, Myers quickly gains inside hand leverage and sits down at the point of attack. His lower body strength allows him to sustain blocks while rarely getting moved off of his spot. If he's initially moved, he quickly resets and re-anchors himself to gain his footing and gain control of the rep. Plays with a good range of motion, showing good footwork while leaving very limited opportunities to defenders to win on pass rush reps. A good communicator that is seen pre-snap calling out protection schemes. High IQ and pre-snap awareness allow him to see blitzes and stunts quickly. Works well with his teammates on combination blocks in the run game, opening up holes at the 1st level. Excellent upper-body power and iron-grip hand strength allow him to latch on without losing sustain. Effective when used to pull in space, showing terrific initial quickness and anticipation to reach 2nd level targets. Powerful in his ability to win against bigger interior players, showing good lower-body explosion to push forward piles in short-yardage situations.

Weaknesses: There's some tightness in his lower body when asked to cross the face of a defender and move his frame. Lacks the lateral agility and quickness to consistently be used to reach/hook block. Uses his length to bail him out quite a bit when he's overmatched athletically against 3-technique defensive tackles. Doesn't always create work for himself when left without an assignment and will be content un-occupied, appearing to have some mental lapses. Could struggle at the next level with his length when leaving his pads up, due to his rare height for the center position.

Best Fit: Center in any scheme

Player Ranking (1-100): 84.3 - Myers is a stud. He's an absolute bully in both the run and the passing games. He's completely maximized his frame out with functional strength. While he's not an elite-level interior athlete, he's solid. He rarely gets exposed. He's smart, long, and strong as an 'ox. '2nd round player.

3 - Trey Smith - Tennessee - 6'6 331 lbs

Strengths: A 4-year starter for the Vols that started his career playing mostly outside at tackle before bumping inside his final 2 years and playing inside. His versatility will likely attract him even further with teams. Built with a tremendous frame, including length, strength, and thickness throughout. The first thing you'll notice is the power that Smith generates when driving from his lower body. He's a powerful drive blocker that generates impressive movement after quickly winning leverage battles and driving backward creating significant movement. His vertical movement when working downhill is excellent as he generates some real 2nd level abilities when working in space. While in passing sets, Smith shows quick feet and patience to quickly get his feet set and in position. Appears to have a good feel for timing his punches to perfection when sitting on rushers. Smith has big, powerful hands that show displacement power in his ability to work as a true mauler.

Weaknesses: The medical is going to be huge for Smith, as he has struggled with blood clots in his lungs during his career causing him to miss game time during his sophomore campaign. When working as a tackle, his lateral movement skills were significantly underwhelming. He failed to get his feet out under him to properly mirror in too much space in the passing game. He will get caught with some balance issues when playing on his toes and waist bending, needing to show some more patience. While his natural size is impressive, he appears to have some sloppy weight that could help him with some mobility concerns.

Best Fit: Guard but can kick outside on occasion

Player Ranking (1-100): 83.9 - The biggest thing with Smith is going to be his medical. If that checks out with no significant long-term health complications he deserves to go in the 2nd round. He has a real understanding of how to play offensive line. Smart, disciplined, strong as an ox, and a fairly good athlete. While he's not the most agile guy and his agility concerns could cause him some trouble against quicker twitch rushers at the next level, he's going to immediately be a top-level run blocker.

4 - Deonte Brown - Alabama - 6'3 364 lbs

Strengths: A 3-year starter for the Tide that took over the starting duties halfway through his sophomore campaign. Brown has experience on both sides of the line of scrimmage, playing both LG and RG. Brown is an absolute monster of a man that is built with giant limbs and a stout physique, capable of controlling the line of scrimmage in both the run and passing games. Brown is at his best when run blocking, where he's able to utilize his natural power to explode off the ball, engaging his lower body torque to clear large pathways in the run game. Not simply a 'power 'blocker as he's often used as the 'pull 'blocker getting in front of outside zone runs and clearing 2nd level defenders. A very capable pass protector that utilizes good knee bend and leverage to absorb blows of oncoming rushers and quickly reset and regain footing. Brown possesses heavy hands to jolt defenders at the line of scrimmage with his initial punch. A real finisher that remains focused on controlling his assignment until the final echoes of the whistle.

Weaknesses: Brown served a multi-game suspension at the end of his sophomore season and the beginning of his junior campaign for undisclosed reasons. Evaluators and scouts will likely want to find out the reasoning behind this. He appears to have some hip/lower body stiffness when failing to get his hands on defenders on the initial rush. He will overset to his outside shoulder and quickly lose inside positioning allowing some QB pressures against quicker-twitch rushers.

Best Fit: Power-blocking guard

Player Ranking (1-100): 83.2 - Brown is a powerful man that will be a dominant run blocker at the next level. While he's not an elite prospect, due to some athletic deficiencies, he's a darn good one! If he continues to get better in pass protection, he will be a high-end interior starter at the next level immediately. 2nd round player.

5 - Creed Humphrey - Oklahoma - 6'5 312 lbs

Strengths: A 3-year starter for the Sooners at center after redshirting his freshman season. Humphrey is a well-built center prospect that has good size for an interior player. Does a great job of easing off the snap of the ball with good initial quickness? Plays with good leverage, despite his size, dropping his pads and maintaining squareness while in pass protection. Very good functional strength throughout his frame allows him to win with power and remain in complete control. He utilizes his heavy hands and length with full extension to stop rushers in their tracks when attempting to rush head-on then perfectly dropping his anchor to sustain. His iron-grip strength in his hands allows him to latch on, rarely losing sustain. Extremely smart and disciplined in his assignments, calling out defensive alignments and properly adjusting the line pre-snap. Leadership qualities are manifest in his continuously pointing to his fellow lineman. Remains patient through reps, rarely getting over his skis. A former wrestler that understands proper angles and technique to win the point of attack and sustain through the duration. In the run game, Humphrey shows good overall athleticism to handle pulls and consistently reach 2nd level defenders. Keeps his lower body engaged through contact, driving with his hip, and pushing forward. Shows good body control and balance when playing in space, keeping a low center of gravity to remain balanced. Makes work for himself when left without an assignment, showing good awareness to assist.

Weaknesses: Humphrey is a left-handed center and will spin the ball in a different direction, which could disrupt a QB's pattern. Has struggled at times in pass protection against angled fronts against rushers that can quickly cross his face, struggling to cross face and remain in a good position. Overall athleticism is functional but not elite and he will struggle if asked to handle too many zone-blocking types of runs. Lateral mobility isn't elite and he will occasionally struggle against quicker interior athletes that can get him caught off-balanced. Doesn't always finish his blocks the way you want him to.

Best Fit: Man-blocking center

Player Ranking (1-100): 82.3 - Humphrey is a solid player that has a lot of big-game experience. He's a smart kid that is tough as nails. While he lacks elite athleticism, he possesses enough functional mobility to have success. He'll be a very good pass protector from Day 1 and a solid 1st level blocker in the run game too. 2nd round player.

6 - Alec Lindstrom - Boston College - 6'4 290 lbs

Strengths: The brother of former Boston College 1st round pick from 2019 Chris, Alex is a highly functional interior player as well. Getting his chance as a redshirt sophomore in 2019, Alec hasn't looked back. Possessing good overall height and length for the position, Lindstrom shows the frame for continued development and weight. Lindstrom is a tough as nails and violent blocker that excels in the running game. Excellent while on the move. Eases out of his stance while showing terrific initial quickness to reach 2nd level blocks, while remaining in control at all times. Possesses the upper-body power to move guys out of the way at the 1st level. Good play recognition abilities in the passing game, quickly reading and reacting to blitzes and stunts. Possesses the power in his lower body to anchor down and hold the point of attack. A very skilled blocker that plays the game with highly refined technical ability, rarely getting beat in any aspect. Remains leveraged at all times, keeping his pads low enough to be able to absorb blocks with ease. If he initially gives up any movement, he quickly shows the ability to re-anchor and recover.

Weaknesses: A bit undersized weight-wise and could stand to gain 10-15 more pounds for the next level to completely fill-out his frame and handle NFL power. Maximizes his overall athleticism but he isn't a great natural athlete. He could get exposed against quicker 3-techniques that could force him to play in space.

Best Fit: Starting Center

Player Ranking (1-100): 81.4 - Similarly to his brother, I love Alec. He's a terrific natural technician that possesses good strength and athleticism. While he isn't elite in either department, he's very very good. And he completely maximizes his natural abilities with 'know-how. 'There's a very very high floor for this player and he will be a Day 1 starter. 2nd round player.

7 - Alijah Vera-Tucker - USC - 6'4 315 lbs

Strengths: Vera-Tucker started all 13 games for the Trojans at guard before transitioning to left tackle for his final season this past campaign. He will likely transition back inside for the next level. Vera-Tucker is built with a compact frame with a low center of gravity. He utilizes his natural leverage advantage and his lower-body anchorage ability to control the point of attack, giving very little movement against bull rushers. An aware blocker that keeps his head on a swivel, always looking for an assignment when left without one. In the run game, he does a nice job of utilizing built-up momentum to wash guys out at the 1st and 2nd levels. Best when playing in a phone booth where he can maintain contact well and minimize spacing to each outside shoulder. Does a nice job of working his hands to win inside hand leverage and sustain the block through the duration of a play? His excellent hand strength allows him to latch on and not let up.

Weaknesses: Vera-Tucker will struggle when asked to do too much when playing in space. He's a limited mover that takes short and choppy steps, looking clunky at times. While his leverage covers up poor technique on many occasions, Vera-Tucker will need to learn how to consistently anchor down and control the point of attack against longer leveraged-athletes. Heavy-footed which limits his ability to play on an island against quicker-twitch 3-techniques. Not great when asked to locate and lock onto defenders at the 2nd level, showing very limited anticipation and change of direction while on the move.

Best Fit: Man-blocking guard but can play tackle as well

Player Ranking (1-100): 79.9- Vera-Tucker showcased some versatility this year showing he can play on the outside in a pinch if needed. While he's a good player that could potentially start inside, he will struggle against longer and more athletic interior NFL athletes. 3rd round player.

8 - Ben Cleveland - Georgia - 6'6 354 lbs

Strengths: A 4-year rotational player for the Bulldogs that begin starting games at right guard for Georgia during the end of his freshman campaign. Built like an absolute brick wall, Cleveland is a monster with tremendous thickness both through his upper and lower bodies. Cleveland is most effective in the run game where he can utilize his big body to blow people off the ball. When given the opportunity to play in space, Cleveland can be devastating at the 2nd level with his ability to drive defenders backward and clean lanes. In the passing game, his point of attack power is on display, showing the ability to anchor down against bull rushes. If he can reach with his initial punch, his displacement ability will stunt rushers instantaneously in their tracks. A finisher that rarely will lose sustain if he's able to get good initial hand placement on rushers.

Weaknesses: Cleveland has had several injuries throughout his college career, missing games for little things here and there. His medical at the combine will be huge for teams. He's struggled with weight, failing to have ideal muscle/fat ratios on his frame, carrying quite a bit of sloppy weight on his frame. Not a smooth mover out of his stance and will get exposed if he's not like in a phone booth. During games against more explosive rushers, Cleveland was constantly on his heels failing to catch his balance. Plays with a narrow stance, limiting his ability to play laterally. He's had some academic issues causing him to miss game time in the past. Has only played 1 position during his career, never having played at any of the other interior positions.

Best Fit: Man-blocking guard

Player Ranking (1-100): 78.0 - Cleveland is limited as a space player and is best served in a simple man or power-blocking system where he can play in tighter spaces. He will get caught flat-footed if he ever has to play on an island. His raw power and strength are rare but his sloppy weight, off the field concerns, and lack of movement ability are serious concerns. 3rd round player.

9 - Michal Menet - Penn State - 6'4 306 lbs

Strengths: A team captain and 4-year starter at center for the Nittany Lions, Menet has been a consistent presence along their offensive line, only missing 1 game since taking over as the starter in his entire college career. Menet is a good-sized prospect that features good width and size for the center position. A highly intelligent blocker that reads things quickly pre-snap while pointing out defensive alignments and communicating with his fellow linemen. Featuring a nasty mean streak, Menet is tough as nails and plays with a violent edge. A well-balanced and functional prospect that has very few flaws on his resume, showing good scheme-versatility to play on any offensive line. Plays like a technician, keeping his pads leveraged and controlling the point of attack. Handles bull rushes nicely by dropping his anchor and staying square. Maintains his balance at all times, rarely getting exposed or getting too aggressive. Good awareness to handle stunts/gains, always keeping his head up and looking for an assignment when he doesn't have one. Works well on combo blocks with his teammates while then climbing the ladder and reaching 2nd level linebackers to open up holes.

Weaknesses: An older prospect who will be 24 during his rookie season. Playing with power is not something that Menet showcased much. Played in a gap-scheme that made him more responsible for playing with technique while utilizing angles in the run game as opposed to clearing rush lanes. Doesn't appear to have the greatest length and he will give up his chest plate on occasion to longer defenders. Can get a bit too narrow and allow his pads to rise mid-play. Has improved in his 2nd level abilities during his years, but he still has some work to do to be an ideal fit in a zone-style system. Has a little bit of stiffness in his hips, failing to redirect his frame in the passing game.

Best Fit: Scheme-versatile center

Player Ranking (1-100): 74.3 - Menet is a really good football player that has very few flaws on his resume. While he's not an overly powerful center nor an elite athlete, he's a technically-sound and consistent performer that rarely makes a mistake. 4th round player.

10 - Jack Anderson - Texas Tech - 6'5 309 las

Strengths: Anderson won the starting job during his freshman season, and other than his injury during his junior season, he's started practically every game at right guard. A big-bodied guard that shows rare length and size for the position. Strength is on display from head to toe. In the passing game, he utilizes his heavy hands to strike opponents and stagger their rushes. A smart and instinctual prospect that reads the game well with good instincts while quickly diagnosing things pre-snap. Appears to have good balance and patience when in pass protection, rarely getting pushed off of his spot. Always looks for an assignment when left uncovered. An absolute mauler in the run game, Anderson loves the physical sides of the game, attempting to bully on every occasion. Generates significant power from his lower body to move piles and push the pocket forward.

Weaknesses: Had a bad shoulder injury during his junior season, causing him to get redshirted and missed the entire season. Plays in a very unusual college-style setup at Texas Tech and will need some time to adapt to a pro-style system at the next level. Lacks elite athletic traits to be successful in a zone-style or play in loads of space. Reach accuracy while on the move is disappointing, missing moving targets on far too many occasions. Allows his pads to constantly rise mid-play limiting his effectiveness when attempting to hit moving targets.

Best Fit: Man-blocking guard

Player Ranking (1-100): 74.1 - Anderson is a tough kid that needs to go to the right offensive line system. He's a limited athlete but he makes up for it with football intelligence and overall toughness. There are traits to work with in Anderson. 4th round player.

11 - Larry Borom - Missouri - 6'6 332 lbs

Strengths: Borom is a versatile offensive lineman for the Tigers that began getting significant snaps towards the end of his freshman season at right tackle. He's also since started games at guard and left tackle as well. Borom is a massive man, showing a rare blend of prototypical size and length for any position along the front. A former high-school basketball player that shows it with his smooth footwork. A nuanced blocker that understands all the technical aspects of playing the position. Keeping his pads down, Borom commits himself to winning the leverage battle despite his tall frame, anchoring down quickly in the passing game while utilizing good knee bend. A technician with his hands, Borom utilizes his length with full extension to keep defenders off of his frame. Shows good ease of movement skills when playing in space, showing the ability to reset his frame if initially beaten. In the running game, Borom also commits himself to placing his hands well, winning inside hand fits and controlling defenders at the point of attack. He understands how to play with angles while winning positioning, opening up holes for his backs at the 1st level.

Weaknesses: Missed several games during his final season with a lower leg injury. Borom is a good athlete but he isn't an experienced move blocker and could struggle in a zone-style system that requires him to continually get out into space, lacking much experience in doing so. Despite his size, he struggles significantly with power. If he's playing against shorter and squatter-built rushers, he will get bullied and moved off of his spot against bull rushes.

Best Fit: Guard

Player Ranking (1-100): 73.4 - An athletically built prospect that is a very skilled pass protector. He's not exactly a bully when it comes to the power parts of playing offensive line and he will need to get better in the running game but he's not a liability either. He's gotten better during each season at Missouri. He could be a Day 1 starter at guard and he could play tackle in a pinch as well. 4th round player.

12 - Landon Dickerson - Alabama - 6'6 326 lbs

Strengths: A former 3-year player at Florida State before transferring and playing his final 2 years with the Tide as the starting center. Dickerson is a versatile prospect that has played at RT, RG, and eventually moving to center. Dickerson has rare size for an interior position, showing tremendous length with the frame for continued mass. A smart and disciplined signal-caller that quickly recognizes things pre-snap, calling out signals, and identifying potential pressure areas for the offensive line. Excellent in the run game, Dickerson commits himself to win inside hand leverage while generating powerful torque from his lower body to move his assignment forward. Has a good understanding of playing with proper leverage and angles, utilizing proper positioning to open up 1st level creases for his backs. Tough as nails, Dickerson does a good job of handling bigger interior defenders with his length, controlling their shoulders pads with full extension while keeping his chest plate clear. Shows some recovery strength to re-anchor if initially giving some movement.

Weaknesses: Has had several injury concerns at Florida State, causing him to be granted a medical redshirt. His medical will be very important at the pre-draft workouts. Not too many interior players have his length, which is good and bad. He's going to have continual leverage concerns, playing with too narrow a base at times, causing him to get caught off balance. Not a great scheme fit for a zone-blocking system as he's far better in tight areas. Overall movement skills are 'OK' but getting him to play in space isn't his strong suit and he's far better at the 1st level.

Best Fit: Center in a man-blocking scheme

Player Ranking (1-100): 72.9 - Dickerson is a positionally-versatile prospect that has the size, strength, and experience playing against top-tier competition. He's likely best suited to play at center at the next level. He's an ideal candidate in a man-blocking scheme. 4th round player.

13 - Trey Hill - Georgia - 6'4 330 lbs

Strengths: Hill took over as a starter on the offensive line during the last few games of his true freshman season, playing at guard in those final four games. As a sophomore he won the starting center job in the spring and hasn't looked back the past two seasons. Hill is built with tremendous compactness and girth through his frame. A powerful man, Hill utilizes his powerful initial punch and heavy hands to slow defenders and erase opponents off the snap of the ball. A nasty finisher that displays the mean streak and toughness on every snap. Showed the ability to handle power against some of the biggest defensive tackles in the SEC, rarely getting beat for lack of strength. Displays the lower body strength and anchorage ability to hunker down and absorb bull rushes. Does a nice job of working combo blocks with his teammates to open up 1st level rush lanes. Powerful at the point of attack quickly winning inside hand fits and utilizing his hips and lower body to drive defenders away. While not the best athlete in space, he has shown some ability to work in the 2nd level.

Weaknesses: Needed to have arthroscopic procedure on both knees following the end of his junior season causing him to miss the last few games of the season. His medical will be very important prior to the draft. Not an elite level athlete and might not be a great fit in a zone-style blocking scheme as his movement ability is his biggest downside. His overall reaction time isn't the greatest and has a tendency to miss some pre-snap changes by the defense, responding a bit late to blitzes. Has had some balance concerns when he plays over his toes, causing him to play belly-to-belly against defenders while leaving his chest plate completely open to longer defenders.

Best Fit: Can play center or guard in a man-blocking scheme

Player Ranking (1-100): 72.1 - If Hill's medical checks out OK he deserves to be a 4th round player. He's a solid and stout interior lineman that has NFL readiness when it comes to the physical areas of the game. He could play center or guard equally as well, which is highly attractive to teams. 4th round pick.

14 - Quinn Meinerz - Wisconsin-Whitewater - 6'3 320 lbs

Strengths: A 3-year starter for Division-3 program Wisconsin-Whitewater, Meinerz has all the makings of the next small-school prospect to successfully transition at the next level. Meinerz is a team captain, possessing all the intangibles scouts look for. Meinerz is built country-strong and that is evident in the amount of functional power he possesses through his frame. Easing off the snap of the ball, Meinerz is quick to widen his base while staying square at the point of attack. His powerful anchor allows him to control the rep, remaining balanced and in control at all times. Former wrestling background is on display with his technical ability to play with angles and leverage. Understands how to utilize his hands, showing good upper-body power in his punch in addition to good placement and strike accuracy. Plays with a real nastiness, always finishing his blocks and rarely letting defenders off of sustain. Tremendous power is shown in the running game, rolling his hips through contact and creating real displacement power through his lower body.

Weaknesses: The biggest concern with Meinerz is going to be his level of competition and transitioning against NFL players from Division 3. It certainly can be done as we've seen with other smaller-school linemen. In passing sets, Meinerz will on occasion overset his feet, getting overaggressive being caught lunging. His mauling/brawling style of play in which he dominated with brute strength will likely need technical refinement for the next level. Not a great mover laterally showing some tightness, and he will struggle in a lot of zone-style runs.

Best Fit: Power-blocking guard

Player Ranking (1-100): 71.6 - Meinerz was a pleasant surprise off the tape. It's no shock that he got invited to the Senior Bowl. He's a very good small-school prospect that absolutely dominated his level of competition consistently. He has the physical traits to transition to the next level. While he's not a great athlete but he's a powerful powerful man. 4th round player.

15 - David Moore - Grambling State - 6'2 350 lbs

Strengths: Hailing from FCS-level Grambling State, Moore has been highly impressive during each of the last few seasons starting inside. Built like an absolute tank, Moore has very little body fat, featuring a rock-solid frame. Moore is a physical specimen that shows rare athletic traits for the position. Loving the physical sides of the game, Moore possesses nastiness coupled with a mean streak, finishing on every snap of the ball. Power is evident in his initial punch, featuring heavy hands with the ability to erase opponents instantly. Iron-grip hand strength allows him to latch on, rarely losing sustain on the counter. Quick feet and good range with impressive balance, agility, and patience in pass protection. Shows a good secondary burst to recover if he is late off the snap. Works well with his teammates on combo blocks. Very good initial movement ability to get off the ball, showing good functional athleticism and lateral mobility to reach and hook in a zone-style system. Commits himself to win hand fits, controlling defenders pads in the run game.

Weaknesses: Moore is still a bit raw and is still learning the finer details of the game, having only started playing football since his junior year of high school. Lacks elite level height for the position. Appears to have some stiffness through his lower body, limiting him when it comes to agility and lateral movement skills. Has had notable leverage concerns throughout his career, playing too high and allowing his pads to rise mid-play. Gets a bit grabby at times when initially beaten. Needs to show better anticipation and change of direction while on the move, far too often getting a bit upright. Don't see the explosive power demonstrated through his lower body to clear run lanes and open up holes. The transition for FCS lineman has proven to be very difficult to the next level.

Best Fit: Zone-blocking guard

Player Ranking (1-100): 70.9 - Moore is a better pass protector than he is a run blocker. While he's a mauler and loves the physical aspects of the game, he doesn't dominate with power in the run game as much as you would like, making me think he's not much of a fit in anything other than a zone-style offensive system. He's a very impressive athlete and certainly has upside. 4th round player.

16 - Tommy Kraemer – Notre Dame - 6'6 320 lbs

Strengths: Kraemer, a versatile starter that has played mostly at RG but has played some tackle as well. Equipped with a huge and compact frame with excellent length, Kraemer is an ideal guard prospect at the next level. A tough kid that has shown reliability for the Fighting Irish offense. Kraemer loves the physical aspects of the game, showing excellent lower-body power and anchorage ability to hold the point of attack. He can fight power with power nicely, as he normally doesn't struggle against power rushers. Is at his best when run blocking. He's not content simply blocking, he takes his battles seriously as he loves steamrolling, especially in the run game where shows the ability to create movement. An excellent help blocker that when he doesn't have an assignment is always assisting and helping his teammates. He plays with excellent anticipation and awareness, always keeping his head on a swivel looking for games or stunts.

Weaknesses: Kraemer is an average athlete that struggles when not playing linear. While he could play tackle in a pinch, his lack of lateral ability would get exposed. He's a waist bender that plays with little natural flexibility. When playing in 1 v 1 pass-rush situations on an island, he can struggle with too much space. Plays too narrow at times, leaving his chest plate far too exposed. Despite his natural strength, he doesn't play with much 'POP 'in his hands to offset or displace.

Best Fit: Zone-blocking guard

Player Ranking (1-100): 70.6 – Kraemer might get drafted higher than he should because of Notre Dame's offensive line pedigree. He's a solid player that deserves a shot at the next level but his lateral mobility is something to be desired. He could be a starter in this league and likely will, but I don't believe he's a great one. 4th round player.

17 - Drew Dalman - Stanford - 6'3 300 lbs

Strengths: A 2.5-year starter for the Cardinals that has started in over 20 consecutive games for Stanford in the middle of their offensive line. While he's played almost exclusively at center, he started a couple of games at right guard during his sophomore campaign as well. The leader of the Cardinals offensive line, Dalman is a highly-functioning and intelligent lineman and signal-caller. Playing in a power-running attack, Dalman is quick to signal and point out things pre-snap to his teammates. Reacts quickly to blitzes or stunts in pass protection, adjusting the front if he needs to. Fires off the ball in the running game, showing good physicality and toughness to finish plays. Maximizes his frame, playing with terrific tenacity and a nasty mean streak. Utilizes his natural leverage abilities to his advantage, getting underneath the shoulder pads of defenders. A real technician in the way he plays, understanding how to play with angles and leverage.

Weaknesses: Dalman lacks the ideal size and length for the next level. While he's gained significant size since coming onto campus, Dalman needs to continue to add to his frame without sacrificing much athletic ability. This lack of size and functional power limits him when attempting to handle larger nose tackles and opening up 1st level holes for his packs. While he's a solid athlete, he isn't an elite lateral moving athlete and shows some tightness through his lower body when working in space.

Best Fit: Scheme-versatile center

Player Ranking (1-100): 70.2 - Even though Dalman played mostly in a power-blocking scheme, he's got enough athleticism that he could be a fit in a zone-style setup as well. If he can continue to gain additional functional strength and mass, he could be a really good starter. 4th round player.

18 - Drake Jackson - Kentucky - 6'2 290 las

Strengths: A 4-year starter for the Wildcats that took over at the center during his redshirt freshman season, never looking back. The anchor for one of the best offensive lines in college football during the last couple of seasons, Jackson is built with compactness and a low center of gravity frame. A tough as nails defender that shows tremendous communications abilities, always calling out things pre-snap and identifying protection schemes and possible pressure points. Does a nice job show awareness for blitzes? Jackson explodes out of his stance in the run game showing good initial quickness to get in space and climb the pocket. Active feet, with good agility and lateral movement skills to quickly cross the face of defenders and work in conjunction with the guard to dominate on combination blocks. In the passing game, Jackson drops his pads and utilizes his natural leverage advantage to hold the point of attack. Strong upper-body allows him to stymie rushers with his devastating punch. He rarely loses the average battle, keeping his knees bent through contact.

Weaknesses: Lack of length causes him to get eaten up by longer and bigger defenders. This is especially evident in short-yardage situations where he gives up far too much movement and he's easily controlled, closing the pocket quickly. Struggles when working in space at the 2nd level, failing to have necessary change of direction ability and ideal length to consistently reach a target. Very susceptible to push-pull pass-rush moves due to lack of length and his over-aggressive nature.

Best Fit: Zone-blocking center

Player Ranking (1-100): 69.3 - Jackson is a consistent performer that has serious size and length limitations for the next level. But despite that, he's a darn good football that never misses a snap. 5th round player.

19 - Aaron Banks - Notre Dame - 6'5 338 lbs

Strengths: Banks took over as a regular starter for the Irish halfway through his sophomore season, having not looked back since, starting 30 consecutive games. He even has some experience kicking outside and playing some snaps in emergency situations at tackle. His extensive experience in the well-drilled Notre Dame offensive system had him used to playing both in zone and power-blocking concepts, presenting schematic-versatility. Banks is a fluid mover that shows some good athleticism in pass sets, showing good lateral agility to mirror in space. Athleticism is on display in the running game as well, showing reliability to be used as the 'move' blocker, fluidly handling space and making good 2nd level contact. Possesses the movement skills and lateral quickness to be used on reach and trap blocks. A smart football player that understands how to utilize good angles to create openings at the first level. Keeps his head on a swivel in passing sets, always looking for an assignment when left without one. Reacts well to blitzes or stunts, quickly recognizing things post-snap. Shows some power throughout his frame with good power in his hands to displace defenders. Remains patient through his sets, rarely oversetting and getting caught off-balanced. A solid anchor allows him to hold the point of attack against powerful interior rushers.

Weaknesses: Not a powerful blocker that is going to drive block and blow defenders off the ball in the run game. Can get a bit lazy with his hand technique, preferring to play belly-to-belly at times while leaving his chest plate completely exposed in the passing game to longer defenders. Poor hand timing and strike accuracy limits his effectiveness at the line of scrimmage. Allows his pads to continue to rise mid-play, causing him to struggle in counter situations.

Best Fit: Versatile guard

Player Ranking (1-100): 69.1 - Banks had a really solid campaign for the Fighting Irish this past season, showing reliability in both the passing and running games. He's not a dynamic interior player that has any defining characteristics, but he's solid, and could be a starter with continued development. 5th round player.

20 - Royce Newman - Ole Mississippi - 6'5 306 lbs

Strengths: A 2-year starter for the Rebels that has extensive experience both at guard and tackle. One of the rare offensive lineman that can play all 5 positions along the offensive line, showing rare versatility. Newman has an excellent frame showcasing tremendous length and size. A fluid mover, Newman shows above-average overall athleticism and smooth footwork when working in pass protection. Has the traits to be a schematic fit for any kind of offensive system. Utilizes full extension to keep his frame clean. Upper-body power is evident with his ability to control and sustain blocks once he reaches them. Has very good lower-body strength to anchor down, rarely surrounding too much ground against bull rushes. Used as the 'move' blocker on reach and hook blocks showing good initial quickness to reach the 2nd level. Has the power to create and open up rush lanes when working in zone concepts.

Weaknesses: Newman will likely play inside at the next level, despite having the experience and the size to play on the outside as well. When playing inside, he's going to need to play with more consistent leverage. His pad level constantly gets him in trouble as he allows smaller defenders to control him at the point of attack. Overall reaction times can be a little slow to react off the snap of the ball, allowing himself to get beat initially. Struggles resetting his pads if initially beaten. A straight-lined athlete that struggles with body control in space. When it comes to the change of directional stuff, his lower-body stiffness is prevalent.

> **Best Fit: Guard**

Player Ranking (1-100): 68.7 - Newman is a versatile prospect that can be a really nice fit in a power-blocking system. But he has the movement skills to play in any offensive system. He certainly has experience in a zone-style system as well. His frame gets him in trouble at times due to his height but he certainly has potential.

21 - Jimmy Morrissey - Pittsburgh - 6'3 305 lbs

Strengths: A 5-year player and former walk-on for Pittsburgh that has started in 47 games at center for the Panthers. A consistent presence that has been one of the best centers in the ACC for four straight years. One of the team leaders that is revered by his teammates and coaches for his leadership abilities. Featuring a squatty and low center of gravity frame, Morrissey utilizes his natural leverage abilities to control the point of attack. He gets low to the ground and maximizes his anchor strength to rarely lose much ground against bull rushes. A fundamentally-sound blocker that utilizes football intelligence and good technique to win. Features a nasty mean streak while playing with good aggression and finishing ability. Playing in a pass-happy offense, Morrissey is very comfortable handling powerfully-built defensive tackles or quicker-twitch 3-techniques. A good mover that shows comfort playing in space and mirroring in 1 v 1 situations. Excellent in zone-runs, showing impressive movement ability to work in space and get to the 2nd level.

Weaknesses: Has dealt with repeated lower-body injury concerns during both his sophomore and junior years, causing him to miss some game time at the end of both seasons. Doesn't have an ideal frame for an interior player, featuring stubbier limbs and failing to have the ideal length to control the snap of the ball. He will lose sustain despite being in good position, due to longer defenders being able to disengage from him.

Player Ranking (1-100): 65.9 - Morrissey is a reliable and stable presence that can be a good fit in a zone-style system. His lack of size and length will cause him to drop further than his tape suggests it should. I wouldn't bet against him though, he's been proving people wrong for a long time. 5th round player.

22 - D'Ante Smith - East Carolina - 6'5 294 lbs

Strengths: A former tight end and 3-year team captain, Smith has played mostly at left tackle, but has also played inside during the earlier part of his career. Took over as a starter during his freshman season, and then starting the entirety of his sophomore and junior campaigns. A wide-bodied lineman, Smith has put on considerable muscle and good weight to play at the next level. Brings versatility to an offensive line, showing comfort and reliability playing both inside and outside. Smith is a rare athlete for the position, showing impressive overall movement abilities. In the running game, he smoothly accelerates off the snap of the ball, rolling his hips forward and driving his legs to steer opponents away from the ball. A physical blocker that will maximize his frame to maul and space clear at the 1st level. Possesses the lateral mobility to consistently reach and hook while on the move, showing good change of directional abilities. Utilizes his natural leverage abilities to hold the point of attack against longer rushers, keeping his knees bent through contact. In the passing game, Smith has the quick feet to mirror and match against explosive rushers. If initially beaten, Smith possesses the recovery quickness to reset.

Weaknesses: Only played in one game this season after missing the rest of the year for an undisclosed injury. Not an offensive fit in a power-type offensive system, simply a zone fit. Has played very little at guard during his career and will likely have to play there due to significant size and length concerns to play on the outside at the next level. Could stand to continue gaining additional weight. Lacks elite power and functional strength, getting overwhelmed at the point of attack against shorter leveraged defenders.

Player Ranking (1-100): 65.5 - An intriguing player, Smith has the athletic abilities to be a nice zone-blocker in the right system. While he's still growing into his frame and is a bit raw, the developmental traits are absolutely there. He's tougher and more physical than you'd imagine for an undersized guy like Smith. 5th round player.

23 - Robert Jones - Middle Tennessee State - 6'4 319 lbs

Strengths: A former JUCO transfer that played his final two years for Middle Tennessee State. At community college, he played as a guard and for Middle Tennessee State he played as a right tackle, showing the positional versatility to play either well. Jones is a smart and intelligent football player that is beloved by his coaches and teammates for his blue-chip and leadership qualities. A wide-bodied prospect that displays prototypical height and length. A powerful man that plays with a violent mean streak on the field, showing terrific explosiveness in the run game. A people mover that rolls his hips forward and driving his legs to steer opponents away from the ball carrier. A finisher that isn't content with his job until the echoes of the whistle. Shows some good 2nd level ability and lateral mobility to be used in reach and hook scenarios. A good athlete that shows match and mirror ability when working in space in the passing game.

Weaknesses: Jones had offseason shoulder surgery following his junior campaign. Doesn't have enough experience at any one particular position, since he's bounced around a bit. Still very raw when it comes to his footwork, routinely getting a bit choppy with his footwork in his pass sets. Needs to understand how to utilize his hands with full extension to control blockers, getting a bit too wide with his strike placement and accuracy.

Best Fit: Guard

Player Ranking (1-100): 64.2 - Jones is a smart kid that is loved by everyone at both colleges he played for. He's versatile and he's as strong as an ox. He needs to get better in pass protection with his technique but he has the athletic profile to get better. 6th round player.

24 - Kendrick Green - Illinois - 6'4 315 lbs

Strengths: Green has started the last 33 consecutive games for Illinois, with the majority of them at guard, but he also started 4 games at center. A former defensive high school player that has transitioned to the offensive side of the ball every early on. Green possesses a nice frame, showing prototypical length and size to play at the next level. His versatility and experience playing in two different positions will be enticing for evaluators. Green plays with a nasty finishers 'mentality, playing until the echoes of the whistle on every snap. Green excels the most in the running game, utilizing his tremendous power at the point of attack to dominate. He rolls his hips forward and drives his legs to steer opponents away from the football, clearing large run lanes. Utilizes his iron-grip strength in his hands to latch onto defenders, rarely letting them out of his sights. In the passing game, Green possesses the length to control and keep defenders off of his frame. Strikes opponents with a powerful initial punch. His excellent lower body strength and natural leverage ability allow him to anchor down, rarely losing any ground.

Weaknesses: Still a giant work in progress in passing sets, lacking ideal lateral movement abilities when playing on an island. His footwork is all over the place, frequently taking short and choppy steps and failing to keep his feet shuffling. He lacks the secondary burst to recover if he is a tick late off the snap. Needs to do a better job with his punch timing and accuracy, getting far too wide with his placement on occasion.

Best Fit: Power-blocking system

Player Ranking (1-100): 63.1 - Green is a powerful man that is very good and refined in the running game. But he will struggle in passing sets at the next level. He needs major refinement with his footwork and I'm not sure if he has the flexibility, agility or lateral quickness to be a starter. 6th round player.

25 - Derek Kerstetter - Texas - 6'5 293 lbs

Strengths: A 4-year starter and team leader for the Longhorns that played mostly as a right tackle but he also has extensive experience at guard and center. A smart and functional lineman that brings about leadership and versatility to an offense, easily transitioning to center this year, looking like an experienced veteran. Kerstetter maximizes his physical tools to the best of his ability, showing to be a reliable pass protector, rarely getting beat with quickness. Remaining patient at all times while staying on the balls of his feet, Kerstetter remains balanced and square, rarely playing over his toes. Good initial footwork when working out of his stance, showing smooth fluidity and some decent agility. In the running game, Kerstetter understands playing with good leverage while sealing off angles with good positioning to open up 1st level openings.

Weaknesses: Kerstetter suffered a very bad ankle injury during his last career game that needed surgery. Kerstetter has had a bit of an up and down career, at times looking like a top-100 player and other times looking like an undrafted player. A bit of a tweener that lacks ideal tools for any position at the next level. While he has the typical size requisites for tackle, he lacks the ideal length to play on the outside and will likely move inside. He fails to have ideal girth and power to play on the inside in a power-blocking system and will likely only be a system fit in a zone-blocking scheme. Size limitations are manifest while on the move, failing to have great change of direction and get-off to effectively be used as a 'move' blocker for an offense.

Best Fit: Swing guard or center. Could also play tackle in a pinch too

Player Ranking (1-100): 57.0 - Kerstetter isn't a bad football player but his lack of elite movement ability, power, size and positional stability makes him a drop a bit for me. If he proves to be healthy during the pre-draft process, he could be a nice swing offensive lineman for a team, allowing coaches to keep him active for his versatility.

26 - Joe Sculthorpe - North Carolina State - 6'3 300 lbs

Strengths: A 2-year starter for the Wolfpack at both center and guard, Sculthorpe shows the versatility to make himself an intriguing option for teams. A former top high-school wrestler, Sculthorpe utilizes his natural leverage advantage and good technique with bent knees to win on most reps. Plays with good leverage, dropping his pads and his anchor to limit the amount of ground he gives up against bull rushes. A technician in his style of play, committing himself to winning hand placement, showing good strike accuracy and timing to slow rushers up. A very good athlete that shows fluidity through his lower body to mirror and handle playing in space against quicker rushers. Good initial quickness and looseness throughout his core to re-direct his frame and recover if initially beaten. Offers upside as a run blocker showing the movement skills, functional balance and lateral mobility to consistent reach and hook block in space.

Weaknesses: Sculthorpe is an undersized prospect that lacks much of a fit in a power-blocking system. He is a stubby-built guy that lacks the ideal length to sustain blocks without losing sustain. Needs to continue to improve his functional power, will get overwhelmed against longer and more powerful nose tackles that can win inside hand placement.

Best Fit: Zone-blocking center

Player Ranking (1-100): 55.6 - Sculthorpe is a good athlete but his lack of size and ideal functional power will cause him to get overwhelmed at the next level. He needs to improve his strength to gain any significant amount of snaps. But he's a good mover and has some upside as a zone-blocker. 7th round player.

27 - Matt Allen - Michigan State - 6'3 303 lbs

Strengths: A 3-year starter at center for the Spartans and younger brother of NFL center Brian, Matt is an experienced and well-accomplished center during his time. At his best when working in the running game, Allen shows good familiarity and comfort when working in zone concepts. Showing good initial quickness out of his stance, Allen shows good body control and change of directional abilities to be effective when used at the 2nd level and working through space. Plays with good fundamentals, including utilizing natural leg bend and hand placement to quickly win control. A strong upper body allows him to latch on while rarely losing sustain. In the passing game, Allen shows good awareness both pre and post-snap to adjust to late blitzes or stunts. Keeps his head on a swivel at all times. Lower body strength is prevalent to be able to hunker down against bull rushes and quickly reset if initially giving up ground.

Weaknesses: Allen has struggled and missed game time during each season of his career. He suffered knee injuries in both knees during both his sophomore and junior seasons, causing him to miss several games during each season. A bit undersized, Matt fails to have ideal size, girth, or length. Lacks great POP in his upper body, failing to offset defenders with his punch. Lack of length is on display against longer defenders that can quickly win inside hand leverage against him. Not a dominant power player and will get overpowered when his pads aren't leveraged, which frequently happens for him. His brothers haven't had much success at the NFL level and that could hurt his draft stock.

> **Best Fit: Zone-blocking center**

Player Ranking (1-100): 54.7 - Allen is a decent center prospect but lacks any clear dominating traits to make him a starter at the next level. He could get better but his lack of great size, athleticism, and his troubled injury history make him especially worrisome. Undrafted free agent.

28 - Sadarius Hutcherson - South Carolina - 6'4 320 lbs

Strengths: Hutcherson took over starting responsibilities towards the end of his freshman season while never looking back. A well-built guard that possesses a sturdy and stout frame. Hutcherson has the experience of playing all over the line of scrimmage, including even playing at LT in 11 games for the Gamecocks. Hutcherson's best position is at guard, where's played most of his time. Known for being a true workout warrior, Hutcherson isn't just workout strong, he's functionally strong. Devastating if he gets his heavy hands-on defenders, Hutcherson never let's go and finishes until the echoes of the whistle. A real force when asked to get to the 2nd level, showing good body control while on the move to clear out 2nd level defenders. Defenders have little chance of moving him off the spot in the passing game when attempting to rush him head-on, showing terrific lower-body anchorage ability.

Weaknesses: Hutcherson has significant movement issues, mostly stemming from his narrow stance and lower body stiffness. He bends at the waist, failing to have adequate flexibility to generate power from his legs. Best when playing in a phone booth in the passing game, if he has to play on an island he will get exposed by quicker twitch rushers. Appears to have some motor issues, looking disinterested in assisting his teammates at times when left without an assignment. Strike accuracy is hit or miss, missing on far too many occasions due to his aggressive nature. Has had several issues with false starts in college.

Best Fit: Power-blocking guard

Player Ranking (1-100): 53.0 - A powerfully-built guy that has all the physicality and strength required to play at the next level, but unfortunately his movement skills and lower-body tightness limits him while pass protecting. He's best in a power blocking system. Undrafted free agent.

29 - Doug Kramer - Illinois - 6'2 300 lbs

Strengths: A four-year starter and team captain for the Fighting Illini at center, Kramer is an experienced and 'NFL Ready' center. A tough blocker that is built with good physicality and compactness through his frame. A well-balanced prospect that shows proficiency in both the running and the passing games. He utilizes his low center of gravity frame to control the point of attack, maintaining good technique with bent knees to get under the pads of larger defenders. Stronger than his size would seem to indicate, showing a nasty initial punch to displace defenders in the passing game. An easy mover in the running game, getting out of his stance quickly and effectively helping on combo blocks and while at the 2nd level. Stays in control and balanced at all times, rarely losing his footing or getting caught off-balanced.

Weaknesses: Has rarely missed a game during his career, but suffered an ankle injury at the end of his junior season causing him to miss the bowl game. Had a big of a disappointing final season. Kramer is an extremely undersized center that lacks the height, weight or the length to be an ideal fit for most teams. He will get overpowered by larger defenders that can win inside hand placement. Strictly a fit in a zone-style system.

Best Fit: Zone-blocking center

Player Ranking (1-100): 52.6 - Kramer has had a nice career in college but he doesn't offer the power or the size to play immediately at the next level. He's going to need to have an impressive preseason to impress coaches. I see him as an undrafted free agent.

TOP-10 Interior Players

1. Wyatt Davis
2. Josh Myers
3. Trey Smith
4. Deonte Brown
5. Creed Humphrey
6. Alec Lindstrom
7. Alijah Vera-Tucker
8. Ben Cleveland
9. Michal Menet
10. Jack Anderson

Chapter 9

———— ❧ ————

Edge Players (4-3 DE's and 3-4 OLB's)

1 - Gregory Rousseau - Miami - 6'5 260 lbs

Strengths: Before sitting out his final season at Miami, Rousseau had arguably one of the best 2019 campaigns for a pass rusher, finishing with 15.5 sacks and 2 forced fumbles. Featuring a mouthwatering physique, Rousseau already possesses an NFL frame with tremendous thickness throughout his frame. Rousseau utilizes every inch of his length, playing consistently with full extension while quickly controlling the shoulder pads of a lineman. Does a nice job of working back towards the ball while utilizing his off-hand to slow down runners with his monstrous tackle radius. An excellent athlete that explodes off the ball displaying tremendous quick-twitch ability. His athleticism is also on display when being asked to drop, showing smoothness and easy movement ability to cover acres of space. Always around the football, playing with nonstop urgency, pursuit, and suddenness. His awareness and HOT motor allow him to quickly locate the ball and work back towards it when playing backside in the run game. Miami moved him all over the defensive front and he showed dominance wherever he played. Impressive overall core and ankle flexibility to allow him to threaten both inside and outside rush lanes.

Weaknesses: Was redshirted his freshman campaign after suffering a bad ankle injury following the first two games. Only has 1 year of college experience, lacking a ton of film in college. Still growing into his frame and will need to continue to learn how to break down blockers, relying far too much on his initial displacement power and length. Lacks ideal polish and pass rush arsenal to bring different plans to the table. Not a bendable athlete and will struggle arcing the corner, due to less than ideal ankle flexion and lower body flexibility. Needs to continue to develop his power game, far too often playing narrow when attempting to bull rush, limiting his ability to push the pocket.

Best Fit: 3-4 OLB or 4-3 DE

Player Ranking (1-100): 86.9 - Rousseau is still raw and isn't quite the full article yet, but he's a very good football player already. I could see some being paranoid for the fact that he only has played in 1 season of college football but I don't believe that's a real reason for concern. He would be a better prospect if he showed a little more elastic flexibility to bend. In the games I watched from 2019, he was the best football player on the field repeatedly. 1st round player.

2 - Patrick Jones II - Pittsburgh - 6'5 264 lbs

Strengths: A consistent pretense for the Pitt defense the last few seasons, Jones came onto the scene strongly in 2019 with 8.5 sacks and 4 forced fumbles putting himself into the NFL Draft discussion. Jones displays prototypical NFL size with an excellent frame and vines for arms. Jones has worked to hone his craft, getting better during each season in all aspects of his game, which is noticeable both on the stat sheet and on the film. As a senior this past season, his explosiveness was on full display. Exploding off the ball, Jones wins reps almost instantaneously with his ability to fire low out of his stance. Not just a 'speed 'rusher, Jones displays an impressive array of moves and counter moves due in part to his quick and explosive hand usage. Loose lower body movements and agility make him a very difficult assignment at the line of scrimmage, causing offensive linemen to completely whiff with their punches. His speed-to-power is devastating, routinely walking lineman into their QB. In the running game, Jones was often used to 2-gap, showing the ability to remain in control and stay disciplined with his hand placement. His twitchy reflexes allow him the ability to quickly diagnose between run and pass and work back towards the ball. Closing speed is on display when chasing running quarterbacks or running backs, showing the ability to make up lost steps quickly.

Weaknesses: While he has impressive overall explosive characteristics, he isn't a natural bender. This limits his ability to affect the outside corner consistently. Overaggressive in his continual desire to rush the passer, his gap integrity will falter, leaving big openings on outside rush lanes. Attempts to always jump the snap count, leading to some poor offsides. Functional strength in both his upper body and lower body could improve. He will get handled in the run game when his leverage isn't on point, leaving his chest plate exposed. He doesn't quite understand how to stack and shed consistently to fight through blocks.

> Best Fit: 4-3 DE

Player Ranking (1-100): 86.6 - Jones is one of the best pure pass rushers in this draft class. He can win in so many different ways. He's absolutely devastating and shooting gaps and getting upfield. His run defense is going to have to improve, but I believe it can with better discipline. 1st round player.

3 - Chris Rumph II - Duke - 6'4 235 lbs

Strengths: A rotational and hybrid chess piece for the Duke defense, Rumph has experience playing all over the defensive front. The coaching staff used him wherever they could find a mismatch. Rumph possesses a long and wiry frame with vines for arms, allowing him to virtually live in the backfield. The definition of quick-twitch, Rumph couples his explosiveness with good natural bend to arc the corner. Has really developed a wide diversity of hand tactics and pass rush moves, showing quick and explosive hands to keep his frame clean. Playing with a relentless motor, Rumph brings it on every snap of the ball. Extremely high football IQ that understands the variety of different roles he's used in, showing good positional awareness and instincts. Despite being undersized, Rumph understands how to convert speed-to-power frequently, possessing a devastating bull rush with good functional strength, capable of walking blockers back to the QB routinely. Effective when used to blitz interior pockets as well, showing good snap instincts and timing to shoot gaps. Very good core strength and flexibility to get skinny through narrow windows or change direction with ease. Reads and processes things very quickly, showing the range and gap discipline to set the edge.

Weaknesses: Took advantage of being a rotational chess piece for the defense, allowing him to stay fresh until he was on the field. A bit of a tweener that lacks an ideal position at the next level due to his lack of bulk and power through his frame. Doesn't have ideal coverage experience to play as a 3-4 OLB and doesn't have the power/strength to play as a 4-3 DE. Even though he's stronger than his size suggests, he will get manhandled against combo blocks in the running game. Needs to continue to improve his upper-body strength as he will fail to get off blocks if blockers can win inside hand leverage and control his chest plate. Can be a bit slow to react off the snap of the ball.

Best Fit: Defensive chess piece that should be a 3rd down rusher

Player Ranking (1-100): 86.3 - The hard thing with Rumph is his ideal position. You'll likely get different responses from different scouts and coaches for where that is. I think he can play in any defense but he needs a forward-thinking defensive coordinator to maximize his natural abilities. And he has a lot of them! Rumph is a dynamic football player and elite rusher that will make a lot of plays in a small number of snaps or in a lot of snaps. 1st round player.

4 - Carlos Basham Jr - Wake Forest - 6'3 281 lbs

Strengths: A 3-year starter for the Demon Deacons that has improved and gotten better in each of his 3 years statistically. A freakish all-around athlete that is built with a long-levered and powerfully-built frame capable of playing all over the line of scrimmage. Basham will be a nice chess piece for a defense that can play in any defensive system and a variety of different roles. Basham had some of his best career games against better opponents including Mekhi Becton last season, showing his ability to compete against the best and have success against NFL players. A smart and instinctual athlete that understands and reads blocking systems quickly in the run game with an understanding of how to break down double teams. Does a nice job of collapsing the pocket in the run game, reading and anticipating well, and closing the pocket with his lower-body strength. Often rushes in a Wide-9 stance showcasing his closing ability when playing further from the ball. Plays with a relentless and hot motor that brings it on every snap of the play. Utilizes his length to control the chest pads of lineman, playing with full extension and controlling the point of attack. His quick and violent hands allow him to dominate on the counter, rarely allowing himself to be controlled for the duration. Possesses some bend in his hips to allow him to turn the corner in a traditional DE stance.

Weaknesses: While he's a freakish athlete, he is faster than he is quick, lacking the elite get-off speed to threaten the tackles immediately. When asked to change direction or play laterally, he shows some tightness through his lower body. Has had some discipline and gap assignment issues when handling misdirection or counter-type runs, falling for the fake. Isn't exactly a dynamic 1v1 pass rusher that is going to threaten continuously with an array of moves and needs to develop more in having a gameplan to threatening a tackle consistently. His functional strength at the point of attack is moderate, lacking elite displacement power. A close but not cigar player that far too often fails to finish the play after getting close, missing several winnable tackles.

Player Ranking (1-100): 85.9 - Bashan Jr is a really good player in a 4-3 system that could be an ideal LDE in that setup. He could potentially play as a 5-technique as well but I'm not sure that would be using him to the best of his athletic abilities. While he's not a great pass rusher, he's just a really good overall football player that is well above average in the passing and running games. If he had more spring in his step, he could be a Top-5 player.

5 - Joseph Ossai - Texas - 6'4 253 lbs

Strengths: A 2-year starter for the Longhorns at outside linebacker, playing in that stand-up role in Texas '3-4 defensive formation. He also has some experience playing at DE with his hand in the dirt when playing in a 4-man front. Ossai originally comes from Nigeria at the age of 10 when he fell in love with American football. Ossai is a good-sized athlete that possesses a lean and athletic frame. A terrific athlete that has a rare blend of length, height, and athleticism. Plays with a 'HOT 'motor and is always in pursuit, going all-out on every snap of the football with tremendous make-up speed. Reads things quickly in the run game. Quick to trigger and get downhill, Ossai is a tackling machine and is always around the football. An explosive tackler that plays like a heat-seeking missile while making contact with runners. When runners pursue outside lanes, Ossai shows the wingspan and upper-body strength to make tackles outside of his frame consistently. Excellent snap anticipation coupled with 1st step quickness to frequently get into the backfield at the blink of an eye. Utilizes his length to quickly control blockers and win inside hand leverage immediately off the snap of the ball. A devastating bull rush created by his speed-to-power ability through his lower half explosiveness. Plays with a variety of other hand tactics, allowing him to bring a different plan of attack on every single rep.

Weaknesses: Plays a little reckless at times, rarely allowing himself to be patient and process before triggering. Has played so many different positions and lacks a refined position in college. Has very limited experience in pass coverage and when he has dropped, he looks completely lost recognizing things in space. Lower body stiffness is manifest when asked to change direction, appearing to lack fluidity when playing laterally or attempting to redirect his frame.

Player Ranking (1-100): 85.3 - There's something about Ossai that truly is special. Yes, he is raw, but man the kid can play. It's rare to see him not near the ball on every single rep. He's so explosive and athletic he's like a blur on film. His first step explosiveness is up amongst the best in this class. 1st round player.

6 - Wyatt Hubert - Kansas State - 6'3 265 lbs

Strengths: A 2-year starter that was also a valuable role player for the Wildcats as a freshman, Hubert has gotten better each and every season, having a tremendous final season as a junior. Hubert is built tough with a well-developed and powerful frame, showing NFL readiness to handle a 'hand in the dirt 'role. Playing like every snap of the ball is his last, Hubert plays with a relentless motor, bringing it on every snap of the ball. A physical defender who plays with aggression and toughness, showing the strength and power to hold the point of attack in the run game. Has experience playing on both sides of the line of scrimmage. He works really well in pursuit, proving to be excellent in pursuit when working backside, showing good closing speed. A reliable tackler that rarely misses an opportunity when he's around the ball carrier, forcefully impacting ball carriers upon impact. Excellent in his ability to fight through blockers, showing the deconstruction ability in his hands and upper-body power to disengage and keep his frame clean. As a pass rusher, Hubert utilizes a wide diversity of hand tactics to attack the pocket in different ways. He does a good job of dropping his pads and playing with leverage, utilizing some bend to grab the edge. Really strong lower-body allows him to utilize a nasty bull rush with his ability to convert speed-to-power and get blockers on skates.

Weaknesses: While he has the 'want 'when it comes to pass-rushing he lacks the ideal athletic ability to be an elite rusher at the next level, despite his gaudy college statistics. There are clear tightness concerns with his lower body, lacking elite change of direction or the ability to redirect his frame. While his floor is definitely high, his ceiling has some limitations, lacking much more physical growth potential. Hubert is strictly a fit in a 4-3 defensive system, failing to offer the pass coverage experience to play in a 3-4 system.

Best Fit: 4-3 LDE

Player Ranking (1-100): 84.4 - I really really like Hubert as a prospect. He's had some tremendous success against very good offensive linemen the last couple of seasons. The guy is just productive every time he plays. He battles his absolute rear off and is likely a guaranteed starter on Day 1 for a defense. While he's not a 10+ sack a year guy, he could be a consistent 5-8 sack a year guy while playing on the left side of the line of scrimmage. Plus he brings leadership intangibles and toughness to a defense. 2nd round player.

7 - Quincy Roche - Miami - 6'3 243 lbs

Strengths: After a nice 3-year career at Temple, Roche transitioned to play his final season with the Hurricanes, playing well and showcasing his ability to play against top-tier competition. Roche is an athletically-built rusher that can play in either defensive setup, showing systematic versatility for the next level. A very explosive rusher that showcases a nice 1st step capable of beating tackles initially. Not a 1-trick pony in his style of play, showing a diverse skill set to win inside or outside. Roche possesses quick and explosive hands, making him a very hard matchup for tackles due to his slippery nature, rarely allowing himself to be sustained. Utilizes all of his length, playing with full extension to keep blockers off of his pads. Has a good understanding of leverage, getting himself down extremely low to minimize his surface area. Disciplined with his eyes, Roche sees things quickly to shoot gaps in the run game routinely. A bendable athlete that shows the elastic flexibility to win outside rush lanes. Plays with a plan at all times, showing the ability to set up his rushes on each subsequent play.

Weaknesses: Has some notable motor concerns where he frequently gives up on plays, not always looking to be involved when it's not an explosive play in the backfield. Could stand to gain an additional 5-10 pounds to have adequate body armor to play with his hand in the dirt in a 4-3 setup. Not a 'power 'player and certainly won't threaten to win with physicality or going through lineman. Change of direction ability appeared suspect when dropping in coverage, showing some tightness and lower-body flexibility concerns. Consistency has been a repeated concern with Roche as he's a bit of a 'flash 'player that will show up big for 1 or 2 plays a game and then disappear for long stretches.

Best Fit: 4-3 Weakside Rusher

Player Ranking (1-100): 83.9 - I was impressed watching Roche, especially this year for the Hurricanes. While he's not the finished product, he certainly has some impressive pass-rush ability. I worry that his motor runs a bit hot and cold and that bumps him down a bit for me. He has the talent to be a 1st round rusher at the next level if he continues to improve as he has throughout his career. I'd feel more comfortable taking him in the 2nd round.

8 - Azeez Ojulari - Georgia - 6'3 240 lbs

Strengths: A 2-year starting redshirt sophomore and former four-star recruit, Ojulari came on the scene in a big way this past year for the Bulldogs, finishing with 12.5 tackles for loss and 9.5 sacks. He also was responsible for causing 4 fumbles. Will only be 20 years old during the start of his rookie season. Brings good versatility to the table with his ability to play in any defensive system or setup. Has experience dropping in coverage, showing good fluidity and movement skills. Ojulari has a nice sized frame with the length for days and room on his physique for additional muscle mass. Has experience playing both with his hand in the dirt or standing up on the edges. A quick-twitch rusher that fires off the ball, showing excellent burst and quickness to quickly get penetration. A very athletic athlete that possesses the long speed with huge stride lengths to quickly close down. His elastic flexibility and ankle flexion allow him to dip his shoulder and bend, frequently challenge outside lanes. Really good POP in his hands, possessing violent hands to knock away would-be blockers, keeping his frame clean. Upper-body power is evident with his tackling ability as well, rarely missing a tackle, showing good fundamentals and wrap-up ability. Plays with a relentless motor, always working tirelessly on every rep. Understands how to work well on stunts with his teammates. Not a slouch in the running game, showing good run instincts while setting the edges.

Weaknesses: Not exactly a 'power 'player and he will get overwhelmed at the point of attack, frequently dropping his head upon contact. Needs to do a better job of working through blocks in the running game, getting hooked far too easily by pulling linemen. Doesn't always appear to have a plan of attack, looking like a chicken with its head cut off while in pursuit. When initially blocked, he doesn't show an ability to consistently have a counter plan for disengaging. Play recognition abilities are a work in progress, he will take himself out of a lot of plays while not recognizing what's going on.

Best Fit: 3-4 OLB or 4-3 RDE (Weak-side)

Player Ranking (1-100): 83.2 - Ojulari began to show his upside this past season for Georgia. He's still a work in progress but the fact that he's only 20 years old and still developing into his frame is very exciting. In his rookie season, he will likely be a rotational pass rusher as he continues to develop into a more seasoned 3-down player. The raw traits are there. 2nd round player.

9 - Jaelan Phillips - Miami - 6'5 266 lbs

Strengths: A former five-star UCLA recruit that played his first two years of eligibility with the Bruins before sitting out a season and playing his final season with the Hurricanes. Phillips possesses really good and prototypical size and length to play in either defensive alignment at the next level. The first thing you'll notice on the tape of Phillips is how quick he is off the ball. He explodes with a terrific 1st step to win immediately off the snap. Drops his pads and shows terrific speed-to-power and significant power through his lower body to generate an impressive bull rush. Commits himself to win inside hand leverage at the snap of the ball to control the rep. Does a nice job of keeping his hands up while rushing to disrupt the timing of the ball to affect the throw. Brings a diverse skill-set to the table as a pass rush with a variety of hand tactics to win at the snap of the ball. Not just a pass rusher, Phillip has shown his ability to maintain discipline and set the edge in the run game. Utilizing his quickness to slip gaps and his core flexibility and strength to get skinny and fight through tight spaces. A good and reliable tackler that exploded upon impact with ball carriers to bring them down with ease.

Weaknesses: Had several concussion injuries at UCLA and contemplated retirement before transferring to Miami. Overly reliant at times on winning with pure athleticism and doesn't show elite bend or flexibility to consistently turn the corner. Has been an inconsistent player on film throughout his career with only 1 solid career season despite his high school pedigree. Has very limited experience in being used in coverage situations.

Best Fit: 4-3 DE

Player Ranking (1-100): 81.9 - Phillips is a hard guy to rank due to his 1-year of production. There's no denying his talent and he's arguably one of the best pure edge rushers in this draft class. There are slight concerns about his former issues with concussions as well. I'd feel comfortable drafting him as a 2nd round player.

10 - Rashad Weaver - Pittsburgh - 6'4 265 lbs

Strengths: Weaver who has been a valuable member of the defensive line since his true freshman season, has come on strong during his senior season. Each year he has shown consistent improvement in his overall production. Weaver has been used on both sides of the line by Pitt's defensive coaches, showing the ability to play both spots, as well as stand up or play with his hand in the dirt. Has even been used at times to drop in cloud coverages in the flats. A well-built prospect that has the size and length coaches look for. His motor runs hot ALL the time, relentless in pursuit on every snap. Weaver is an absolute load to handle. Active, heavy hands allow Weaver to quickly shed and disengage while rushing the passer, utilizing a nasty rip move when taking outride rush lanes. I love how active he is to disrupt throwing lanes, always getting his hands up and jumping to disrupt the pass. A real power rusher that shows some speed-to-power ability coming out of his stance and displaying real leg drive when equipping his lower body into rushes on his bull rush. Upper body power allows him to keep his frame clean while rushing the passer, showing the strength in his hands to keep his frame clean and offer some counter ability. Explosive power is evident in his ability to bring ball carriers down, launching them into the ground.

Weaknesses: Missed his entire junior campaign after tearing his ACL. Doesn't appear to always have great play recognition or awareness, over pursuing at times in the opposite direction of the ball carrier. This makes him highly susceptible to play fakes, option-style runs, or misdirections. Plays narrow and upright in the run game, making him an easy target, completely exposing his chest plate and easily cleared out of the run lanes. Gap integrity and setting the edge are struggles for Weaver as he looks far more interested in attacking the pocket on every snap, even in running scenarios. Not a true 'bendable 'edge rusher that is going to offer any kind of consistent ability to threaten outside edges.

Best Fit: LDE in a 4-3

Player Ranking (1-100): 79.3 - Weaver is a powerful man that is an absolute bully when attacking the passer. He's a bit frustrating in the run game because he will leave giant holes on the edges after crashing hard inside. He brings tremendous toughness and physicality to a defensive line. Ideally, he's suited as a 4-3 LDE but he could gain 10-15 pounds and play a 5-technique in a 3-4. He has the size, power, and length to do it.

11 - KwityPaye - Michigan - 6'4 272 lbs

Strengths: Paye began getting some starts during his sophomore season but took off in 2019 where he started almost every game. He finished his junior year with 12.5 tackles for loss, 6.5 sacks, and over 50 tackles. Paye is a thickly-built edge defender that shows incredible strength and weight distribution throughout his frame. Moves all over the defensive front and has the power and strength to even kick inside. The first thing you'll notice about Paye is how 'HOT 'his motor runs, playing relentlessly on every snap of the ball. Paye plays with very active and quick hands, showing the ability to almost always keep his frame. A slippery rusher that plays with good leverage and loose lower body movements that make it very difficult for a lineman to consistently sustain him. Good awareness and to quickly locate the football and work his way back towards the ball. Core flexibility and strength allow him to get shoot gaps and get skinny through tight, congested spaces in the middle of the defense. In the running game, Paye shows his anchorage ability to control the point of attack and absorb pulling guards in space. Stays square through contact, rarely losing balance.

Weaknesses: While Paye has active hands, his length isn't ideal and he will get controlled at the point against longer tackles. A 'power 'player that lacks the ideal elastic flexibility or ankle flexion to offer consistent penetration from bending or winning the arc around the corner. Lacks any kind of definite plan when rushing the passer. Quicker than he is fast, lacking the closing speed and the length to make plays backside or close off perimeters lanes if any missteps are made.

Best Fit: 4-3 LDE

Player Ranking (1-100): 79.1 - Paye has really improved as a football player each season. He looked good as a senior despite only playing in 4 games. He doesn't have any elite characteristics but he's equally adept in the running and the passing game. He certainly has the developed frame to play at the next level. 3rd round player.

12 - Shaka Toney - Penn State - 6'2 238 lbs

Strengths: A 4-year contributor for the Nittany Lions that has garnered more and more success with each subsequent season. An athletically-built rusher that shows good overall weight distribution with additional room for more muscle. Toney's a pass rusher, simple as that. Playing his best as a wide rusher or a 9-tech, his explosive characteristics make him dynamic in pass-rush situations. The definition of quick-twitch, Toney gets to full speed in an instant. Not just explosively quick, Toney displays the closing speed to make up ground quickly while working plays backside as well. He is one of the best bendable athletes in this class, showing the ability to constantly threaten the arc and win the outside corner, due in part to his loose hips and ankle flexion. Very active and explosive hands allow him to utilize a variety of pass rush moves to swipe defenders hands and keep his frame clean at the line of scrimmage. A high motor guy that plays with nonstop intensity. Toney shows good play recognition and quickly will sniff out plays in the backfield on occasion.

Weaknesses: Suffered from some minor injury concerns during his career, including a knee injury during his junior season. Was suspended by team coaches for the bowl game during his freshman season. An undersized athlete that simply is a situation pass rusher at this point for the next level. Reliant on winning on his initial explosiveness, lacking any kind of counter plan if his shoulder pads are controlled. His lack of functional strength causes him to get completely overwhelmed at the point of attack in the run game, lacking the anchorage strength to hold the point of attack when attempting to play face-up. Gets caught too upfield when playing in the running game, taking him completely out of position. Not the most reliable or forceful tackler, and will allow additional yardage after contact.

Best Fit: 3-4 OLB or 4-3 Situational Rusher

Player Ranking (1-100): 78.0 - The problem with Toney is he rushed mostly from a wide-9 stance which isn't always translatable to the next level because very few teams allow their rushers to play that far outside. There's no doubt he's a dynamic rusher but he's a liability at this point in the running game. 3rd round player.

13 - Victor Dimukeje - Duke - 6'2 265 lbs

Strengths: A rare 4-year starter for the Blue Devils that has been a mainstay for their defensive line since his freshman campaign, having never missed 1 start. Has gotten better during each campaign, showing tremendous improvement in each subsequent year. Built with a compact and stacked physique, showing muscularity and strength throughout his frame. A coaches 'favorite that is one of the hardest workers on the team and incredibly smart both on and off the field. Playing with a relentless motor, Dimukeje is a dynamic football player that brings it on every snap. A terrific athlete with great speed, Dimukeje shows the ability to anticipate the balls 'snap with excellent explosive characteristics in his lower body to generate good penetration. A fluid mover that displays loose hips and core flexibility. A bendable athlete that shows elastic flexibility when turning the corner and threatening outside rush lanes. His quick and explosive hands allow him to quickly knock away would-be blockers, keeping his frame clean through contact. Proficient when working in stunts with his teammates, utilizing his terrific closing burst to get into the backfield. In the running game, he does a nice job of setting the edge and forcing inside rush lanes. Disciplined in all areas of the game, Dimukeje isn't easily fooled by misdirections or option-style runs. A reliable tackler that has racked up high tackles each season, showing good wrap-up mechanics.

Weaknesses: A lot of his production during his last couple of seasons was taking advantage of mismatches, such as TE's attempting to block him, or on manufactured plays, such as stunts. Reliant on winning on the 1st move, lacking the counter plan to win on the 2nd move, if initially blocked. Needs to do a better job of stacking/shedding in the run game, allowing himself to sit on blocks for too long. A finesse rusher that lacks any kind of ability to win with power on any of his pass rush moves.

Best Fit: 4-3 DE

Player Ranking (1-100): 77.3 - A really good rusher that offers intriguing characteristics as a football player. No one will work harder than Dimukeje on and off the field. He needs to improve in the running game, but he's an explosive athlete that will generate significant playing time quickly.

14 - Joe Tryon - Washington - 6'4 262 lbs

Strengths: Before sitting out his final season at Washington, Tryon came onto the scene in a big way for the Huskies defense with 8 sacks during his sophomore campaign. Possessing an 'NFL ready physique, 'Tryon shows the length, strength, and filled-out frame to compete in multiple defensive systems at the next level. Playing a hybrid type of role, Tryon shows comfort and experience playing on the line of scrimmage with hands in the dirt, standing up, or even dropping to more of a zone type of cover guy. Good when working backside, showing his excellent athleticism and catch-up speed to make plays in front of him. An explosive athlete that shows quick-twitch ability to explode off the line of scrimmage. He couples that with his snap awareness to oftentimes be the 1st one to get a jump at the line of scrimmage. Functional athleticism will allow him to be used in a variety of roles for a defense, including dropping in coverage. He shows the fluidity of movement and range to handle playing in space. Active hands upon contact, always looking to keep his frame clean. Shows impressive ankle flexion to win outside rush lanes when threatening the corner.

Weaknesses: Only has 1 full year of starting experience. Tryon is still a work in progress when it comes to run support, failing to adequately handle gap assignments or hold up at the point of attack. He will easily get washed out of plays when attempting to play across the face of defenders at both the 1st and 2nd levels. When attempting to set the edge, Tryon fails to be able to utilize his entire wingspan to use his off-hand to slow runners down on the perimeter. When pass-rushing, Tryon is a one-trick pony that is overly reliant on winning with speed, lacking any kind of counter plan. Doesn't quite understand how to fire low out of his stance, far too often looking content rushing completely upright, failing to minimize surface area.

Best Fit: 3-4 OLB or 4-3 DE

Player Ranking (1-100): 76.3 - I like Tryon quite a bit as an athletic type of guy that is still learning to play the position. He's not the finished article but he has the build and athletic traits to get better with more experience and coaching. I would love to see him in a 3-4 defense due to his experience in dropping back in coverage. His 1st step quickness is very very appealing as a pass rusher but he needs to learn to win in other ways. 3rd round player.

15 - Hamilcar Rashed Jr - Oregon State - 6'3 254 lbs

Strengths: Rashed Jr came out of seemingly nowhere to be one of the best rushers in the Pac-12 during his junior season, finishing with 14 sacks, 2 forced fumbles, and 22.5 tackles for loss. An athletically-built rusher that displays a lean physique with little body fat, displaying above-average length for his size. Plays mostly in a stand-up role for their defense. Rashed Jr is a relentless worker that plays with a 'HOT 'motor on every snap of the ball. Explosion and athleticism are the names of the game for Rashed as he certainly is a quick-twitch edge defender. Not a '1 trick pony either 'as he often displays a nice combination of both inside and outside rushes, keeping offensive tackles guessing at all times and putting them on their heels. For being an undersized guy, Rashed Jr definitely displays some power in his lower power, generating terrific torque from his lower body on his bull rushes to walk lineman into the QB. Loose hips allow him to keep his frame clean, offering good counter ability. Processes things nicely in the run game, showing good gap integrity and patience while allowing plays to come to him, rarely being out of position.

Weaknesses: An undersized player that could stand to still gain an additional 10-15 pounds to play at the next level and fill out his frame without sacrificing his quickness. Despite his overall athleticism his overall snap anticipation and timing are very poor, oftentimes being the last one to get a jump at the line of scrimmage. While he's an explosive rusher, he isn't exactly an elite bendable athlete and he struggles to arc the corner and winning purely on speed in college. Lacks the ideal ankle flexion to consistently win the outside lane. His lack of functional strength will be exposed in the run game at times, getting completely washed out by pulling linemen. Has some zone dropping experience but he didn't appear to have a good understanding of proper positioning.

Best Fit: 3-4 OLB

Player Ranking (1-100): 76.2 - Rashed Jr is a really good pass rusher that will offer immediate upside as a rookie in subpackages to rush the passer. He doesn't offer enough run-stuffing abilities or pass coverage abilities to offer much on 1st and 2nd downs at this point in time. I would like to see him continue to add strength and size to his frame. 3rd round player.

16 - Joshua Kaindoh - Florida State - 6'7 265 lbs

Strengths: Originally a five-star recruit, Kaindoh has dealt with ups and downs so far but there's no denying the level of talent he has. Possessing a freakish frame with ideal prototypical 'hand in the dirt 'size, Kaindoh possesses the length/width/height combo that makes evaluators drool. A versatile chess piece that was utilized all over the defensive front, playing in a variety of different positions. He would occasionally drop into coverage at times, showing good football intelligence and movement skills to handle patrolling the flats, limiting available spacing. A rare athlete that shows tremendous quick-twitch ability with rare get-off. He's able to close down quickly with his long strides. Despite his height and frame, he shows the rare ability to dip and bend, threatening the arc routinely. Plays with a relentless motor at all times. Has a plethora of pass rush moves, bringing a plan and a counter plan on every snap. Converts speed-to-power effectively with his bull rushes, walking offensive lineman back with great lower body power. Production doesn't tell the story with how disruptive Kaindoh is, he's constantly around the football. Possesses good power at the point of attack, dropping his pads and maintaining leverage. Does a nice job of utilizing his length to disrupt passing lanes. Not strictly a north/south athlete, he does a nice job of playing laterally when asked to change directions.

Weaknesses: Suffering a serious leg injury causing him to miss almost the entire 2019 season. He's also dealt with several other nagging injuries causing him to miss games in each season. To say Kaindoh's college career has been underwhelming would be an understatement. He's been mostly a rotational player when he has played, never starting more than a few games in a season during his four-year college career. A 'flash 'player that will make a ton of 'WOW 'plays but doesn't consistently affect a game. Needs to do a better job of being effective in the run game, taking himself out of far too many plays, lacking gap integrity and discipline.

Player Ranking (1-100): 75.1 - Kaindoh is a really really tough guy to rank because of his upside. He possesses traits and athletic potential that probably no other edge rusher in this class does. But the problem is, it's all potential and very little production. The fact that he's only started in a handful of games during his career is very worrisome. I'd be interested to see how his medical comes out. With his ceiling, I couldn't pass him up in the 3rd round. The kid is insanely talented.

17 - Dayo Odeyingbo - Vanderbilt - 6'5 280 lbs

Strengths: A 3-year starter for the Commodores, Odeyingbo saved his best season for his last season, having a tremendous senior year, continuously standing out despite his team being terrible. Displaying a rare combination of size, length, and strength, Odeyingbo has a 'first off the bus 'physique that evaluators will fall in love with. He shows the experience and the versatility to play both as a 3-4 DE or a 4-3 DE and not looking out of place in either spot. Has the lower body anchorage ability to set the edge against double teams if playing as a 5-tech. Will kick inside in clear pass-rushing situations showcasing his athleticism and core flexibility to fight through congested spaces and make plays in the backfield. Does a nice job of utilizing his length to disrupt the QB's sight of vision, knocking down balls or affecting the throw in some way. Brings a large diversity of different hand tactics to his pass rush repertoire, including a devastating push/pull move. An explosive quick-twitch rusher that will be a mismatch no matter where he plays along the line of scrimmage. A very good counter rusher that has surprising agility and change of directional ability for a guy of his stature. A difficult guy to sustain for some time due to his upper-body strength and length to control the chest plate of blockers. Very active and is always around the football, displaying a tremendous motor at all times. Catch-up speed is excellent, making up ground very quickly. Relentless in pursuit in the running game, making a lot of tackles while chasing down backside. Good instincts, physicality, and gap integrity in the running game, usually being at the right place at the right time.

Weaknesses: Tore his achilles prior to the draft and will likely miss his rookie season. A late bloomer that had very minimal production during his first few seasons with the Commodores and some could be concerned he's a 1-year wonder. Still, a bit raw and is continuing to adjust and grow into his frame, as he's gained around 30 pounds of muscle since entering the program. A bit of a tweener that lacks a true refined position at the next level. Picked up the majority of his production when kicking inside and taking advantage of opportunities against inferior interior athletes. Would like to see him continue to refine his pass rush abilities with a larger arsenal of moves to fully maximizes his functional athleticism and explosiveness.

Player Ranking (1-100): 74.9 - Hard to find a lot of negatives about the player other than the injury. His film during his first couple of seasons was just 'OK 'and he didn't make enough plays, although he would flash on occasion. This year, he proved to be on a whole other level despite the subpar play around him on the Vanderbilt defense. He stood out in every game. It's rare to find a guy like Dayo that has the size, athleticism, and length to be a dominator in all aspects of a football game. He could stand to continue to refine his pass rush moves and abilities but he's a dang good football player! 4th round player. He was a borderline 1st rounder for me before the injury.

18 - Payton Turner - Houston - 6'5 270 lbs

Strengths: A 4-year contributor for the Houston defense that has shown the versatility and comfort to play along multiple spots along the front. Turner has been stellar his last two seasons, especially his final year, despite only playing in 5 games. In those 5 games, he finished with 5 sacks and 10.5 tackles for loss. Versatility is the name of the game for Turner, having experience playing as a 5-tech DE, a stand-up DE, or even as a 3-technique DT. Possessing a rare frame, Turner has tremendous size, featuring vines for arms and excellent height. He perfectly utilizes his height and length to disrupt by knocking balls down or disrupting the QB's vision when he can't reach the QB. An extremely hard worker, Turner plays with relentless energy on every snap of the ball. As a rusher, Turner keeps his frame clean by utilizing his length to control the point of attack, limiting the linemen's opportunities to win inside hand fits. Not just a hard worker, Turner has excellent 1st step quickness to immediately get penetration into the backfield. Moves well laterally for his size, showing good agility and range when forced to move off his spot. Good pass rush arsenal, understanding how to use his quick and active hands. Can make plays extended and outside of his frame.

Weaknesses: Likely best projects as a 5-technique at the next level but he needs to gain substantial lower-body strength to hold up in the running game. He will get easily blown off the ball when attempting to take on combination blocks, failing to drop his anchor. Needs to understand how to drop his pads and play with leverage in the run game, allowing his pads to rise mid-play.

Best Fit: 5-tech DE or 4-3 DT (3-technique)

Player Ranking (1-100): 74.7 - Turner was impressive this year for Houston and has a ton of developmental upside to continue to get better with more work on fundamentals and added lower body strength. He's a natural pass rusher and has the rare length to make a ton of plays. 4th round player.

19 - Ronnie Perkins - Oklahoma - 6'3 247 lbs

Strengths: Perkins has been a valuable member of the Sooners defensive line since his freshman year, where he was named an All-American, playing significant snaps the 2nd half of his freshman season. An athletically-built edge defender that has experience playing both in 3 and 4 man fronts for the Sooners. An explosive rusher that shows good short-area quickness off the snap of the ball. Understands how to attack a lineman, varying up his reps and utilizing many different inside and outside moves. Good hand tactics allow him to know away would-be blockers. Loose-hipped in space affording him the ability to bend through difficult angles. A relentless rusher that makes a lot of plays on broken-down coverages due to his never giving up on a play. Perkins shows good instincts and play recognition, gearing down in the run game and quickly locating the ball. He patiently allows plays to develop while fighting for inside positioning. Does a nice job of containing the edges and not getting manipulated on option plays or misdirection runs. Strong upper-body allows him to consistently be reliant as a tackler, routinely bringing backs down.

Weaknesses: Was suspended for multiple games this past season due to failing a drug test at the end of his sophomore campaign. Allows his pads to rise mid-play, playing with far too narrow a base. Perkins is a little light in the lower half, lacking elite lower body power to handle the point of attack in the run game. He will get overmatched in the running game by a lineman that can win inside hand fits and plow him off the line of scrimmage. Lack of lower body strength limits his options as a power rusher, failing to offer any kind of push with his bull rush. Slow reaction times off the snap of the ball, and is usually the last one on the line to get a jump at the ball.

Best Fit: 4-3 DE (Weak-side)

Player Ranking (1-100): 74.2 - Perkins has been consistent for the Sooners the last 3 seasons. He's been good from Day 1. He needs to get stronger if he plans on being an every-down defender at the next level. His narrow base and lack of great functional strength limit him on 1st and 2nd downs. But there's no denying he's a talented rusher. 4th round player.

20 - Jayson Oweh - Penn State - 6'5 252 lbs

Strengths: A rotational player for the Nittany Lions before his redshirt sophomore season in 2020 where he finally got a chance to start regularly. Despite being a rotational player his first two seasons, Oweh still put up solid production in limited snaps. Oweh has prototypical edge rusher size with a muscled-up physique with additional room on his frame for more muscle. Oweh is known on campus as a workout warrior with tremendous strength and power in his frame. Has the ability to be a scheme versatile prospect, playing in any defensive system. Oweh is an athletic freak, displaying tremendous athletic abilities for his size. Eats up cushioning and space in an instant, quickly closing down. Always in pursuit and attempting to get in on every single tackle. Potential is through the roof with more playtime. Not just an athlete, Oweh is a blue-chip prospect that plays with a relentless and hard-working motor, going 100 MPH on every snap of the ball. Shows some elastic bend to capture the edge and grab the outside lane with good ankle flexion, shoulder dip, and hip mobility. Speed-to-power is manifest when bull rushing tackles, putting them quickly on skates. In the running game, Oweh utilizes his natural athleticism and make-up speed to make plays backside while in pursuit.

Weaknesses: Oweh is still very very raw and doesn't quite know how to best use his physical tools yet. A bit of a 1-trick pony as a rusher and he fails to have much of a counter plan other than winning with his speed rush. If he's initially blocked, Oweh will stay blocked, failing to disengage with good hand usage. A liability at this point in the running game, failing to show play-recognition abilities and fails to locate the ball. His failure to deconstruct blocks while working back towards the ball limits his effectiveness in pursuit. While his 1st step is elite, his snap anticipation and poor reaction times limit his ability to quickly win the snap.

Best Fit: 4-3 DE (Can play 3-4 OLB as well)

Player Ranking (1-100): 73.2 - Oweh will likely get drafted high due to his rare athleticism but he didn't always show it on the field. He's still very very raw. He's a bit of a straight-line athlete that needs continued refinement in playing the position. There's clearly tremendous upside but he's going to need more time as he didn't have a ton of snaps in college. 4th round player.

21 - Jordan Smith - UAB - 6'6 255 lbs

Strengths: A former four-star Florida Gators recruit that ended up going the JUCO route before finally catching on playing his final couple of seasons with UAB, in the Conference-USA. Smith stands out immediately on tape for his frame and rare wingspan. He understands how to utilize his long arms to control the snap of the ball, quickly winning and controlling the pads of blockers. He utilizes his speed-to-power to generate significant power from his lower body coupled with good 1st step quickness to produce a devastating bull rush. Terrific bend throughout his frame allows Smith to threaten outside rush lanes, showing lower-body flexibility to arc the corner. A dominant run player that shows terrific strength to hold the point of attack and maintain gap integrity. Utilizes full extension with his club hand to keep his outside arm free to slow runners up on the perimeter. Twitchy reflexes allow him to quickly diagnose and recognize things both post and pre-snap. Has shown on some occasions his ability to drop in space and handle the flats.

Weaknesses: Was suspended at Florida due to his involvement in the credit card fraud scam. Off-the-field concerns and maturity issues will need to be examined. Overall pass-rush stats aren't great, lacking top-end production especially from not coming from one of the better conferences. A 1-trick pony as far as a pass rusher, attempting to win solely with speed outside rushes. Lacks any kind of counter plan when blockers can get under him and control him.

Best Fit: 4-3 LDE

Player Ranking (1-100): 72.4 - Smith is a really good player against the run and he shows upside as a pass rusher. While he's not refined in the pass rush department, he has the natural tools to get better. Intriguing prospect. If his off-the-field concerns are minimal he's a 4th round player.

22 - Patrick Johnson - Tulane - 6'3 255 lbs

Strengths: A 3-year starter for Tulane that rose to prominence following his stellar sophomore year in which he finished with double-digit sacks and 4 forced fumbles. Johnson is a stoutly-built edge defender that displays a muscled-up physique capable of playing in any scheme at the next level. Johnson played standing up at Tulane in a 3-4 outside linebacker role. The first thing you'll notice about Johnson is his explosiveness, showing tremendous twitch ability. He may have the best 1st step in the entire draft class, showing elite explosion coupled with terrific closing speed. If offensive tackles don't quickly win the hand battle against him, they'll be on their heels the rest of the play. Generates significant displacement power from his lower body, converting speed-to-power and walking offensive tackles into their QB. He has experience playing in coverage as well, showing some smoothness in patrolling the field in the flats. Has been lined up in man coverage against bigger slot receivers, showing rare movement skills for a guy of his size. An outstanding tackler that appears to love the physical parts of the game, delivering some big blows when attacking the ball carrier.

Weaknesses: Racked up a lot of his production against inferior competition. Overly reliant on winning with his 1st step and with speed, failing to offer much of a backup option with his hands. Needs to do a better job of deconstructing when breaking down blocks in the run game, getting stuck for far too long. Mental processing ability is a bit slow to react to things happening in the backfield. He's often fooled on play-action or misdirection type of plays. Pursuit angles when working back towards the football aren't always the best, lacking urgency and intensity chasing down plays backside.

Best Fit: 3-4 OLB

Player Ranking (1-100): 71.2 - An explosive rusher that has improved during each year in college. He's ideally suited in a 3-4 defense where he can stand up and rush in clear passing situations. He's one of the most explosive rushers in this class. 4th round player.

23 - Big Cat Bryant - Auburn - 6'5 250 lbs

Strengths: A 4-year rotational player for the Tigers that took over full-time duties during his junior season. Bryant is considered the 'Bucks 'for the Tigers, being used mostly standing up in a 2-point stance but plays with both hands in the dirt. Possesses good overall size for the position, showing translatable traits to play at the next level. A hard-working presence that shows a relentless nature on every snap of the ball. Good explosiveness coming off the edge, showing quick-twitch ability to threaten outside rush lanes. Does a nice job of dropping his pads and playing with leverage. Has experience dropping in zone coverage and patrolling the flats. Does a nice job of maximizing his frame in the run game, setting the edge, and showing discipline in gap control. Lower-body strength is evident when getting double-teamed, staying square, and not allowing himself to be completely washed out.

Weaknesses: There have been concerns about his overall 'game-shape 'in the past and whether he can contribute and be more than a rotational player. His production over the years has been marginal at best, never posting big numbers. Reliant far too much on his explosiveness than having any kind of plan. Coaches are going to want to him develop more of an arsenal so that he can have an actual diversified plan when attacking the pocket. Gets into too many personal battles when attempting to get off blocks almost as if he's stuck in the mud. Hand placement and timing are inconsistent.

Best Fit: 4-3 DE or 3-4 OLB

Player Ranking (1-100): 67.3 - Flashes at times but he is far too inconsistent to be a consistent starter at the next level. His lack of production despite the number of snaps he's gotten is disappointing at best. But he certainly has an athletic profile to continue to improve as long as he stays healthy.

24 - Charles Snowden - Virginia - 6'6 232 lbs

Strengths: A rare 4-year starter for the Cavaliers that has been a mainstay for their defense during every season. Built with ridiculous length, Snowden is a complete size mismatch for opposing tackles. Playing on both sides of the line of scrimmage, Snowden plays mostly standing up in a 3-4 defensive system. A really good athlete that fires off the ball in the passing game showing terrific explosiveness while utilizing full-armed extension to keep his frame clean. Closing speed coupled with rare length allows him to be effective when working backside and chasing down plays. Does a nice job in the run game of holding the point of attack and maintaining outside rush lanes with his insane tackle radius. Snowden will utilize his off-hand to stab blowers while utilizing his other hand to slow down runners that attempt to run head-on. Shows a surprising amount of spring in his step and lateral mobility to play with smoothness coming out of his stance, showing the traits to drop in zone coverages. When used in zone, Snowden's length allows him to minimize openings in the flats. Utilizes his length consistently at the line of scrimmage to alter the QB's line of vision, forcing bad throws.

Weaknesses: Undersized and needs to gain considerable size and strength to play at the next level. Very raw as a pass rusher, lacking elite bend or ankle flexion to threaten outside rush lanes with any kind of consistency. Lacks any kind of counter plan to win once initially blocked. Needs to do a better job of breaking down blockers, upper-body strength is subpar. Leverage and pad level are going to be consistent problems with Snowden when having to deal with 'move 'blockers that can get under his pads.

Best Fit: 3-4 OLB

Player Ranking (1-100): 66.4 - Snowden shows plus athleticism with the rare length that make him an intriguing next-level option for a team. He's still raw as a pass rusher and doesn't quite know how to utilize all of his physical traits, but he shows upside. 5th round player.

25 - Malcolm Koonce - Buffalo - 6'3 250 lbs

Strengths: Koonce began receiving significant snaps during his sophomore year, while greatly impressing. Then during his junior season, he completely broke out, leading the MAC conference in sacks with 8 in addition to 3 forced fumbles. A well-built prospect with prototypical size and girth throughout his frame. A versatile rusher that will attack the pocket from the ground or in a 2-point stance as well. As a pure rusher, Koonce displays the terrific quick-twitch ability to generate significant pressure almost immediately into the backfield. Also, he shows agility, loose hips, and elastic flexibility to bend and threaten outside rush lanes. Has a plan to win every single rep, showing a variety of pass-rush moves. Has a dynamic spin move that he'll use to his inside or outside shoulder to keep his frame clean. Understands how to utilize his length in all aspects of the game, including disrupting the QB's passing lanes. He utilizes his strong upper body and aggressive hands to knock away would-be blockers, including cut blockers with relative ease. He commits himself to win inside hand fits, allowing him to quickly control the shoulder pads of offensive lineman in the run game, staying square and keeping his off-hand free. Disciplined with his eyes in the run game, maintaining good positioning against RPO's and misdirection-type plays, rarely allowing himself to be caught too far up the field on run plays.

Weaknesses: Needs to be a more consistent tackler, far too often failing to wrap up and allowing runners out of his grasps. Hasn't competed against top-tier competition. Lower body strength isn't great and will struggle anchoring in the run game when needing to hold the point of attack. Needs to continue working on developing a counter plan if initially sustained on his rushes, appearing to run out of ideas if he's initially blocked. Will over pursue QB's by taking too far a rush angle to the outside, leaving the edges open for running QB's to evade and pick up yards down the field.

Best Fit: 3-4 OLB

Player Ranking (1-100): 66.2 - Koonce is an intriguing mix and a good blend of explosive twitch and power. He's been really solid at the MAC level but transitioning to the NFL could be a transition. Let's hope he's got some former Buffalo Bull Khalil Mack to his game.

26 - Jonathon Cooper - Ohio State - 6'3 254 lbs

Strengths: A former five-star high school recruit that brings big leadership and potential to the table. Cooper is a 5th year senior and team leader who was able to get a medical redshirt in 2019 after suffering a nagging high ankle sprain that plagued him all season. Cooper brings a plethora of physical tools to the table, featuring a stacked physique and ideal size for any defensive system. Cooper brings significant blue-chip characteristics to a defensive, battling his butt off and playing with a 'HOT 'motor on every snap of the ball. There's very noticeable power throughout his frame, especially in his upper body. An excellent counter rusher that brings a 'Plan B 'to the table. A very difficult guy to sustain through the duration of his play, due to his heavy hands and upper body strength to disengage. Commits himself to playing with good leverage, equipping his strong lower half into his bull rushes to close the pocket quickly. Twitchy reflexes with very good instincts and awareness, quickly locating the ball and working in pursuit in the run game. Remains in control and balanced on every play, rarely getting toppled over or pushed out of the play. Has experience and comfort dropping in zone, showing good cover instincts and awareness to play in space.

Weaknesses: Cooper's medical is going to be very important. His level of pass-rushing production never quite matched his 'potential 'as he only has 9 career sacks through his five years of playing significant snaps. A 'close but no cigar 'player that fails to finish plays, getting close on so many plays. Doesn't play with full extension at times, allowing blockers into his chest plate far too easily. Lacks the explosive twitch to be a top-tier rusher, failing to generate any kind of speed rush ability. Not a great bender, failing to have the elastic flexibility to threaten corners. Has some tightness in his lower body, struggling to redirect his frame or change direction if moved off of his spot.

Best Fit: 4-3 LDE

Player Ranking (1-100): 65.5 - It's hard not to like Cooper. Everyone that knows Cooper loves him. Is he a great pass rusher? No. But he's got enough intangibles and upside to continue to develop, despite his 5 years of college experience. I think he could be a nice day 3 pickup for a team and rotational defensive lineman for a team. 5th round player.

27 - William Bradley-King - Baylor - 6'4 254 lbs

Strengths: A graduate transfer to Baylor that played over 3 seasons with Arkansas State before transitioning over and playing his final year for the Bears. A good-sized athlete with a long and lean muscled-up physique that has worked hard to continue to add solid muscle to his frame. Bradley-King has the experience and versatility to be a systematic and schematically-versatile prospect having experience playing both as a standup linebacker in a 3-4 system or playing with his hand in the dirt. I was impressed with the power and strength he plays with despite being a little undersized. Heavy-handed with excellent 'POP' and jolt power to displace and cause blockers to get caught off-balanced. Lower body strength is on display when setting the edge, rarely getting pushed off of his spot. Maintains discipline and integrity in the running game, showing the football intelligence and instincts to remain in good position against running QBs or misdirection-type plays. Plays with a HOT motor and never gives up on a play, making a lot of plays when chasing backside. Really good snap instincts and timing to get a good jump at the line of scrimmage. Engages his lower half when utilizing his bull rush, showing good speed-to-power to walk offensive lineman back into the QB. Has shown the ability to drop in space comfortably and handle the flats in a zone situation.

Weaknesses: Bradley-King is likely a better fit in a 3-4 system at the next level due to his lack of ideal bulk to play on the line of scrimmage. Didn't quite have the season many were hoping for at Baylor after transferring, underwhelming a bit production-wise against better Big-12 competition. A bit of a 'jack of all trades master of none' player that fails to excel in any one area. His overall athleticism is just 'OK' and he fails to win consistently on athleticism, despite being a little undersized. Not a quick-twitch rusher that is going to offer much bend the arc potential. He fails to bring a wide diversity of pass rush moves to the table, attempting to win mostly with power.

Best Fit: 3-4 OLB or 4-3 LDE

Player Ranking (1-100): 64.3 - Bradley-King is loved by teammates and coaches for his hard-working and leadership qualities but he's not a top-tier NFL prospect. He has a unique skillset considering he wins mostly with power, despite being undersized. I love his upper-body strength and ability to be effective in the run game but he's simply not a great pass rusher. 6th round player.

28 - Adetokunbo Ogundeji - Notre Dame - 6'4 256 lbs

Strengths: Not officially being a regular starter until his final season at Notre Dame, the 5th year senior and team captain greatly excelled, saving his best for last, finishing the season with a highly respectable 6 sacks. Ogundeji possesses an outstanding and prototypical physique with compactness and muscular development throughout. A blue-chip prospect, Ogundeji brings a tireless motor to the table on every snap of the ball. He's often running down the field 20+ yards in pursuit, making some tackles from his pure hustle. Lower body strength is prevalent in every game tape, both in the running game and the passing game. Comfortable handling double teams, Ogundeji drops his anchor while maintaining positioning to set the edge. Understands playing with leverages to put blockers on skates. In the passing game, he brings an effective bull rush to the table with his ability to convert speed-to-power from his lower half.

Weaknesses: Only has one full year of starting experience and has been limited to mostly a rotational player in his first few seasons. Most of his problems stem from the fact that he isn't a great athlete. A hustle pass rusher, failing to have ideal quick-twitch or bendability to arc the corner. Almost all of his sacks are coverage sacks where the QB has held onto the ball. Fails to have any kind of counter plan when initially blocked, lacking the change of directional ability or the hand usage to disengage. Doesn't always reliably wrap-up in the run game, missing some tackles due to poor form.

Best Fit: 4-3 LDE but could gain 10+ pounds and play as a 5-tech

Player Ranking (1-100): 62.6 - Ogundeji had a nice season but he's not a great overall prospect. Scouts and evaluators might fall in love with his frame but he just doesn't show any kind of consistent ability to win or offer much as a pass rusher, despite his 6 sacks this past season. 6th round player.

29 - Daelin Hayes - Notre Damn - 6'4 261 lbs

Strengths: A 5th year senior that was able to take a medical redshirt season. Hayes has been a contributor to the Fighting Irish's defense during each of the last 5 seasons, showing reliability and versatility for their defensive front. Built with a stout frame, Hayes has all of the length needed to be either a 4-3 hand in the dirt defensive end or a 3-4 outside linebacker for the next level. Shows experience and comfort when being asked to drop in zone coverage, showing good cover awareness and instincts when playing in the flats. Good upper-body POP in his hands to deliver some initial displacement power when taking on blocks. A good overall athlete that brings an arsenal of pass rush moves, including a nice spin move that he frequently uses on counters. Shows some bend in his lower body to arc the edges and get underneath blockers. A very disciplined player that maintains gap integrity when holding the point of attack, rarely getting faked by RPO's or misdirection-type runs.

Weaknesses: Missed almost all of the 2019 season after tearing his labrum. Has been mostly a split carries player throughout his career, sharing snaps while on the field. This has allowed him to stay fresh and be effective when playing. Lacks a plan at times when rushing the passer, attempting to win on pure athleticism on most reps. His overall run defense is disappointing, showing some functional strength deficiencies. A good athlete but not great, and lacks the dominant physical profile that allows defenses to have a specific plan for him at the next level.

Best Fit: 3-4 OLB

Player Ranking (1-100): 61.2 - Hayes is a good player that has versatility and comfort being used in different roles. While not overly explosive, he can occasionally generate some penetration with his diverse arsenal of moves. Has a chance to catch on in camp. 6th round player.

30 - Jamar Watson - Kentucky - 6'3 244 lbs

Strengths: A 4-year contributor and full-time starter for the last two years for the Wildcats, Watson is an experienced and consistent performing edge defender in the SEC. The former partner in crime with follow Wildcat and Top-10 draft pick last year Josh Allen, Watson has some very similar traits. Built with a long and rangy physique, possessing vines for arms. An excellent athlete that hasn't quite tapped the surface of his overall ceiling quite yet. Watson explodes low out of his stance, possessing a good 1st step and putting linemen on their heels almost instantly. Utilizes his speed to threaten the arc and winning outside rush lanes, or will set up his rushes and counter back to the inside. Good lower-body power allows him to generate some speed-to-power when bull rushing. Has been used in several different coverage alignments, including dropping in zone as well as covering in man-to-man at times as well.

Weaknesses: Functional strength is minimal at best. It limits him as a power player and makes him somewhat 1-dimensional as a finesse rusher at this point. He can be very frustrating as a tackler, failing to always wrap-up securely and allowing additional yardage after contact. Overall production in college was 'OK 'but nothing reminiscent of a top-flight edge rusher in college football. Doesn't appear to have any kind of plan of working through blocks and disengaging once initially blocked. Gets into too many personal battles with his hands, lacking good technique, timing, and placement.

Best Fit: 3-4 OLB and rotational rusher

Player Ranking (1-100): 60.3 - Watson is an experienced SEC defender that has flashed against good competition on occasion. He's just far too inconsistent and needs continued refinement when it comes to his technique. Upper-body strength and overall confidence in the running game needs work. At this point, he will need to earn his keep on special teams and as a rotational rusher. 6th round player.

31 - Deangelo Malone - Western Kentucky - 6'4 230 lbs

Strengths: Malone is a 4-year contributor for the Conference-USA program Western Kentucky. He burst onto the scene after a stellar sophomore campaign where he finished with 60 tackles, 6 sacks, and 2 forced fumbles. He had an even more impressive junior campaign. A schematically-versatile defender that has played all over Western Kentucky's defensive front, including playing as a stand-up linebacker as well. A long and rangier built defender, Malone has the vines defensive coordinators love. These long arms allow him to control the snap of the ball, quickly winning leverage. If initially hooked or reached, his length allows him to quickly shed and disengage, offering upside as a counter rusher. Utilizes his length to close off parts of the field, engaging his full wingspan and tackle radius to make plays outside of his frame in the running game. Upper-body strength is apparent when bringing ball carriers down with relative ease. Good when working back towards the ball backside, showing his closing speed to make up lost ground and trip backs up.

Weaknesses: Had had several injury concerns during his career, including a high ankle sprain his sophomore season. He also needed offseason shoulder surgery in 2019. Will need to gain additional functional strength and size to play consistently on 1st and 2nd downs at the next level. Would like to see him continue to add to his pass rush arsenal and is fairly reliant on 2 or 3 moves strictly at this point. Has major gap discipline issues, venturing too far away from the football due to poor angles and discipline. For as lean as Malone as, he's not quite as explosive as you'd like to see. That is worrisome especially considering he will likely need to bulk up a bit and could lose even more quickness.

Best Fit: 3-4 OLB

Player Ranking (1-100): 58.4 - Malone is a good player that has had nice production during the last couple of seasons. He's got good length but at this point, he's strictly a subpackage rusher due to his size and inability to offer much on 2nd and 3rd downs.

32 - Micheal Clemons - Texas A&M - 6'5 270 lbs

Strengths: A 2-year starter for the Aggies, that was a former JUCO transfer, has served as the teams 'defensive captain this year as well. Improved each season for the Aggies and had his best year as a senior in 2020, finishing with impressive overall production. Built with a sturdy and long frame and toughness throughout, Clemons is 'NFL Ready 'to handle different defensive systems during the next level. Strength and physicality are where Clemons excels the most. A hard-working and blue-chip prospect that will give 100% on every single snap of the ball. Excellent at the fundamentals of the game, including a reliable tackler that rarely allows runners out of his grasps. Shows some good athleticism and quickness off the snap of the ball, firing low out of his stance. Quick hands allow him to keep his frame free at all times. Has the necessary anchor strength to hold the point of attack in the running game, remaining square and disciplined at all times.

Weaknesses: Suffered a bad foot injury before 2018, causing him to take a medical redshirt season. Missed 2 games in 2019 for an undisclosed injury. Far too comfortable playing belly to belly and not utilizing full arm extension, allowing defenders to hook his pads far too easily. Not a bendable athlete and is far too upright when rushing the passer. Hand strength and POP in his hands is virtually non-existent. Needs to do a better job shedding in space while in pursuit. Had a bad habit of dropping his head upon contact.

Best Fit: 4-3 DE

Player Ranking (1-100): 56.4 - Clemons is a solid overall prospect but lacks elite athleticism to be a consistent NFL pass rusher. A team leader and a tough kid that is worth taking a chance on. But his injury history will need to be looked at. 7th round player.

33 - Jeremiah Moon - Florida - 6'6 228 lbs

Strengths: A 4-year rotational player for the Gators who has been used all over the defensive front for them. Built with an NBA player with a long, lean, and limber physique showcasing substantial room for additional muscle growth in an NFL strength and conditioning program. Moon has arms for days allowing himself a monstrous tackle radius to shorten the field and cut off outside rush lanes. Often used in 'cloud coverage ' assignments to wall off entire sides of the field. Not just a 'straight-line 'athlete as he does have a bit of change of directional ability to his game, showing some interesting intrigue in a 3-4 set up as a potential cover player. It's clear Moon loves the game as he battles and works hit butt off, maximizing his ability on every single snap. His closing speed allows him to be effective when working plays backside or blitzing or attacking the pocket on 3rd downs.

Weaknesses: Moon needs to add substantial strength and bulk for the next level if he wants to be able to handle the NFL rigors. A 'flash 'player that made the majority of his plays when no one was in front of him and where he was completely unblocked. A limited player when working through blocks, lacking the counter ability or the strength in his hands to break down blocks. Lacks any kind of plan when rushing, appearing to offer very little other than simple speed rushes. Lacks the necessary functional strength to fight off or even handle the slightest of jams on the line of scrimmage.

Best Fit: Special Teams and Developmental 3-4 OLB

Player Ranking (1-100): 54.2 - It's possible someone takes a risk on Moon with his size and length but he's going to need a solid year in an NFL strength and conditioning program before he can be asked to contribute. He's a developmental player in the truest sense of the word.

34 - Elerson Smith - Northern Iowa - 6'7 262 lbs

Strengths: Smith began getting significant playing time for the FCS program Northern Iowa during his sophomore season, never looking back. He's been dominant, racking up 14 sacks, 21.5 tackles for loss, and 5 forced fumbles back in 2019. Smith has put on 40+ pounds since his freshman year and he still has additional room in his frame for substantial more muscle without sacrificing athleticism. Defensive coaches have used Smith in a variety of different roles, including even 2-gapping at 5-technique. Built with tremendous length, Smith is a load to handle for offensive tackles. When fully extended, Smith easily controls the pads of blocks and utilizes a devastating push/pull move to create for himself. Smith possesses an impressive 1st step with the ability to generate some speed-to-power to walk lineman back into the QB with his bull rush. Despite his frame, Smith does a nice job of playing with leverage and keeping his pads low when firing out of his stance to control the point of attack. In the run game, Smith shows good play recognition abilities and quickly locates the ball. Shows twitchy reflexes with the ability to diagnose and work his way back towards the football. His large tackle radius allows him to close perimeter lanes and reliably wrap-up runners in the running game.

Weaknesses: Smith is still quite undersized for his position and needs to continue to add strength and muscle to his frame to play at the next level. Functional strength is a continued problem for Smith, most notably in his lower body. He lacks the ability to hold the point of attack while taking on offensive lineman, even tight ends at times. Anchor strength and lower body power are sufficient at best. A stiff athlete that struggles when asked to play laterally, proving to be tight hipped in space. Doesn't always appear to have much of a counter plan when initially blocked, lacking the upper-body strength or the secondary quickness to get off blocks and keep his frame clean.

Best Fit: 4-3 DE

Player Ranking (1-100): 53.5 - Smith is a good prospect but not one of the best FCS prospects in this class. He's still raw and needs continued development in the finer aspects of playing the game. A very straight-line athlete that will struggle when asked to change direction. And he will be a major liability at the point in time in the run game. Undrafted free agent.

35 - Tarron Jackson - Coastal Carolina - 6'3 260 lbs

Strengths: A 4-year contributor to the defense, Jackson burst onto the draft scene after his junior year where he finished with 10 sacks and 13 tackles for loss. Jackson possesses a compactly-built and stacked physique from head to toe, showcasing all the physical tools to play at the next level, including vines for arms. When looking at players in the Sun Belt you look for domination against the competition and Jackson did that. He looked like a man amongst boys at times. A powerful rusher that shows the ability to win more with finesse and speed or pure power. Explosive off the line of scrimmage, Jackson shows quick-twitch ability to instantly win the rep against tackles and penetrate the backfield. Shows good lower body looseness with the ability to change direction and work laterally while on the line of scrimmage. Accelerates fluidly to chase ball carriers from behind the backside. A reliable tackler, that rarely lets runners out of his grasps once he gets a hold of them.

Weaknesses: Transitioning from the Sun Belt Conference will be a big jump up for Jackson. A bit undersized for the position. Has had two different seasons in college cut off due to season-ending injuries. He also played through an entire season, as a sophomore, where he battled a knee issue. Jackson got by mostly on pure athletic traits, lacking nuance and refinement in his play. He will need to learn how to better utilize hand technique when fighting through blockers at the next level. A major liability at this point in the run game, failing to have the lower-body strength, awareness, and anchor ability to hold the point of attack when taking on blocks. Mental processing skills and play-recognition abilities in the running game are also suspect.

Best Fit: 4-3 DE

Player Ranking (1-100): 53.1 - Jackson has physical tools but lacks the refinement necessary to play at the next level. He's going to need to come a long way when it comes to his run defense if he wants to get drafted. Undrafted free agent.

TOP-10 Edge Players

1. Gregory Rousseau
2. Patrick Jones II
3. Chris Rumph II
4. Carlos Basham Jr
5. Joseph Ossai
6. Wyatt Hubert
7. Quincy Roche
8. Azeez Ojulari
9. Jaelan Phillips
10. Rashad Weaver

Chapter 10

Defensive Tackles (Includes 3-4 DE's)

1 - Christian Barmore - Alabama - 6'5 311 lbs

Strengths: A rotational player for the Tide during his redshirt freshman season, Barmore took the next level at a starter in 2020 as a redshirt sophomore. Barmore has a tremendous and rare frame, showcasing long limbs and a powerful upper-body. Possesses the frame to be a systematically-versatile defender. Plays like he's shot out of a cannon on every single rep, possessing a tremendous motor. Can be dominant in the passing game, showing to be a disruptive presence from all different defensive alignments. Moves incredibly well for his size, showing good snap anticipation coupled with violent POP in his hands. Lower body power is manifested on bull rushes, keeping his legs churning through contact to close the pocket. There are several times where he will rush as the '0 'and generate pressure while double-teamed. Barmore understands leverage, firing out of his stance low and with dropped pads, making it hard for a lineman to control him at the point of attack. Fluid in space, showing impressive lateral quickness to be used on angled-fronts or stunts. Quickly reads things in the backfield, showing the twitchy reflexes to quickly diagnose. Shows a diverse skill set with his hand usage, bringing several hand tactics to the table to keep his frame clean. Rarely gets stuck on blocks, showing the upper-body strength and violent hands to quickly disengage.

Weaknesses: Production-wise Barmoreisn't going to blow anyone away, failing to rack up high tackle numbers, pressures, or sacks. Fails to finish plays despite how often he reaches the backfield. He's been used almost always as a rotational player, never having to play for significant amounts of snaps continuously. Plays a bit recklessly losing where the play is and could stand to be a bit more disciplined especially in the run game. Barmore has some notably sloppy fat in his midsection that he can clean up. Not a refined or reliable tackler in the open field, whiffing on several running plays.

Best Fit: 4-3 DT or 3-4 DE (He can truly play anywhere)

Player Ranking (1-100): 87.6 - He's a very hard player to rank because of his versatility. Ideally, I'd love to see him in a 1-gap system where he can constantly thrive in the backfield perhaps as a 4-3 three-technique DT. But to be honest, he could have success anywhere he's played. He's got the size, explosiveness, and motor to be effective. This guy lives in the backfield! He still needs to be a better finisher and more disciplined in the run game. I just wish he was on the field more often and didn't miss so many snaps. 1st round player.

2 - Jaylen Twyman - Pittsburgh - 6'2 290 lbs

Strengths: Before opting out of the 2020 season, Twyman came onto the scene following a terrific 2019 sophomore year, finishing with 10.5 sacks from an interior position. Tyman is built with a low center of gravity frame, possessing a lean physique with a tapered midsection and virtually 0 bad fat on his frame. It's not farfetched to say Twyman brings very similar qualities to his biggest inspiration, former Pittsburgh defensive lineman Aaron Donald. A really good athlete with quick-twitch ability to be a disruptive interior pass rusher at the next level. Twyman brings a diverse skill set to the table with the focus being on his excellent hand usage at the line of scrimmage, which allows him to utilize a full range of pass rush moves. Always has a plan to attack and set up his rushes, quickly reading the backfield and firing low out of his stance. Good initial quickness coupled with snap awareness to time the snap count and shoot through gaps into the backfield. Twyman isn't simply successful when playing in 1 spot, showcasing the ability to get moved all over the interior front. A tireless worker both on and off the field always looking to get better at his craft, playing with a 'HOT 'motor on every snap of the ball.

Weaknesses: A 1-year starter that only was a role player during his freshman campaign. I noticed on quite a few occasions his ability to process things in the running game wasn't great, putting himself behind the 8-ball when it comes to positioning. During the duration of games, his pads tend to rise, limiting his ability to get off blocks and have a counter plan. Overly reliant on winning on the initial move, lacking elite levels of lateral quickness and power to win after initially squaring up to lineman. Size and length aren't elite for the position which will likely only make him a suit in a 4-3 system.

> **Best Fit: 4-3 DT (3-technique)**

Player Ranking (1-100): 86.3 - Despite his lack of tremendous experience, he showed to be a really good overall football player. Far more advanced in his ability to rush the passer than have a notable presence in the running game at this point. But he's definitely a 3-down player that will improve with additional experience. I love his upside as a rusher. Late 1st round player.

3 - Daviyon Nixon - Iowa - 6'3 305 lbs

Strengths: A former JUCO transfer, Nixon started his final two seasons for the Hawkeyes, exploding during his final season as a senior in 2020. Despite the shortened campaign, Nixon finished with 13.5 tackles for loss, 5.5 sacks, 1 interception, and a forced fumble. Nixon is a massive man, that displays tremendous all-around size with good muscular distribution along his frame. Nixon is a systematically and schematically-versatile prospect that can play anywhere along the defensive front. Nixon is an explosive athlete that doesn't look like he's a 300-pound man with the way he moves. Playing with urgency at all times, Nixon utilizes his quick-twice explosiveness to fire off the ball, both in the running and passing games. Possessing a wide diversity of pass-rush moves, Nixon shows a good understanding of how to keep blockers guessing at all times. He utilizes his quick and explosive hands to knock away would-be blockers. Understands how to break down blockers as a defender, rarely getting hooked or sustained. Sees things quickly, showing excellent read/react abilities to quickly process. Does a nice job of utilizing his powerful mitts to control the point of attack in the run game, playing with full extension, and keeping his off-hand clean. Power is evident throughout his frame as he shows the lower body power to hold the point of attack when handling double teams.

Weaknesses: Nixon has been a bit of a 1-season wonder with only one full season of good production at the top level. Appears to have some 'motor 'issues where he runs out of gas and is content sitting on a blocker for far too long. Doesn't possess top-tier length and this could cause some challenges in a 2-gap system.

Best Fit: 4-3 DT (3-technique)

Player Ranking (1-100): 84.3 - Nixon is an absolute beast to have to handle. He's got so much power throughout his frame that he's a real challenge to have to handle in 1 v 1 situations. As a 3-technique DT, he could be extremely devastating if he continues to develop the way he's been. 2nd round player.

4 - Marvin Wilson - Florida State - 6'4 319 lbs

Strengths: A team captain and full-time 2-year starter for the Seminoles that also contributed during his first two years as well, racking up some impressive statistics for an interior player. Wilson possesses tremendous thickness through his frame with wide shoulders and long limbs. The way Wilson moves for a guy of his size is nothing short of spectacular, combining his snap anticipation and good quickness to often get himself into the backfield before you can blink an eye. Wilson is a dynamic 1-gap penetrator that deconstructs blockers with his upper-body power and strength. His diverse set of hand tactics allow him to attack in a wide variety of different ways, including his favorite punch-pull move that is devastating. A fluid mover that shows some good lateral movement abilities to play in space. Plays with overwhelming power at the point of attack, completely enveloping lineman with strength, length, and hand POP. Has a good understanding of playing with leverage to put blockers on skates. Provides good gap integrity and discipline to rarely get moved off of his spot. Utilizes his length to disrupt passing lanes as evidenced by his high numbers of batted balls each season.

Weaknesses: Missed the final few games of the 2019 season due to suffering a hand injury and needing surgery to fix it. Suffered a leg injury and needed surgery during his final season causing him to miss the final several games of the year. Wilson has shed some sloppy weight during his career and will likely need to shed a bit more at the next level with some untidy core weight. Needs to show the same amount of commitment in the run game as he does in the passing game. Could stand to improve his eye discipline in the run game, seemingly a bit late to respond to plays that go in the opposite direction.

Best Fit: 3-tech DT in a 4-3 system

Player Ranking (1-100): 79.8 - Wilson is a really solid and dynamic leader for the Seminoles defense. He's been good for 3 seasons now. He isn't just a pass rusher but that's his best aspect of playing football. He will get better in the run game and he needs to if he wants to be an elite interior player. 3rd round player.

5 - Tedarrell Slaton - Florida - 6'5 330 lbs

Strengths: A 4-year rotational defensive lineman for the Gators defense that has played a valuable role in their defensive setup despite not being a 'production 'guy. Built like an absolute monster, Slaton looks more like an offensive tackle with tremendous overall length and size. Utilizing his size in every sense of the word, Slaton shortens the field with his wingspan. He utilizes his size to constantly be disruptive to the QB, staying in his line of vision to disrupt the timing with his length. Does a nice job of utilizing full arm extension to lock out his arms and control the point of attack while taking his off-hand to slow down runners. Not a limited moving space-eater, Slaton shows some good get-off for a guy of his size. Brings some pass-rushing moves to his game, including a nice swim move as well as impressive gap shooting abilities to split double teams. When dropping his pads, Slaton is an immovable force that will take on double teams with ease in the running game.

Weaknesses: Slaton is limited to a 2-down player likely at the next level, rarely staying on the field for long stretches for the Gators defense. He's had several minor injury concerns throughout his career, missing games in each of his 4 seasons. Will have notable leverage concerns due in part to his frame, far too often giving up his chest plate to blockers, limiting his ability to offer much once sustained. Limited counter ability due to lateral tightness in his hips and heavy feet.

Best Fit: NT in either system

Player Ranking (1-100): 78.3 - Slaton is a better player than I expected on film. He will make the field smaller for a defense and will occasionally show some pass-rush ability while playing in the middle of the defense. He's not an interior prospect but he shows some upside if he continues to grow into his frame. 3rd round player.

6 - Jay Tufele - USC - 6'3 305 lbs

Strengths: A solid 2-year contributor to the Trojans defense, Tufele in a rotational role had solid numbers with 7 sacks and 64 tackles before opting out of his final season. Tufele has a very stout and compact build, showing the frame to be a positionally and schematically-versatile guy that can present an intriguing 2-gap or 1-gap penetrating option for a defense. Tufele showed success wherever he played along the Trojans defensive front. An above-average athlete that shows good gap penetration skills in which he combines his snap anticipation and 1st step quickness to get a good jump off the ball. A difficult guy to handle when he fires off the ball with good leverage, showing power at the point of attack with really strong upper body power and hands to fight through blockers. A warrior that plays with a relentless motor and passion for the game, always in pursuit despite not having stellar production. Good ball locator that shows a commitment to keeping an eye on the ball and working back towards the ball. Really good mental processing ability to quickly read/react and beat blockers and ball carriers to the spot, showing tremendous reactionary ability and instincts.

Weaknesses: Was mostly limited to a 2-down role quite a bit at USC while getting taken off the field on key passing downs. Consistency is the major issue with Tufele as he frequently will go missing for long stretches of a game. More of a 'gap shooter 'than a true pass rusher. He lacks any kind of consistent pass rusher ability or plan to set up his rushes to win in different ways. Inconsistent in playing with leverage, far too often standing upright when attacking the pocket and barely getting any movement off the ball. Lacks elite size and length to consistently make plays outside of his frame.

Best Fit: 4-3 DT or 3-4 NT

Player Ranking (1-100): 77.3 - Tufele's best quality is his versatility and block shedding ability. His powerful upper body, motor, and deconstruction ability will allow him to make plays at the next level. He's not a dynamic player but he's likely going to be a starter immediately in a 2-down role. Hard not to like the player though. Battles his butt off on every play and will give an occasional pressure in the passing game. 3rd round player in any system.

7 - Tyler Shelvin - LSU - 6'3 346 lbs

Strengths: Before opting out prior to his final season, Shelvin was an impressive interior starter and five-starHigh School Prospect for LSU. An unsung hero that showed up in a big way during his sophomore campaign and LSU's title-winning season. Regularly drawing double teams from opposing lineman, Shelvin is a powerful and massive man that has incredible thickness and power throughout his frame, rarely allowing himself to get moved off of his spot. Shelvin handled all of the dirty work for the LSU defense, clogging up space at the 1st level and keeping linebackers free at the 2nd level. For a guy of his size, Shelvin consistently moves well, showing good initial get-off to push the pocket forward and get off single blocks. Really powerful hands and active hands allow him to control the point of attack and keep his frame mostly clean. Will be a dominant run stuffer at the next level due to his anchorage power, balance, and gap integrity. Possesses a nonstop motor that fires out of his stance with good leverage to almost always pushing the pile forward.

Weaknesses: Very limited as a pass rusher at the next level and will likely be a 2-down player that will be taken off of the field on clear passing downs. Production is not the name of the game for Shelvin, with only 1.5 career sacks during his 2 years at LSU. Limited when asked to play with range (anything outside A-Gap responsibilities) or to close down outside rush lanes, lacking the tackle radius or the lateral change of direction to play sideways. Limited as a counter player and if he doesn't get initial penetration, he will sit on blocks for the duration.

> **Best Fit: NT in either scheme**

Player Ranking (1-100): 76.3 - Shelvin no doubt was quietly responsible for much of the success of LSU's defense in 2019. While he's likely a 2-down player at the next level, he will be a dominant interior run defender for a team. He's no slouch for a guy of his size and his workmanship and power will allow him to make some plays but he will contribute and open up things even more for his teammates. 3rd round player.

8 - Levi Onwuzirike - Washington - 6'3 290 lbs

Strengths: A 3-year contributor for the Huskies that chose to sit out his final year of eligibility. An athletically-built interior player that shows the versatility to play in any defensive system and multiple positions and alignments. A consistent player that has shown improvement during each of his campaigns, Onwuzirike is a hard-working and flexible prospect. Combining good snap anticipation, initial quickness, and awareness, Onwuzirike will threaten the pocket frequently from wherever he is playing. Has a good understanding of how to set up his rushes with hand placement, committing himself to proper technique, and winning the hand battle to control the point of attack. A loose-limbed athlete that shows fluidity in his lateral movements, presenting a difficult matchup for a lineman to sustain. Shows some impressive lower-body strength, generating some good speed to power and exploding out of his stance while utilizing natural momentum. A technician in the way in which he plays, showing a wide and diverse range of pass rush moves to attack the pocket. Good in the run game when working through blockers, showing the awareness and strength to deconstruct blocks while keeping his eyes on the ball to work towards the football.

Weaknesses: His tape is much more impressive than his production, Onwuzirike has never had big production despite frequently standing out on film. Gets close to making the play a lot, but rarely finishes plays. While he played quite a bit of a 2-gap in college, he lacks the ideal frame to consistently take on double teams at the next level. Doesn't have any dominating physical traits and is a bit of a 'good at everything great at nothing' player. Has had some leverage concerns when shooting out of his stance too upright.

Best Fit :3-Technique DT

Player Ranking (1-100): 75.8 - A really solid player that could be an immediate starter at the next level. Unfortunately, I believe sitting out this year will likely hurt him because he didn't get a chance to showcase that he can be a dominant interior force. 3rd round player.

9 - Marlon Tuipulotu- USC - 6'2 308 lbs

Strengths: A former five-star recruit for the Trojans and three-year starter along the defensive line, Tuipulotu has been a valuable cog in the heart of the USC defense. Built with a compact and sturdy frame, Tuipulotu is an absolute load to have to handle. Utilizing his natural leverage advantages, Tuipulotu fires low off the ball, maintaining the point of attack at all times. Shows some twitchiness off the ball with good initial quickness to fire into the backfield. Will command double teams in the running game. A reactionary player that has good instincts and reflexes to quickly diagnose. Plays like his hair is on fire on every snap, showing nonstop hustle, willing to constantly work in pursuit. A slippery player to have to block, showing good body control and lateral quickness to keep his frame clean, rarely getting hung on blocks. Does a nice job of breaking down blockers with quick hands. Understands how to convert speed-to-power with his low leveraged frame, producing a devastating bull rush, capable of closing the pocket quickly on passing downs. Solid production behind the backfield despite playing as mostly as a nose tackle.

Weaknesses: Has had his fair share of injury concerns early in his career, including knee and back issues. He needed back surgery during his freshman season, missing almost the entire season. Slightly undersized to play as a typical nose tackle lacking ideal height and length. Will struggle a bit when plays go away from his frame, failing to have the tackle radius or the range to consistently make plays along the perimeter. Besides a bull rush, he offers very little else in the terms of a pass rush repertoire.

Best Fit: 4-3 DT (1-technique)

Player Ranking (1-100): 75.3 - Tuipulotu is an absolute battler! While he's not a great pass rusher, he's worth having on the field on 3rd downs because of his ability to close the pocket. A very difficult guy to move off of his spot that will be a dominant run stuffer in the middle of the defense. Really good football player. 3rd round player.

10 - Darius Stills - West Virginia - 6'1 281 lbs

Strengths: A 2-year starter for the Mountaineers that has produced immensely during each of the last two years, finishing with double-digit sacks totals combined. Stills is a squatty-built defender that remains low out of his block, showing tremendous lower point strength at the point of attack to absorb blocks and stay balanced through contact. A positionally and schematically versatile defender that generally plays in the middle of the 3-man front for the Mountaineers, showing nose tackle ability in either system. Despite playing out of position and having to 2-gap quite a bit, he still produced consistent production. Utilizes his natural leverage advantage to instantly win the point of attack battle against bigger, stronger interior players. Stills 'best trait is his explosive twitch out of his stance, showing really good 1st step quickness to get good initial penetration. Impressive core flexibility and balance to be able to get skinny through narrowing gaps. Possesses a wide diversity of moves and hand tactics when attacking the pocket. Moves well laterally, showing loose limbs and agility.

Weaknesses: Stills lacks the prototypical interior defensive tackle build for the next level, lacking great length and overall size. If he wants to continue playing in the middle of a 3-man front at the next level he's going to need to put on substantial weight. Over pursues plays due to aggressive pursuit angles, taking himself out of plays. Technique in the running game is sporadic at best, leaving his gap assignments consistently unfulfilled as he attempts to attack the pocket time-after-time. While pass-rushing, he's very reliant on winning on the initial move and needs to develop a counter plan to disengage against more athletic interior players.

Best Fit: 4-3 DT (3-technique)

Player Ranking (1-100): 75.0 - Stills is a really good pass rusher with excellent explosive-twitch. While he can play other positions, his explosive nature would best be served in a 1-gap system where he can shoot gaps and attack the pocket. 2nd round player.

11 - Cameron Sample - Tulane - 6'3 274 lbs

Strengths: A 4-year contributor to the defense, Sample took over as a regular starter towards the end of his true freshman campaign. He played mostly outside for the Tulane 3-4 defense and bumped inside in sub-packages. Has had really solid production levels during each season, both in tackle totals and in stops behind the line of scrimmage. Sample has an impressive power-packed frame with very good overall weight distribution. If he can't get near the QB while rushing, he shows excellent awareness to disrupt the pass by keeping his hands up. Excellent snap timing and anticipation to get a good jump off the snap of the ball. Sample moves well, showing very good lateral agility and change of directional ability to be effective when having to redirect his frame. Brings a wide diversity of pass rush attacks. Understands how to utilize his hands in both the running and passing game. Very powerful upper body and hands allow him to control blockers. Utilizes his natural leverage advantages to control the point of attack against blockers and put them on skates.

Weaknesses: Sample dealt with a knee injury in 2018 that slowed him down in both 2018 and 2019. Hasn't competed against top-tier competition where you can see his levels of power in comparison to NFL lineman. On occasion will show a lack of play awareness, getting lost in the scuffle and losing track of the ball carrier. Will take overaggressive pathways to the ball, leaving his gap responsibilities in the run game. Doesn't have the ideal length to play as a 5-technique at the next level and will struggle to make stops in the run game outside of his frame.

Best Fit: 4-3 DT (3-technique)

Player Ranking (1-100): 74.8 - Sample has been very impressive during his career. While his production isn't elite, he is very disruptive. And he does it wherever he's lined up. I'd love to see him play as a 1-gap penetrating 3-technique DT at the next level. That'll fully allow him to utilize his upper-body strength and quickness to make stops in the backfield, both in the run game and passing games.

12 - Alim McNeill - North Carolina State - 6'2 320 lbs

Strengths: A 3-year contributor to the Wolfpack's defensive line that has played in every single game of his career. McNeill took over the starting responsibilities halfway through his sophomore season. Had a stellar sophomore year, finishing the season with 5.5 sacks and 7.5 tackles for loss. A mountain of a man, McNeill possesses rare athletic characteristics for a man of his frame. Moves well, showing good explosiveness off the snap of the ball and good closing speed to quickly makeup steps. Displacement power is evident in his bull rush, showing good speed-to-power and showing the ability to walk centers/guards backward. Has experience playing in both 3 and 4 man fronts, showing systematic versatility. Possesses the power in his lower half to play in a 2-gap system, with the ball awareness and anchor ability to sustain combination blocks without getting blown off the ball. But McNeill excels when playing as a 1-gap penetrator with his ideal mix of burst and short-area quickness that allows him to consistently slip gaps. Possesses the core flexibility and strength to get skinny through narrowing windows. Loose hips and good lateral quickness allows him to work well with teammates to be dynamic on stunts. Controls the point of attack with a commitment to utilize full extension and keep his chest plate clean.

Weaknesses: Inconsistent pad level that allows his pads to rise mid-play, limiting his counter ability. Doesn't make as many plays as his athletic traits suggest he should, missing a lot of opportunities in the running game. Could stand to react quicker to running plays, appears to have some slight mental lapses when reacting to misdirection-type plays. A lot of his success rushing is predicated on slipping gaps and he fails to consistently win with technique and good hand usage. Doesn't possesses elite length, limiting his potential as a nose tackle for the next level.

Best Fit: 4-3 DT (1 or 3 technique)

Player Ranking (1-100): 73.8 - McNeill had a stellar sophomore season and a somewhat down junior season. He has some good athletic traits to work with. He's been a bit 'hit or miss 'but as a whole, I believe there's definitely upside to work with. I like his ability to play at multiple spots along the formation. 4th round player.

13 - Kyree Campbell - Florida - 6'4 295 lbs

Strengths: Campbell has played a significant role for the Gators defense in each of the last three seasons, playing a valuable nose tackle role in the middle of their defense. Campbell missed a few games during his career and his loss was very apparent along the defensive line. While not a production machine, Campbell was often the glue that held the Gators defense together, opening up opportunities for his teammates. Possessing outstanding size, Campbell possesses the length and the power-packed frame to be a fit in any defensive setup. While playing mostly in the nose position, Campbell's strength and lower body power were on display, frequently handling double teams. He brings terrific snap anticipation and timing to get a really good jump off the ball, showing good initial quickness and movement skills. Plays with a good bull rush to collapse the pocket when he's used on 3rd down. Does a really nice job of dropping his pads to play with good leverage, making him a force to be reckoned with in the running game. Shows excellent hand strength and disengagement ability to shed blockers and finish plays.

Weaknesses: Missed the first three games of the 2020 season with a minor injury. Besides his bull rush, Campbell offers very little else as a pass rusher, likely making him strictly a 2-down player at the next level. While Campbell displays good initial quickness, his overall range is limited while in pursuit, failing to offer any kind of recovery ability. An upright rusher that lacks any kind of bend in his frame.

Best Fit: NT in either defensive system (Can play 0, 1, or 5-technique DE)

Player Ranking (1-100): 72.2 - Campbell is one of those football players that never gets the glory but if you really watch him play, he's a darn good football player. You need a guy like this on your defensive line because he will consistently push the pocket and force extra attention. While he's likely not a guy that can play on 3rd down, he's good enough on 1st and 2nd downs that he's worth a 4th round pick.

14 - Tommy Togiai - Ohio State - 6'3 292 lbs

Strengths: A significant 3-year contributor to the Buckeyes defensive line, Togiai is more than just a 'space player. 'Togiai had a breakout year in his final season for the Buckeyes. Possessing a compact and stout physique, Togiai is a powerful man that has rare functional strength throughout his frame. Utilizing his natural leverage advantage, Togiai fires low out of his stance controlling the point of attack. Possesses an immovable body that will force double teams in the run game with his ability to win positioning and hunker down with his lower body power. Excellent overall in the running game, minimizing available gap openings through the 'A 'and 'B 'gaps. Showed impressive pursuit and recovery bursts when playing backside, making plays along the perimeters. A technician with his hands, showing good anticipation and timing to work through blockers while keeping his frame clean. Not simply a straight-line runner, there's some looseness in his frame, showing some lateral mobility.

Weaknesses: Was mostly a rotational player his first two seasons on the defensive line, only getting one full year of starting experience. Lacks elite length for the positioning with a smaller than ideal tackle radius, limiting his potential ability to play in a 2-gap role. A low ceiling pass rusher that will likely be strictly a 2-down player at the next level due to his lack of overall pass-rush upside.

Best Fit: 4-3 DT or 3-4 DE

Player Ranking (1-100): 71.2 - Togiai is one of the strongest players in this draft class. He's a powerful man that will regularly force double teams in the running game. He's no slouch as an athlete either. He's a very good 2-down player, and for that, he deserves to be a 4th round pick.

15 - Osa Odighizuwa - UCLA - 6'2 280 lbs

Strengths: A 4-year contributor to the Bruins defense that has been a solid stalwart of their defensive line. Also, the brother of NFL player and former Giants draft pick, Owa. Built with tremendous stoutness through his frame and excellent length, featuring over 84" arms. A workout warrior that has incredible lower body strength, shining through when handling double teams. He utilizes his natural leverage advantage coupled with his anchorage strength to rarely get moved off the spot in the running game. Good explosiveness and 1st step quickness that could nicely translate to a 1-gap interior position at the next level. Plays with good core flexibility and strength to get skinny through expiring gaps. A very good bull rusher that understands how to generate speed-to-power to put blockers on skates in the passing game. Does a nice job of utilizing his length to disrupt throwing lanes. Plays with a relentless motor and is always in pursuit, often catching backs 20-30 yards down the field. Size, length, and power make him effective in any defensive system.

Weaknesses: Lacks ideal height for the position. Played mostly as a base defensive end in college and will likely have to transition to playing inside in a base defense. Not a bendable athlete that will be able to generate any kind of consistent pressure if playing as an end, failing to offer the flexibility to threaten the corners. Overall pass rush production has been subpar throughout his career, offering little else other than his bull rush. Appears to have significant awareness issues, frequently losing track of the ball carrier and running in the wrong direction. Doesn't consistently play with good hand placement and technique.

Best Fit: 4-3 DT, 4-3 LDE or 3-4 DE

Player Ranking (1-100): 70.8 - Odighizuwa is a powerfully-built prospect that has some versatility with his size and length that allows him to be a scheme fit for any defense. While he's not a greatpassrusher, he doeshavesomeexplosiveness to work with. He's a tremendously powerful guy that could be a nice inside player at the next level. Or he could play as a base DE and kick inside in sub-packages. 4th round player.

16 - Khyiris Tonga - BYU - 6'4 321 lbs

Strengths: A rare 4-year starter for BYU in the heart of their defense, Tonga is a massive massive man that shows rare physical traits to go along with his frame. Not a "sloppy weight" big man, Tonga shows good overall weight distribution throughout his frame. A really good overall athlete that shows surprisingly nimble feet and lateral quickness. Tonga does a nice job of dropping his pads and playing with leverage despite his height. Exploding out of his stance with a solid 1st step, Tonga will blow up the pocket and force double teams. While he never produced big production, he forced offensive lines to pay him extra attention. In the running game, he commits himself to quickly locating the ball carrier while showing good play-recognition and awareness. Quick to drop his anchor when playing with power at the point of attack, Tonga shows good balance through contact. Capable of playing in a 2-gap system with good range and instincts. He utilizes his length and wingspan to slow down ball carriers. Excellent in short-yardage situations, forcing runners to ignore the A gap.

Weaknesses: A belly-to-belly defender that will leave his chest plate completely exposed in the running game, allowing blockers to win inside hand fits easily. Production has been very very limited during his career, lacking any kind of nuance or pass-rush plan, and will likely be a 2-down player at the next level. Despite his size and strength, Tonga misses a lot of tackles surprisingly, not always using the best of wrap-up fundamentals. Has struggled with conditioning and getting noticeably worn down towards the end of games.

Best Fit: NT in either scheme

Player Ranking (1-100): 70.4 - Tonga is a big man that moves incredibly well. He could end up being a starting nose tackle if he can maintain the right condition and size. If he stays around the 320 mark I think he could end up being a solid 2-down starter in this league. 4th round player.

17 - Ta'Quon Graham - Texas - 6'3 290 lbs

Strengths: A 4-year contributor to the Longhorns defense, Graham has started in 24 games during his career, but having a significant role since his sophomore season. A team captain for the team, Graham possesses a really intriguing frame for the next level, showcasing excellent overall size with room for added growth to be a systematically-versatile prospect. A very good athlete for his size, moving impressively for a man of his size, showing the range to be effective along multiple spots on the front. Tremendous motor and plays like his hair is on fire on every snap of the ball. Looseness is evident through his frame as he shows no signs of struggling when needing to redirect his frame to play laterally. Possesses the recovery speed to quickly accelerate and fluidly chase ball careers down from behind. Possesses good reflexes coupled with twitchy reflexes to quickly diagnose and make stops behind the backfield.

Weaknesses: A 'potential player 'that never quite lived up to his former high-school billing while at Texas as a pass rusher, failing to record more than 2.5 sacks in a campaign. While he flashes his athletic profile on occasion, he never consistently showed it through the duration of a game. Significant functional power concerns, failing to have the ideal 2-gap lower body strength to anchor unless considerable strength is gained. Allows blockers to easily get underneath his pads, coming out of his stance far too high in the run game when playing face-up. Doesn't appear to have a great deal of confidence in his hand usage, failing to bring much of an attack arsenal.

Best Fit: 4-3 DT (3-technique)

Player Ranking (1-100): 69.7 - Graham shows good potential with a nice frame but his tape is all over the place. He never quite showed consistency or an ability to affect a game as much as his 'athletic talent 'says he should. He certainly has room for added development as he's put on sizable amounts of muscle onto his frame since being at Texas. 5th round player.

18 - Bobby Brown III - Texas A&M - 6'4 325 lbs

Strengths: A 3-year contributor to the Aggies defense that has started almost every game for their defense during the last two seasons. Possessing a big-bodied frame with terrific width and rare length to play at the next level. His blend of size and length makes him a schematically and positionally-versatile defender to fit any defense. Has improved with his versatility this past season, showing that he can be more than just a run stuffer. He does a nice job of timing the snap count and getting a good jump at the line of scrimmage when rushing the passer. A really good athlete for his size that shows good initial quickness and explosiveness to shoot through gaps. Plays with a relentless motor on every snap of the ball, making a lot of plays in pursuit. Shows good power and strength through his frame to be able to hold up at the point of attack against combination blocks if attempting to 2-gap.

Weaknesses: Brown struggles against leveraged blockers that can get underneath his pad level. Poor ball instincts post-snap and awareness lead to disappointing pursuit angles. This causes him to miss several tackles due to improper positioning when attempting to bring down a ball carrier. Poor gap control and discipline have led to many unfulfilled assignments in the running game, leading to big plays through interior gaps. Still raw in his development when it comes to utilizing his hands and keeping his frame clean through contact. There's definitely some tightness through his frame and in his hips, failing to offer much of a counter plan if initially blocked.

Best Fit: 4-3 or 3-4 NT

Player Ranking (1-100): 68.3 - Brown III is a big-bodied man that has developed his frame from a defensive end into a defensive tackle the last few seasons. While he's lost a bit of his athleticism, he still shows above-average explosiveness for a 320+ pound interior defender. He needs to improve in the run game, but he does show some impressive pass rush ability. 5th round player.

19 - Cory Durden - Florida State - 6'5 315 lbs

Strengths: A 2-year contributor for the Seminoles that exploded onto the scene following his stellar 2019 season where he finished with 5 sacks and 6.5 tackles for loss. Durden is built with rare size and length, being an ideal fit for a 3-4 defensive end at the next level. But he has experience playing in both schemes at Florida State during his time. A really impressive pass rusher that plays with a diverse skill set of moves, showing good initial quickness and core flexibility to shoot gaps and get skinny through tight windows. Understands how to set-up his rushes, showing a plan at all times and capitalizing against any over-aggressive lineman. Not a narrow or straight-lined athlete, Durden shows rare lateral mobility and flexibility when it comes to getting under blockers. A threat on stunts due to his ability to make up ground and quickly close on the quarterback. Does a nice job of utilizing his length to disrupt at all times, frequently getting his hands up and disrupting the quarterback's vision. Controls the pads of blockers with his length, allowing himself to get significant movement on his bull rushes. Large tackle radius and wingspan allows himself to cut off and seal rush lanes;

Weaknesses: Only played in 3 games during the 2020 season before opting out for the remaining of the season. Despite his terrific 2019 season, Durden played with an injured shoulder and will need to get it evaluated. Durden is very very tall for an interior player in a 4-man front and he will struggle with his large surface area. He allows shorter, interior blockers to easily get underneath him and control him at the point of attack. He's generally bullied off the line of scrimmage in the run game. Balance through contact is a challenge for Durden due to his height. Durden has had some trouble with consistency when it comes to wrapping up and securing tackles once he gets his hands on runners despite his large tackle radius. Lower body strength and anchorage ability to hold up at the point of attack is 'OK' at best and he needs to strengthen his anchor, especially if two-gapping. Overall motor is just 'OK' and he appears to get gassed very quickly in games.

Best Fit: 4-3 DT (3-technique) or 3-4 DE (5-technique)

Player Ranking (1-100): 65.3 - Durden's size is a plus and a negative all at the same time. He has the perfect build to be a 3-4 DE but he lacks ideal lower body strength to hold up consistently at the point of attack. He'll most likely be suited immediately to play inside in a 4-3 defense where he can just focus on shooting gaps and disrupting with his length. 5th round player.

20 - Lorenzo Neal Jr - Purdue - 6'3 315 lbs

Strengths: The son of former NFL great, Neal Jr is a completely different type of player that plays in a much different position. A 5th-year senior, Neal has shown to be a reliable plug in the middle of Purdue's defense. Experience playing at the nose tackle role in both a 3-4 and a 4-3 defense, Neal Jr displays the big-bodied frame to handle the same duties at the next level. Unlike most NT's in the NFL, Neal doesn't take snaps off, showing excellent conditioning. He plays every single down, showing the defense's reliance on his play. Shows the lateral mobility, awareness, and change of directional abilities to handle a 2-gap role. He moves surprisingly well for a guy of his size showing a good overall burst while firing out of his stance. Athleticism and closing speed are on display when making plays on backs or running QB's while chasing down backside. Active and quick hands allow him to keep his frame clean when attacking the pocket. Hand usage is also impressive when he's stacking/shedding in the run game working through blockers. Does a nice job of firing low out of his stance and playing with good leverage showing the power to dominate big interior players and pushing them off their spot.

Weaknesses: Was able to get a medical redshirt after missing his entire 2019 season after needing knee surgery. Play-recognition abilities to quickly process and anticipate plays aren't as good as you would hope for someone playing the middle of the defense. Anchorage ability and lower-body strength are mediocre, getting handled at times by combination blocks and completely washed out of the play. Overall production is mediocre despite the number of snaps he plays on, lacking any kind of pass rush ability.

Best Fit: NT in either scheme

Player Ranking (1-100): 64.4 - Neal Jr offers upside athletically but he's not quite as strong or as mentally-aware you would like. His production in the Big-10 was just OK. He likely will be limited to a 2-down role at the next level assuming he makes the team. 6th round player.

21 - Jerome Johnson - Indiana - 6'3 304 lbs

Strengths: A 5th year senior for the Hoosiers, Johnson has been a mainstay of their defense for the last three seasons, posting reliable production during each. As a junior, Johnson had his 'coming out party 'finishing with 7.5 tackles for loss and 5 sacks. Johnson has been outstanding against top-tier competition, having some of his best games against Ohio State's top-tier offensive line. Johnson is a good-sized prospect possessing width and very good length for a 3-technique defensive tackle. He's shown the ability to play in a 2-gap system as a nose tackle at times as well. Fires off the ball low, showing really good initial quickness to get quick penetration. Does a nice job of timing the snap count, showing good snap anticipation and timing. Shows good core flexibility and strength to get skinny and fight through tight spaces. A battler that brings it on every snap, working his butt off, and is always in pursuit when working backside. Possesses power through his frame and isn't easily moved off of his spot in the running game.

Weaknesses: The Hoosiers defense rotates their defensive line constantly so Johnson wasn't required to stay on the field for significant amounts of snaps. Has some stiffness to his frame, lacking ideal change of directional abilities. This limits his ability on the counter. Needs to understand how to utilize his hands when in block deconstruction, failing to disengage in ample time. Took advantage production-wise of missed assignments and hustle, not because of 'true 'pass-rush ability.

Best Fit: 4-3 DT (Can play either 1 or 3 technique)

Player Ranking (1-100): 64.2 - Johnson has been very solid for the Hoosiers during each of the last few seasons, showing reliability and consistent production. While he's not athletically a dynamic interior prospect, he possesses the power and size to play all along the interior of a defensive line, preferably in a 4-3 system. 6th round player.

22 - Naquan Jones - Michigan State - 6'4 340 lbs

Strengths: A 4-year contributing role player for the Spartans defensive line, Jones is a mountain of a man that spearheads the middle of their defense. Not a waste of space in the middle of the defense, Jones shows the athletic traits that match the size gifts. Equipped with a good 1st step, Jones shows some good initial quickness to shoot gaps and play skinny through narrowing gaps. Has the versatility of being used all over the defensive front, Jones shows systematic and schematic versatility for the next level. Where Jones shines is in the run game where he demonstrates his upper-body power to deconstruct and shed blockers. Utilizes his long arms to keep his frame clean and his quick hands to give himself some separation. Heavy-handed with the ability to lodge real displacement power when making contact.

Weaknesses: Despite being a four-star recruit, Jones has never really has had a lead dog situation, almost playing as a rotational player in every game during his career. That will lead some to question his abilities to play more than 30-40% of snaps. Limited pass rush arsenal that has rarely caused the QB to move off of his spot, Jones looks stuck in the mud when attempting to generate any kind of movement while attacking the pocket. A stiff-hipped and linear athlete that lacks the change of directional ability when having to cross face. A 2-down player at the next level.

Best Fit: 4-3 DT (1-technique)

Player Ranking (1-100): 63.4 - I like Jones as a 1-technique at the next level. He's a really good player against the run, showing good strength and the ability to play through blocks. While he's not a 3-down player he doesn't need to be. He has a real understanding of how to utilize his hands to keep his frame clean. He will be a solid run stuffer. 6th round player.

23 - Malik Herring - Georgia - 6'3 283 lbs

Strengths: A rotational player for the Bulldogs before beginning to start some games as a junior while greatly impressing. A nice chess piece that can play any position along the defensive front, playing in Georgia's hybrid defensive front. Herring is a big-bodied bruiser that works his tail off on every snap of the ball, showing tremendous blue-chip characteristics. A good athlete for his size, showing good initial quickness to shoot gaps or get some good initial penetration. Nice combination of snap timing and anticipation to quickly get a good jump at the line of scrimmage. Not overly consumed with production, showing to be a trustworthy teammate, willing to handle the dirty work, and 2-gap to open up things for his teammates. Disciplined in his gap assignments, Herring quickly locates the ball and anchors down showing good lower-body strength to maintain the point of attack. Strong upper-body power is evident when tackler, rarely letting runners outside his grasps.

Weaknesses: A limited all-around athlete that fails to utilize some of his natural gifts routinely. While he displays some pass rush moves, he appears to be content just playing belly-to-belly when attacking the passer. Slow reaction and reflexes limit his ability to make plays once diagnosing. Doesn't have a true position since he played all over the place. Gets stuck on blocks for far too long due to lower body stiffness and lack of fluidity through his frame.

Best Fit: 4-3 DT (1-technique) or 3-4 DE (5-technique)

Player Ranking (1-100): 62.4 - Appears to enjoy playing 2-gap while plugging up the running game. Not going to offer much else in the passing game so his role will likely be limited to 2 downs in the NFL. 6th round player.

24 - Xavier Kelly - Arkansas - 6'5 311 lbs

Strengths: A former four-star recruit for the Clemson Tigers, Kelly transferred to play his final year of eligibility for the Razorbacks. While with the Tigers, Kelly was a rotational player that never was counted on to start consistently. With the Razorbacks this year, he fits perfectly into their 3-man front scheme, allowing him to play as a 5-technique defensive end. Kelly is gifted with excellent size and length, making him a scheme fit for any defense. Does a nice job of holding the point of attack and winning inside hand leverage in the run game while keeping his off-hand free to make the stop. Strong upper-body allows him to win on the counter, ripping with his arms and disengaging to keep his frame clean. Plays with a 'HOT 'motor on every snap of the ball, always in pursuit and never giving up. Excellent lower-body power enables him to generate some speed-to-power on his bull rushes, closing the pocket quickly.

Weaknesses: Production has been subpar throughout his career, offering very little in the pass rush department. Far too content playing belly-to-belly in the game, bouncing off blockers and leaving his chest completely exposed. His gap integrity isn't always the best, especially when playing in a 3-man front, choosing to crash down hard inside and leaving the outside completely wide open at times. Appears to have some sloppy weight on his frame, minimizing his lateral movement ability. A linear athlete that struggles with lateral movements.

Best Fit: 3-4 DE or 4-3 DT (1-technique)

Player Ranking (1-100): 61.2 - I thought Kelly played well this year for the Razorbacks. He played mostly as a 5-technique and it allowed him to utilize his 2-gap ability and be an effective run stuffer. He's going to offer little rushing the passer but he's got excellent power throughout his frame to be a good 2-down player.

25 - Jared Goldwire - Louisville - 6'6 305 lbs

Strengths: A former JUCO, Goldwire was used in a rotational role as a junior for the Tigers defense before transitioning to a full-time starter at nose guard during his final year as a senior. The first thing you'll notice with Goldwire is his massive frame, showing vines for arms and tremendous height. His frame allows him to be equally attractive in any defensive system. Goldwire utilizes his length effectively at the length of scrimmage to disrupt the QB's vision and alter the throwing motion of the QB. Goldwire is very good in the running game, especially when playing backside. He's able to utilize his rare tackle radius to continuously make plays outside of his frame. Plays with a HOT motor, accelerating fluidly to chase ball carriers down from behind. A reliable wrap-up tackler. Does a nice job of controlling the pads of blockers, keeping his frame clean while playing with full extension. Appears to have twitchy reflexes with the ability to quickly read and diagnose things in the running game.

Weaknesses: Goldwire lacks a true position even though he has the frame to play in any. He will likely be a better fit in a 3-4 defense as a 5-technique two-gap DE. Needs to continue to strengthen his lower half, lacks a great anchor. Very limited as a pass rusher, lacking any kind of explosive twitch to win on pure athleticism. Needs to learn how to utilize his hands better, far too frequently getting stuck on blocks. His main issue is his repeated issues with his pad level, playing far too upright. This limits his ability to play with any kind of lateral quickness or counter abilities. He will allow lineman to get underneath him and put him on skates quickly when playing face-up.

Best Fit: Developmental 3-4 DE

Player Ranking (1-100): 59.4 - Goldwire has an attractive frame but he's still growing into it. He needs to continue to add lean muscle mass to his frame while strengthening his base. He could be a really nice 3-4 DE if he continues to get stronger to be able to handle 2-gap responsibilities at the next level.

26 - Mustafa Johnson - Colorado - 6'2 290 lbs

Strengths: A former JUCO transfer that started his final couple of seasons with Colorado, greatly impressing when doing so. A thick-framed defensive lineman that shows above-average length and plays with comfort at any position along the defensive front, having moved everywhere. He's even been used to stand up and attack the pocket as a standup rusher. A team leader and coaches 'favorite that has impressed the Colorado coaches immensely during his time. Johnson displays good football awareness, reading his keys and locating the football quickly. Plays with a relentless and non-stop motor, showing the ability to win in a variety of different ways. Strong at the point of attack, partly due to his thick lower body and strength to be able to handle double teams.

Weaknesses: Lacks elite size and is a bit undersized for the position. Has dealt with some lower-body injuries in both his ankles and knees causing him to miss a few games while at Colorado. Has had sloppy weight issues throughout his career, limiting his overall movement abilities. A subpar athlete that struggles when asked to play laterally, showing some tightness throughout his frame. Limited makeup speed when working back towards the football. Has racked up loads of production on designed plays, such as gains and blitzes where he was uncovered.

Best Fit : 3-4 DE (5-technique)

Player Ranking (1-100): 55.6 - Johnson is a 7th round player that can offer some upside in a 3-4 defense. He's going to need to continue to improve his frame and clean up some of his bad weight. He displays some strength, length, and physicality to 2-gap in a 3-man front.

27 - Carlo Kemp - Michigan - 6'3 286 lbs

Strengths: A 5th-year senior, 3-year starter, and defensive co-captain for the Wolverines, Kemp has been a key cog in their defensive line in each of the last few seasons. Kemp is an athletically-built interior defender that shows excellent thickness throughout his frame. Playing both as a 1-tech and a 3-tech, Kemp is ideally suited as more of a 3-tech at the next level due to his athletic nature. A very good athlete that shows excellent quickness out of his stance to generate initial penetration. At his best when working with his teammates on loops. Michigan oftentimes slants their front, allowing him to slip through gaps and utilize his explosiveness to generate pressure. A high-motor player that battles his butt off on every snap of the ball, showing nonstop pursuit when working back towards the ball. Maintains good gap integrity in the running game, showing the lateral mobility and awareness to redirect his frame and stay in a good position.

Weaknesses: Despite the amount of playtime, he's had over the last several seasons the amount of production he's had has been very minimal despite playing in a 1-gap role quite a bit. Deal with nagging lower-body injuries during the 2019 campaign. Gets stuck on blocks, failing to have any kind of shed ability to disengage. Below average pass rusher that lacks any kind of plan, especially if attempting to counter. Anchor strength is below par, getting completely blown off the ball at times.

Best Fit: 4-3 DT (3-technique)

Player Ranking (1-100): 54.3 - Kemp has loads of experience in the Big-10 but he goes missing for giant chunks during games. He has some explosive characteristics but he's not ready for valuable snaps at the next level.

TOP-10 Defensive Tackles

1. Christian Barmore
2. Jaylen Twyman
3. Daviyon Nixon
4. Marvin Wilson
5. Tedarrell Slaton

6. Jay Tufele
7. Tyler Shelvin
8. Levi Onwuzirike
9. Marlon Tuipulotu
10. Darius Stills

Chapter 11

Middle Linebackers

1 - Micah Parsons - Penn State - 6'3 245 lbs

Strengths: A dynamic 2-year starter for the Nittany Lions that before sitting out his final year in 2020 absolutely dominated. As a sophomore, he had 109 tackles, 14 tackles for loss, 5 sacks, and 4 forced fumbles. Possessing a stacked frame, Parsons shows prototypical length and compactness for the position with virtually minimum body fat. A tremendous and twitchy athlete that couples his sideline-to-sideline explosiveness with his rare read/react instincts to put himself into good positions routinely. Parsons utilizes his tremendous wingspan in all aspects of the game, most notably when it comes to his tackle radius, showcasing excellent wrap-up abilities while rarely missing a tackle. Mental diagnosis abilities and football intelligence are sky high with Parsons as he routinely puts himself into good positions, reacting quickly to route concepts and the development of plays. Excellent when asked to take on blocks and play face-up against blockers, showing impressive upper-body power and block deconstruction abilities. His former experience at defensive end in high school is evident in the way he rushes the passer, showing the ability to penetrate and attack both inside and outside rush lanes. Has shown some flashes of man cover abilities, but shines the most when he's able to sit back and read passing cues while in zone.

Weaknesses: There are times on film where you question his overall looseness through his lower half, looking a bit stiff when attempting to change direction. This would likely show up more if he was asked to handle additional man coverage responsibilities. His aggressive nature will cause him to overrun the ball and wash him out of plays. This also leads to him biting down hard on play-fakes, not always the most disciplined in his assignments. Can take overaggressive pathways to the ball on occasion.

Best Fit: 4-3 MIKE or 3-4 ILB

Player Ranking (1-100): 88.9 - Hard not to love Parsons. He's one of the cleanest and best all-around players in this draft class with virtually one of the highest floors imaginable. At the very least he will be a solid NFL starter at the next level but most likely much, much more. 1st round player.

2 - Dylan Moses - Alabama - 6'3 240 lbs

Strengths: A dominant presence along the Tide's defense, Moses has impressed during each of his 3 years on the field. Built with a V-Tapered and stacked frame, Moses shows the athletic physique with more than adequate size to play in today's NFL with additional room in his frame for continued muscular development. Versatility is the name of the game for Moses, showing the physicality to stack the box and shed blockers in the running game while also showing the looseness and lateral movement ability to cover in space. Plays with tireless energy and passion for the game, going 100 MPH on every snap of the ball, always around the football. A true sideline-to-sideline athlete that possesses outstanding range and body control to close down large sections of green in a flash. Plays like a hammer in search of a nail in every facet of the game, successfully being used as an oncoming blitzer, showing terrific instincts and closing speed to rush the QB into making a decision. A violent and physical tackler that rarely misses once he gets his hands on runners, utilizing his lower-body torque and momentum to violently bring ball carriers to the ground. A gap shooter that shows no hesitancy in the hole. Showed some upside when being used in all kinds of defensive coverages for the Alabama defense, including playing man against tight ends. Used at times as a QB spy, rarely allowing running QB's to escape and gain additional yards down the field.

Weaknesses: Moses, unfortunately, tore his ACL before his junior campaign, causing him to miss the entire 2019 season. He's struggled at times during the 2020 season, appearing to have nagging issues with his knee. He's overly reliant on his athletic qualities to overcompensate for some of his lapses in concentration and play recognition. His overaggressive nature causes him to bite hard on double moves and RPO's against disciplined QB's leaving large gaps in the middle of the field. Would like to see him learn some more pass rush variety rather than simply attacking the pocket straight-up with speed. When in coverage, Moses will get caught looking quite a bit forgetting his assignment and leaving some spacing.

Best Fit: 4-3 MIKE, WILL or 3-4 ILB

Player Ranking (1-100): 84.6 - Moses can play both as an off-ball or on-ball linebacker in any defensive system. He has the playmaking abilities coupled with the size and athleticism to have success in any spot. I would love to see him play in space as a 4-3 MIKE but some teams might prefer seeing him playing off the ball and flying downhill constantly as opposed to taking on blocks. I'm a bit worried about his knee issues going forward and his medical will be very very important. Either way, he's dynamic and should be a 1st round player.

3 - Cameron McGrone - Michigan - 6'1 236 lbs

Strengths: A former five-star high school recruit and 2-year starter for the Wolverines at middle linebacker that has played a valuable role for them on special teams his first two seasons as well. McGrone has a low-center-of-gravity cut frame with squatty legs possessing impressive next-level readiness. Possesses the traits to be equally effective and systematically-versatile in both a 3-4 and a 4-3 defense. The first thing you'll notice with McGrone is his athletic nature, showing terrific burst and acceleration out of his stance to quickly trigger and get downhill. Plays like his hair is on fire on every snap, playing like each snap is his last one. The sideline-to-sideline range is prevalent on every rep, showing the ability to cover large sections of green in the blink of an eye. Lower body flexibility and hip mobility are evident when asked to change directions, rarely losing any built-up momentum. Keeps his pads leveraged through contact, showing the ability to stay on his feet when deconstructing. Good upper-body power allows him to shock blockers upon impact. Will make plays on every snap if not continuously accounted for due to his instincts and playmaking nature. A sound tackler that reads his keys well and quickly closes gaps. Strong at the point of attack due to his compact frame and strength in his anchor. Will only be 20 years old on draft day.

Weaknesses: Missed some game time during his junior season for an apparent upper-body injury that was not disclosed. Can get overaggressive at times, making him susceptible to double moves and misdirection-type plays. Needs to do a better job of reading his keys pre-snap, but that will likely come with more experience and playtime. Would do a better job of staying disciplined and patient in running plays, far too often attempting to shoot gaps as opposed to maintaining gap integrity. Has struggled at times in man coverage against backs and tight ends and will need to get a bit more fluid when working through transitions.

Best Fit: 4-3 MLB (Mike)

Player Ranking (1-100): 83.5 - McGrone is a really intriguing prospect that has all the physical tools teams will want in a linebacker. He's still a bit raw and will need to improve in the mental areas of the game, but that will likely come with more additional game time. The sky is the limit with McGrone. 2nd round player.

4 - Jamin Davis - Kentucky - 6'4 234 lbs

Strengths: Davis somewhat came out of nowhere this past season to be one of the best linebackers in the SEC, finishing with over 100 tackles, 4 tackles for loss, 1.5 sacks, 3 interceptions, and a forced fumble. Davis has a solid and chiseled frame, possessing excellent height and length to play in the middle of a defense at the next level. He also possesses room in his frame for additional muscle mass. Davis is also a dynamic special teams player for the Wildcats, producing several big plays during his career. Davis is a terrific athlete that displays the functional movement abilities and range to play as a MIKE at the next level. He closes down so quickly with his long strides, making him a very good blitzer when working through the 'A 'gap. Length and recovery speed allows him to chase down plays backside and cut off perimeter lanes in the running game. Shows zero hesitancy in the hole and can really lay the wood, delivering bone-rattling hits due to his acceleration and compact frame. A reliable wrap-up tackler that rarely letters runners out of his grasps, utilizing his massive tackle radius to bring down outside of his frame. Plays the game with nonstop violence, urgency, and aggression. Possesses natural instincts that allow him to be properly positioned. A smart kid that reads his keys while utilizing excellent eye discipline, rarely getting fooled.

Weaknesses: Needs to continue adding functional strength and weight onto his frame. When he's playing in space he can allow his pads to rise a bit, causing him to get blown off the ball by pulling linemen. Has very little experience in pass coverage and was used far more to attack the pocket. A 1-year starter that exploded out of nowhere this year before being a backup in his first few years at Kentucky.

Best Fit: 4-3 MIKE or 3-4 ILB

Player Ranking (1-100): 82.1 - This kid is really really good. One of my pet cats in this draft. Yes, he's still raw but he's going to get better and better with more game time. The athleticism, frame, and downhill nature of Davis make me think he could be an immediate starter as a MIKE linebacker in a 4-3 defense. The sky is the limit. 2nd round player.

5 - Baron Browning - Ohio State - 6'3 241 lbs

Strengths: Browning is a 4-year rotational player for Ohio State that shined in limited snaps when given the chance. Was tremendous for the Buckeyes in playoff game and the championship. Built with tremendous size and twitched-up explosiveness, Browning possesses the frame to play inside at the next level in any defensive system. Athleticism and speed were on full display during his junior season where he made 11 plays behind the line of scrimmage, 5 of them being sacks. Equipped with a good burst, Browning shows the 1st step quickness coupled with good length to quickly make plays in the backfield. This is especially true when attacking the pocket, showing terrific core flexibility and instincts to shoot gaps and stay skinny through narrowing gaps. Excellent overall range and body control allow him to cover giant sections of green. A physical, downhill thumper that gets to top speed quickly, generating POP on contact when hitting a back. Not just quick, Browning shows fluidity in his movement with excellent overall lateral mobility to be able to handle different coverage situations.

Weaknesses: Suffered a bad core injury that he missed some time with during his junior campaign. I'm very concerned why Buckeyes coaches didn't trust him to start more games considering his athletic profile and how well he played when he was on the field. A 'FLASH'player that thrives on continually making big plays instead of being a reliable and consistent player. Due to his aggressive nature, he will take poor pursuit lanes to the football, and gap containment will sometimes be a problem for him. Play recognition and football IQ are a serious question mark with Browning, always in 'catch-up'mode instead of utilizing instincts and awareness to be in a good position.

Best Fit: 4-3 or 3-4 ILB

Player Ranking (1-100): 79.7 - Browning is a talented physical specimen that lacks some of the mental readiness to be an 'NFL Ready'prospect. He certainly flashes and has all the physical tools you'd like to see. He could be a good value on Day 2 of the draft. I'd take him in the 3rd.

6 - Nick Bolton - Missouri - 6'0 232 lbs

Strengths: Bolton has been a starter for the Tigers at the interior of their linebacker core during each of the last two seasons. He also has some experience playing as the SAM as well. Possessing a short and low center-of-gravity frame, Bolton utilizes his natural leverage to his advantage. Playing far more physical than his size would suggest, Bolton is quick to trigger and get downhill to deliver punishing blows to ball carriers. Good pre-snap awareness and snap anticipation to quickly recognize things develop and get a good jump at the snap of the ball. Stays patient at all times, allowing himself to maintain good gap discipline while funneling runners in the direction he wants them to go. Quickly processes things post-snap, doing a nice job of locating the football and working through the trash back to the ball. A fairly good athlete that covers ground in a flash, showing good makeup speed. Keeps his pads leveraged in the running game, allowing himself to generate good explosiveness through his lower body and finish tackles with reliability. Maximizes his frame when bringing down ball carriers outside of his frame. Shows good spatial awareness when in zone, knowing exactly who to pass and who to cover.

Weaknesses: Bolton lacks the ideal and prototypical build of a 4-3 MIKE linebacker, lacking the necessary length to play for many NFL defenses. Lack of length is evident when taking on blockers in space, failing to keep his frame clean through contact. This limits him in block deconstruction, failing to get off blocks quick enough. He's much more comfortable when being used in zone, failing to have the sticky abilities in man coverage to stick with his assignment. This in part, is due to his lack of agility and looseness through his lower half, struggling in transition. Not a great short-area quickness athlete and will fail to play in too much space. Will take overaggressive pathways to the football at times in pursuit, causing him to take himself out of plays.

Best Fit: 3-4 ILB

Player Ranking (1-100): 79.4 - Bolton lacks the ideal size and speed to play as a rangy 4-3 MIKE. But he absolutely can be a really solid starter in a 3-4 system. While he's not a dynamic athlete nor does he have a great frame, Bolton is tough! He's a leader, plays with a chip on his shoulder and he makes plays. He can be a dynamic special teams player from Day 1 too. 3rd round.

7 - Paddy Fisher – Northwestern - 6'4 239 lbs

Strengths: A 3-year starter and team captain for the Wildcats that has been highly productive during each campaign, tallying 315 tackles, 20 tackles for loss, 3 interceptions, 8 passes defended, and 9 forced fumbles. Featuring a physically-imposing build with a tall and filled out frame, Fisher shows NFL readiness. Plays with a nose for the ball, utilizing his field vision, range, and anticipation to put himself into good positions. A physical linebacker that plays with constant urgency, quickly getting downhill, wasting very steps, and rolling his hips through 2nd level contact. He has improved each season in his ability to break down and deconstruct blockers, showing violence in his upper-body to shed quickly. A large tackle radius that generally shows reliability to make tackles outside of his frame. Couples his physicality with his excellent grip strength to frequently rip at the ball, as evidenced by his 9 forced fumbles. A tone-setter for the middle of the defense. Utilizes his height to disrupt throwing lanes and maintains good awareness of passing lanes. Is comfortable when dropping in zone, gaining good depth on his drops, and keeping his eyes zeroed in on the QB's throwing motion.

Weaknesses: Fisher has improved in his ability to drop in zone, but he's still a work in progress with his overall coverage ability. He was never used in man coverage drops and likely would struggle if tasked with doing so. He's a marginal athlete that minimizes his deficiencies with his instincts and anticipation abilities. He will have pad level issues due to his frame, and he will have to focus on not raising them mid-play. When his pads are high, he's a very easy 2nd level contact to hit in space for pulling guards and centers.

Best Fit: MLB in either scheme

Player Ranking (1-100): 78.4 – I like Fisher quite a bit. He's a dynamic tone setter that has gotten better in each season at Northwestern. Some might argue he's not a 3-down linebacker because of his inefficiencies in coverage, but I believe he's good enough to play all 3 downs. 3rd round player.

8 - Nate Landman - Colorado - 6'3 235 lbs

Strengths: Landman was exceptional during his sophomore campaign, finishing with over 100 tackles, 4 sacks, 2 interceptions, and 1 forced fumble. Playing as the middle linebacker for the Buffaloes, Landman shows good overall toughness, leadership and instincts for the position. Possesses an impressive frame with above-average length. A tough as nails defender, constantly playing with a relentless and nonstop motor, showing tremendous urgency and intensity at all times. An excellent communicator that quickly organizes the defenses while recognizing things pre-snap. Landman shows good eye discipline and patience while diagnosing, maintaining good awareness, and read/react abilities to maintain proper positioning. Quick to trigger, Landman gets downhill in a flash while showing excellent reliability as a tackler to wrap-up with good positioning. One of the best tacklers in this draft class, Landman utilizes his entire tackle radius to make plays outside of his frame. Has all the traits of a dynamic and top-end special teams 'player at the next level.

Weaknesses: Landman has regressed production-wise during his college career since his sophomore season. Coaches will have to decide if that has to do mostly with Colorado's defensive changes, before his junior season, or just a lack of physical ability. Strictly a north/south mover that has limited movement skills and physical traits to be a 3-down player. His stiffness is apparent throughout his lower body when asked to transition in space. Lack of great closing speed limits his sideline-to-sideline mobility. A clunky runner that looks like a laborer when asked to play in large spaces.

Best Fit: 3-4 ILB, 4-3 MIKE or 4-3 SAM

Player Ranking (1-100): 74.6 - Landman is a really good football player that is quick to get downhill. Very physical and aggressive. He will at the very least be a dynamic special teams player on all units. But I believe he has the physical tools and experience to be a solid 2-down linebacker at the next level immediately. 4th round player.

9 - Tuf Borland- Ohio State - 6'0 229 lbs

Strengths: A 4-year contributor and two-time captain for the Buckeyes defense that has played in virtually every game during those 4 seasons, starting most of them the last 3 seasons. A consistent presence for their defense, Borland has shown incredible toughness in playing through injuries or while not fully recovered from previous injuries. A physical specimen, Borland is always around the ball, quickly triggering while reading his run keys and getting downhill. Plays with good play-recognition, quickly seeing things and anticipating allowing him to maintain good positioning. Does a nice job when playing through the trash, quickly locating the ball carrier and working in pursuit while keeping his frame clean. Limits false steps, rarely taking himself out of plays. Very powerful POP in his hands, jolting opponents with his powerful punch that leaves them staggering. Utilizes his short-area quickness and leg drive to deliver explosive pop-on contact when hitting ball carriers in the hall. Maintains good discipline on play-fakes and misdirection, rarely getting fooled.

Weaknesses: Borland isn't a traditional MIKE linebacker and lacks ideal size and length. His stubby frame limits his ability to get off blocks, getting stuck for far too long while failing to be able to disengage when playing head-on against blockers. Not a great point of attack player with a mediocre power profile overall. Limited as a 3-down player as he wasn't generally tested in a ton of coverage scenarios. In obvious passing situations, he was taken off the field by the coaches. Appeared to regress in production and overall play-making abilities his final two seasons. Lack of length limits his abilities to make plays outside of his frame. A solid athlete but isn't spectacular.

Best Fit: 4-3 MIKE or 3-4 ILB

Player Ranking (1-100): 73.9 - Borland is a decent middle linebacker prospect but his overall lack of size and length limits his ability to play with range and be used for all 3 downs at the next level. He will be an immediate high impact special teams player. 4th round pick.

10 - Ernest Jones - South Carolina - 6'2 230 lbs

Strengths: A 2-year starter for the Gamecocks who has been a reliable performer in the middle of their defense, racking up nearly 200 tackles the last two seasons combined. Jones is a good-sized linebacker that has the desired build to play in any defensive system. A downhill, physical thumper that loves the physical aspects of playing football, and it is clear in his style of play. A tackling machine that is almost always around the football due to his acute diagnosis skills and his mental processing abilities to quickly read and react. Quickly triggering in the run game, Jones shows no hesitancy in the hole when coming up to fill a gap. Smart and intelligent, Jones is a good defensive leader and signal caller, keeping his defense organized at all times. Works well in space, quickly sorting through the trash and working his way back towards the football. Plays with a 'HOT 'motor and brings it on every snap of the ball, showing good body control to play in space.

Weaknesses: Struggled with an injury towards the end of the season that he played through. Jones should continue to add muscle and weight to his frame to handle the roles of an inside linebacker. Despite his physicality, he appears to struggle when breaking down blocks in space, failing to utilize full extension to keep pulling linemen off of his frame. A decent athlete but he's much better in straight-line scenarios, when he has to work laterally, lower body stiffness appears significantly present. Will get exposed in some coverage scenarios due to lack of agility and speed and failing to have the ideal closing quickness to make up ground if initially granting any separation.

Best Fit: Middle Linebacker in any system

Player Ranking (1-100): 73.2 - Jones had a very solid last season with the Gamecocks and stood out despite playing on a team that won only a couple of games. He's a tough-as-nails linebacker that won't struggle with the physical areas of the next level. But he isn't an elite athlete and will struggle to play in too much space. 4th round player.

11 - K.J. Britt - Auburn - 6'0 239 lbs

Strengths: Britt took over as a starter during his junior season, greatly impressing while finishing with 68 tackles, 10 tackles for loss, 3.5 sacks, and 2 forced fumbles. A team leader and natural-born leader, Britt brings terrific intangibles to a defense. Built with a compact and wide frame, Britt brings NFL readiness to handle the rigors and physicality for the next level. Britt has played all over the linebacker front for the Tigers defense, playing mostly in the middle, but he's been used as a WILL and a SAM as well. The signal-caller for the defense, Britt brings football intelligence and communication abilities to a defense, constantly barking orders and making adjustments to his teammates. A real student of the game, Britt anticipates plays before they happen, allowing him to be in proper positions to make plays. Rarely getting fooled, Britt shows confidence in reading keys and being used as a QB spy against athletic QBs. A real gap penetrator that shows good acceleration to shoot gaps and get into the backfield as evidenced by his sack numbers and tackle for loss numbers. Looks very confident when handling zone coverage duties, maintaining good spatial awareness while limiting effective openings. Plays through his tackles well, rarely allowing ball carriers out of his grasps.

Weaknesses: Britt missed most of his final season due to surgery on his thumb after suffering ligament damage. Has only started 15 games during his career, playing almost exclusively in a backup role in his first couple of seasons. Lacks ideal length to block deconstruction, allowing pulling linemen to quickly win hand placement to blow him off the ball. His lack of length shows up when attempting to make plays outside of his frame as well, failing to have an ideal tackle radius. Appears to have some tightness when handling man coverage responsibilities, allowing quicker targets to quickly separate on him when breaking underneath. Takes overaggressive pathways to the ball carrier, taking him out of plays. Can get a bit too reckless while on the move, not appearing to always have the greatest of vision when working back in pursuit.

Best Fit: 4-3 MIKE or 3-4 ILB

Player Ranking (1-100): 71.3 - I love Britt's leadership and his play recognition abilities as a linebacker. While he's not a great athlete he's fairly solid when playing in zone. He has 3-down upside but at this point he's likely just a 2-down linebacker. 4th round player.

12 - Ventrell Miller - Florida - 6'1 230 lbs

Strengths: A 2-year starter for the Gators at middle linebacker and before that, he has been a core special teams player. Played mostly at MIKE in the Gators 3-4 defense, Miller possesses the athletic ability to play in any defensive system. Very quick when playing in a straight line, showing good short-area quickness to close quickly on plays. Allows things to develop in front of him, maintaining sound gap discipline and integrity. Disciplined when in coverage, showing good decisions, and rarely being fooled by misdirections or play-action type plays. When in coverage, he appears to maintain proper spacing to minimize available openings. Solid range allows him to play sideline-to-sideline. Excellent blitzer that allows his acceleration, timing, and core flexibility to shoot gaps and get quickly into the backfield. Strong upper-body allows him to take on blocks when his leverage is right, and make plays on the ball carrier. Good when working through space, keeping his frame clean, and finding his way to the ball carrier. Experienced in man coverage, showing the closing speed to remain in the hip pockets of running backs down the field.

Weaknesses: Was suspended his entire freshman season for his involvement in the fraud scandal. His overall instincts and ability to read/react quickly to things are just average at best. He tends to be a tick late to the play due to poor processing abilities. Lacks great overall length for the position and he will be eaten up at the point of attack by pulling linemen, failing to have the length to keep his frame clean. Needs to do a better job of dropping his pads when attacking a ball carrier, causing him to miss some tackles or get dragged for additional yardage. His overall motor doesn't appear the best and he fails to always work in pursuit, seemingly giving up on plays. A bit of a stiff lateral athlete, appearing to need to gear down extensively before changing directions.

Best Fit: 3-4 ILB and special teams '

Player Ranking (1-100): 66.4 - Miller will be a terrific special teams player for a team from Day 1. He could eventually be a starter in a 3-4 defense for some teams. 5th round player.

13 - Drew Seers - Lindenwood - 6'1 227 lbs

Strengths: An All-American Division II player for school Lindenwood, Seers has been a reliable presence for their defense the last 3 years and on their special teams 'units. He was also used as the teams 'punter as well. An absolute tackling machine, finishing with nearly 200 tackles during his junior season. Seers is a smart and instinctual linebacker that quickly reads things pre and post-snap. He plays with tremendous urgency and a relentless motor. His read and reaction abilities allow him to constantly be in good positions to make plays, breaking quickly on the ball carrier. Launches himself into ball carriers with his compact frame. Utilizes his natural leverage abilities to stay leveraged in space, staying underneath pulling lineman in the run game, while keeping his frame clean. Shows zero hesitancy in the hole in the running game, quickly crashing down hard inside and utilizing good wrap-up fundamentals to bring ball carriers down.

Weaknesses: Seers is a bit undersized to play on the inside at the next level, lacking elite height, weight, or length. Transitioning from Division II could be a major challenge for Seers. He lacks great overall physical traits, failing to have ideal athleticism or range. Has improved some in pass coverage but he still lacks ideal lateral movement skills to handle man responsibilities, and he looks lost while in zone drops as well.

Best Fit: 3-4 ILB

Player Ranking (1-100): 63.4 - Seers is an intriguing small-school prospect that could be a really nice special teams player from Day 1 with developmental upside to playing a role as a 3-4 ILB down the road. 6th round player.

14 - Justin Hilliard - Ohio State - 6'1 227 lbs

Strengths: A former five-star recruit and a sixth-year player with the Buckeyes, Hilliard has had an injury-plagued career. He was granted an additional year of eligibility due to his myriad of injuries. Hilliard has been a major special teams contributor practically since Day 1 on campus. Hilliard is stacked physically, possessing a power-packed frame with very little body fat on his frame. A twitchy linebacker that possesses solid overall movement skills with good lateral range to play sideline-to-sideline. A high football IQ allows him to quickly recognize things to put himself in good positions, showing good read and react abilities. Shows good hand strength and POP to be able to keep his frame clean when working through the trash, rarely getting hung up on blocks. A reliable wrap-up tackler that fully maximizes his tackle radius to make plays away from his frame. Shows good zone fundamentals when dropping, playing with a good understanding of spatial awareness.

Weaknesses: There's no getting away from his injury past, having missed game time during every year of his 6-year career, including 3 season-ending injuries. Even when he did play, he's almost exclusively been a rotational player. A bit of a tweener that has played at several different linebacker spots, failing to settle in at any particular spot. Appears to have some stiffness when asked to change directions, likely due to multiple lower-body injuries. Quicker than he is fast, lacking ideal athleticism and range to play as a MIKE in a 4-3. Struggled when asked to handle man coverage responsibilities, lacking the recovery speed to catch-up if initially beaten.

Best Fit: 3-4 ILB or 4-3 SAM

Player Ranking (1-100): 61.4 - Hilliard was a glorified high school prospect before having a very underwhelming college career due to all the injuries. He showed up some for Ohio State in his final year, having some big-time plays in the playoff game against Clemson. It's hard to believe he's completely past all his injuries but he's worth king in the 6th round. Could be a nice reliable rotational linebacker and special teams 'stud.

15 - Zach McCloud - Miami - 6'2 235 lbs

Strengths: A rare 4-year starter and former four-star high school recruit for the Hurricanes that has played in the heart of their defense the last several seasons. Positional versatility is the name of the game for McCloud, as he's played several different linebacker roles for the Hurricanes during his time. McCloud is a physical presence that will inch forward pre-snap and get downhill in a flash. A good and reliable tackler that shows finishing ability and good fundamentals, rarely missing a tackle. Utilizes built-up momentum to generate good torque from his lower power to drive runners down. Good upper-body power allows him to fight through blockers, rarely staying sustained through contact. Keeps his shoulder pads down through contact, remaining in control and leveraged.

Weaknesses: Had a left wrist injury in 2018 that caused him to miss spring practice. Redshirted in 2019 due to not getting any playtime by Hurricanes coaches. Size doesn't match his physicality and McCloud is a bit undersized, lacking the ideal length to disrupt passing lanes. An average and strictly north/south athlete that shows stiffness throughout his frame to play laterally. Very limited experience or natural ability to play in any kind of coverage. Easily manipulated by smart QB's that understand how to utilize their eyes, getting McCloud completely out of position while in coverage.

Best Fit: 4-3 MIKE or 3-4 ILB

Player Ranking (1-100): 56.4 - McCloud had a much better senior year this season but he's still limited as a 3-down player. His best chance of making an NFL roster will be on special teams.

TOP-10 Middle Linebackers

1. Micah Parsons
2. Dylan Moses
3. Cameron McGrone
4. Jamin Davis
5. Baron Browning
6. Nick Bolton

7. Paddy Fisher
8. Nate Landman
9. Tuf Borland
10. Ernest Jones

Chapter 12

Outside Linebackers
(Strong Side or Weak Side)

1 - Chazz Surratt - North Carolina - 6'2 227 lbs

Strengths: The former starting QB for the Tar Heels before transitioning and playing his final two years at linebacker, showing tremendous promise and upside for the position. An athletically-built linebacker that shows long limbs and good overall body composition with little unnecessary body fat. Surratt is only going to get better with additional game time, showing one of the higher ceilings in this draft class. One of the most impressive aspects of Surratt's game is his pass-rush ability, finishing with 31 pressures during his junior campaign. He shows the core flexibility, ankle flexion, and loose limbs to turn the corner and continuously threaten both outside and inside rush lanes. A really impressive athlete that shows the lower body explosiveness to spring himself in any direction in space. Possesses the range and body control to cover in acres of space. Looks outstanding in zone drops, showing comfort, awareness of passing lanes, and fluidity in his drops. Plays with urgency and little hesitancy when asked to fulfill an assignment or close down a pursuit lane. Really impressive diagnosis abilities allow him to utilize his athleticism to put himself into great positions.

Weaknesses: Was suspended for 4 games during his sophomore campaign for selling team shoes. He also suffered a bad wrist injury as well during that season. He is still learning the position and that is evident in his inabilities to consistently deconstruct blockers to keep his frame clean while in space. Tackling is a problem for Surratt as he's very inconsistent. There will be times when he looks reliable and other times when he fails to wrap up consistently in space.

Best Fit: 4-3 WILL

Player Ranking (1-100): 85.8 - I like Surratt quite a bit. He seems like he's always at the right place at the right time. His raw athletic gifts coupled with his pass-rushing ability and natural cover awareness skills makes him a prime 1st round quality player. He's only going to get better and I couldn't believe how good he was at linebacker practically from Day 1.

2 - Jabril Cox - LSU - 6'3 233 lbs

Strengths: A 3-year starter for North Dakota State before transitioning to LSU and playing his final year for the Tigers. Cox has a long, rangy, and athletic frame to be an ideal modern and versatile linebacker for today's NFL. Cox is an athletic freak, displaying insane explosiveness and overall athleticism. He utilizes his explosive traits to play sideline-to-sideline, showing outstanding range to play at every level of a defense. Relentless while in pursuit, utilizing his closing speed to make plays in the running game from the backside. A fluid athlete that shows loose hips and flexibility to cross the field without needing to gear down while in transition. Shows upside in block deconstruction, utilizing full extension to lock out his arms and keep blockers off of his frame. Excellent and natural in coverage, utilizing his length to disrupt at the catch point and force pinpoint passes by the QB. Comfortable when lining up against backs in the flat or even play man coverage against tight ends. Does a great job of working back towards the ball, taking acute angles to the football when working through the trash. Shows to be proficient in the mental side of the game, reading his keys and rarely making any mistakes. A large tackle radius allows him to force poor running lanes, showing the ability to close off the perimeter. Shows some ability to attack the pocket as an extra rusher on 3rd downs, utilizing his terrific closing bursts to push the QB off of his spot.

Weaknesses: An inconsistent tackler in space and will frustrate with his inability to bring down securely. While he does flash the ability to breakdown blockers, he needs to continue to add functional strength to his frame to handle working through blocks at the next level. Very narrow bone structure with not too much room for added muscle on his frame. Lower-body strength is minimal at best, and if he's reached at the 2nd level by a pulling guard, he will get engulfed.

Best Fit: WILL LB in a 4-3

Player Ranking (1-100): 84.5 - Cox is an outstanding athlete that is a rare size, length, and speed maven. His coverage skills are off the charts for a linebacker. While he needs significant power and functional strength added to his frame, his ability to play 3 downs and close down entire sections of the field makes a versatile defensive piece. 2nd round player.

3 - Jeremiah Owusu-Koramoah - Notre Dame- 6'1 225 lbs

Strengths: A 2-year starter at outside linebacker for the Fighting Irish, Owusu-Koramoah has proven to be the perfect commodity for today's NFL. A small but athletically-built linebacker that plays with rare physical tools for the position. An explosive athlete that will immediately make a defense faster, possessing ridiculous blur speed. Played as a 'jack of all trades 'player for the Irish defense, playing in the slot at times and rushing as an extra rusher at other times. An impressive cover guy that shows the ranginess and fluidity through his movements to turn and run with tight ends up the field without losing any ground. Excellent body control while taking acute pursuit angles to the football, often beating backs to the spot. Does a nice job of keeping his frame clean through traffic and navigating through the trash. Don't let his size fool you, he is a strong kid that plays bigger than his listed size and is a reliable tackler in space. Quick to trigger, he sees and recognizes things pre-snap and then shoots gaps and makes plays. This is especially notable when he gets sent to attack the pocket, showing impressive short-area quickness to quickly generate pressure from all angles.

Weaknesses: At times he has a bad tendency to get into too many personal battles while breaking down blocks, failing to locate the ball carrier, and missing the opportunity to set the edge. Will over pursue plays at times, running past the play. Some teams may be worried about his overall lack of size, failing to have traditional linebacker size, and is built more like a safety. Will get overaggressive in coverage, leading to some misses when he attempts to jam at the line of scrimmage. Not a guy you want having to handle or consistently take on blocks in space, he will get overpowered due to a lack of elite lower-body strength.

Best Fit: 4-3 WILL

Player Ranking (1-100): 83.2 - Owusu-Koramoah is a talented athlete that brings so much athleticism and playmaking abilities to a defensive. He will be loved by the coaching staff because of his hardworking and instinctual abilities to play all over the defense. Love this kid. 2nd round player.

4 - Zaven Collins - Tulsa - 6'4 260 lbs

Strengths: A mostly 3-year starter for Tulsa that has consistently been one of their best players both on special teams and on defense. A well-built prospect that shows a good overall build for the next-level with good height, size, and power through his frame. His versatility is tremendous, oftentimes lining up standing up as a linebacker, moving inside as an interior linebacker, or putting his hand in the dirt and rushing. Appears to be very comfortable when dropping in space, showing good spatial awareness and comfort when handling zone coverage. Terrific instincts, showing good read/react abilities to place himself around the ball constantly. Agility and lateral quickness are prevalent throughout his frame, showing the ability to change directions seamlessly. Has the movement skills and fluidity in the transition to even cover some larger receivers or tight ends in man-to-man situations. Rare ball skills for a player of his size, showing good body control in space to contort his body to makes plays with his back to the ball. Aggressive at the catch point as evidenced by his interceptions tallies and pass breakouts. Inches forward on clear running plays, reading his keys and showing good play-recognition abilities. Elite mental processing and twitchy reflexes allow him to beat backs to the spot and generally showing good reliability as an open-field tackler. High IQ football player that was relied upon as the signal-caller and defensive team leader.

Weaknesses: As a pass rusher, Collins is raw and his lack of top production signifies that. He doesn't possess much of a pass-rush plan and lacks refinement with his hand usage. Tends to be more of a 'avoid 'player in space as opposed to consistently taking on guys head-on. Lacks great hand strength to offer much 'POP' when taking on pulling lineman. Will struggle consistently getting off blocks, failing to quickly shed sustain. Not a downhill physical player in the run game.

Best Fit: 4-3 off-ball or 3-4 standup

Player Ranking (1-100): 82.0 - Collins has been tremendous for Tulsa the last few seasons. He's a rare cover linebacker that possesses defensive lineman size. He can be used as a chess piece for a defensive at the next level. I believe he can play in any system but his best attribute right now is his coverage ability and he needs to be utilized to be able to do that. 2nd round player.

5 - Garret Wallow - TCU - 6'2 230 lbs

Strengths: A 3-year starter for the Horned Frogs, Wallow has been an unstoppable force along their defense, playing mostly in a nickel coverage role. A former safety that has worked hard to put 20+ pounds on his frame since entering the TCU program. A perfect fit for today's modern fit NFL, Wallow possesses a safeties' frame with good compactness and toughness throughout. An absolute tackling machine, Wallow has combined for well over 200 tackles the last two seasons, despite playing in one abbreviated season. A 'jack of all trades 'athlete that plays best in space, bringing tremendous versatility to a defense. Aggressive post-catch showing a good knack for ripping out the ball and causing fumbles. Looseness is prevalent through his lower body as he looks so smooth when asked to cross-field and change directions. Dynamic when triggering downhill and blitzing, showing terrific instincts, timing, and short-area quickness to get into the backfield. Wallow excels in all types of coverage scenarios. In zone, he possesses a natural feel for depths, showing good spatial awareness and instincts to limit available spacing. While in man, he shows the movement skills and the speed to handle tight ends or running backs with relative ease.

Weaknesses: Still relatively new to the position and is a bit raw when it comes to some of the finer nuances of playing the position. Tends to be more of a 'react 'player that always plays in catch-up mode as opposed to having natural levels of instincts to be in the right place at the right time. His overaggressive nature causes him to attempt to jump routes and crash down hard on play-fakes or misdirection-type plays, making him susceptible to double-moves. Doesn't limit movement or steps when in pursuit, taking far too many false steps. Play strength isn't always ideal, as he will struggle routinely tackling bigger backs in the hole, showing some hesitancy in the hole.

Best Fit: WILL LB (Weak-side LB)

Player Ranking (1-100): 81.4 - Wallow is still a 'work in progress 'but his athleticism and coverage abilities make him a very very intriguing fit for today's NFL. His lack of reliability in open-field situations is a bit scary but he makes A LOT of plays. 2nd round player.

6 - Kuony Deng - California - 6'6 250 lbs

Strengths: A JUCO transfer from Community College that started at linebacker immediately after transitioning to Cal. Dang was incredibly successful right away, starting in every game and finishing with 120+ tackles, 8 passes defended, and 3 sacks. Built with rare overall size and tremendous length, Deng is a defensive mismatch no matter where he plays. A dynamic and explosive athlete that shows the rare fluidity, pure speed, and sideline-to-sideline ability to be a dynamic defense presence wherever he plays. Loose-hipped in space, showing more than just linear athletic characteristics, displaying tremendous agility and lateral mobility. Not just an athlete, Deng also packs power through his upper body. Impressive when used as a blitzer where he showcases his timing and instincts to attack the pocket. When playing in space, Deng has SHOCK hand strength to deliver striking blows to unsuspecting blockers. He does a good job of fighting through blocks and keeping his frame clean as he works through the trash in the middle of the field. Loads of experience when dropping in space, showing good awareness of passing lanes with the long arms to contort in space to knock down throws. He does a nice job of utilizing his length and tackle radius to slow down runners and cut off perimeters lanes, forcing runners back inside.

Weaknesses: A slender frame that is still growing into his body and could stand to gain additional mass to play inside at the next level. Suffered a season-ending injury in his sophomore year in community college that was undisclosed. The mental areas of the game are where Deng struggles, mostly due to his overaggressive nature. His pursuit lanes will at times leave something to be desired, not always reading his keys accurately and attacking the wrong gaps. Mental processing abilities are suspect, biting very hard on QB fakes and play-action, leaving entire sides of the field exposed. An inconsistent tackler that needs to do a better job of dropping his pads when wrapping-up, allowing additional yards after contact on too many occasions. In coverage, he shows inconsistencies and a lack of confidence to challenge the receiver at the catch point, failing to showcase any kind of ball skills. A bit of a tweeter that lacks a true position at this point.

Best Fit: 4-3 SAM or 4-3 MIKE

Player Ranking (1-100): 79.3 - Deng doesn't have a true position at the next level but he might be best suited in either a 4-3 SAM or MIKE role. As a MIKE, he can utilize his range and playmaking abilities to cover loads of space. As a SAM he could be effective when taking on blocks with his upper body power. 3rd round player.

7 - Monty Rice - Georgia - 6'0 238 lbs

Strengths: A 3-year starter at inside linebacker for the Bulldogs that rose to prominence following his stellar junior campaign where he finished with 90 tackles. A compact and thickly-built kid that shows the size and football IQ to be a schematically-versatile guy that can be attractive in any defensive system with his skill set. A downhill thumper that will quickly get downhill in the run game and lay the wood. Rice is a rangy athlete that shows the terrific range and body control with a good 1st step to catch up and close giant gaps down the field. Does a nice job of or sorting through the trash and taking good pursuit lanes to the football? Maximizes his frame with his aggressive mindset, showing the physicality and strength at the point of attack that will translate at the next level. Very comfortable when working in space in coverage, showing proficiency both in zone and man. Shows looseness throughout his lower body to change direction without needing to gear down. Used quite a bit to attack the interior of the pocket, generating several interior pressures with good acceleration and timing.

Weaknesses: Missed the final 5 games of the 2018 season with a knee issue. While the functional strength is there, Rice lacks ideal measurements for many scouting departments that will require certain attributes. Inconsistent tackler, will occasionally fail to drop his pads and allow additional yardage after contact. Needs to do a better job of breaking down blocks in the run game, far too often getting stuck when playing head-on. Athleticism is good but needs to do a better job of reading his keys and recognizing things sooner.

Best Fit: 4-3 WILL or 3-4 ILB

Player Ranking (1-100): 77.5 - I like Rice best as a 4-3 WILL (weak-side) but he can also play as a 3-4 ILB and be very good there too. He flashes impresses coverage ability overall but he needs to do a better job of seeing things develop quicker. This will allow him to make more plays. 3rd round player.

8 - Merlin Robertson - Arizona State - 6'3 250 lbs

Strengths: Robertson has been a starter for the Sun Devils since his true freshman season in 2018, producing some big-time moments for their defense throughout. A well-built prospect that has an excellent build with good compactness and length for an interior linebacker in any scheme. Came onto the scene as a freshman and looked like a man amongst boys at times with his overall athletic ability, competitive drive, and leadership abilities. A very good sideline-to-sideline athlete that shows an impressive secondary burst to click-and-close and take acute angles to the football. Does a nice job of working through the trash and keeping his frame clean to evade blockers. Utilizes his built up momentum and lower body torque to generate explosive pop-on contact when delivering blows to ball carriers. A smart football player that does a nice job of reading his keys and diagnosing both pre and post-snap to allow him to be in good positions to make plays. Has impressed with snaps when used as a blitzer, showing good snap timing to jump the count and quickly generate interior pressure.

Weaknesses: After being one of the best freshman defenders in the PAC-10, Robertson hasn't quite improved his levels of production. Struggles when dropping into coverage, not having natural movement skills or understanding spatial awareness or proper positioning in his zone drops. An upright player that plays with a narrow base, leaving his chest plate far too exposed for pulling lineman. He struggles with balance when attempting to play through blockers due to his lack of consistent leverage. Lacks great flexibility and lateral movement ability, getting hung up on blocks and staying for far too long. Doesn't have as much functional strength as his size suggests he should, lacking the hand strength or downhill nature to fight through blockers.

Best Fit: 4-3 SAM

Player Ranking (1-100): 73.2 - I like Robertson as a SAM linebacker that can occasionally be used in coverage and occasionally be used to attack the pocket. He presents real 3-down ability. He's a natural pass rusher and had 5 sacks his freshman season. A good overall athlete that should immediately win special teams reps.

9 - Tony Fields II - West Virginia - 6'1 222 lbs

Strengths: A 3-year starter in the Pac-12 for Arizona before transitioning to West Virginia and playing his final season of college. Fields has been tremendous and consistent for both the Wildcats and the Mountaineers, playing in every single game during his college career, finishing with at/around 100 tackles each campaign. Has proven the ability to generate significant pressure when being used as a pass rusher, both inside and outside. Plays the position completely in control, remaining on the balls of his feet and instinctually reacting. Always playing with a 'HOT 'motor, Fields plays with terrific intensity and urgency. Sees things develop quickly, showing terrific eye discipline. Fields is comfortable in coverage, showing proficiency and fluidity throughout his movements to cover both in man and zone situations. When in man coverage, Fields fights for everything, showing terrific hand strength and timing to rip at the ball and disrupt the balls 'arrival. Always in pursuit with good catch-up speed to work back towards the ball carrier and close down. Takes good and direct pathways to the football, wasting very little movement and showing ranginess in his overall movement skills.

Weaknesses: An undersized linebacker at the college level that will need to gain considerable gain and bulk to play at the next level, especially in an inside role. Good overall athleticism but lack of lateral mobility can slow him down when not playing north/south. Lack of overall power and strength is especially evident when attempting to work through blocks, getting completely bullied at the point of attack. When in coverage he tends to always keep his back towards the ball instead of getting his head turned around to play the football. Is prone to some poor tackle misses against bigger ball carriers.

Best Fit: 4-3 WILL or MIKE

Player Ranking (1-100): 72.4 - I like Fields the best at WILL linebacker because I think he possesses the movement skills and the upside as a coverage linebacker that doesn't have to fight through blockers as much. He can utilize his quickness and closing speed to always be around the football. I like Fields and he's incredibly reliable and consistent! Always around the football. 4th round player.

10 - Amen Ogbongbemiga - Oklahoma State - 6'1 235 lbs

Strengths: A two-year starter and defensive team captain in the middle of the Cowboys defense, Ogbongbemiga has been fantastic in each of those seasons. In those combined years, he finished with 180 tackles, 20.5 tackles for loss and 7.5 sacks, and 4 forced fumbles. Born in Nigeria, Ogbongbemiga is the cousin of NFL player Emmanuel Ogbah. Built with an athletic frame, Ogbongbemiga is built more like a safety than a traditional linebacker. A modern linebacker that displays twitchiness through his frame. Shows solid range and sideline-to-sideline ability with good change of directional ability. Makes up ground quickly while in pursuit with good recovery speed to close down. A tackling machine that utilizes his natural instincts and play-recognition abilities to put himself at the right place at the right time. Not always the prettiest of tacklers, but he gets the job done more often than not. A very effective blitzer that does a nice job of working stunts, showing terrific closing bursts and timing to get home. Has extensive cover experience both in man coverage and in zone. He looks far more comfortable in man coverage. Remains disciplined on most occasions with trained eyes, rarely biting on misdirection or play-fakes. Plays with a nonstop motor.

Weaknesses: Approaches tackles far too upright, causing him to allow additional yards after contact. Struggles while in zone, failing to have an ideal feel for proper depth on his drops. He lacks proper adequate spatial awareness, frequently leaving big gaps in coverage. Undersized as a traditional MIKE in a 4-3, lacking the ideal girth or the length. Struggles when having to take on blocks in the run game, failing to offer any kind of deconstruction abilities to shed.

Best Fit: 4-3 WILL (Weak-side)

Player Ranking (1-100): 72.1 - Ogbongbemiga is a tackling machine that has a place on a football team due to his athleticism, extensive cover experience, and effectiveness as a rusher. He's best suited either as a 4-3 WILL. This will allow him to run free to the ball, where he truly excels. 4th round player.

11 - Pete Werner - Ohio State - 6'3 242 lbs

Strengths: A 3-year starter for the Buckeyes at off-ball linebacker, playing in the SAM role for the defense. Werner has been a consistent presence for the last 3 years, showing similar levels of production during each campaign. A thickly-built prospect that shows NFL size and readiness physically for the next level. Physicality is the name of the game for Werner, displaying tremendous upper-body strength to take on blocks and deliver some powerful 'POP ON 'contact with his hands to keep his frame clean. Werner plays with a 'HOT 'motor, showing terrific urgency and suddenness to his game. Reads his keys well to quickly process and diagnose, allowing himself to be in good positions. Showed during his sophomore season an ability to get home on blitzes, finishing with 3 sacks. Has a ton of experience in coverage, showing some instincts and discipline to handle tight ends on shallow routes. A reliable wrap-up tackler that utilizes good fundamentals and technique.

Weaknesses: While experienced in coverage, Werner's lower body stiffness is exposed, most notably in man coverage. His lack of flexibility and fluidity limits his ability to play laterally in all aspects of the game, including playing in too much space. Doesn't always take the most direct pathways to the football while in pursuit. Overall athleticism is subpar as a whole, lacking the true sideline-to-sideline abilities to be a true 3-down player at the next level.

Best Fit: 4-3 SAM Linebacker

Player Ranking (1-100): 71.2 - Werner is a physical downhill thumper that will offer 2-down ability in 4-3 defenses. He's shown some rush ability at times and is experienced in coverage, but he lacks the athleticism and lateral movement skills to be asked to do so effectively at the next level. 4th round player.

12 - Riley Cole - South Alabama - 6'2 242 lbs

Strengths: A 5th year senior for Sun-Belt program South Alabama, Cole has started 3 of his last 4 seasons for the program after missing most of his sophomore season due to injury. Cole was an absolute production machine his final year, finishing with 96 tackles, 6.5 tackles for loss, 2 sacks, and 2 forced fumbles. Originally recruited by Alabama, Cole is a work out warrior, proving to be a rare athletic specimen. Cole played in a hybrid role, being used both to rush the passer and as an inside linebacker. A versatile chess piece that has proven to be effective in a wide range of coverage situations (both zone and man), showing outstanding sideline-to-sideline range and agility to cover tight ends or running backs out of the backfield. Closing speed is evident with his ability to beat running backs to the perimeter lanes. When playing as a rusher, Cole utilizes his terrific get-off to quickly arc the corner and threaten outside rush lanes. Possesses the natural instincts that allow him to beat blockers to the action. Plays with relentless energy, almost always in pursuit and around the football. Possesses all the physical traits to be a dynamic special teams player immediately.

Weaknesses: Has suffered multiple injuries during his career, including tearing his ACL during his freshman year. He suffered another bad lower-body injury his sophomore campaign causing him to miss all but a few games. Can be overaggressive at times, taking poor pursuit angles to the football while chasing the ball carrier. A bit of a tweener that lacks a true defined position for the next level. Needs to continue to gain functional strength, weight, and power to be able to handle the point of attack stuff in the running game. Hasn't competed against the top-tier competition in the Sun-Belt.

Best Fit: WILL LB and special teams maven

Player Ranking (1-100): 70.1 - Cole is an intriguing prospect that has the developmental upside to be a real game-changer at the next level. I love his upside as a WILL (Weakside OLB) in a 4-3 system. His athleticism, rangiess, and coverage ability can be maximized there. He will have some challenges with the jump up in competition but if he can gain some experience in a defined position and finally find a home, he will excel. 4th round player.

13 - Derrick Barnes - Purdue - 6'1 245 lbs

Strengths: Barnes has been a 4-year significant contributor to the Purdue defense, splitting time up at both linebacker and defensive end. He's had solid production during his career, finishing amongst the leaders on the Purdue defense both in tackles and in sacks during his sophomore and junior seasons. Featuring a stout and wide frame, Barnes has more than enough power and strength in his power-packed body. As a rusher, Barnes is very effective when working in combination with other linemen on stunts. He has a knack for timing the snap count showing good instincts and reaction times to get a good jump. Utilizes his natural leverage advantage to get underneath the pads of blockers, keeping his frame clean. A downhill thumper that excels at the physical aspects of the game, showing good point of attack power to handle double teams. Very good upper-body strength allows him to deconstruct while taking on blocks, keeping his frame clean through contact. A reliable tackler that shows good wrap-up abilities once he gets his hands on a runner.

Weaknesses: Unfortunately, due to transitioning back and forth between positions, Barnes hasn't had significant time to develop at linebacker. A bit of a tweener that lacks a true refined position. Has a bit of a stubby build, lacking ideal length to play in too much space or to handle consistent rushing off the edge at the next level. This lack of length limits him when attempting to make plays outside of his frame, lacking the tackle radius to close perimeter lanes. Lacks ideal athleticism to be a great rusher at the next level, failing to have the short-area quickness or explosive twitch to offer much as a 3-4 OLB.

Best Fit: 4-3 SAM or 3-4 ILB and special teams' maven

Player Ranking (1-100): 68.4 - Barnes lacks a true position and I see his best fit as a 4-3 SAM with his abilities to play through blocks. He's a 'tough as nails' prospect that shows excellent POP in his hands to keep his frame clean when working back towards the ball. He can occasionally be used to rush the passer as a SAM, allowing him to potentially be a 3-down player. Not a player you want handling too much space. 5th round player.

14 - Isaiah McDuffie - Boston College - 6'1 224 lbs

Strengths: A 3-year starter for BC, McDuffie capped off his college career with another stellar season in 2020, finishing with over 100 tackles, 6.5 tackles for loss, 3 sacks, and an interception. McDuffie started his college career as a terrific special teams player. An undersized off-ball linebacker, McDuffie is a modern fit for today's NFL, showing tremendous versatility. McDuffie routinely will line up in man coverage, even covering receivers at times. He's a terrific athlete showing fluid movement abilities to chase-and-run against dynamic receivers, showing good change of directional abilities and agility. Also shows the ability to line up in the box and play the run or be used as a QB spy. In the running game, McDuffie plays with tenacity and a violent downhill nature, utilizing his explosiveness to generate devastating pop-on contact. Excellent while in pursuit, quickly locating the ball carrier and working his way back. Plays with nonstop urgency and a relentless motor.

Weaknesses: Missed most of his junior season after suffering a knee injury. Has some issues with gap assignments and eye discipline as he repeatedly struggled on RPOs against running QB's that could cause him to bite hard. Struggles consistently breaking down as a tackler if he doesn't have built-up momentum. Very undersized and still could stand to gain additional bulk at the next level. Not a guy you want having to take on pulling lineman at the 2nd level struggles shedding and getting off blocks when he isn't able to run free.

Best Fit: 4-3 WILL (Weak-side linebacker)

Player Ranking (1-100): 67.3 - McDuffie is a really good all-around athlete that displays good versatility to eventually be a 3-down linebacker. He had a tremendous season this year for BC. He's likely going to need to win a role on special teams early on. He can push for snaps on defense likely by his second season in the NFL. 5th round player.

15 - Antjuan Simmons - Michigan State - 5'11 225 lbs

Strengths: A 4-year contributor to the Spartans defense and 2-year starter, Simmons has been the leading tackler and team leader for their defense during each of the last two seasons. Simmons displays a lean and athletic-frame, ideally suited to play an outside role at the next level. A tackle for loss machine, Simmons utilizes his natural read/react abilities and short-area quickness to quickly diagnose and make plays behind the line of scrimmage. A very fluid athlete that shows a good understanding of how to play in acres of space, flying around the football and showing good range and body control. Keeps his pads leveraged at all times, allowing him to get skinny and play through narrow gaps and make plays coming downhill in the hole. A very good and natural blitzer that shows good instincts and timing to get into the backfield quickly. Relentless in pursuit, understanding how to keep his frame clean through contact to work in the middle part of the field. Despite being undersized, he is fearless in the hole, showing 0 hesitancy. Has extensive experience both in zone and in man coverage scenarios.

Weaknesses: Played in a unique defensive system for the Spartans with only 2 linebackers on the field and will likely have to transition to an outside role at the next level. While he's gained substantial muscle and weight the last few seasons, he's still very undersized at this point and coaches will want him to completely maximize his frame. Lacks the length to make plays outside of his frame or seal off perimeter runs. Quicker than he is fast, and could struggle making up ground in coverage if initially beaten. Doesn't always read his keys well and can be overly aggressive with his pursuit angles, leading to some bad misses or exposed gaps on the field. Easily manipulated in pass coverage and will bite hard on play-action type plays. Struggles when attempting to play face-up against pulling linemen, getting blown off the ball in the run game, failing to disengage.

Best Fit: Off-ball linebacker. Ideally a 4-3 WILL (Weak-side)

Player Ranking (1-100): 65.6 - Simmons is an intriguing prospect that has immediate upside on special teams. While he's a good athlete, he's not a great athlete, despite being significantly undersized. With too much additional muscle mass or bulk, he could lose the athleticism he does have. There's no denying he is an instinctual football player that makes a ton of plays behind the line of scrimmage. He's versatile with his coverage experience as well. 5th round player.

16 - Anthony Hines III - Texas A&M - 6'3 230 lbs

Strengths: A former five-star recruit that saw significant game time during his true freshman season, greatly impressing immediately and being a part of the All-SEC freshman team. Hines then improved even more in his only year of starting as a sophomore with over 70 tackles and 10.5 tackles for loss. Hines is a physical presence that has a nice frame with continued size for additional growth. A very good player against the run that couples his aggressive downhill nature with good short-area quickness to deliver devastating blows to ball carriers. A reliable tackler that can make plays outside of his frame. Shows decent range and body control when working in space and sorting through the trash. Possesses the upper-body power to handle playing through blockers, showing some disengagement power in his hands to deconstruct blocks. Has the lower body strength to handle gap assignments without getting blown off the ball in the run game.

Weaknesses: Hines opted out of the 2020 season. He also missed the entire 2018 campaign after suffering a bad leg injury in camp. Hines played in the middle of the Aggies defense but will likely have to transition to an outside role at the next level. Despite his high school accomplishments, he failed to play in enough snaps to show 'NFL Readiness.' He was exposed quite a bit when having to handle coverage responsibilities, looking out of his depth, and getting exposed. Needs to do a better job of keeping his pads leveraged, playing far too high in space, and easily getting reached by pulling blockers.

Best Fit: 4-3 SAM or 3-4 ILB

Player Ranking (1-100): 56.4 - The frustrating thing for evaluators with Hines is there is very very little tape to get of the player. While he flashes physical prowess and upside as an athlete, his lack of experience is very troublesome. Unfortunately, he opted out this year because I believe it could have helped him prove his NFL credentials. He's a 7th round player based on tape.

17 - Grant Stuard - Houston - 6'0 230 lbs

Strengths: Stuard is a jack of all trades defender for Houston that has been moved all over the place on defense for them. Experience playing on all the special teams' units. On defense, Stuard has been moved all over, playing in the nickel and then as a WILL outside linebacker during his final season. A versatile chess piece that possesses the football intelligence to be used in a variety of roles at the next level. A terrific special teams player due in part to his aggression, toughness, and physicality, showing 0 hesitancy to play through blockers. This trait shows up at linebacker as well, playing with a fearlessness when filling gaps and plugging holes to trigger downhill. Stuard plays with good read/react ability, quickly recognizing things and then utilizing his short-area quickness to quickly close down in pursuit. He brings 3-down ability with his vast experience in man and zone coverage, routinely lining up and handling tight ends and slots. Shows the cover instincts and lateral agility to mirror in space, playing with quick feet and route-recognition abilities. A solid athlete that can play with some sideline-to-sideline range.

Weaknesses: Stuard is still developing his frame and putting on weight and could stand to gain additional size and muscle for the next level if he's going to play in a linebacker role. Very short arms. Very raw and still learning how to play linebacker. Lacks the ideal length to impact plays outside of his frame, possessing a limited tackle radius. Needs to do a better job of utilizing his hands in space to disengage and keep his frame free while working through the trash.

Best Fit: 4-3 WILL and special teams

Player Ranking (1-100): 56.3 - Stuard shows upside with some nice athletic traits and coverage experience, but he's still a giant work in progress as a linebacker. He's brand-new to the position and needs continued development. In the meantime, he could be a solid special teams player as he potentially develops more to win snaps on defense.

TOP-10 Outside Linebackers

1. Chazz Surratt
2. Jabril Cox
3. Jeremiah Owusu-Koramoah
4. Zaven Collins
5. Garret Wallow
6. Kuony Deng
7. Monty Rice
8. Merlin Robertson
9. Tony Fields II
10. Amen Ogbongbemiga

Chapter 13

Cornerbacks

1 - Patrick Surtain II - Alabama - 6'2 202 lbs

Strengths: The son of former All-Pro defensive back with the same name, Surtain II is an 'NFL ready' prospect and former five-star recruit out of high school. Surtain has tremendous size for the position, with a rare wingspan and a muscled-up physique. Surtain has experience lining up all over the defensive formation for Alabama, playing both outside and in the slot. Surtain loves to play the game physically, showing tremendous aggression and physicality when lined up in press. Very comfortable in man-to-man showing refined jam technique with the strong upper body to disrupt and re-route at the line of scrimmage. An absolute bully that loves to play aggressively, making the intended receiver fight for every single ball at the catch point. Physicality is also on display through receiver stems, knowing exactly what he can and cannot get away with. Sinks in his stance, remaining patient and under control at all times. Excellent ball skills and leaping ability allow him to play effectively with his back to the ball, timing the balls 'arrival to perfection to knock it away. A quick-twitched athlete with good reactionary ability and processing skills that allow him to shadow in space, showing the smoothness and loose limbs to remain on the hip pocket of receivers through transitions. Smart and instinctual when in zone coverage, allowing him to read keys and quickly diagnose. Physicality shows through in the running game with good wrap-up technique.

Weaknesses: Needs to do a better job of working through blocks in the running game, getting hung up and stuck on blocks for far too long. Doesn't always take the more direct pathways to the football in pursuit. His overaggressive nature can sometimes get him in trouble with being a bit too handsy down the field, leading to some penalties. Quicker than he is fast and will struggle on some deeper routes where he will occasionally grant some separation to speedier straight-lined athletes. Make-up speed isn't ideal and if he's initially beaten by a quicker receiver, he will have difficulty making up ground. Can be caught looking on occasion at the QB, granting some separation at the top of the route.

Best Fit: Press-man corner

Player Ranking (1-100): 92.1 - Surtain II is a gifted athlete that displays all the physical traits you want in a next-level corner. While he's not an elite speed athlete like we've seen from some top-10 cornerbacks the last several years, he is one of the most well-rounded when it comes to technique, physicality, and overall athleticism. 1st round player.

2 - Caleb Farley - Virginia Tech - 6'2 207 lbs

Strengths: A former high school QB that transitioned to WR and then transitioned to CB after arriving at Wake Forest. Farley was tremendous in 2019, finishing with double-figure pass deflections and 4 interceptions. Farley sat out his final year in 2020. Farley is a well-built corner that shows the tremendous size, length, and strength for the position, perfectly capable of handling bigger receivers at the next level. Despite having a minimal amount of experience at the position it is barely noticeable, Farley is 'NFL Ready 'with the perfect amount of physicality, functional athleticism, and mental processing capabilities. An advanced student of the game that displays good route recognition abilities in combination with anticipation. A natural when it comes to his all-around movement abilities. Click and close ability is tremendous, showing fluidity and locking himself in step for step against tight ends and receivers on in-breaking routes. If initial separation is given, Farley has the ability to utilize his closing speed to minimize openings. Hyper-aggressive in run support showing fearlessness, toughness, and good wrap-up abilities to rarely let someone out of his grasps. Will fight through blockers in pursuit. Love the confidence in which he plays at the line of scrimmage, not afraid to get right in the face of receivers, and staying square. Really good ball skills down the field with an impressive ability to find, judge and disrupt the ball at the catch point.

Weaknesses: Has dealt with several injuries during his time in college, including tearing his ACL during the 2017 season as well as missing the final two games of 2019 for back spasms. Still learning the finer nuances of playing the position such as utilizing his hands properly while in press. Tends to bite a bit on double moves and will get caught looking on occasion. Not the most comfortable when being asked to play in zone or off-coverage, giving a bit too much space and not fully recognizing zonal spacing.

Best Fit: Press-man corner

Player Ranking (1-100): 90.2 - There's very little not to love about Farley's game. He's only going to get better at the next level with more experience. He has everything you want in a player, including the athleticism and physicality for an NFL player. 1st round pick.

3 - Jaycee Horn - South Carolina - 6'1 202 lbs

Strengths: A 3-year starter for the Gamecocks that has started almost every game of his career, since his true freshman season before opting out for the last few games of the SEC season. Horn is a well-built kid with a rock-solid, filled-out frame with ideal prototypical length. The son of former Saints 'wide receiver Joe Horn, Jaycee certainly possesses NFL bloodlines. Horn is an alpha that plays with an ultra-aggressive mindset, playing super chippy and aggressive from the get-go. He's oftentimes lined up against the opposing teams ' number 1 receiver and he relished every minute of it, following them all over the field. He loves to win the mental side of the guy and wear opposing receivers out. Horn is terrific in man-to-man coverage, showing ultra twitchy reflexes and instincts to almost always time the balls 'arrival to perfection. A fluid mover that shows good fluidity and is seamless while in transition with his back to the ball. Hip flexibility is excellent, showing the ability to mirror when working laterally. Varies up his jam technique at the line of scrimmage, making receivers uncomfortable off the snap of the ball. Will occasionally get beat early on in a rep with speed but he shows the makeup speed to close on the football and catch-up. Horn never gives easy receptions, showing strength and physicality at the catch point to fight for everything. Prefers to give the QB no option to throw in his direction because he gives up such little space at all levels of the field. Appears comfortable in zone coverage while keeping things in front of him with good route recognition and instincts. Quick to trigger downhill in the running game, showing good short-area quickness and aggression when going for the ball. Aggressive hands and will go for the ball when wrapping up, as evidenced by his multiple forced fumbles. Smart and hard worker that clearly is a film-junkie as evidenced by his ability to recognize things very quickly in a route.

Weaknesses: Horn is overly physical to a fault and gets called for a lot of holding calls with slight pulls on jerseys. A very good athlete but not elite. This will likely limit him to an outside position at the next level due to his size and struggles against some elite-level speed receivers that will pull him on underneath routes. Ball production before his junior season was nonexistent, with no career interceptions prior despite starting. Despite showing willingness and aggression in the run game, he's a bit of an ankle swiper that will allow some players to stay on his feet and pick up additional yardage.

Best Fit: Outside corner

Player Ranking (1-100): 87.8 - I really really like Horn. He's got the alpha dog mentality and that's exactly what you want in an NFL cornerback. He's a smooth athlete and will fight for absolutely everything. He will wear receivers out at the next level. 1st round player.

4 - Israel Mukuamu - South Carolina - 6'4 205 lbs

Strengths: Mukuamu has been one of the best players on the Gamecocks defense in each of the last two seasons, showing the positional versatility to play both at corner and safety. The first thing you'll notice about Mukuamu is his frame, showcasing length for days and incredible height. Despite his wiry frame, Mukuamu will not be bullied, showing outstanding physicality in all aspects of playing the position. Outstanding as a press-man corner where he can bully smaller receivers with his wingspan, limiting their ability to release off the line of scrimmage effectively. Very good in zone as well when he can keep his eyes in the backfield, allowing him to utilize his natural instincts. Stays in phase with receivers throughout their stems and if initially granting any separation, he has the makeup speed co quickly recover. Excellent ball production, getting his hands on a ton of balls with his combination of instincts and length. Shows the comfort and experience in playing both on the outside or inside. A mentally alert guy that reads/reacts quickly showing tremendous recognizing skills and processing speed. A fluid mover that moves impressively both vertically and laterally for a guy of his size. Rarely gives up an uncontested ball, makes receivers fight for everything. Is at his best down the field with his combination of wingspan, ball skills, and leaping ability. Very aggressive and physical in run support, showing fearlessness when triggering downhill. He perfectly utilizes his tackle radius to make plays outside of his frame.

Weaknesses: Mukuamu has a long and rangy high-cut physique, reminiscent of a track athlete. Those types of athletes tend to struggle with injuries, and he's already had some nagging injuries he's worked through. Mukuamu is a gambling type that likes to keep his eyes roving in the backfield which often gets him in trouble and he gets caught looking on occasion, especially on play fakes and double moves. I would like to see him utilize his size more on the line of scrimmage with better hand technique to slow down more explosive receivers. Far too often he gives up too much inside leverage, leading him to get caught on his heels and giving up inside access. His long speed is just 'OK 'and will struggle to catch up if initially beaten. His tackling will leave you frustrated, looking passive, and disinterested when runners are coming downhill at him.

Best Fit: Zone corner or free safety

Player Ranking (1-100): 83.4 - I like Mukuamu and think with his combination of size and length he could be a really really good football player. His positional versatility and experience both while in zone and man makes him even more exciting. He will give up 5-10 yard routes routinely which can be frustrating. But he's excellent down the field and his length will give even the biggest of receivers trouble at the next level. 2nd round player.

5 - Asante Samuel Jr - Florida State - 5'10 184 lbs

Strengths: Son of former NFL Pro-Bowl corner, Samuel Jr is a valuable 3-year player for the Seminoles that begin getting significant snaps during his true freshman campaign. Samuel Jr, built like his father, is an undersized but highly competitive and tenacious playmaking corner. Samuel excels the most when he's able to play off-man, allowing him to utilize his natural instincts and twitchy reflexes to make plays on the ball. Has experience playing both in the slot and on the outside. Showcasing terrific mental alertness and self-assured confidence, Samuel Jr sinks in his stance and stays on the balls of his feet at all times remaining in control. Read/react abilities are terrific, showing the short-area quickness combined with anticipatory skills to close on the ball quickly. Moves well in all directions, showing good fluidity and change of direction to flip his hips and mirror in space. Very disciplined and was entrusted to frequently shadow and cover the opposing teams ' number 1 receiver wherever he lined up. Excellent in the run game, completely maxing out his frame with really impressive physicality. Utilizing really good wrap-up abilities and fearlessness to take on running backs on the perimeters. Several reps on tape where he successfully took on blocking TE's in space and deconstructed with success.

Weaknesses: Samuel Jr is undersized obviously and isn't a typical outside corner for today's NFL. Struggles when matching up against bigger receivers on the outside that can utilize their frames to post-up at the catch point or win inside positioning. Mostly just an off-man corner and wouldn't fit a scheme for a press-man defense with very little jam experience on tape. Overall ball production was a bit disappointing during his time, despite showing improvement in 2020.

Best Fit: Slot corner and occasional outside reps

Player Ranking (1-100): 82.7 - Samuel Jr is a talented read/react cornerback that will make a lot of plays for a defense. He's terrific and natural in coverage. Depending on the defensive coaches and their comfort level with his lack of size, he might strictly be an inside cornerback at the next level. I believe he could play outside in certain situations but is better suited inside, especially against NFL-sized athletes. 2nd round player.

6 - Paulson Adebo - Stanford - 6'1 190 lbs

Strengths: Adebo came to prominence during his freshman campaign when he lit up the Pac-12 with 20 passes defended and 4 additional interceptions. After a somewhat disappointing 2019 campaign, Adebo decided to also opt-out of the 2020 season to prepare for the draft. Built with a long and rangy physique,

Adebo shows the looseness and fluidity expected to play at the next level. His experience as a track and field athlete are constantly on display with his above-average athleticism, rarely allowing any separation on vertical routes. Former high-school receiver traits are also on display with his ball skills, showing receiver-like ball tracking abilities when the ball is in flight and the ability to run routes better than the receiver on occasion. Is at his best in press coverage when he can control the rep, dictating where the receiver goes to, showing tremendous physicality, and maximizing out his frame. Fearless in his abilities to play against the run, reading things quickly and shooting downhill even when taking on bigger backs in the hole. Very good in transition, showing loose hips to mirror in space and limit separation given in man coverage situations.

Weaknesses: Suffered an undisclosed injury at the end of the 2019 season causing him to miss the final few games of the season. Doesn't always possess the greatest play recognition abilities with a really bad habit of biting on double moves and falling hard on play fakes and misdirection-type plays. Footwork is a major concern for Adebo as he's a bit clunky out of his backpedal, allowing some separation almost instantaneously. Strictly an outside corner at this point, lacking the ideal short-area quickness to handle quicker receivers on the inside. Long-speed isn't as good as you would expect for a track and field athlete.

Best Fit: Outside press-man corner

Player Ranking (1-100): 81.4 - Adebo is a solid cornerback prospect with excellent length, ball-hawking abilities, and playmaking skills. While he's a good athlete, he's not an elite one. He needs to clean up some of his poor techniques, most notably with his footwork. He could be a solid outside starter though that will make a lot of plays for a defense, as evidenced by his ball production numbers in college. He will give up plays as well. 2nd round player.

7 - Greg Newsome III - Northwestern - 6'1 190 lbs

Strengths: Newsome took over as a starter during the end of his freshman campaign, starting in his final 4 contests. He's gotten progressively better and better each season. Possessing a long and rangy physique, Newsome displays prototypical man coverage size with good length. Frequently shadowing the number one receiver on the opposing team, Newsome plays with swagger and self-assured confidence. He's comfortable playing on either side of the line of scrimmage in a variety of coverage setups but appears most comfortable in off-man. Newsome has terrific anticipation and read and react abilities, quickly diagnosing with his play-recognition abilities to click and close on the football. This has been evidenced by his 16 passes defended in the last 11 games. A very good athlete that has impressive top-end speed, rarely granting any kind of separation against all types of receivers. If initially loses any ground, his recovery abilities allow him to quickly make-up ground. Plays with good physicality, both through the contact window and throughout the route, rarely allowing a reception that isn't contested. A terrific mirror cover corner that stays on the hip pocket of his assignment at all times, showing the rare foot quickness and looseness through his lower body to stay square, even on lateral routes. Maintains excellent eye discipline at all times, rarely biting on double-moves or play-action type plays.

Weaknesses: Suffered a groin injury during his final game of the season in the Big Ten championship game, causing him to miss the rest of the game and the bowl game. Despite getting his hands on a number of balls, he fails to consistently finish with turnovers. Has a bit of a wiry frame and could stand to gain additional functional strength for the next level to be able to better assist in run support. Appears to be content allowing a number of underneath receptions when dropping in zone coverage.

Best Fit: Off-man corner

Player Ranking (1-100): 80.7 - Newsome is a really really good football player. I love the swag and confidence he plays with, showing fearlessness at all times. He's got the natural movement abilities to be an eventual #1 corner for a team. I love Newsome and think he should be a 2nd round draft pick. If he finished more plays with turnovers and was a little better in run support, he'd be a 1st rounder.

8 - Tyson Campbell - Georgia - 6'2 185 lbs

Strengths: Campbell has taken over as one of the starters in the Bulldogs secondary since his freshman campaign, starting in most of his games since the last 3 seasons. Built with a long and prototypical corner frame, displaying top-notch height and length. Campbell is a tremendous athlete for the Bulldogs and is one of the best speedsters on the team, showing the ability to run vertically with the fastest NFL receivers. Not just long speed, Campbell keeps his frame leveraged at all times while remaining low in his stance and playing on the balls of his feet. Appears comfortable in press-coverage showing good jam technique to disrupt and re-reroute. Has loose hips and lower body flexibility that allow him to transition and play seamlessly while changing directions. Closing speed and short-area quickness allow him to quickly make-up any lost ground. Does a nice job of utilizing his long arms to disrupt at the catch point, making it difficult for receivers to make clean catches. While he's not the most stoutly built defender, he maximizes his frame out with physicality. Fearless when coming downhill in the run game, Campbell shows fearlessness taking on larger backs on the perimeter. A large tackle radius allows him to make plays outside of his frame in the run game.

Weaknesses: Campbell missed 5 games during his sophomore season due to a foot injury. Campbell gets caught looking quite a bit into the backfield, allowing him to give up some spacing and losing track of his receiver. Gives inside leverage down the field too often on underneath routes. Balance at the top of his routes doesn't appear to be the best as he sometimes loses his footing. Struggles when it comes to zone coverage. Average zonal instincts and spatial awareness, leaving large gaps opened down the field. Overall ball skills aren't great and he struggles down the field with his back to the ball, losing track of the football in mid-flight. Could stand to gain additional functional strength and size.

Best Fit: Press-man corner

Player Ranking (1-100): 80.1 - Campbell is a terrific athlete and is one of the best raw athletes at the position in this draft class. He's still raw when it comes to overall abilities and could stand to refine himself a bit. I like his upside as a press-man corner in the right defensive formation. 2nd round player.

9 - Elijah Molden - Washington - 5'10 190 lbs

Strengths: Continuing in the long line of successful Washington defensive backs, Molden was incredible in his final season as a junior before opting out of his final season in 2020. Built with a squatty and low center of gravity physique, Molden shows tremendous short-area quickness and fluidity in the way he plays. Grading out as one of the best pure cover corners in college football by many, Molden displays stick cover characteristics in his ability to lock on hip to hip with receivers in man coverage. Excelling in his footwork, Molden takes very few wasted steps in coverage, showing fluidity in transition and rarely losing any ground when having to flip his hips. For being a smaller guy, Molden shows terrific ball skills both with his back to the ball and when the play develops in front of him, finishing with 16 passes defended and 4 interceptions during his junior season. Possesses excellent cover awareness, combining his anticipation with instinctive abilities to put himself into great positions down the field. In the run game, Molden was very impressive for a guy of his size. Fighting through blocks with some deconstruction ability to break through blocks, Molden shows toughness and reliability as a tackler.

Weaknesses: The biggest concern for Molden is his lack of outside experience. Is he limited to a 'niche 'role simply playing inside? While his short-area quickness is terrific his long speed appears to be just subpar and he could get beaten vertically if taken up the field. A role player during his first two seasons at Washington and only has 1 full year of starting experience.

Best Fit: Nickel player that could play as a situational safety as well

Player Ranking (1-100): 79.9 - I like Molden quite a bit. He's a playmaking defensive back that makes plays all over the field. His mirror ability is rare in the way he limits spacing for receivers. Rarely will he allow any separation in man coverage. But he's not simply a 'cover guy. 'He's a playmaker too. 3rd round player.

10 - Kary Vincent Jr - LSU - 5'10 185 lbs

Strengths: A 3-year contributor to the Tigers defense that came to prominence during LSU's title-winning season in 2019 where he played almost exclusively as the nickelback for the Tigers. Vincent Jr opted out before the 2020 season choosing to prepare for the 2021 NFL Draft. A member of the LSU track team, Vincent Jr is explosive, showing terrific athletic abilities. As a junior, Vincent Jr showcased impressive statistics, finishing the season with 8 passes defended and an additional 4 interceptions. Vincent is at his best when he's playing closer to the line of scrimmage where he can show off his terrific instincts and short-area quickness to close on the football. I like him best when playing off-coverage where he can show off his anticipatory skills coupled with his change of directional skills to quickly close on the football. While in man, Vincent Jr shows sticky coverage traits with fluidity and ease of movement when having to flip his hips. He competes for everything both when his back is towards the ball or when the ball is in front of him. His strong hands allow him to compete for the football at the catch point. His good ball skills allow him to time and track the balls 'flight to perfection. A willing tackler that maximizes his frame out when having to handle the dirty work in the run game.

Weaknesses: While he was used as a single-high safety at times for the Tigers, he looked quite uncomfortable when doing so. Due to his undersized nature and lack of ideal physical traits, he's best suited as a slot inside corner solely at the next level. While he's a willing tackler, he appears to struggle to bring guys to the ground, allowing them additional yards after contact. His aggressive nature makes him susceptible to double moves biting frequently.

> **Best Fit: Slot player or he plays as a subpackage safety**

Player Ranking (1-100): 79.1 - A similar player to Molden, but Vincent Jr is a better all-around athlete. Molden is a better pure cover guy and a more physical and stouter built player. Vincent Jr will best be served with a defensive coordinator that can find a way to use him and get him on the field. He could be a real game-changer if used in sub-packages near the line of scrimmage. 3rd round player.

11 - Trill Williams - Syracuse - 6'2 198 lbs

Strengths: A three-year starter for the Orangemen that has played both outside corner and in the nickel, before transitioning to safety for his final season, before opting out. Williams is built with outstanding size, showing excellent length and good overall weight distribution. Scouts will love Williams 'versatility to play all over the defensive secondary, showing success wherever he's played. Williams is a tremendous all-around athlete that displays all the explosive characteristics you look for. Equally adept and comfortable in both zone and man coverage. Long speed is frequently on display when in pursuit, frequently catching guys from behind. If initially beaten at the line of scrimmage in coverage, his recovery bursts allow him to quickly recover. Not just fast, Williams displays the short-area quickness and lateral agility to mirror the quickest of slot receivers. Very good flexibility through his hips, effortlessly flipping his hips and changing directions. A very physical defender that loves to get in the face of receivers when lined up in coverage, overwhelming slot receivers at the line of scrimmage while disrupting their routes. Physicality is also prevalent at the catch point where he utilizes his length to time the balls arrival to perfection, knocking it away. Large tackle radius assists him heavily in run support, showing the ability to slow runners down while extended. While in zone, Williams shows natural instincts and good route intelligence to recognizing things quickly. Has a natural feel for drops and zonal spacing?

Weaknesses: Can get overly reliant on his natural athletic abilities, getting a little bit clunky with his footwork when working out of a backpedal. Has far more experience playing in the slot than anywhere else and could stand to gain additional experience with his skillset on the outside. His long-levered frame tends to play a little bit too high at times, allowing shorter receivers to win inside leverage on him. While he's very physical in run support, his tackling fundamentals aren't great, frequently arriving too high. He will frequently allow runners to gain additional yardage after contact. Will routinely take overaggressive pathways to the ball when working as a safety.

> **Best Fit: Versatile chess piece. Likely best as a slot corner**

Player Ranking (1-100): 78.7 - Williams is more athlete than he is football player right now. He was one of the bright spots of the Syracuse defense, frequently showing up. He's such a versatile player that I'd imagine coaching staffs will have different ideas on how to properly utilize him. The idea of him being a 'shadow' corner and manning up against opposing teams 'best receivers isn't a bad idea. He has the versatility and the comfort to play anywhere. An exciting prospect with a HUGE ceiling. He will just need more time. 3rd round player.

12 - Shaun Wade - Ohio State - 6'1 195 lbs

Strengths: Wade was a former five-star recruit coming out of high school. Built with a prototypical NFL frame, Wade possesses both the size and the length teams covet. Experienced playing both on the inside and on the perimeter, Wade possesses the versatility for any kind of defensive system and anywhere along the defense. The first thing that stands out about Wade is how well he moves. A twitchy athlete that possesses the lower body explosiveness to spring in any direction to attach himself hip-to-hip in coverage with receivers in man coverage. Loose limbs and lower body flexibility allows him to fluidly transition and redirect his frame without needing to gear down. Shows an impressive secondary burst to recover if he takes any false steps in his backpedal. Mentally alert, wasting very little time to break on the ball, timing the balls 'arrival to perfection. Terrific reaction times and processing abilities allow him to recognize things quickly. Does a nice of utilizing his length to disrupt at the line of scrimmage to re-reroute. Also shows good physicality with his length at the catch point to rip at the ball. Very impressive when used in zone coverage, showing terrific patience and understanding of route concepts with good spatial awareness. Quick to trigger in the run game, Wade shows fearlessness when working downhill to take on blockers with physicality. Has a good feel for keeping his frame clean and consistently wrap-up with good technique.

Weaknesses: Missed his entire freshman season after tearing an abdomen muscle, causing him to be redshirted. Most of Wade's experience came while playing in the slot. Had a slightly disappointing senior campaign and appeared to look disinterested in the physical areas of the game, perhaps due to thinking about the NFL Draft. Overall ball production numbers weren't as great as you would expect for someone with his ability. He needs to do a better job of finishing plays and attacking the football in the air. Hand technique at the line of scrimmage can get lazy at times, giving some easy and free releases off the line of scrimmage.

Best Fit: Slot corner but can play outside too. Might move to safety

Player Ranking (1-100): 78.0 - Wade is a talented and instinctual player that shows really impressive overall athleticism and football intelligence. He's a playmaker that appears to make plays every time he's on the field. If he had a better senior season he'd be a 1st rounder but I'd take him in the 2nd round. Outstanding football player. Shutdown slot corner that will get better and better on the outside with more reps.

13 - Rodarius Williams - Oklahoma State - 6'0 193 lbs

Strengths: Williams, the brother of Browns 'CB Greedy Williams, is a rare 4-year starter for the Cowboys that has loads of experience and reliability rarely having missed a snap during his career. Williams is a versatile corner that played mostly off-man coverage his first few years at Oklahoma State before transitioning mostly to a press-man corner during his final season. Built with a long-levered frame with solid length and weight distribution, Williams shows the size and movement ability to play both inside and outside at the next level. A twitchy guy with excellent instincts and reflexes to read/react quickly to the ball. Williams remains bent at the knees and eagerly inches forward to the line of scrimmage. A mentally alert guy that plays with a nonstop motor, energy. swag and confidence. Disruptive at the line of scrimmage, Williams commits himself to physicality at the line of scrimmage to alter and disrupt. Appears to have a really good understanding of route concepts both in zone and when playing press-man, oftentimes beating the receiver to the spot of the ball. Rarely will he not compete for the ball upon arrival, showing good awareness and hand strength to rip at the ball. Ease of movement is evident in the way Williams plays, showing the loose hips to cross-field and cover inside routes. Not passive in the run game, showing fight when breaking through blocks.

Weaknesses: There are some concerns about his overall athleticism, including his top-end speed but it didn't appear to be exposed much in college. A lankier built guy that has the frame for additional growth and strength to be added onto his frame to compete against bigger NFL possession receivers. More of a 'cover' corner than a ball-hawking corner. Ball production is modest at best with only 2 career interceptions before his senior season.

Best Fit: Versatile CB that can play in any system

Player Ranking (1-100): 77.9 - Williams was good in his final year at Oklahoma State. He's gotten better on film each year and will contest everything thrown in his direction. While not exactly a 'playmaker 'like his brother, he's a really solid cover corner that will compete for snaps very early on. 3rd round player.

14 - Keith Taylor - Washington - 6'3 191 lbs

Strengths: Taylor took over the starting duties for the Huskies during his junior campaign, where had a solid overall campaign. Possessing a rare frame with good length, Taylor shows the ideal physical profile to play as a press-man corner. Display his long-levered frame, Taylor doesn't move like a slouch. He is incredibly fluid both on vertical plains as well as laterally, showing loose limbs and flexibility throughout his frame when being asked to cover against in-breaking routes. He also displays the makeup speed to regain any lost steps when in pursuit. While he's at his best in press-man situations, he does show some comfort when being asked to drop and disguise into zone coverage. Disciplined with his eyes, maintaining good positioning down the field, and rarely being fooled by double moves or play-action type of plays. Long speed is very good, rarely losing any ground down the field in vertical situations. Very clean with his footwork, wasting very few steps, and transitioning nicely out of his backpedal. Contests everything down the field and is very comfortable with his back towards the ball.

Weaknesses: As per typical with a guy of his size, leverage and maintaining a low stance when being asked to flip his hips can sometimes be delayed causing him to give up some easy inside access against shorter and quicker receivers. I would like to see him utilize his length more consistently both at the line of scrimmage and when competing at the catch point, most notably against smaller targets. Play strength needs to continue to grow as he grows more into his frame. Not great in the run game, showing some passive characteristics to avoid getting himself hurt.

Best Fit: Press-man boundary corner

Player Ranking (1-100): 77.2 - I like Taylor quite a bit as a boundary corner. He's really good when receivers attempt playing on a vertical plain. He will grant some separation if receivers take him inside, but it's fairly rare. Really good player and could start at the next level.

15 - Eric Stokes - Georgia - 6'1 185 lbs

Strengths: Stokes has been a valuable role player for the Gators since his freshman season but taking over the starting role during his sophomore season and never looking back. Stokes has good overall size and length for the position with the frame for continued muscular development to add more functional strength to his frame. Stokes has experience playing in every kind of coverage for the Bulldogs but impresses the most when he can play in a press-man system. Stokes has improved during each of his seasons and showed during his junior campaign that he has some ball skills as evidenced by his interception tally and 2 defensive returns for touchdowns. Stokes maximizes his frame with physicality in man coverage, showing the 'want 'when it comes to getting his hands on receivers to disrupt them at all levels. Excellent football intelligence with good route-recognition abilities to see things very quickly. An easy mover that shows fluidity through a variety of different points, showing enough functional athleticism to mirror without granting any kind of separation on deeper routes. Possesses enough recovery speed if initially granting separation to catch-up to the ball carrier. Utilizes his length well at all levels, with the ability to high-point and attack the ball in the air against receivers. Agility and lower-body flexibility manifest in Stokes when working in-and-out of transitions.

Weaknesses: Stokes biggest issue is the lack of overall power in his frame to play with physicality at the next level. This shows up when attempting to play in run support, lacking the ability to fight through blockers and keep his frame clean when working downhill. When attempting to tackle, Stokes shows willingness but he will allow them to gain additional yards after contact. Struggles at times against a quicker receiver that will take him across the field laterally, allowing them to gain inside leverage and win positioning quickly. Has a habit of getting handsy down the field and knocking out receivers' arms when the balls 'about to arrive. When in zone coverage, he appears to have some slow processing abilities to quickly react to close down insufficient time.

Best Fit: Press-man corner

Player Ranking (1-100): 77.1 - Stokes is a really solid cover corner. His ball skills were a serious question mark before his junior season but he proved this year he has them. He needs to continue to add functional strength to his frame for the next level. But he certainly has the desire to play with physicality. Like Stokes quite a bit. Could be a starter on Day 1. 3rd round player.

16 - Thomas Graham Jr - Oregon - 5'11 193 lbs

Strengths: A 3-year starter for the Ducks that had equally and similar production years during each of those campaigns before opting-out for his final season. A squattier built guy that is built with some compactness through his frame. The first thing that stands out about Graham is his ball production, finishing with double-digit production during each season. This is in fact due to his excellent ball skills where he shows his ability to time the balls 'arrival to perfection while disrupting at the catch point. A fluid mover that shows comfort when playing both off man and in man coverage showing the instincts and reactionary abilities to click/close in an instant. Explosive movements in his backpedal with the ability to smoothly transition out and into top gear. A solid athlete that shows above-average long speed to stick to speedier receivers on vertical plains. Shows a good secondary burst to close cushions or recover after false steps.

Weaknesses: Graham is limited to an outside role at the next level, failing to have the ideal short-area quickness and agility to play against in-breaking routes. Very limited in the running game, getting completely exposed at times whiffing on tackles, even when coming downhill. Gives up far too many easy yards in zone or off-man coverage, oftentimes unnecessarily. Very susceptible to double moves down the field. Not a great 'cover' corner, failing to mirror on far too many occasions.

Best Fit: Off-man or Zone corner

Player Ranking (1-100): 76.4 - A solid player that shows some coverage ability. The problem with Graham is he doesn't excel in any one thing and lacks the ideal measurables for a typical starting CB. He might be limited to a defensive system where he can play zone or off-man. 3rd round player.

17 - Shakur Brown - Michigan State - 5'10 190 lbs

Strengths: After taking over the starting responsibilities during his sophomore year, Brown rose prominently during his final year, starting every game as a junior. Despite only playing in an abbreviated season this year, Brown still finished with 5 interceptions. Ball skills are prevalent as evidenced by his production numbers, showing good route-recognition abilities and patience at all levels of a route. He utilizes his football IQ and ball tracking abilities to watch the receivers 'eyes to effectively turn at precisely the right time to make a play on the ball. A big-play guy that has experience in the return department as well, proving to be dynamic every time he gets the ball in his hands. A terrific and fluid moving athlete that shows the change of directional abilities coupled with agility and flexibility to flip his hips with ease, proving to be a reliable man cover corner. His mirroring abilities allow him to match stride for stride all types of receivers, including explosive route-runners. Brown doesn't need to gear down when working in transition. Fearless in run support, despite being undersized, showing 0 hesitancy when working back towards the football.

Weaknesses: Has very limited game experience, only having about 12 career starts. Missed half of his sophomore season due to injury. An undersized prospect that lacks the ideal build to play on the outside at the next level. Will get overmatched against bigger and more physical corners. Brown lacks great strength and aggression both at the line of scrimmage and at the catch point. Has played almost exclusively in man coverage, having very little experience in off-man or zone. Quicker than he is fast and could be exposed against long strides in vertical settings.

Best Fit: Man-to-man corner

Player Ranking (1-100): 74.8 - Corners that make plays are very very valuable these days. His ball skills are amongst the best in this class. But his lack of ideal size and schematic flexibility will cause him to drop off many teams 'draft boards. I wish he had more experience and game tape but unfortunately, he doesn't. I love how fearless he is in run support. 4th round player.

18 - Camryn Bynum - California - 6'0 198 lbs

Strengths: After originally opting out during his senior season, Bynum came back to play the final 4 games of the season. A 4-year starter, Bynum is a consistent and reliable performer, showing very few flaws in his game.

Built with a developed frame, showing good muscular distribution and compactness. Functional strength is apparent in his abilities to handle run support, showing to be a reliable open-field tackler, playing with aggressiveness when coming downhill. Excels the most while playing in a wide variety of zone coverages. Excellent when playing in Cover-2 concepts, showing terrific agility to close quickly. Also has a good understanding of playing in Cover-3 and even in quarters coverage, showing the ability to cover deeper routes. Has a very good understanding of route concepts, maintaining good leverage while attaching himself to the hip pocket of receivers down the field. Rarely allows receivers to separate on him when attempting to cross his face. Plays with relentless physicality both at the line of scrimmage and throughout the stem. Very good ball skills, in part, due to his innate ability to locate the football with his back to the ball and disrupt at the catch point. Times 'the balls 'arrival excellently, utilizing his ability to key in on the receiver's arm and eyes to time it to perfection.

Weaknesses: Before his senior season, Bynum suffered a lower-body injury in the offseason in which he was recovering from. One of the frustrating things for Bynum is he doesn't always finish plays, he gets his hands on a lot of balls, but fails to turn them into consistent turnovers. When handling press coverage, Bynum appears to struggle with his hand accuracy, frequently whiffing at the line of scrimmage. Shows some lower-body stiffness and tightness when attempting to change directions, and will get exposed against more savvy route-runners. Strictly a perimeter corner. Lacks elite functional athleticism and long-speed to handle speedier vertical options up the field.

Best Fit: Zone corner but could transition to a FS role

Player Ranking (1-100): 74.2 - Bynum is a physical presence that excels further away from the football when things are in front of him. His lack of athleticism will get exposed if he handles press man coverage responsibilities. He has very impressive ball skills and cover awareness though. Good football player. 4th round pick.

19 - DJ Daniel - Georgia - 6'0 183 lbs

Strengths: A former JUCO prospect that transferred to play his final two years of eligibility for the Bulldogs. Daniel possesses an ideal mix of size, length speed, and physicality to play at the next level. Built with a long-levered frame and athleticism throughout, Daniel commits himself to maximize the possibilities with his frame. Impressive in his usage of his entire wingspan at the line of scrimmage, jamming, and re-rerouting receivers. Despite limited interception numbers, Daniel does do a nice job of timing the ball at the top of the route upon the balls 'arrival to knock the ball away at precisely the right time. Plays with good physicality in all aspects of the game. Especially notable is his physicality in the run game, playing downhill and crashing hard on ball carriers. A terrific athlete that possesses top-end speed for a cornerback, rarely allowing any separation on vertical routes. If initially granting any separation, Daniel's closing speed will quickly close it. Not just a speed athlete, also possesses the rangy and elastic flexibility through his hips to limit separation on in-breaking routes across the field.

Weaknesses: Ball production numbers have been modest at best with 0 career interceptions during his 2 seasons with the Bulldogs. Has a bad habit of grabbing when panicked, leading to some poor holding and pass interference calls. Not as proficient in zone and lacks the instincts and feel for proper cushioning and spacing, granting too much separation at times. Needs to do a better job of not oversetting his feet outside on crossing routes, allowing receivers initial separation at the top of their stems.

Best Fit: Outside corner in a man-to-man system

Player Ranking (1-100): 73.3 - Daniel has impressed for Georgia when he's played. He will likely get drafted higher due to his elite athleticism and speed. While he's not an elite playmaking corner, he will get better after gaining more experience against top competition. His speed gives him the necessary 'potential' to continue to get better with proper fundamentals work.

20 - Marco Wilson - Florida - 6'1 191 lbs

Strengths: A rare starter from Day 1 during his true freshman season, Wilson was a highly-touted four-star recruit that has been a consistent mainstay for the Gators since. The younger brother of former Gator and NFL cornerback, Quincy Wilson. Possessing a long and rangy physique, Wilson possesses the physicality and length to be an effective boundary corner at the next level, as he was in college. Best used when playing in off coverage but can play on the line as well. Also has shown his ability to kick inside and play in the slot, most notably his junior season. A twitched-up athlete that shows impressive long-speed to run downfield with speedy receivers in man coverage, rarely granting any separation. Quick reflexes allow him to mirror in coverage, matching foot movements precisely. Short-area quickness allows him to close down on balls at the catch point, showing impressive timing and instincts to knock the ball away. Very sudden when working in-and-out of transitions, showing terrific lower body explosiveness and lateral mobility to change directions while remaining leveraged. Above-average ball skills and does a nice job of tracking the ball down the field to high-point when competing with receivers. Not a slouch in the run game and will show physicality and 'want' when it comes to supporting. Very good in blitzing situations, showing the knack for timing it and quickly getting into the backfield.

Weaknesses: Tore his ACL during his sophomore season, allowing him to be granted a medical redshirt season. Will struggle if asked to play in a press-man system with very little experience utilizing his hands at the line of scrimmage. When he does use them, he looks awkward and fails to disrupt routes. Lanky frame will cause him to get overmatched by bigger, possession receivers. Very focus entirely on vertical routes while maintaining outside leverage at all times, making him susceptible to inside routes when he will give up easy access.

Best Fit: Off-man corner

Player Ranking (1-100): 72.8 - Wilson is a good athlete that displays excellent fluidity and length. He's not an elite athlete or cover guy but he's very solid. He has a defined role for the right team in the right defensive setup. His versatility having experience playing all the cornerback positions is a major plus. 4th round player.

21 - Benjamin St. Juste - Minnesota - 6'3 200 lbs

Strengths: Originally a four-star recruit by Michigan and playing immediately as a true freshman for the Wolverines, St. Juste transferred to the Gophers the following year, starting during his final 2 seasons. In his first year with the Gophers, St. Juste flashed big-time potential, finishing the year with 45 tackles and 10 passes defended. Featuring a rare long-levered frame and vines for arms, St. Juste is a perfect fit for today's NFL to match up with larger receivers. A physical kid that loves to play bump-and-run coverage, showing the athletic profile to handle speedier downfield. Long strides that eat up chunks of green in no-time. Proficient in both press-man and off-man. He understands how to utilize his length to disrupt both at the line of scrimmage and at the catch point. Good ability to utilize his physicality through a receivers 'stem to remain hip-in-hip with the intended target. Then he perfectly times the balls 'arrival to compete at the catch point, ripping and competing for everything. Excellent in the running game, showing the ability to fight through blocks and keep his frame clean in pursuit. Does a nice job of getting his frame low to take out the ankles of ball carriers.

Weaknesses: Missed his entire sophomore season in 2018 with a nagging hamstring injury. Overall ball production during his 3 seasons has been very minimal, failing to record an interception during his career. A high-levered frame that struggles against shiftier receivers that can quickly get him on his heels and win inside leverage on underneath routes. Can miss with his hands at times, getting him caught flat-footed and granting some initial separation. Gets a little too handsy down the field, remaining overly physical after the contact window. Not a thumper in the run game, allowing runners to gain additional yardage after contact.

Best Fit: Outside man corner

Player Ranking (1-100): 72.4 - St. Juste impressed me quite a bit when watching his tape. His length and long speed are very good. He's so difficult to play against with his combination of physicality and length. He will make receivers fight for absolutely everything. He will grant separation at times but he generally recovers quickly. I love how willing and aggressive he is in run support. 4th round player.

22 - Kelvin Joseph - Kentucky - 6'1 197 lbs

Strengths: After being a four-star prospect in high school, Joseph signed on with LSU and played one season there before sitting out a season and entering the transfer portal to Kentucky. Joseph only played in 9 games for the Wildcats but greatly impressed when doing so, finishing with 4 interceptions, one of which he returned for a touchdown. Joseph is built with prototypical size for the next level, showing good length and height to play on the outside. Joseph is a tremendous athlete, possessing top-flight speed to play bump-and-run man coverage down the field against elite NFL athletes. Not just straight-line speed, Joseph has fluidity throughout his lower body, showcasing the ability to mirror on in-breaking routes. Flashes really impressive ball skills this season, showing his magnetism to the ball. He has a rare blend of timing and anticipation to quickly break on the ball with his back towards the ball. Doesn't shy away from the physical aspects of the game, showing to be a reliable tackler in run support.

Weaknesses: Very minimal game time and experience for Joseph in college, having only started a handful of career games. Personal and character concerns will need to be looked into with Joseph. There were clear concerns with Joseph at LSU, as he repeatedly entered the transfer portal. Teams will likely want to dig into what the problem was. He also had several really poor discipline penalties for Kentucky this past season, penalizing his team in really inopportune times.

Best Fit: Outside man-to-man corner

Player Ranking (1-100): 71.5 - A very hard guy to rank due to lack of overall game tape. Plus I don't know the full extent of his off-the-field concerns. There's no denying his talent levels. He has VERY few flaws on the field. But he has significant unknowns when it comes to off the field. It's clear to see why he was so highly regarded in high school though. Based on what I do know, I'd take him in the 4th round.

23 - Aaron Robinson - Central Florida - 6'0 190 lbs

Strengths: A former Alabama four-star recruit that ended up transferring following his freshman season. Built with the desired height and a long-levered frame, Robinson shows the experience and versatility to play at any of the cornerback positions. He starred his last few years playing mostly at nickel back. Robinson has impressive ball skill showing good diagnosis ability to read the balls 'flight and make plays on the ball as evidenced by his high passes defended each of the last two seasons. Robinson is a scrappy and feisty defensive back that loves to get in the face of opposing receivers at the line of scrimmage and jam them at the line to re-reroute them. Competes for absolutely everything. He moves like a guy that isn't over 6 feet, showing spring in his steps and looseness in his backpedal and side to side movements. Straight-line speed appears to be very good, rarely did I see him grant any separation down the field. Shows aggression and physicality in the run game and isn't afraid to put his neck in to make a tackle.

Weaknesses: Battled a bad injury during his sophomore season, causing him to miss the beginning of the season. His physical and aggressive nature gets him in trouble quite a bit as he loves to get grabby at all levels of the field. Is a ball watcher, always looking back at the QB, allowing himself to get beat at the top of routes. Needs to finish more plays, he has dropped several very catchable interceptions.

Best Fit: Man-to-man corner

Player Ranking (1-100): 71.0 - Robinson is a really interesting prospect that has some developmental upside. He has looked really good in each of the last two seasons for Central Florida. The fact that he's got the size, athleticism, and fiery nature makes me love him. 4th round player.

24 - IfeatuMelifonwu - Syracuse - 6'3 212 lbs

Strengths: The brother of NFL player, Obi, Ifeatu is similarly a very rare and athletically-built prospect. A 3-year contributor to the Orange, Melifornwu possesses ridiculous physical tools in his arsenal. Built with a tremendous long frame, Melifonwu has the size and the athleticism to smoothly transition to the next level. He utilizes his athleticism to play quite a bit of man coverage for the Orange, showing the ability to match up against bigger receivers and tight ends while limiting separation. Really good long speed allows him to track receivers up the field vertically with minimal separation. His wingspan and length make him a difficult assignment for receivers because he's frequently able to disrupt both at the line of scrimmage and at the catch point to knock the ball away. Understands how to place his hands when playing in press-man, disrupting and re-routing smaller receivers. The unique blend of ball skills and read/react abilities allow him to break quickly on routes. Moves well through his transitions, showing looseness through his frame to change direction and accelerate fluidly.

Weaknesses: Has missed some game time during his career for lower-body injuries. His frame will make playing with leverage a constant chore, allowing himself to play far too narrow when fighting through blockers. Appears to have some mental lapses when plays aren't directly in his direction or when he's playing in off-man or zone. Lacks the physical demeanor and the toughness to be an effective player against the run, getting completely blown off the ball by pulling lineman. Can struggle with balance against shiftier receivers that will easily win inside leverage on in-breaking routes. Has to continue to gain strength through his frame to be a more effective player in the running game.

Best Fit: Outside press-corner

Player Ranking (1-100): 70.4 - Melifonwu has a rare frame and tremendous length for the position. His lack of elite physical traits to be the 'alpha 'make me wonder if he can ever be a top-end corner. He struggles when it comes to strength and playing with power. 4th round player.

25 - Mark Gilbert - Duke - 6'1 175 lbs

Strengths: Gilbert quickly rose to stardom during his sophomore campaign and was arguably one of the best defensive backs in football in 2017, finishing with 6 interceptions and 15 passes defended. Unfortunately for him, it went downhill for him immediately after. But there's no denying there is talent in this football player. Gilbert is the cousin of NFL great Darrelle Revis. As a prospect, Gilbert has a nice-sized frame, featuring a long and rangy physique with room for additional mass. Gilbert is so refined with his movement skills and footwork, rarely wasting any steps. He remains leveraged at all times while remaining in the hip pocket of receivers, showing terrific agility to mirror in space. Sticky in man coverage, Gilbert excels when playing on an island, showing the route recognition abilities in combination with the fluid hips to change directions while decelerating. Remains disciplined with his eyes, not biting on double moves, and showing the closing burst to quickly recover ground and time the balls 'arrival to perfection. Tremendous ball skills, showing impressive reactive abilities and ball tracking skills to locate the ball when his back is to the ball. Utilizes his length to high point the ball and out jump receivers. Maximizes his frame out with physicality, both at the line of scrimmage or at the catch point. Will compete for everything, playing through the wide receiver's hands. Aggressive in run support and comes downhill on screens.

Weaknesses: An older prospect that will be 24 during his rookie season. Has dealt with major injury after major injury in college, having only played in 4 games the last 3 seasons. He's had multiple hip surgeries. His medical before the draft is going to be the most important thing for Gilbert. He's very skinny and needs to gain significant amounts of muscle to handle the physicality of bigger NFL receivers. Willing in run support, but struggles disengaging if blocked in pursuit. Is quicker than he is fast, not a great overall straight-line athlete, and will likely be hampered even more with the multiple lower-body injuries. Can get a little bit grabby on vertical routes.

Best Fit: Outside press-man corner

Player Ranking (1-100): 70.2 - A very good man cover corner that displays rare footwork and refinement in the technical areas of the game. If he didn't have the injury-troubled past and continued to get better from his sophomore season, he'd be a Day 1 player. I would take a gamble on a player of his talent all things considered in the 4th round.

26 - Ambry Thomas - Michigan - 6'0 189 lbs

Strengths: Before opting out of his final season with Michigan, Thomas had a solid junior campaign for the Wolverines defensively playing as a corner. In his first two seasons with the Wolverines, he was a dynamic kickoff return specialist before focusing on just defense in his final year. Good overall frame with a solid wingspan with room for additional growth and muscle. Thomas is at his best closest to the line of scrimmage, playing in press-man coverage partly due to his abilities to utilize excellent hand technique at the line to disrupt and redirect receivers. Also possesses the versatility and experience in playing off-coverage and zone coverage as well in Michigan's defense. A solid athlete that shows above-average long speed coupled with solid short-area quickness to stay on the hip pocket of most receivers. Shows the flexible joints to change direction and accelerate fluidly. Plays well as a perimeter corner with a good understanding of how to utilize the sidelines to close off routes. A willing supporter in the run game that shows little hesitancy when having to take a back on in the open field.

Weaknesses: Thomas features an undersized and wiry type of frame making some worry about his abilities handling NFL wide receivers, especially in the style in which he plays. He was outmuscled at times in the Big-10 most notably at the catch point where bigger-bodied receivers would post up him routinely. While he's a willing run supporter, he will get eaten up at first contact when having to fight through blocks. His ball skills are 'OK' but not spectacular and he is prone to losing track of the ball in the air, failing to always attack the football at the catch point.

Best Fit: Outside press-man corner

Player Ranking (1-100): 69.3 - A really good athlete that will immediately provide special teams 'value as a return specialist. His coverage skills are pretty solid but not great. He can fight for a role for a team early on but most likely it'll be as a #4 or 5 cornerback. He will have to prove he can handle the physical areas of the game in training camp. 5th round player.

27 - Tre Brown - Oklahoma - 5'10 188 lbs

Strengths: Brown has been a reliable presence for the Sooners defense in each of the last two seasons, starting in practically every game. Brown has dual-threat versatility, having impressive abilities as a return specialist as well. Brown is an outstanding athlete, combining short-area quickness with the long speed to makeup ground in an instant. This will enable him to be effectively play both inside and outside at the next level, although he played primarily on the outside in college. Might be one of the fastest corners in this draft class. Stays on the balls of his feet at all times, showing terrific closing bursts. Impressive ball skills as evidenced by his 29 passes defended the last three seasons. Possesses an innate ability to find, judge and disrupt at the catch point as precisely the right moment. More aggressive than you would expect for his size, showing physicality both at the line of scrimmage and through routes. Plays with a 'HOT' motor and is always working back towards the football in the running game, showing fearlessness when it comes to sacrificing his body, making many impressive plays tracking down ball carriers from behind. A reliable wrap-up tackler in run support.

Weaknesses: Will give up receptions constantly to bigger targets that can box him out at the catch point. Has major size concerns if he's going to play exclusively on the outside as he did in college, especially against NFL-sized outside possession receivers. Has some struggles when it comes to changing directions fluidly and will get caught out of position and caught trailing receivers quickly that are more nuanced route runners. Can be very grabby down the field. Strictly a man coverage fit for the next level.

Best Fit: Man cover corner

Player Ranking (1-100): 68.9 - I wish Brown had more experience playing inside because he has the movement abilities that make me think he could do so with additional development. His ball skills have gotten better during each season which shows he's only going to continue to get better. His lack of size while playing in the way in which he plays, doesn't bode well for the next level unless he develops as an inside cover guy. But his upside as a return specialist is very enticing. 5th round player.

28 - Deommodore Lenoir - Oregon - 5'11 203 lbs

Strengths: Lenoir has started every game in each of the last few seasons for the Ducks, proving to be one of the best playmakers in the Pac-12. Built with a squatty and low center of gravity frame, Lenoir is built with NFL strength and toughness. A consistent performer during each of his campaigns with very comparable production lines during each season. Lenoir has experience and comfort playing both inside and outside. Tough as nails, showing physicality and willingness to fight through blocks and come downhill to make big stops in the running game. Lenoir shines the most in off or zone coverage alignments where he can utilize his eyes, instincts, and click/close ability to bait the QB into making a throw and then beating the ball to the spot. Despite not being the longest or the tallest guy, Lenoir is impressive in the air with his vertical leaping ability to go snatch the ball out of the air against taller targets. Has a really good understanding of route development and route concepts to recognize things quickly. While not being an outstanding overall athlete, Lenoir flashes impressive recovery speed to quickly recover any lost steps. A feisty and fiery competition that shows the flexible joints, fluidity, and anticipation to make a lot of plays at the next level.

Weaknesses: A big risk-taker that is a gambler on every snap, leading to some big plays and some big losses. Lenoir's overconfidence gets the best of him, getting too reliant on reading and reacting to every single QB motion that he will get baited easily down the field. Will give up some separation on shorter to intermediate-based routes and is oftentimes is in catchup mode. Lacks the ideal measurable to be a boundary corner at the next level and could be limited by some as strictly a subpackage inside player.

Best Fit: Inside or outside off-man corner

Player Ranking (1-100): 67.9 - Lenoir is a solid prospect that shows the versatility to play in any defensive system. While he lacks elite characteristics, his playmaking skills and instincts allow him to be in a great position to make a lot of plays. I could see him carving out a valuable role on special teams 'immediately and work his way to win valuable snaps very quickly. 5th round player.

29 - Emmanuel Rugamba - Miami (OH) - 5'11 190 lbs

Strengths: A former Iowa player that transferred to Miami (OH) after losing his starting job at Iowa. Rugamba opted out of his final year of eligibility, playing his last year of college football in 2019 as a junior. After having an impressive junior season, Rugamba put himself back on the NFL Draft radar after finishing with 85 tackles and 9 passes defended. Rugambaisn't the biggest guy, more of an athletically-built prospect, but he completely maximizes his physique when it comes to playing with toughness. Tremendous physicality when it comes to the running game as evidenced by his high tackle numbers. Squeezes out running lanes and plays like a hammer in search of a nail in his ability to get downhill quickly and forcefully wrap up. When in man coverage, Rugamba shows physicality at the line of scrimmage with good hand technique to re-route and jam receivers. Does a good job of utilizing the perimeters to cap off routes. Has some experience in zone coverage and while it's not his specialty, he does show some instinctive traits and the closing speed to close gaps in a flash.

Weaknesses: Was suspended for a game at Iowa for a violation of team rules. Ball production is minimal with only 3 career interceptions. His overaggressive nature is apparent on double moves and play-action type of fakes, oftentimes biting hard and losing his man down the field. Not the biggest or the longest guy and could struggle against bigger possession receivers that can box him out at the catch point. He needs refinement in zone coverage and lacks ideal footwork in his backpedal. A solid athlete but not a spectacular one and will get exposed against top-tier speed.

Best Fit: Press-man corner

Player Ranking (1-100): 67.5 - Rugamba showed this in 2019 that he deserves to play at the next level despite his disappointing Iowa career. He is a solid prospect that could compete right away for a role on defense. I love his toughness and physicality with which he plays. 5th round player.

30 - Robert Rochell - Central Arkansas - 6'0 195 lbs

Strengths: One of the most intriguing FCS prospects in the entire draft, dominating his level of competition as evidenced by his ball production with 10+ career interceptions during his career. Built with prototypical NFL size, featuring good length and an absolutely stacked physique. Rochell is an athletic freak that also features for the track and field team. Known for his explosive characteristics, Rochell is one of the fastest and best athletes in this draft class. Playing almost entirely as an outside boundary corner, Rochell utilizes his length to close off and seal boundaries. His length also allows him to get physical at the line of scrimmage, utilizing strong hands and good jam technique to disrupt and re-route. Not scheme-specific, Rochell can play both in press-man situations or even play off-man coverage or zone. Not just athletic, Rochell is aggressive and physical when it comes to run support and competing at the catch point. His former wide receiver experience comes to play when it comes to his ball tracking abilities.

Weaknesses: Raw as raw can be in every aspect of the game. Gets by with his physical characteristics at the FCS level, but far too often fails to utilize proper anticipatory abilities to put himself into good positions. His eyes can deceive him at times, not always reading things properly and overrunning plays while in pursuit. Very grabby down the field, failing to always trust his technique. Allows his pads to rise while trailing, which limits his ability to mirror when playing laterally. Shows some willingness in the run game, but lacks ideal instincts to put himself in the right gaps.

Best Fit: Developmental boundary corner

Player Ranking (1-100): 66.2 - Rochell is an intriguing prospect that has the size and raw physical traits to be a fun developmental prospect. He's going to need some time and NFL coaching, but there are traits to work with. 5th round player.

31 - Olaijah Griffin - USC - 6'0 175 lbs

Strengths: A former five-star high school recruit and son of multi-platinum artist Warren G, Griffin was one of the best two-way players in the nation, having experience both at WR and QB. As a sophomore at USC, Griffin showed off his upside, finishing with 37 tackles and 9 passes defended. Griffin has been used on kickoff returns as well for USC. Playing mostly as a boundary corner, Griffin shows the self-assured confidence and swagger to play on an island. Entrusted with covering the larger section of the field for USC, Griffin shows terrific speed and lower body explosiveness to spring himself in any direction. His quick feet allow him to mirror in space, showing loose body movements to mirror while remaining on the hip pocket of receivers at all times. Route recognition abilities and mental alertness are on display at all times with his understanding of route development and concepts. Highly aggressive at the catch point, showing his former receiver skills on display to time the balls 'arrival to perfection to knock it away. Has shown impressive fearlessness in the run game, reacting without hesitation and willing to take out the legs of bigger runners in the hole.

Weaknesses: Griffin has struggled with disc injuries in his back causing him to miss several games during his sophomore season. Possesses a very wiry frame for the next level and needs to put on an additional 10-15 pounds. Overall ball skills haven't been proven in interceptions, failing to have elite and developed ball skills when his back is to the ball. Will get dominated at the catch point against larger receivers that can effectively box him out.

Best Fit: Outside corner

Player Ranking (1-100): 65.9 - Griffin is a talented athlete there's no denying that. But his back issues and his lack of ideal size and functional strength make me worry if he can hold up at the next level. His athleticism and physical traits warrant him a 5th round pick, assuming his back checks out 'OK 'at the medical checks.

32 - T.J. Carter - Memphis - 5'11 190 lbs

Strengths: A 4-year starter for Memphis that has impressed during each of his campaigns showing tremendous maturity and experience. Built with an athletically tapered frame and a compact shape. The thing you'll notice right away about Carter is the confidence in which he plays. Memphis coaches repeatedly left him in acres of space 1v1 in man coverage, showing their complete reliance to shut down ½ of the field. His ball production and tackling numbers were solid posting double-digit passes defended and 60+ tackles during those seasons as well. Confident in his press technique at the line of scrimmage, showing strong hands to alter and disrupt. Will compete at the catch point, showing good anticipation abilities and timing. Fearless in the way he plays showing a downhill nature to come and assist in run support. Manipulates QB's with his eyes, testing them to see if they'll throw it in his direction. Impressive footwork out of his backpedal, remaining patient and in control. Transitions smoothly without wasting any steps, showing impressive mirror abilities.

Weaknesses: Missed some game time during his final year for an undisclosed injury. Despite his experience, he makes far too many common simple mistakes especially on crossing routes where he will give easy inside access too often. Doesn't look overly comfortable reading the game in zone coverages, failing to properly adjust to spacing and route concepts. He is very grabby down the field and has gotten called for several holding and pass interference calls. Overall athleticism is 'OK 'but isn't top-tier and he will get exposed at times against AAC receivers in space. Has missed many interception opportunities that have fallen right in his lap, dropping some terrible opportunities. Lacks ideal measurables to be an outside corner to compete against bigger NFL possession receivers.

Best Fit: Press-man corner

Player Ranking (1-100): 65.3 - Carter is a good player that has a lot of experience. He is known to be a favorite of the coaching staff and will work his butt off. He has physical limitations but he makes up for it with his film work and his desire to be good. He's worth a gamble in the 5th round.

33 - Bryan Mills III - North Carolina Central - 6'1 180 lbs

Strengths: After being a JUCO prospect, Mills played his final season as a junior for MEAC-program North Carolina Central. He greatly excelled his junior season, finishing with 5 interceptions and 13 passes defended before opting out before his senior season. Mills has a long and rangy frame with enough room for continued development and muscular growth. He utilizes his length to control receivers at the line of scrimmage, showing good press ability to disrupt and re-route at the line of scrimmage. Physical at the catch point as well, utilizing his length and strong hands to knock the ball out upon arrival. Mills is a highly intelligent football player that has an advanced understanding of route concepts, showing good recognition abilities to read/react quickly. Good ball skills, showing excellent cover awareness and down the field instincts. Sinks in his stance and stays on the ball of his feet to remain under control at all times, remaining patient as routes develop.

Weaknesses: Mills is very skinny and needs to continue to add additional muscle mass to his frame to play at the next level. Played almost entirely in man coverage in college, having very little off-man or zone experience. The competition jump to the NFL level from the MEAC-conference is going to be very large. His overall functional strength is minimal and he needs to gain additional lower and upper body power to be able to offer anything in run support. Overall athleticism is just 'OK 'and he struggles against speedier receiver. There are noticeable stiffness concerns through his lower body. He will allow separation on shifty receivers that can take him laterally across the field.

Player Ranking (1-100): 61.3 - Mills has very good size and physicality for the position. The problem is, his physicality is going to be significantly offset when competing against higher levels of competition. He needs to gain substantial strength and weight to play consistently at the next level. 6th round player.

34 - Darren Hall - San Diego State - 5'11 189 lbs

Strengths: Starting his career at safety before transitioning to cornerback and starting in 3 consecutive years for Mountain-West program San Diego State. A ball production machine that has tallied 25 passes defended the last three years in addition to 6 interceptions and 3 forced fumbles. The definition of versatile, Hall has experience playing at every position in the secondary. He is comfortable in the slot but typically plays on the perimeter. Excels the most in off-man or zone. This allows him to utilize his natural instincts and feel for developing routes. Excellent route anticipation, reading his keys, and then quickly closing down with excellent short-area bursts to make plays on the ball. Terrific click and close ability are very good. A loose athlete that appears to have flexible joints to change directions with ease. Loves baiting QB's into throwing in his direction and then making a play on the ball. Loves getting aggressive in run support, playing with tireless energy while working in pursuit.

Weaknesses: A 'bend but not break' corner that will give up a lot of plays underneath. Lacks great size and has stubby length. Despite his ball production numbers he struggles when his back is to the ball on deeper-developing routes. On far too many occasions, he fails to get his head turned around while the ball is in the air. Needs refinement when working out of a backpedal, takes far too many wasted steps, and is always in catch-up mode. A gambler that is overly aggressive to a fault and is susceptible to double moves and play fakes. While he's willing in run support, he approaches tackles far too high, allowing additional yardage after contact.

Best Fit: Zone or off-man corner or could bump back out to FS

Player Ranking (1-100): 60.7 - Hall is a good athlete and a big-time playmaker. There are developmental traits with him for sure. He will give up a lot of plays but he makes a number too. A fun player that is worth a pick in the 6th round.

35 - Nashon Wright - Oregon State - 6'4 187 lbs

Strengths: A former JUCO prospect, Wright started the last two years with the Beavers. Previously a wide receiver, Wright's offensive background is certainly on display in the way he plays the position. Blessed with tremendous height and length, Wright showcases the frame to handle NFL size. Has had excellent ball production numbers the last two seasons, combining for 5 interceptions and 11 passes defended. A very good athlete that displays impressive long speed, eating up large sections of grass with his stride lengths. Does a good job of keeping his pads down, allowing him to cross-field and change direction. Has some good looseness through his frame, showing comfort to flip his hips on lateral-breaking routes without gearing down. Has handled both man and zone concepts, looking comfortable at both. A student of the game that anticipates and recognizes things quickly. Very physical at the catch point, utilizing his length to play through the receiver's hands. Tracks the ball down the field like a receiver, quickly locating the ball and then high-pointing it to perfection. Very disciplined in his assignment, rarely biting down the field by QB play-fakes or double moves.

Weaknesses: Wright is very very wiry and needs to continue to grow into his frame and add sizable amounts of muscle. His lack of functional strength is on display in the running game, getting completely handled by receivers in pursuit, lacking any kind of shed abilities if engaged. As a tackler, he's an ankle biter, failing to consistently wrap-up securely. His jam technique is very poor, frequently missing at the line of scrimmage. Will struggle against shorter and quicker receivers that can win leverage on inside or underneath routes.

Best Fit: Outside corner

Player Ranking (1-100): 59.3 - Wright is an intriguing prospect. His frame and his speed are very very exciting. But he's still very raw. His lack of functional strength and reliability in the run game will likely limit him to a practice squad early on for a team. But I'd still take a chance on him in the 7th round.

36 - Mike Hampton - South Florida - 6'1 190 lbs

Strengths: A 3-year starter for AAC-Conference South Florida that has been one of their best players each of the last few seasons. A rangier built guy that has more than enough height and length for the next level. Led the AAC in breakouts during his sophomore season with 18 passes defended. USF plays mostly in a Cover-3 defensive system where Hampton is left practically on an island on one side of the field, showing complete reliance on him. Very comfortable in man-to-man situations, showing fluidity and explosiveness to spring himself in any direction, attaching himself to the hip pocket of opposing receivers. Elastic flexibility is evident through his hips as he fluidly and seamlessly transitions into full stride, rarely granting any kind of separation. Not just a short-area quick guy, Hampton appears to have excellent long-speed. A quick-footed guy that wasted very little motion out of his backpedal, showing to have good overall footwork. Fiesty and competitive and will battle at the catch point for every single ball.

Weaknesses: After his stellar sophomore year, Hampton's production has dropped off quite a bit overall, failing to record an interception in each of the last two seasons, as well as decreased passes defended. An older prospect and will be a 24-year-old rookie. A lankier guy that needs to add additional muscle and size for the next level to compete against bigger outside possession receivers. Has struggled in the running game due to his inconsistent physicality, failing to accurately deconstruct and fight through blockers.

Best Fit: Outside boundary corner

Player Ranking (1-100): 57.4 - I like Hampton quite a bit. Unfortunately, he hasn't always had the best of showings against the better opponents, but he has really impressive overall size and athletic characteristics. 7th round player.

37 - Mark Webb - Georgia - 6'1 210 lbs

Strengths: A former four-star wide receiver high school recruit, Webb ended up transitioning to a cornerback very early on during his freshman season. As a freshman, Webb was a very good special teams' player before eventually winning some defensive snaps during his sophomore season. Having mostly played in the STAR (a cross between a nickel corner and a safety) role for the Bulldogs defense, Webb has shown his versatility and football intelligence to pick up things quickly. Webb has very good size for the position, featuring the frame for additional growth and vines for arms. A physical kid that doesn't shy away from run support, showing fearlessness and good reliability to wrap up and bring runners down. While playing closer to the line of scrimmage this year, Webb showed his ability to get in the faces of receivers and tight ends to disrupt their route. Has shown good short-area quickness, lower body flexibility and agility to handle the lateral aspects of playing on the inside. Often tasked with covering athletic tight ends, Webb didn't shy from the physicality or the willingness to compete at the catch point. Webb impressed when covering arguably the best tight end in the nation, Kyle Pitts.

Weaknesses: Webb is still very raw and is still learning the finer nuances of playing on the defensive side of the ball. He's not a traditional cornerback and has played almost entirely inside and closer to the line of scrimmage, making some feel he's more of a safety than a cornerback. Ball production numbers have been vastly underwhelming with only 1 career interception. Webb isn't a top-end athlete and will allow separation against better targets down the field in vertical settings.

> **Best Fit: Developmental corner or safety**

Player Ranking (1-100): 56.8 - I could see coaches/scouts looking at Webb at different spots along the defense. He certainly has the football IQ to pick up things quickly. He's still learning when it comes to playing in the secondary and will require some growth pains but he's a solid football player. The physical traits are there to be a solid special teams player, he just needs time to win snaps on defense. 7th round player.

38 - Tre Norwood - Oklahoma - 6'0 192 lbs

Strengths: A 3-year contributor to the Sooners defense that brought himself strongly onto the draft scene following a very impressive final junior season. He was a ball production machine, finishing the season with 5 interceptions. A hybrid defensive back that played both in the nickel and as a free safety, showing his versatility for the next level. Possessing a prototypical frame with additional room for more growth, Norwood has the ideal size to play at the next level. Most comfortable playing off-man when in the nickel. A magnet to the football that displays natural ball skills when in coverage, showing good cover awareness and field vision. An instinctual athlete that possesses good timing and anticipation to break on the ball, with very good click and close abilities. Flexible joints to change direction and accelerate fluidly when in transition. Can handle larger possession receivers in the slot or quicker, agile receivers as well. Reliable hands to finish interceptions. A mentally alert player that plays with self-assured confidence.

Weaknesses: Missed the entire 2019 season after tearing his ACL in spring practices. Has worked hard to bulk up and gain muscle since coming onto campus but he needs to still add additional muscle and strength to play. A liability in the running game, lacking the functional strength or the ability to fight through blockers. Really short arms. Approaches tackles far too high, bouncing off at times. Has a bit of a reckless and kamikaze style of play, allowing his eyes to deceive him at times, frequently getting caught looking into the backfield. A true gambler that will make plays but give up giant plays in coverage as well. Quicker than he is fast, Norwood will get exposed playing further away from the football, lacking ideal range to handle vertical routes. Struggles at the catch point against bigger-bodied receivers that can out muscle him. Strictly a slot corner when in coverage with practically no outside experience.

Best Fit: Nickel corner

Player Ranking (1-100): 56.2 - Norwood had a very impressive season this year ball production-wise. He is a playmaker that will frustrate at times but 'WOW 'at other times. He needs continued development and added bulk onto his frame. 7th round player.

39 - RachadWildgoose- Wisconsin - 5'11 197 lbs

Strengths: After being a rotational player during his freshman season, Wildgoose got his chance as the starter during his sophomore campaign in 2019. Built with a compact frame, Wildgoose shows some impressive NFL-quality traits to play at the next level. A physical corner that loves to compete at all areas of the game. Showing fearlessness in the running game, Wildgoose is quick to trigger and get downhill, delivering some big blows to ball carriers. Maximizes his frame by extending and making plays outside of his frame. Aggressive in man coverage at the line of scrimmage, getting right in the face of receivers to re-route and disrupt. Will fight for every ball, forcing receivers to outmuscle him at the catch point. Grants very little separation in man coverage, forcing QB's to avoid him for most of the games in which he started in. Shows good short area quickness with the flexible joints to change direction and accelerate fluidly.

Weaknesses: Missed most of his final season as a junior due to some injury and sickness concerns, choosing to opt out the final part of the season after playing in just 2 games. Doesn't have a lot of game time due to only having 1 year of starting experience. Lacks ideal overall size and length for the position. More of a cover guy than an elite playmaker, causing many to question his overall ball skills with only 1 career interception. Has very much been a hot and cold player during his career, making several boneheaded mistakes and/or penalties that cost the team in inopportune times. Quicker than he is fast, Wildgoose lacks elite vertical speed and will grant some separation against speedier up-the-field targets.

Best Fit: Outside man cover corner

Player Ranking (1-100): 55.4 - A very good cover corner that unfortunately doesn't have a lot of game tape on his resume. He's a good player but isn't a great one. He's simply a man cover corner. 7th round pick.

40 - DicaprioBootle - Nebraska - 5'10 195 lbs

Strengths: A 4-year contributor and a team captain to the Cornhuskers defense that has been a starter for every single game since the beginning of his sophomore campaign in 2018. Bootle is built with a compact and low center of gravity physique. An aggressive athlete that is fearless in the run game, quickly getting downhill with 0 hesitancy. Bootle is a quick-twitch reactionary player that moves with effortless fluidity. Comfortable when playing inside or outside and in man or zone. Easing out of his backpedal and transitioning into full speed, Bootle wastes very little time or motion. Very feisty and competitive when the ball is in the air, showing good timing and reflexes to time the balls 'arrival to perfection to knock it away. Good mirror ability due to his loose limbs, quickness, and agility. This enables him to remain in the hip pocket of receivers in press coverage.

Weaknesses: Bootle's ball skills are very subpar, rarely allowing himself to track the ball accurately and make a play to locate the ball in flight. He tends to always keep his back towards the ball and play the receiver. This is very evident in the fact that he hasn't had "1" interception during his 4-year career at Nebraska, especially considering he's gotten his hands on well over 20 passes defended. Lack of length is evident when trying to deconstruct blocks, failing to offer any kind of shedding ability once reached in space. Poor technique when attempting to bring down bigger backs, failing to drop his pads and bouncing off tackles. Quicker than he is fast, his long speed was exposed at times against bigger, straight-line athletes. Will occasionally flip his hips too quickly causing him to get caught out of position on in-breaking routes. His size limits him to likely a nickel role at the next level.

Best Fit: Nickel corner

Player Ranking (1-100): 54.6 - Bootle's size likely will limit him to nickel responsibilities at the next level. Unfortunately, Bootle is a very very poor tackler and that will hurt his chances to get drafted. He has some impressive movement ability but his lack of size and physicality could cause him to get undrafted. He will likely be an undrafted free agent grade for me.

41 - Chris Wilcox - BYU - 6'2 195 lbs

Strengths: A 3-year starter for the BYU defense, Wilcox has shown experience and consistency during his time with the team. A former high-school top track athlete, Wilcox possesses a long and lean high-torso track physique. Wilcox certainly possesses the size, length, and speed combination teams are looking for. Is at his best when playing in a press-man scenario, showing the ability to bully smaller receivers with his length at the line of scrimmage. Does a nice job when utilizing the boundaries to seal off routes. He has the speed to not allow any kind of vertical separation down the field. Mentally alert showing the secondary burst to close cushions or recover after any false steps.

Weaknesses: Suffered a bad low leg fracture during the end of the 2018 season causing him to miss the entire 2019 season as well, due to having his surgery in the spring prior. Wilcox isn't a playmaker, failing to record an interception during his college career. His ball-hawking skills are a serious question mark, as he regularly attempts to play the receiver with his back towards the ball as opposed to timing the ball and competing at the catch point. Still very raw, and will struggle against shorter and shiftier receivers that can cause him to overset to the outside and put him on his heels when forcing him to play laterally. His aggressive style will lead him to some holding calls and getting overly grabby down the field. Needs to continue to add functional strength to his frame for the next level.

Player Ranking (1-100): 53.6 - A talented athlete that is still getting refined in the position. Has all the measurables you like to see in a player but still needs major development to play against top-tier competition. Undrafted free agent.

42 - Tay Gowan - Central Florida - 6'2 185 lbs

Strengths: Before sitting out the entire 2020 season, Gowan was a 1-year starter for Central Florida. He was originally a Miami (OH) recruit but transferred to community college after his freshman season. Gowan is a long and rangy built corner that had a very sold 1-year college resume. Playing as a perimeter corner, Gowan shows his good sideline awareness, wingspan, and body control. Closing burst is evident when closing gaps and working his way back towards the football. Excels in zone coverage showing a good understanding of route concepts and development, putting himself in good positions to make plays. A twitchy athlete that shows good instincts and route recognition to jump routes and maintaining proper cushioning in coverage. Utilizes his length well at both the line of scrimmage and at the catch point, showing physicality at all levels. Flashes good ball skills with the ability to track the ball down the field and high-point the football.

Weaknesses: Has only played in 12 career college games with very minimal game time to view. Has a very skinny and rangy physique and will struggle without additional muscle at the next level. Jam technique when in man coverage is very poor, as he will get bullied by bigger receivers. Not as fast as you'd like him to be, and will grant initial separation rather quickly to speedier receivers. Overly aggressive to a fault and will bite hard on double moves or misdirection-style plays. Passive when it comes to initiating contact in the run game, tends to stay away from physical contact.

Best Fit: Perimeter zone corner

Player Ranking (1-100): 53.5 - Gowan is a long and rangy corner that lacks any defining physical traits. He's not overly physical nor is he a great athlete. He needs to go to the right system to have a chance to make the team. Undrafted free agent.

43 - Jerry Jacobs - Arkansas - 5'11 203 lbs

Strengths: Jacobs has had a frenzied college career, originally a JUCO prospect for Arkansas State before transitioning as a graduate transfer and playing his final season for the Razorbacks. Jacobs has a stoutly-built frame, showing good muscularity and size. Possesses very good ball skills, as evidenced by his 4 interceptions, 8 passes defended, and 1 forced fumble in his only full season against Division-1 competition in 2018. Jacobs best fits in a zone-style defense where he can utilize his playmaking abilities and natural instincts to make plays on the football. Possesses a high football IQ showing good recognition of route concepts with good play recognition abilities which allows him to make plays on the football. Disciplined with his eyes, Jacobs reads his keys and quickly closes down. Mentally alert that plays with self-assured confidence.

Weaknesses: Tore his ACL in 2019 and missed the last few games of the season for Arkansas State. Only played in 3 games for Arkansas his final season, choosing to opt-out for the remainder of the season. Has only started 1 full season in the last 3 years. Lacks ideal and prototypical height and length. Appears completely passive in the running game, choosing not to get his hands dirty. Just an 'OK 'athlete that fails to have the long speed to be able to carry receivers up the field. Struggles against savvy route runners that can quickly get him on his heels and create separation. Needs to play better when his back is turned to the play.

Best Fit: Outside zone corner

Player Ranking (1-100): 53.1 - Jacobs doesn't have a draftable grade. He had a nice year with Arkansas State in 2018 but he's just been 'OK 'the last two seasons in the few games he's played in. He fails to have ideal size or great athletic traits to have a fit for most defenses. His lack of tackling ability limits him even more when playing in a zone-style defense. Undrafted free agent.

TOP-10 Cornerbacks

1. Patrick Surtain II
2. Caleb Farley
3. Jaycee Horn
4. Israel Mukuamu
5. Asante Samuel Jr
6. Paulson Adebo
7. Greg Newsome III
8. Tyson Campbell
9. Elijah Molden
10. Kary Vincent Jr

Chapter 14

Safeties

1 - Andre Cisco - Syracuse - 6'0 209 lbs

Strengths: A 2-year starter that has played ever since his true freshman campaign, winning significant snaps on defense from Day 1. Cisco is a well-built prospect that has good next-level size showcasing good compactness through his frame. Cisco is a ball hawk as evidenced by his gaudy ball production numbers in each of his seasons, finishing with 13 interceptions, 14 passes defended, and 2 forced fumbles during only 24 career college games. A dangerous threat for QBs every time the ball is remotely close to Cisco due to his ability to snatch the ball out of mid-flight with some spectacular diving catches on his resume. Instinctual at all areas of the game showing tremendous awareness to locate the football, both in the run game and the passing game. Evidence of film study is prevalent with the way Cisco plays, showing the ability to quickly recognize and anticipate developing plays. Mentally alert and possesses twitchy reflexes, remaining on the ball of his feet to quickly time the balls 'arrival. Very good when his back is to the ball, utilizing his innate ability to find and judge the ball to challenge receivers in the air. Used at times in the slot, showing the ability to rough up slot receivers at the line of scrimmage to disrupt their routes. Lower body movements are smooth, showing good flexibility and hip mobility to transition and change direction with ease. Fearless when coming up and supporting in the run game, showing an aggressive downhill nature to attack runners in the hole.

Weaknesses: Missed almost his entire final season after suffering a lower-body injury during warmups, choosing to opt out the remaining of the season to prepare for the draft. Also missed 3 games in 2019 for another lower-body injury. Cisco's biggest concern is his inability to consistently wrap-up, routinely missing tackles in space. He's too content attempting to ankle swipe or drag down as opposed to forcefully utilizing his lower body to drive runners down. His poor pursuit angles lead to opportunities for additional yardage in the open-field for runners. Struggles breaking down blocks in the open field, failing to get off and properly disengage in ample time. Can get overaggressive on occasion, leading to him getting manipulated with pump-fakes and play-action type of plays down the field.

Best Fit: All-around safety

Player Ranking (1-100): 85.3 - Cisco is likely the best playmaking ball hawk in this entire draft class from the secondary. The fact that he had an interception on more than half of his games in college is ridiculous.

There's no denying his ability to be around the football. He needs to improve his tackling fundamentals though. 1st round player.

2 - Trevon Moehrig - TCU - 6'2 202 lbs

Strengths: A former highly-touted cornerback recruit that has transitioned to safety at TCU. Moehrig has played valuable snaps since his freshman year, where he was also voted the team's 'most valuable special teams 'player. Exploding during this sophomore year, Moehrig finished the season with 62 tackles, 4 interceptions, 11 passes defended, and 2 forced fumbles. A good-sized athlete that displays an athletically-built frame with good overall muscularity and length. Playing in a deeper role, Moehrig typically plays as a single-high safety showing the effectiveness to cover large sections of grass with good overall athletic ability. Loose-limbed, Moehrig shows fluidity in his movements, remaining on the balls of his feet, and displays good twitchy reflexes to quickly react. Possesses the flexible joins to change directions with ease and accelerates fluidly out of his stance. Recovery speed is good, and when beaten initially, he's shown the ability to make up ground and play the ball in flight. Highly intelligent, Moehrig is seen communicating with his defense pre-snap. Very comfortable in a wide range of coverage setups, showing good instincts and route recognition when in zone coverage. Initiates contact well at the balls 'arrival to play through the receiver and knock the ball away. Quick to trigger in the run game, Moehrig will deliver punishing hits when squared. Aggressive and physical, always around the ball carrier, getting in on several tackles.

Weaknesses: Moehrig loves to go for the big hit but he's not a secure wrap-up tackler and as the last line of defense, it can be a bit troubling. This is partly due to his troublesome angles while in pursuit, leading to difficulties when approaching runners. Has very little experience being used in man coverage situations and likely won't offer much as a nickel man cover guy. Overall play strength could stand to gain some improvement, he will get occupied while working downhill through traffic, possessing little ability to keep his frame clean. Doesn't possess elite top-end safety range in coverage.

> **Best Fit: Single high or Cover-2 safety**

Player Ranking (1-100): 83.7 - Moehrig has been impressive at TCU. He's one of the rare deep cover safeties in this draft class that can really play. His leadership traits, reliability having never been hurt, and athletic abilities and instincts make him an immediate next-level starter. His special teams 'value makes him an even higher commodity. 2nd round player.

3 - Richie Grant - Central Florida - 6'0 200 lbs

Strengths: A 3-year starter and 4-year contributor toe AAC-Conference Central Florida. Grant came onto the scene after a stellar sophomore campaign where he logged over 100 tackles, 6 interceptions, and 2 forced fumbles. Grant has good overall size and length to play both deeper and closer to the line of scrimmage. Grant is an explosive athlete that shows looseness and elastic flexibility throughout his lower body that allows himself to spring in any direction with ease. Not just quick, Grant shows really good closing bursts to the football which allows him to close down zone cushions and make-up ground on any lost steps. When used in man situations, Grant shows some mirror ability with impressive change of direction to accelerate fluidly in and out of transitions. Shows comfort when in zone looks, quickly reading the QB's arm motions to anticipate on routes and breaking. Grant uses his explosiveness to generate significant power through his hips to generate some bone-crushing collisions and hits, showing aggressiveness when coming downhill in the running game. Appears to be at his best when working either as a single-high or playing in a Cover-3 cloud defensive formation.

Weaknesses: While Grant has good size, some might be worried that his downhill nature could cause him some injury concerns competing against bigger NFL athletes, lacking ideal body armor on his frame. His aggressive nature causes him to get caught ball-watching in the backfield, making him susceptible to double moves and play-action type of plays. His hands are a major question mark as he has dropped several catchup interceptions during his time. While he's an aggressive tackler, sometimes his pad levels are far too high and his overaggressive nature leads him to bounce off of bigger backs, lacking ideal wrap-up fundamentals.

Best Fit: FS

Player Ranking (1-100): 82.1 - I really really like Grant. He's got the right combination of consistency, size, explosive characteristics, and football IQ. While he has some concerns and I would like to see him gain 5-10 more pounds of muscle, he should be a Day 1 starter for most teams.

4 - HamsahNasirildeen - Florida State - 6'3 213 lbs

Strengths: A full-time 2-year starter for the Seminoles that has been tremendous during each of the seasons, finishing with just under 200 tackles during those years combined. His physique looks like it was built in a lab with true athletic gifts showing tremendous thickness and length from head to toe. Overall athleticism is through the roof for a guy of his size, showing the short-area explosiveness coupled with really good long speed. Tremendously versatile, showing the ability to line up in single-high, as a subpackage linebacker, or even in slot coverage. Has some Isaiah Simmons to his game with the ability to line up anywhere on the defense and make plays. A high motor player that works his butt off on every snap of the ball. His length allows him to stay square in coverage and play laterally when asked to cross face and cover in-breaking routes against tight ends or backs. Quick to get downhill, Nasirildeen triggers quickly when firing into the backfield to close gaps in the running game. Excellent when working back towards the ball, showing the athleticism to make up lost ground and make plays backside in the running game.

Weaknesses: Tore his ACL at the end of his junior season causing him to miss some games during the 2020 season as well. Struggles when his back is towards the ball, failing to quickly locate the ball in flight. A 'jack of all trades 'athlete that lacks a true position for the next level. When in coverage, he needs to learn some of the finer nuances, such as footwork when working out of a backpedal. Would struggle to play too deep in coverage, lacking the necessary range, field awareness, and ball-hawking ability. Looks for the big collision instead of the reliable form tackle, which is mostly due to the rise of his pads, Nasirildeen's leverage when taking on backs in the hole is far too high. When blitzing, he never seemed to have much of a plan, failing to disengage once initially reached by backs.

Best Fit: Hybrid S/LB

Player Ranking (1-100): 81.8 - Lacks a true position or an 'elite' trait other than the fact that he's a really good athlete and he's got a tremendously gifted physique. He needs to continue to learn to harness it and find a bonafide role sooner rather than later if he wants to flourish. He will make defensive coaches salivate with his 'potential' but they will have to show the same levels of patience. 2nd round player.

5 - Paris Ford - Pittsburgh - 6'0 190 lbs

Strengths: A former four-star recruit that has been a starter for the Pittsburgh defense in each of the last two seasons. Came onto the scene in a big way during his sophomore season, where he finished with 90 tackles, 3 interceptions, 1 defensive touchdown, 9 passes defended, and 3 forced fumbles. Ford is a long and rangy built safety that completely has maximized his frame out with top-end physicality and athleticism. A playmaker that has proven his abilities to create big defensive plays during each of his seasons, utilizing his terrific field vision to put himself in good positions to make plays. A very good and rangy athlete that has been used in a variety of different scenarios for their defense, playing mostly in a deeper role. Fluidity through his frame and excellent speed allow him to offer upside in both zone and man coverage. Highly competitive and tough, Ford is quick to trigger and get downhill. Exploding into ball carriers, Ford is a big hitter that utilizes his short-area quickness and explosiveness to drive with his hips, rarely letting a runner out of his grasps. Has very good recovery speed capable of making plays in pursuit from the backside. Excellent zone instincts when playing closer to the line of scrimmage due to read/react abilities to make plays on the ball coupled with good route instincts. Reads things quickly and takes good 1st steps to the ball. A defensive leader and good communicator that keeps the defense organized pre-snap. An excellent blitzer that utilizes his explosive nature to quickly generate pressure. Plays with a 'HOT' motor and is always in pursuit.

Weaknesses: Opted out for the final few games of the 2020 season to focus on the NFL Draft. His reckless nature could be troublesome with his skinnier frame at the next level. He's still a bit raw when it comes to the cover aspects of playing safety, needing to show more patience before triggering at times. Has made most of his plays when closer to the line of scrimmage and when playing deep, he needs to do a better job of making plays on the ball by recognizing route concepts. He appears to have some slight mental lapses the further he is away from the ball. Has had several issues catching the football on clear-cut interception opportunities. A diver at times when tackling, leading to missed opportunities and runners being able to jump over him or avoid him.

Best Fit: Versatile safety that has physicality and movement abilities to be used anywhere

Player Ranking (1-100): 81.2 - Ford is a really good player. He's physical and plays with a chip on his shoulder. He's excellent against the run and shows the athleticism to be a successful player against the pass as well with more experience. But he was will some struggles if relied on too heavily in the passing game. 2nd round player.

6 - Jevon Holland - Oregon - 6'1 200 lbs

Strengths: A 2-year key contributor and defensive team leader for the Ducks defense that had a stellar first two campaigns where he finished with a combined 9 interceptions. He was also used as the main punt returner as well during his sophomore campaign. Holland is a well-built prospect that shows the length and weight distribution to play on the back end of a defense or closer to the line of scrimmage if needed. Good ball skills when playing face-up in the defense, showing good instincts and closing bursts to quickly diagnose where the QB is going with the football. Versatility and football intelligence is the name of the game for Holland, showing comfort and experience playing in a cover-2, single-high, box player, or in the nickel. Remaining on the balls of his feet and disciplined in all aspects of the game, Holland will rarely get caught out of position. In the run game, Holland does a really good job of locating the football and fighting through blocks by stacking/shedding to make the stop. A willing tackler that drops his pads and utilizes good fundamentals to bring ball carriers to the ground. A really solid athlete that shows his recovery speed when chasing down plays backside or when needing to recover after false steps. Smooth and fluid in his footwork, opening up his hips and transitioning with ease.

Weaknesses: A steady player but lacks any elite characteristics for a safety other than athletic abilities. While he played mostly in the nickel role, he isn't exactly great in man coverage. He will need to improve this if he wants to play in a deeper role at the next level. Gets caught flat-footed quite a bit by in-breaking routes, losing his receiver in space. He struggled badly when his back was toward the football, failing to have elite instincts and confidence in his ball tracking abilities to time the balls 'arrival to make plays down the field.

Best Fit: Box Safety

Player Ranking (1-100): 80.2 - I like Holland quite a bit but I don't believe he has the cover awareness or the instincts to play in the deeper halves at the next level. He's a solid athlete as seen when chasing plays down, but he's more reactive than anticipatory, limiting his range. He's one of the best tackling safeties in this class and he will make a lot of plays near the line of scrimmage on defense and a ton on special teams 'as well. 2nd round player.

7 - Ar'Darius Washington - TCU - 5'8 179 lbs

Strengths: A redshirt sophomore, Washington took over as the deep safety in the Horned Frogs defense during the end of his redshirt freshman season. He immediately sprung himself into the draft discussion after finishing with 5 interceptions and 46 tackles despite playing in a limited role most of the season. Washington is a dynamic football player that jumps off the screen in every game, playing with nonstop urgency and energy. His movement abilities are very good, showing blur quickness and explosiveness. Fluid through his motions, showing flexible joints and looseness in his frame to change direction on a dime. As a run defender, Washington shows 0 hesitancy coming up in the hole, delivering knock-out blows. A reliable last line of defense that utilizes acute angles to take direct pathways to the football. His read and react abilities allow him to quickly close down and key in on runs, quickly triggering and getting downhill. His coverage awareness abilities are very good, especially further away from the football. He shows good route recognition with a real understanding of route concepts to put himself into good positions. Attacks the football in the air, showing good competitiveness and timing at the catch point. Flashes good man coverage abilities with the experience and comfort to go into the slot and handle quicker receivers.

Weaknesses: After his tremendous success during his redshirt freshman campaign, Washington's sophomore season didn't quite live up to the billing, failing to record an interception in 9 starts. The immediate concern for Washington is his size, failing to have NFL measurements, or anywhere close to it for that matter. Teams began targeting him quite a bit and utilizing larger targets to mismatch on him in the slot. He routinely gets boxed out at the catch point against bigger targets. Has had some eye discipline issues due to repeatedly getting caught looking into the backfield. This ultimately causes him to grant some separation down the field. Really struggled consistently wrapping up during the 2020 campaign, whiffing on a number of tackles. Struggles when working through traffic in the run game, getting hooked and stuck on blocks due to his lack of length. Quicker than he is fast and appeared to struggle when chasing down long striders that got behind him.

Best Fit: Deep-lying FS

Player Ranking (1-100): 79.7 - Really fun player to watch on tape. If he had a better sophomore campaign he could be an early Day 2 player, but he seemed to regress a bit in 2020. He's always around the football! There's definitely developmental traits there, considering he's had less than a year and a half of starting experience. 3rd round player.

8 - Caden Sterns - Texas - 6'1 207 lbs

Strengths: A 3-year starter and team captain for the Longhorns that has started since his freshman season, having arguably his best year as a freshman with 4 interceptions and over 60 tackles. Built with good size, Sterns possesses a prototypical NFL safety physique with good compactness and length. A highly competent safety that plays with a terrific football IQ while showing good leadership intangibles. Sterns is at his best in coverage, showing proficiency in all types of coverage. He's played both in single-high looks as well as dropping to cover shallow zones. He also will kick inside and cover the slot on occasion. A very good athlete that shows terrific functional movement skills with good quickness, loose hips, and flexible joints to change directions. When covering in man, he shows the quick feet to limit separation and remain in the hip pocket of receivers. When playing deeper and further from the ball, Sterns possesses the body control and the range to cover a lot of ground and quickly close. He reads his keys well while reading the QB's arm motion to quickly anticipate and attack the football. Will compete at the catch point showing good physicality with the ability to play through receivers and knock the ball away. Generally speaking, he's a reliable tackler that will utilize good wrap-up technique.

Weaknesses: Despite his great size, his physicality and toughness aren't prevalent in the way he plays. Most notably in the run game, he tends to be a drag-down tackler that will allow additional yardage after contact. Doesn't appear to have any 'POP' in his hands when initiating contact. Can be a little late at diagnosing plays in the running game, failing to be in proper positions to make plays, and getting into 'catch-up' mode. Struggles when lineman can get their hands on him, failing to have the power in his upper-body to disengage. This limits him when used as a blitzer as he will easily get blocked by running backs or tight ends.

Best Fit: Cover-2 or Single-High Safety

Player Ranking (1-100): 77.5 - Sterns is much much better further away from the ball. His lack of physicality and functional strength will get exposed if he's too close to the line of scrimmage. While further away, he can utilize his athleticism and cover awareness to make plays down the field. 3rd round player.

9 - Richard LeCounte - Georgia - 5'11 190 lbs

Strengths: A 4-year contributor and 3-year starter for the Bulldogs that has been proven to be one of the most consistent and well-rounded players on their defense during each of those campaigns. LeCounte had his best year as a junior where he finished with 4 interceptions, 2 forced fumbles, 3 fumble recoveries and 3 more passes defended. LeCounte is a team leader and the signal-caller for the Georgia secondary, communicating with his teammates at every step. LeCounte is an instinctive player that understands the mental side of the game, reading cues and route concepts to put himself into good positioning to make plays. Has good internal instincts, field vision, and processing ability to beat the ball to the target. A high-IQ player that quickly processes things in the backfield and commits himself to the play while wasting very limited time or steps. LeCounte, while not the most athletically gifted, works his tail off and maximizes his physical abilities on every snap. Takes good pathways to the football when the ball is in flight, reading the QB's arm motion in the backfield.

Weaknesses: Suffered a shoulder injury in a motorcycle accident during his senior season that will need to be looked into. LeCounte is good at everything great at nothing player that fails to overly impress in any one area of his game. Undersized, lacking great measurables, LeCounte could stand to gain additional muscle and functional strength for the next level. Pad level when approaching tackles is sporadic, far too often playing with high pads which limits his ability to use proper fundamentals to bring ball carriers down. Overall range is OK but it isn't anything to ride home about, lacking great athletic characteristics to cover loads of green. A willing tackler but lacks the confidence in his strength to bring down ball carriers with consistency in 1v1 situations, oftentimes dragging down as opposed to using proper technique.

Best Fit: Single high and special teams

Player Ranking (1-100): 76.8 - LeCounte is a smart and experienced safety that has a good understanding of the mental side of the game. He will be a great teammate and a solid NFL starter at the next level. He's not a game-changer but he's consistent and will help stabilize and organize a defense. 3rd round player.

10 - JaCoby Stevens - LSU - 6'1 216 lbs

Strengths: A former freshman receiver that transitioned to safety following his freshman campaign for the Tigers. Stevens is one of the leaders of the team and thought of very highly by both the community and the LSU coaching staff. After a stellar junior season, Stevens put himself very high on the NFL Draft map, finishing the season with 90+ tackles, 5 sacks, and 3 interceptions. To put it simply, Stevens is an incredibly versatile chess piece that defenses are looking for in today's NFL. Built with a completely stacked physique, Stevens shows prototypical NFL size to play down in the box and close to the line of scrimmage to disrupt. Used frequently in man coverage and zone coverage situations to line up against athletic tight ends, showing the size and physicality to match up against the best of them. A solid straight-line athlete that shows discipline and precision in the way he plays the game, rarely getting fooled on misdirections or option-style runs. A reliable wrap-up tackler that utilizes his entire wingspan to seal off edges and force poor rush lanes in the running game. Appears at his best in zone coverage, remaining in control at all times and showing a good understanding of zonal spacing and depths. Will compete for the ball at the catch point, showing good aggression and hand stretch to rip at the ball to dislodge it at precisely the right time. Has loads of special teams experience on all of LSU's units.

Weaknesses: A build-up speed athlete that lacks great initial quickness or short-area bursts to cover the entire field, most notably if asked to play in a single-high scenario. Overall range and cover awareness are limited when playing in acres of space, appealing to have some lower-body stiffness. Gets caught flat-footed when attempting to read things in the backfield waiting to "see it before he reacts." While his sack numbers have been impressive, he doesn't exactly have a plan when attacking the pocket, failing to utilize his hands to disengage or fight through initial blocks. Play recognition abilities need work, as he fails to see keys and quickly recognize things.

Best Fit: Box Safety or Dime Linebacker

Player Ranking (1-100): 75.8 - Stevens is a really good football player that does all the basic things well. Physicality, toughness, hard-working, and a real leader. His size and length make him a fun chess piece for a defense, but he's limited as a pure cover safety. He struggles the further away he is from the ball. Keep him close to the line of scrimmage and use him to attack the pocket and handle gap assignments. 3rd round player.

11 - Tyree Gillespie - Missouri - 6'0 207 lbs

Strengths: A 2+ year starter for the Tigers that has progressively improved during each season, showing to be one of the mainstays of the Missouri defense. Built with a filled-out frame, Gillespie possesses the desired and prototypical size for the next level. Physicality is the name of the game for Gillespie. A dominating physical presence, Gillespie possesses good versatility to play closer to the line of scrimmage or in a single-high deeper role as well. An explosive athlete, Gillespie sees things in a flash, showing tremendous read/react abilities to close on the ball at precisely the right time. A magnet to the ball due to his cover awareness and field vision. Impressive range when playing further from the ball, showing the anticipatory abilities in addition to the closing speed to cover the entire field. He utilizes his explosiveness to generate explosive pop-on contact when reaching ball carriers, consistently laying the wood. A finisher that stings in run support and reacts without hesitation, rarely missing an open-field opportunity. Takes good pursue angles to minimize yardage opportunities. An excellent special teams player that has extensive experience.

Weaknesses: Ball production numbers have been greatly disappointing as Gillespie has 0 career interceptions during his time with the Tigers. Lacks ideal length, has stubbier arms. Will occasionally fall victim to double-moves, biting on fakes down the field. Was ejected for a game due to a violent targeting hit.

Best Fit: Single-high safety

Player Ranking (1-100): 75.1 - Gillespie has been part of one of the best safety duos in college football the last couple of seasons. A terrific athlete while playing with tremendous toughness, Gillespie is one of the rangier safeties in this draft class. While his lack of ball production numbers prevents him from being one of the top safeties in this class, Gillespie has very few flaws. He should be a Day 1 starter for most defenses. 3rd round player.

12 - Talanoa Hufanga - USC - 6'1 215 lbs

Strengths: A 2-year starter for the Trojans that brought himself into the draft discussion following a spectacular sophomore season. Despite missing a few games during his sophomore season, he still finished with nearly 100 tackles, 7.5 tackles for loss, 3.5 sacks, and 2 forced fumbles. A versatile chess piece for the Trojans defense, Hufanga has played all over the defensive formation, including in the box, on the edge of the defensive formation, and as a deep-cover safety. One of the best and more sure-handed tacklers in this draft class, showing his ability to utilize reliable wrap-up fundamentals when playing in the box. He completely maximizes his tackle radius to make plays both inside and outside of his frame. When coming downhill, Hufanga is a force to be reckoned with, delivering explosive POP-on contact through his upper body and hands. This allows him to comfortably play through blockers and keep his frame clean through contact to work through the garbage. Comfortable when being used in man coverage against tight ends, showing good fluidity through his movements to mirror in space.

Weaknesses: Struggled with some injury issues during his sophomore season causing him to miss some game time. (Concussion and shoulder sprain) Before his junior season, his ball production numbers were modest at best with 0 career interceptions. This lack of ball skills shows up frequently when in coverage, he's not a natural with the ball in the air and his lack of ball skills and comfort with the back towards the ball is evident. Quicker than he is fast, Hufanga lacks the long strides to make up ground when playing in catch-up mode. This limits him when taking bad angles to the ball. Not much of a candidate to play in a deep-lying role due to lack of range to cover ground.

Best Fit: Box safety or dime linebacker

Player Ranking (1-100): 74.3 - Hufanga is good at what he does. And that's certainly playing in the running game. He's a violent and physical kid that is best maximized closer to the line of scrimmage. He will be an instant impact special teams 'player from Day 1 for a team as well. 4th round player.

13 - Joshuah Bledsoe - Missouri - 5'11 201 lbs

Strengths: Bledsoe has been a valuable cog in Missouri's defense since his true freshman season, progressively winning over more and more snaps until winning the starting job toward the end of his sophomore season. Bledsoe is built with an athletic frame, showing enough compactness and width to play closer to the line of scrimmage or further in the back end. He's played mostly in coverage, excelling most while handling a variety of cover responsibilities. He oftentimes plays as a nickel corner, covering in the slot, both against tight ends and shifty slot receivers. Bledsoe is a very good athlete that shows desirable range to cover large sections of the field. Shows natural coverage instincts, impressing greatly with his ability to find the football with his back towards the football, as evidenced by his 16 passes defended the last two years. Highly intelligent that reads things well as plays develop to anticipate and react quickly. Doesn't shy away from the physical aspects of playing safety, showing 0 hesitancy to trigger and get downhill. Takes good angles in pursuit while cutting off lanes.

Weaknesses: While he's a solid cover safety, his overall ball skills and finishing ability are a huge concern mark due to his lack of ball production numbers, only finishing with 1 career interception. While he's a physical player, Bledsoe plays far too upright when working in run support. This causes him to struggle to disengage while working through the trash, getting hung up on blocks. It also causes him to enter tackles far too high, failing to bring down consistently. Appears to have some stiffness concerns when asked to change direction, getting caught out of position, and allowing separation against quicker slots when getting taken laterally.

Best Fit: FS

Player Ranking (1-100): 73.4 - Bledsoe could serve a nice role in today's NFL. He's got more than enough athleticism, physicality, football smarts, and coverage ability. He can be used as an extra corner or handle deeper halves coverages as well. While I wish he finished more plays with high ball production numbers, he's a reliable safety that rarely is out of position. 4th round player.

14 - Lamont Wade - Penn State - 5'9 192 lbs

Strengths: A 2-year starter and former five-star prospect for the Nittany Lions, Wade had an impressive first year of starting during his junior season finishing with 67 tackles, 4.5 tackles for loss, and 2 sacks. A former cornerback that has transitioned to playing mostly in a box safety role. Also was the teams 'primary kickoff return specialist during his senior season. He will occasionally drop deeper and play in a single-high look as well. Wade is a short and athletically-built safety that brings a diverse skillset to the table. Don't let his size fool you, Wade is a physical and tough kid. His former cornerback abilities allow him to effectively be used in a nickel role, covering slot receivers. Fearless in the running game, showing good reliability and physicality to take good angles to the ball carrier. He quickly recognizes things, diagnosing, and working his way back to the football. Twitchy reflexes and anticipation allow him to sniff out screens and misdirection-type plays when working in the box. Aggressive with his hands, routinely ripping at the football to attempt to create turnovers, forcing 4 fumbles during his career. A solid athlete that possesses short-area quickness to quickly close on plays. This is especially evident in his abilities to attack the pocket while blitzing, showing good quickness and timing to generate pressure.

Weaknesses: Overall ball skills are just OK, as he has only recorded 1 career interception despite playing a role during 4 seasons. Despite his willingness and instincts in run support, he routinely whiffs on tackles, failing to accurately wrap-up. Quicker than he is fast and will get exposed if having to play deeper in coverage, failing to have the long speed or the range to cover large sections of green. Struggles against shiftier route runners that will cause him to get caught flat-footed at the top of routes.

Best Fit: Zone safety that can play in the box as well

Player Ranking (1-100): 72.1 - Wade is a hard projection because he has some terrific mental tools, including his instincts, smarts, and anticipation. But he has serious physical deficiencies, including his lack of reliability when tackling and his overall ranginess. In the right fit, I think he could be a nice piece for a defense. 4th round player.

15 - Reed Blankenship - Middle Tennessee State - 6'1 200 lbs

Strengths: A rare 4-year college starter that is a team leader and dominant presence for MTSU's defense. Has been one of the best defensive and most consistent players in the All-Conference USA. Blankenship is built tough, showing good compactness in his frame, showing the capabilities to handle the NFL rigors both in deep halves or closer to the line of scrimmage. A high energy and effort prospect that shows excellent field vision and awareness to put himself near the football on almost every snap. A coaches 'favorite due to his relentless work ethic and high football IQ and character. Appears to have a good understanding of spatial awareness when in zone coverage, looking comfortable while dropping in space, and rarely being at the wrong depth. Aggressive when coming downhill in run support and acts without any hesitation when filling gaps. Shows to have loose limbs and comfort when asked to flip his hips, rarely wasting any movements or taking false steps in coverage. When playing as a single-high, Blankenship shows good range and athleticism to quickly close on the ball.

Weaknesses: Missed the last few games of his junior season after a season-ending ankle injury. Needs to show more physicality upon the balls 'arrival, far too often allowing the receiver to make the catch instead of competing. Dips his head when tackling, always going for the big-hit instead of consistently utilizing good form to wrap-up. Doesn't always take the cleanest and most efficient pathways to the football getting caught up in the mud on far too many occasions. Has several poor drops on film when in position to make the play.

Best Fit: SS that plays deeper

Player Ranking (1-100): 70.3 - Blankenship is a really solid and fluid athlete that shows physicality with an aggressive downhill nature to come up and hammer some nails in run support. I'm really intrigued by the prospect and think he will be a great special teams player on Day 1 and push for snaps on defense very early on.

16 - Brady Breeze - Oregon - 6'0 198 lbs

Strengths: A valuable contributor for the Ducks that came onto the scene in a big way during the 2nd half of his junior campaign where he took over full-time starting responsibilities. Built with good overall size and weight distribution while carrying virtually only necessary body fat. Has a knack for being around the ball as evidenced by his 3 defensive/special teams 'touchdowns last year for the Ducks, 1 of them on an interception the other 2 from fumble recoveries. An excellent special teams player that has been used successfully to block punts. Breeze is tough as nails, showing terrific downhill ability to come up into the box and fight through blockers to make stops in the running game with good form technique. His strong upper-body combined with proper leverage and physicality allows him to keep his frame clean in space and flow back toward the football. Breeze flashes impressive ball skills with his back toward the ball, showing the ability to find and locate the ball quickly and then time the balls 'arrival to perfection by knocking it away. Versatile in his ability to play in man coverage, in the box, or even as a single-high safety. When he's playing in a deeper role, Breeze's click/close ability is on full display, showing the ability to quickly read keys and put himself into position to make plays.

Weaknesses: Size is good but isn't elite, lacking ideal length to be a dominant force further away from the football. Doesn't appear to have ideal levels of athleticism or range when playing deeper in a Cover-2 or Single-High situation. It appears especially when he's in man coverage, he will struggle to stick with his assignments due to some lower-body tightness. Range is 'OK 'but lacks the ideal change of direction and transitional quickness to play in large gaps of green.

Best Fit: Box safety and special teams 'maven

Player Ranking (1-100): 69.5 - Breeze on Day 1 will be a dominant special teams 'player with his physicality, toughness, and overall playmaking skills. He's limited athletically as a deeper halves safety like he played in college. I think he will likely be a better player transitioned to playing closer to the line of scrimmage, which will allow him to make impacts in the running game and utilize his instinctive characteristics. 5th round player.

17 - Kolby Harvell-Peel - Oklahoma State - 6'0 210 lbs

Strengths: A 2-year starter for the Cowboys that had his breakout year during his sophomore campaign, finishing with over 70 tackles, 5 interceptions, 13 passes defended, and 2 forced fumbles. A very stout and compactly-built safety that has more than enough muscle to play at the next level. Cowboys coaches used him in a variety of ways, showing good versatility both in deep looks like a single high, and coming down and covering in the slot on occasion. Effective when used to attack the pocket, showing good timing and closing speed to affect the QB while blitzing. Tremendous ball skills and production allow him to make several plays on the ball. Very physical when playing closer to the box. Quick to trigger, he gets downhill in a flash and drives runners down through his hips. A very reliable tackler both inside and outside of his frame. Has experience playing both in zone and in man coverage. Comfortable covering receivers in the slot with good straight-line speed to be carried up the field. Very good in zone when he's allowed to see plays develop and utilize his closing bursts to make plays on the ball. A leader for the defense, showing a high football IQ and constantly keeping the secondary organized and lined up properly.

Weaknesses: Tore his ACL on the very last play of the 2019 season. He really struggles when he's asked to play laterally and flip his hips. There's clear stiffness through his lower body and he will struggle to mirror if taken across the field. Struggles when having to navigate through space as he will get hung up on blocks for far too long. Has some discipline concerns when in coverage, leading to frequent bites on double-moves, allowing separation down the field. Not great when his back is towards the ball, looking uncomfortable and giving up separation down the field.

Best Fit: Box safety

Player Ranking (1-100): 69.3 - Even though Harvell-Peel is experienced playing deeper, he's more effective closer to the line of scrimmage. He's able to utilize his physicality and stout physique to be effective in the running game. He can be used on shorter zone drops to cover in space as well. 5th round player.

18 - Shawn Davis - Florida - 5'11 199 lbs

Strengths: Davis took over full-time starting responsibilities for the Gators during his junior season where he excelled, finishing with 51 tackles and 3 interceptions. Made his mark as a freshman as one of the best special teams 'players on the team and eventually won some snaps. A reliable communicator that keeps the defense organized and disciplined. Davis safety experience mostly stems from playing in both a single-high and as a deep halves safety in a cover-2 system. A reactionary athlete that shows terrific click/close abilities and lower body explosiveness to spring himself into any direction. He combines that with his flexible joints to change direction and accelerate fluidly in transition without needing to gear down. Closing burst is a major plus, getting himself to top-speed in a flash. Possesses the secondary burst to close cushions or recover after false steps. A high football IQ allows him to possess a good understanding of route developments, allowing him to get a good jump on routes. Showcases upside with his ball skills and body control to be able to play with his back to the ball while tracking the balls 'arrival and competing at the catch point.

Weaknesses: Missed a few games this past season due to an undisclosed injury and has had a repeated injury history with little things here and there. An undersized safety that lacks ideal measurables, both in terms of height and length for the next level. Leads with his head as a tackler, always going for the big hit instead of utilizing proper wrap-up technique, leading to several missed tackles. Needs to gain additional functional strength and likely weight to have more confidence to be effective closer to the line of scrimmage. Has a bad habit of attempting to always intercept the ball with one hand, leading to needless drops and missed opportunities.

Best Fit: Free safety in a deeper role

Player Ranking (1-100): 66.9 - Davis is a really good athlete that displays loose limbs and fluidity throughout his frame. He's a bit overconfident at times and misses plays he really should make. His tackling concerns are real and until he gains some additional functional strength I don't see him improving in that aspect. But there's upside as a pure cover guy. 5th round player.

19 - Christian Uphoff - Illinois State - 6'3 213 lbs

Strengths: After the FCS season was pushed off until the spring, Uphoff declared for the draft. Starting two years for the Redbirds, Uphoff is one of the best FCS prospects in this draft class. A dynamic return specialist. Featuring a long-levered frame, Uphoff has tremendous height and size. A very good athlete, Uphoff displays the long speed to compete with the best athletes at the next level. Versatility is tremendous, showing the experience to play in a variety of coverage setups. When handling slot duties, Uphoff looks like a natural, pressing with good jam technique and handling tight ends or slot receivers. Good ball skills down the field, shows good anticipation and timing to break on the ball quickly, oftentimes baiting the QB into throwing in his direction. Good agility and lower body flexibility to change direction with ease, flipping his hips and staying in phase with receivers on lateral routes. Fearless and disciplined in run support, utilizing his closing burst and length to seal off perimeter lanes. Is quick to trigger and plug holes when maintaining gap integrity.

Weaknesses: Transitioning from the FCS level has been challenging for defensive players. Very slight frame and despite his size, he lacks length. His lack of functional strength and power will limit him when having to deconstruct and fight through blocks. Despite having the willingness in run support, his poor pad level and technique will cause him to bounce off bigger backs. He misses a lot of tackles.

Best Fit: Return specialist, special teams units, and developmental safety

---

Player Ranking (1-100): 65.1 - Uphoff is an interesting player that has developmental upside with his athleticism. He's raw and needs to get stronger for the next level but he has coverage traits that will be desirable for teams. 5th round player.

20 - Damar Hamlin - Pittsburgh - 6'1 201 lbs

Strengths: Coming to Pittsburgh as a top high school cornerback, Hamlin transitioned over to safety the last few seasons. Possessing a long and rangy physique, Hamlin plays all over the defensive formation, bringing tremendous versatility. A major four-year contributor to the defense, Hamlin has gotten progressively better during each season. An absolute tackling machine, Hamlin excels the most when playing in run support while down in the box. High tackle for loss numbers each season due to his tremendous anticipatory abilities and instincts. An aggressive downhill tackler, Hamlin shows 0 hesitancy when coming in the hole. Excellent read/react ability, utilizing his tremendous short-area quickness to quickly close on the ball. A loose-limbed athlete that shows good flexibility to sink his hips and change direction with ease. In the passing game, Hamlin shows good comfort to handle tight ends. Extremely intelligent with impressive route recognition abilities. Very good ball skills, showing a natural feel when his back is towards the ball. High-end up ball production with over 20 passes defended the last 3 seasons in addition to 5 interceptions.

Weaknesses: A very slight frame that is built more like a cornerback than a safety at this point. Hamlin had a core injury requiring multiple surgeries, causing him to miss quite a bit of game time both in 2016 and 2017. When playing in man coverage in the slot, Hamlin appeared to struggle to handle quicker receivers that could easily separate on lateral routes. Lack of functional strength is apparent when working back towards the football, getting hung up and stuck on blocks, failing to disengage. Has had several on-field discipline issues. Repeatedly allows his eyes to deceive him, biting hard on play-fakes and misdirections. He also has had some very poor defensive penalties. An average overall athlete, lacking the ideal long speed to handle top-end speed threats.

Best Fit: Box safety / nickel corner

Player Ranking (1-100): 64.6 - Hamlin could be a really solid box safety due to his anticipatory skills and instincts but he desperately needs to get stronger and improve functional strength. Until then, he's likely going to win snaps playing in some coverage responsibilities, possibly handling tight ends or bigger receivers. 6th round player.

21 - Eric Burrell - Wisconsin - 6'0 195 lbs

Strengths: A 3-year starter for the Badgers defense and team leader, Burrell has shown the ability to be a valuable cog in their defense. Burrell showed up during his junior season where he finished with 55 tackles, 2 sacks, 2 interceptions, 6 passes defended, and 2 forced fumbles. Versatility is the name of the game for Burrell, having played in the box, as a deep halves safety, or even in the slot. Wherever he's played he has shown the ability to be one of the better cover safeties in this class. He's at his best in zone coverage, showing a real feel for proper zonal depth. A real magnet to the football due in part to his cover awareness, field vision, and range. Plays far bigger than his size, showing physicality in all aspects of the game, getting downhill and fearless when working through blocks to be effective in the running game. A really effective blitzer that shows good timing and disguising abilities to affect the pocket whenever he is sent. Plays with a relentless motor and is one of the most tireless workers on the field in pursuit.

Weaknesses: Was ejected for a game during the 2019 season for targeting. Burrell wins mostly with instincts and toughness and isn't an elite-level athlete. He will struggle winning game time on the field due to his lack of elite range or short-area quickness to make plays on the ball. A rangier built guy that could stand to gain additional weight and size, especially in the manner of physicality that he plays with. Inconsistent leverage concerns are evident when attempting to break down as a tackler. Takes overaggressive angles to the football, which causes him to over pursue and having an over-reliance on his closing speed.

Best Fit: FS further away from the ball

Player Ranking (1-100): 64.2 - Burrell is very comfortable in zone coverage but at the same time he lacks the elite range to play as a really deep safety. Ideally, he would be used in a Cover-2 or Cover-3 system where he isn't necessarily the last line of defense. He can occasionally come up and blitz or play in the box as well. 6th round player.

22 - Tariq Thompson - San Diego State - 6'0 200 lbs

Strengths: A rare 4-year starter for Mountain West program San Diego State that has been a consistent performer for them during each campaign, finishing with double-digit interceptions numbers during his career. Thompson possesses good overall size for the position with a tapered midsection and plenty of room for additional muscle mass. Thompson has a knack for being around the football, show terrific ball-hawking attribute, in part due to his terrific awareness and field vision. Not content with receivers doing damage upon receiving the ball, Thompson goes out of his way to rip at the ball and force the turnover. Utilizes good fundamentals when breaking down as a tackler, wrapping up securely. Excellent ball skills with the innate ability to find, judge, and disrupt at the catch point. Shows lower body explosiveness and leaping ability to high point the football and win the ball at the top against receivers. Thompson inches forward when playing deeper, sinking in his stance and staying on the balls of his feet at all times. A springy athlete that shows good straight-line speed to quickly close down. Comfortable in zone, showing a good feel for zonal spacing, oftentimes disguising it well pre-snap.

Weaknesses: Thompson still needs to continue to maximize his frame and add additional muscle mass at the next level. Functional strength and physicality aren't great and he will need to continue to improve them. Not overly aggressive in run support, failing to offer much when initially contained and blocked, lacking any kind of hand strength to disengage.

Best Fit: FS that can cover

Player Ranking (1-100): 63.3 - Thompson is an impressive cover safety that shows good awareness and understanding of route concepts to remain in control and in a good position to make plays. He's a good athlete, albeit not a great one. Physicality and functional strength need to improve for the next level. 6th round player.

23 - AashariCrosswell - Arizona State - 6'0 205 lbs

Strengths: A former four-star high school player, Crosswell has proven to be a reliable hybrid defensive chess piece for the Arizona State coaches. A two-year starter for the Sun Devils, Crosswell was excellent as a true freshman finishing with 4 interceptions and 9 passes defended. Built with good size, Crosswell possesses good compactness and toughness through his frame. A versatile prospect that has shown the ability to cover in the slot or play in the box in run support. In run support, Crosswell shows fearlessness when working downhill and is a very reliable open-field tackler, rarely missing when he gets his hands on a runner. Comfortable when handling slot duties in coverage, staying mentally alert at all times and playing with self-assured confidence. Has shown good ball skills with impressive ball tracking abilities due to his natural cover awareness.

Weaknesses: Crosswell was serving an indefinite suspension by the team for conduct reasons and it was likely one of the main reasons he declared for the draft. Crosswell was beaten out in preseason for the starting role prior to his final season and played very few snaps in the opening game, before sitting out the rest of his junior season. After a really promising freshman season, Crosswell never quite showed the improvement or consistency coaches were looking for. Not an overly rangy safety that can play in acres of green, better when playing closer to the line of scrimmage. Overall athleticism is just 'OK' and he fails to have ideal change of direction, long speed or agility to impact things further away from the football.

Best Fit: Box safety that can occasionally play in the slot

Player Ranking (1-100): 61.5 - Crosswell has a lot of questions to answer in regards to the way he left the program. College coaches Herm Edwards and Antonio Pierce will be consulted and highly regarded in regards to their opinion of Crosswell. There's certainly impressive traits that have flashed during his career but it's unfortunate we didn't get a chance to see them this year. There's no doubt he's a versatile prospect with upside at multiple spots along the defense. Based on what I do know, I'd take him in the 6th round.

24 - Divine Deablo - Virginia Tech - 6'3 226 lbs

Strengths: A former wide receiver that transitioned to playing safety following his freshman year with the Hokies. Deablo took over as the starter during his redshirt sophomore campaign and flashes some significant upside in doing so. The first thing you'll notice with Deablo is his 'first off the bus physique.' He's absolutely stacked from head to toe, showing the ability to be used even as a subpackage linebacker at the next level, as he did at times for the Hokies. He's a jack of all trades player that can be used effectively in the box to consistently take on blocks and fill gap assignments. Deablo is surprisingly comfortable playing even as a deeper safety, showing a natural feel and instincts when it comes to coverage. When tasked with handling tight ends, he showed the frame to be able to handle the physical aspects of it. A really good athlete that shows sideline to sideline range to cover large sections of the field. A reliable tackler that rarely misses when allowed wrap-up.

Weaknesses: While he shows impressive upside in zone coverage and playing deeper, he's a major liability at this point in time if he's matched up in man coverage situations. He lacks fluency in his hips and lateral mobility to be able to mirror in space. Was responsible for a ton of big plays in coverage, failing to accurately make plays on the ball despite being in a good position. Mental processing abilities and play recognition leave quite a bit to be desired as he's often the last one to the spot. Fails to drop his pads when tasked with gap assignments, leaving his chest plate completely exposed for blockers to easily control. Despite his size, he doesn't always show the functional athleticism or strength you would expect.

Best Fit: SS that can play as a shallow zones safety

Player Ranking (1-100): 59.3 - Deablo is a frustrating player because he looks the part but doesn't always play the part, with far too many mental lapses and delayed response times. There are some developmental traits and natural athleticism that will make him an appealing fit for teams. He just needs to make more plays. 7th round player.

25 - James Wiggins - Cincinnati - 6'0 205 lbs

Strengths: Wiggins is a 2-year starter for the Bearcats that came onto the scene as a sophomore where he finished with 54 tackles, 4 interceptions, 1 defensive touchdown, and 2 additional forced fumbles. A compactly-built safety, Wiggins shows tremendous strength and physicality through his frame. Wiggins is known on campus for being one of the most impressive workout warriors throughout college football. An athletic specimen that isn't just weight-room strong, Wiggins shows the functional strength on the field as well with his ability to come downhill and lay the wood on ball carriers. Lower body explosiveness is evident in his excellent long speed as well as his short-area quickness to close plays down in an instant. Comfortable with his back to the ball showing good ball tracking ability to make plays after timing the balls 'arrival. Versatility to play in different coverage schemes or play in the box and playing closer to the line of scrimmage. Has experience playing as a nickel man corner and showing to be fairly adept at mirroring quicker receivers.

Weaknesses: Suffered a torn ACL before his 2019 season causing him to miss the entire season. Wiggins overall athleticism and closing speed get him out of a lot of trouble, lacking the ideal instincts and spatial awareness to put himself into proper situations to make plays. Only has 1 full year of starting experience in college.

Best Fit: Deep safety

Player Ranking (1-100): 58.3 - Wiggins is an athletic specimen that has shown impressive flashes during his minimal playing time. The question is, can he stay healthy? If he can he has the potential to be a quality NFL starter at safety. He certainly has the physical tools to get there.

26 - Marcus Murphy - Mississippi State - 6'1 200 lbs

Strengths: A 3-year contributor for the Bulldogs that has been a valuable role player both for the defense and on special teams'since his true freshman season. A former West Point QB that switched to the defensive side of the ball upon arriving at Mississippi State. A smart and versatile prospect that has shown the ability to play all over the defensive front, including playing closer to the line of scrimmage. A good-sized athlete that possesses a nice safety frame, showing compactness and toughness throughout. Comfortable in a variety of different coverage setups, showing good anticipation and cover awareness with his back towards the ball. Maintained good positioning and instincts when handling zonal drops or nickel responsibilities. A physical thumper that isn't afraid to get downhill in the run game, proving to be a reliable open-field tackler.

Weaknesses: Was suspended for 8 games during his sophomore season for a violation of team rules. Has only started 9 career games. Is still learning how to play on the defensive side of the ball after playing on the offensive side of the ball before arriving with the Bulldogs. Ball production numbers have been greatly underwhelming as he has questionable ball skills. Murphy is a limited athlete that plays far better in small spaces, appearing to have minimal range when playing in too much space.

Best Fit: Special teams and backup safety

Player Ranking (1-100): 54.3 - Murphy could still get better considering he is still learning the position but he hasn't been exceptional in any one area. He's a developmental prospect that could win a role on special teams early on.

TOP-10 Safeties

1. Andre Cisco
2. Trevon Moderig
3. Richie Grant
4. HamsahNasirildeen
5. Paris Ford
6. Jevon Holland
7. Ar'Darius Washington
8. Caden Sterns
9. Richard LeCounte
10. JaCoby Stevens

Chapter 15

❧✖☙

Conclusion

And that's a wrap! There you have it, my 2021 NFL Draft Guide. I hope you enjoyed it and found this to be a significant resource for you during the 2021 NFL Draft. And you're anything like me you'll find yourself looking at this not just this year but in 2022, 2023, and years into the future. Where was Dan right, where was Dan wrong....

This guide was truly designed to be the ultimate compliment for you during all 3 days of the draft. While I can't promise to cover every single draft pick and it's also possible some of the guys I ranked and listed won't be drafted at all. That's the NFL draft for you. It's unpredictable and that's why we love it so much.

I put my heart and soul into this draft guide like never before! I did all the possible digging on every single one of these players I could find with the available resources I had. If I missed anything it wasn't for lack of digging or trying. As always guys, I'm here to chat and connect with you. I'd love to help answer questions from a fellow draft nerd. The best place to find me is on Twitter @DTPDraftScout

And once again I have to say it: thank you from the bottom of my heart. You've allowed me to turn a fun little side project into a passion of mine.

If you could all do me a favor and PLEASE leave me a review on Amazon, it would mean the absolute world to me! And as always, thanks to every last one of you guys for grabbing my draft guide. If any of you need help with anything in the future let me know and I'd be more than honored to help you out. Honestly,

Daniel Parlegreco

Chapter 16

Glossary of Terms and Top 50 Big Board

0 Technique (Zero Technique DT) – A DT who is required to play two different gaps. They are lined up directly over the center. They can be in a 3-4 or a 4-3 system. They are the biggest guys on the defensive side of the ball. They are generally extremely powerful and clog the middle of the field. They generally are not required to rush the passer, nor are they very good at it. They are also called nose tackles as well.

1 Technique (One Technique DT) – A DT that generally is required to take on multiple blockers and open things up for his fellow defensive lineman. They play on either one of the outside shoulders of the center and are not directly over the center like a 0 technique. They generally are also referred to as nose tackles as well. A 1 technique is always partnered up with a 3 technique DT as well. The 1 technique is more powerful, stronger and a better player against the run. The 3 technique is more explosive and a better pass rusher.

2 Technique (Two Technique DT) – A DT that plays head up directly over the guard. They have more gap assignments and are generally required to handle both the 'A' gap between the guard and the center in addition to the 'B' gap between the guard and the tackle. They are usually required to be incredibly stout and constantly take on double teams.

3 Technique (Three Tech DT) – Plays on the outside shoulder of either guard. They are the penetrating and more explosive DT that is a better pass rusher. They don't have much responsibility in the way of gap control, and generally are 1-gap players. Think of guys like Warren Sapp and Aaron Donald.

3-4 OLB – Plays mostly on the line of scrimmage but standing up on the outside. These guys are generally your best pass rushers in a 3-4 system. They can be used in coverage at times as well. They are similar to 4-3 DE's but differ because of the defensive scheme your defense employs. 4-3 DE's are required to put their hands on the ground and are relied upon to be generally bigger, longer and stronger against the run. Depending on the defensive coaches and their philosophies, most guys are capable of playing either as a 4-3 DE or a 3-4 OLB depending on what defensive system your team plays.

4-3 OLB – These guys aren't your pass rushers. They consist of both the Will linebacker and the Sam linebacker. The Will (Weak Side) is generally the more athletic, sideline to sideline LB who is faster and can cover better. The Will plays on the weak side of the formation. The Sam (Strong Side) linebacker is the guy that's asked to play closer to the line of scrimmage to play the run more. They play on the strong side of the formation.

Cover 2 – Two deep-lying safeties who each cover half of the field.

Cover 3 – Rather than covering ½ the field like a Cover 2, a Cover 3 requires 3 deep playing guys who each takes a 3rd of the field.

Dime Defense – Has 6 defensive backs on the field, only 1 linebacker and 4 rushers on the line. Used in passing situations or long yardage situations.

JUCO – Transferred from a junior college program.

Mike Linebacker – Quite simply the middle linebacker on your team.

Nickel Defense – Has 5 defensive backs on the field, 2 linebackers and 4 rushers on the line of scrimmage. Used in passing situations or when teams are in 3 receiver sets.

Nickel Linebacker – When a team is playing in nickel, there are 2 linebackers on the field. These linebackers are the best on the team in space, and can really cover and run.

Quick Twitch (Twitchy) – Meaning a guy who is explosive off the snap of the ball. They possess above-average quick-twitch fibers, meaning they are more explosive in their lower bodies.

Rangy – Good length but lacks great bulk on his frame. Almost like a wiry-built guy who lacks the ideal weight on his frame.

RPO – A popular new term in the NFL referring to run pass option plays. It's when the QB goes to the line of scrimmage with both a run and a pass play. He generally decides based on the defensive look whether to run or pass.

Sam Linebacker (Strong Side Linebacker) – Stronger, bigger guy who is required to play closer to the line of scrimmage. Generally, has more assignments in the run game.

Single High Safety – Deep covering safety who plays deep by himself and covers the entire field. Generally, is a safety who plays with outstanding range and instincts. Think Earl Thomas.

Slot Cornerback (Nickel Corner) – A cornerback who plays inside and covers the receivers closest to the line of scrimmage. These cornerbacks are usually smaller, quicker and more agile.

Sub-packages – Any package which is different from your base defense. Your base defense is either a 3-4 or a 4-3. Every team has sub-packages that are generally required to be used in certain game situations, such as nickel or dime defense. Most teams in the NFL play in their sub-package almost 50% of the time.

Will Linebacker (Weak Side Linebacker) - More athletic outside linebacker who plays on the weak side of the formation in a 4-3 defense.

Top 50 Big Board

1. Trevor Lawrence
2. Penei Sewell
3. Patrick Surtain II
4. Ja'Marr Chase
5. Caleb Farley
6. Christian Darrisaw
7. Kyle Pitts
8. Trey Lance
9. De'Vonta Smith
10. Micah Parsons
11. Jaycee Horn
12. Zach Wilson
13. Christian Barmore
14. Gregory Rousseau
15. Justin Fields
16. Patrick Jones II
17. Rashod Bateman
18. Chris Rumph II
19. Jaylen Twyman
20. Carlos Basham Jr
21. Chazz Surratt
22. Rashawn Slater
23. Joseph Ossai
24. Andre Cisco
25. Najee Harris
26. Jaylen Waddle
27. Wyatt Davis
28. Dylan Moses
29. Jabril Cox
30. Travis Etienne
31. Wyatt Hubert
32. Alex Leatherwood
33. Josh Myers
34. Daviyon Nixon
35. Trey Smith
36. Quincy Roche
37. Samuel Cosmi
38. Trevon Moderig

39. Cameron McGrone
40. Israel Mukuamu
41. Pat Freiermuth
42. Deonte Brown
43. Azeez Ojulari
44. Jeremiah Owusu-Koramoah
45. Dyami Brown
46. Asante Samuel Jr
47. Cornell Powell
48. Creed Humphrey
49. Jamin Davis
50. Richie Grant

Made in the USA
Middletown, DE
25 April 2021